Advance Praise for *Confronting Saddam Hussein*

"The Bush Administration's invasion of Iraq in 2003 tops any list of strategic failures in the long history of American foreign relations. Conversely, Mel Leffler tops any list of the nation's finest scholars of American strategic decision-making. The two come together in this gripping, illuminating, fair-minded, and undoubtedly landmark exploration of how American leaders, at the height of their power and influence yet simultaneously driven by fear, got it all so very, very wrong."
                —**Jeffrey A. Engel**, Director, Center for Presidential History

"The war in Iraq was a disaster that diminished American power and divided the American people. Leffler explains how a fearful, well-intentioned, but poorly informed president led our country down this damaging road. This book is essential reading for any leader who hopes to avoid disaster, and any citizen who wants to elect better leaders."
—**Jeremi Suri**, author of *Civil War by Other Means: America's Long and Unfinished Fight for Democracy*

"*Confronting Saddam Hussein* offers a welcome antidote to flip assessments of the Bush administration's decision to invade Iraq in 2003. Mel Leffler's provocative new account shows that the invasion was not a result of cartoonish bumbling or single-minded warmongering, but rather careful debate poisoned by a disastrous mix of fear and hubris."

—**Nicole Hemmer**, Director of the Carolyn T. and
Robert M. Rogers Center for the Study of the Presidency,
Vanderbilt University

CONFRONTING
SADDAM HUSSEIN

CONFRONTING SADDAM HUSSEIN

GEORGE W. BUSH AND
THE INVASION OF IRAQ

MELVYN P. LEFFLER

OXFORD
UNIVERSITY PRESS

OXFORD
UNIVERSITY PRESS

Oxford University Press is a department of the University of Oxford. It furthers
the University's objective of excellence in research, scholarship, and education
by publishing worldwide. Oxford is a registered trade mark of Oxford University
Press in the UK and certain other countries.

Published in the United States of America by Oxford University Press
198 Madison Avenue, New York, NY 10016, United States of America.

CIP data is on file at the Library of Congress

ISBN 978–0–19–761077–0

DOI: 10.1093/oso/9780197610770.001.0001

Printed by Lakeside Book Company, United States of America

For my younger brother, Fred,
who died too young
and whose friendship and love
sustained me in good times and bad

CONTENTS

PREFACE

On September 11, 2001, I walked by the White House at about 8:20 A.M. on a beautiful, cloudless, sunny Tuesday morning. I recall the light traffic on the street, the relative tranquility, as I meandered alongside the Treasury Building and turned right on 15th Street to head to the Woodrow Wilson International Center, located in the Ronald Reagan Building on Pennsylvania Avenue. It was the onset of a new academic year, and I hoped to use my time as a Visiting Scholar to make progress on my book dealing with the Cold War. Shortly after I arrived, I noticed a small group of people standing in a lounge watching television. I had been at the Wilson Center many times, and I had never noticed anyone doing this. I joined them to see what was going on, and watched repeated pictures of a jet flying into one of the towers of the World Trade Center in New York City. The horrifying, spectacular scene was mesmerizing. Hushed, a group of us stood there together. After listening to commentators speculate about what had happened, I think I walked away, and then returned—I don't really remember. But, then, I watched another jet crash into the second tower, and saw the ensuing chaos as flames engulfed the upper floors and the towers collapsed.

The Wilson Center closed. Rumors circulated that the Reagan Building might be a target of another attack. I do not recall being scared, just shocked. I left around noon to walk to my apartment, about a mile away. The streets were eerily quiet, deserted. I called my daughter who lived a few blocks away. She came over and we spent the evening watching the same scenes again and again on television. We did not talk much. We were too absorbed in our own thoughts. What did it mean? Why did it happen? What next?

The rest of the year remains a blur. I tried to stay focused on my research, but it was not easy. Every day there were rumors of new terrorist attacks. Routines at the Wilson Center were disrupted when letters with anthrax spores circulated in the mail and killed some postal workers. Government buildings, including the Wilson Center, instituted new regimes of security. Book deliveries from the Library of Congress were disrupted, and internet access was restricted. These personal inconveniences were inconsequential, as larger developments unfolded. President George W. Bush launched the Global War on Terror, overthrew the Taliban government in Afghanistan, declared new threats from an "Axis of Evil," and identified Saddam Hussein's Iraq as a gathering menace that had to be confronted.

I went to England for the 2002–2003 academic year to be the Harmsworth Professor of History at the University of Oxford. The big event of the year for a Harmsworth Professor is the so-called inaugural address, then occurring, paradoxically, at the end of the year. I had every intention of crafting my Harmsworth Lecture around the research I was doing on the Cold War. But during the fall of 2002, I was beleaguered by British students and scholars pressing me to explain why the Bush administration was discarding the doctrines of deterrence and containment, and embracing preemptive wars. I did not enjoy the position I was in—trying to elucidate, and often forced to defend, the logic of policies I did not fully grasp nor necessarily support.

My best friend, the late philosopher John Arthur, who was also spending the year at Oxford, asked me one day why I was planning to give my Harmsworth Lecture on the Cold War. Nobody, he mused, cared about the Cold War any more. Talk about recent events; put 9/11 in historical perspective, he insisted. John enlisted my wife to join him in the campaign to shift the focus of my lecture. I did, reluctantly. In May 2002, I presented my Harmsworth Lecture on "9/11 and American

Foreign Policy." Unintentionally, that talk reshaped the trajectory of my interests over the next twenty years.

Although I returned to the United States and finished my book on the Cold War, I also began to write short articles on the Bush administration's foreign policy. I contested the idea that his policies constituted a radical turn or spectacular aberration. Unilateralism, pre-emption, military preponderance were not new phenomena, I argued; nor was the quest for a liberal, open international marketplace. I was not seeking to excuse, praise, or criticize the president and his advisers; I was just trying to place their actions and predilections in historical perspective.

I met Eric Edelman in 2009. Eric was a professional foreign service officer, but had had a unique career, among other things, working for Deputy Secretary of State Strobe Talbott during the administration of Bill Clinton and then serving on the staff of Vice President Dick Cheney in 2001 and 2002. After being appointed ambassador to Turkey, he returned to Washington and served as the under secretary of defense during the second Bush term, 2005–2008. As an undergraduate student at Cornell University, my alma mater, Eric had taken courses with the renowned historian of American foreign policy Walter LaFeber. He had been in the discussion section of my closest academic friend, Frank Costigliola, and they had retained some ongoing contact as Eric went on to graduate school in history at Yale and then shifted to a foreign service career. Through Frank and through my connections at UVA's Miller Center for Public Policy, I was introduced to Eric.

One day we had lunch together at the Boar's Head Inn. Eric surprised me. Although he had spent the last thirty years working in the government, he was incredibly well versed in the academic literature on American foreign policy. He was intimately familiar with my own writings. I told him I had written a bit about the Bush administration and was pondering the idea of a big book about the profound impact of 9/11 on American foreign policy, resembling a volume I had written about the transformation of American foreign policy during the Truman years. He strongly encouraged me to do so. I told him the big constraint was the paucity of primary source documents because so few of them were declassified. Acknowledging that was a huge impediment, Eric said that if I embarked on the project he would help me secure interviews with many of the leading policymakers in the Bush administration, his former colleagues.

I was intrigued. I felt challenged. I had not relied on interviews for my previous books, and I wondered how much I would gain from talking to former policymakers whose ability to spin, I wagered, might exceed my ability to probe. However tempting, I also wondered if interviews could adequately substitute for real documents, the hundreds and hundreds of archival boxes that I routinely examined for my previous books. Whether they could or could not, I doubted that Eric would make good on his promise to arrange interviews, or whether I would have the gumption to go ahead with them.

Eric did carry out his commitment. He quickly introduced me to Paul Wolfowitz, the former deputy secretary of defense; Scooter Libby, Vice President Dick Cheney's chief of staff; and Steve Hadley, President Bush's former national security adviser. Other friends introduced me to Richard Clarke, the counterterrorism expert on the staff of the National Security Council. Lee Hamilton, the former congressman and director of the Wilson Center, helped facilitate an interview with General Colin Powell, who had served Bush as secretary of state. Bob Jervis, an acclaimed scholar of international relations and expert on the CIA, put me in contact with Michael Morell, the president's CIA briefer, with whom I had two long, productive interviews. And on it went. I began talking to these policymakers, officials, and analysts in 2010, and have been doing so, off and on, for more than ten years. Some of them, like Wolfowitz and Libby, I interviewed multiple times at the very outset of this project. Others, like William Burns, the assistant secretary of state for Near Eastern Affairs, and Condoleezza Rice, Bush's national security adviser, I spoke to much more recently on the phone or by a Zoom video link. Still others, like Steve Biegun and Elliott Abrams, I talked to over long lunches.

The interviews were fascinating. I quickly realized that I could not write a comprehensive overview of the administration's foreign policies, but would need to narrow my focus. To interviewees, I made it clear that I was a historian trying to figure out what seemed among the most momentous decisions of the twenty-first century: the articulation of a global war on terror and the invasion of Iraq. I emphasized that I hoped to write a book, but I was in no hurry. I told my interviewees that I had no fixed views and that I wanted to understand what happened. I stressed that I still hoped to secure lots of important documents through declassification requests that other scholars and institutions, as well as I, were submitting. I made it clear that I had read extensively in the excellent journalistic literature that already had appeared. Much of that literature was critical, and my questions sometimes irked my interlocutors. Forget everything I had read, Scooter Libby said to me one day.

I had no intention of doing that. My questions invited officials to tell me what they thought they were trying to do and why. I encouraged them to describe the environment in which they were working, the emotions they felt, and the pressures they encountered. I asked them about the policy process, about who was making policy, and how decisions were shaped. I questioned them about President Bush, his role, and his strengths and weaknesses. I focused a lot on the "intelligence" information they were gathering and examining and how it shaped policy outcomes. I queried why things went so wrong, so quickly, once the Iraqi regime was toppled.

Most of Bush's advisers were eager to talk and inform. They seemed exceptionally willing to explain important and complex decisions to an academic who they regarded as open-minded. Occasionally, they expressed frustration, even bitterness, with colleagues in other departments; sometimes, they stridently defended what they did; at other times, they lamented policy outcomes that they still could not quite grasp. Frequently, they told me that it was good I was speaking to them, that the written record would never illuminate precisely what they had experienced.

I did not believe that last comment. I had spent most of my academic career examining documents in archival boxes. I was, and remain, a firm believer in the power of written evidence. Policymakers themselves often do not realize how much gets written in complex bureaucratic environments where officials must inform one another about what has occurred. I made a commitment to myself to examine as much of the written record that I could access. My interviews—and those being conducted by the entirely separate Miller Center oral history project on the Bush administration—would supplement and complement the written record, not replace it. I filed requests for documents. Although some of them still have not been acted upon, most of them have been denied in part or in full. But I was helped by other scholars and organizations, especially the National Security Archive. They, too, were seeking to illuminate the documentary history of the Bush administration. They filed freedom of information and mandatory declassification requests. Documents started to appear in the internet reading rooms of government agencies and on the website of the National Security Archive. Several policymakers like Donald Rumsfeld, the secretary of defense; Douglas Feith, the under secretary of defense; and Bill Burns used their influence to secure the declassification of key documents that enriched their own accounts of the history of the administration.

Most important, the British parliament authorized a special inquiry to investigate the decision of Prime Minister Tony Blair to align Britain with the US invasion of Iraq. Under the leadership of Sir John Chilcot, his investigative committee, including eminent historians like Lawrence Freedman and Martin Gilbert, interviewed every leading British policymaker, secured the release of hundreds of documents and reports, and published a voluminous, comprehensive analysis of British policymaking. These interviews and memoranda often revealed a tremendous amount about the Bush administration's thinking and calculations.

Among other things, I came to understand how much the two leaders—Bush and Blair—detested Saddam Hussein, and how much their view of his defiance, treachery, and barbarity affected their calculations. I realized that the story of intervention could not be told without illuminating the Iraqi tyrant's role and agency. His record and his behavior made a difference, and had to be integrated into any overall analysis of US decision-making. Many Iraqi records, including tapes of some of the Iraqi dictator's conversations, were seized by US forces, and dozens of Hussein's colleagues and advisers were captured and interrogated by US officials and intelligence analysts. Saddam Hussein himself spent years in prison, during which he was interviewed extensively. He talked at length about his challenges, ambitions, setbacks, and aspirations. Although incomplete, scholars can gain valuable insights into what the Iraqi dictator was thinking and doing, and how his actions affected the calculations and decisions of US officials.

This book seeks to explain the most consequential US foreign policy decision of the twenty-first century. Although reeling from the attack on 9/11, at the time the Bush administration decided to invade Iraq the United States remained the world's hegemon with unparalleled military power and unchallenged economic superiority. The terrorist attack, moreover, aroused sympathy from around the world and modulated simmering resentment of its so-called hyperpower. But a decade or so later, much had changed. With the United States still mired in Iraq— now fighting the Islamic caliphate, or ISIS—its standing in the world had been tarnished, its power challenged, its economic dominance receding, and its internal cohesion fraying. The war in Iraq demoralized the American people, intensified their partisan divisions, and shattered trust in their government. Abroad, it alienated key allies, aroused widespread anti-Americanism, and devastated its moral authority. It destroyed many lives, and consumed enormous resources, energy, and time. It distracted attention from the challenges in Afghanistan, the rising power of China, the swelling anger inside Russia's Kremlin, and the growing warnings about climate change. Rather than abetting the overall war on terrorism, it complicated that struggle, fueling Muslim grievance, and attracting adherents to join a holy, bloody struggle. In the long history of the United States, then, the Iraq War may well be seen as a critical turning point, the onset of a trajectory into a far grimmer future than that anticipated at the end of the Cold War, just a decade or so before.

The aims of this book are straightforward. I want to examine why the United States decided to invade Iraq and why the war went awry so quickly, leading to tragedy for Iraqis and Americans. I try to correct some widely held misconceptions, yet also confirm some of the established wisdom. I place President Bush at the center of the policymaking process where he unquestionably belongs. I stress his fears, his sense of responsibility, and his concerns for homeland security. I discuss his war plans and his strategy of coercive diplomacy. I emphasize the distinction between his motives and his goals, and explain how a war for security morphed into an exercise in nation-building and democracy promotion without adequate preparation. I highlight the dysfunction within the administration and explain why things went awry so quickly. The invasion of Iraq turned into a tragedy, but not, as some accounts have it, because of an inattentive chief executive, easily manipulated by neoconservative advisers.

Over many years, my commitment to this project has been sustained by my growing conviction that too much of the history of the Bush administration has been entwined with partisan, personal, and ideological battles that have made it difficult both to empathize and criticize. I try to do both. Too many accounts that stress the lying, the manipulation, and the preconceived predilections of officials obfuscate the real lessons of the tragic intervention in Iraq.

As I explain in my conclusion, it is consoling to think that if we had had smarter, more honest policymakers all would have turned out well and good. The truth of the matter is that it is hard to garner accurate information and to assess it objectively. It is hard to measure threats. It is hard to deal with unpredictable, brutal, defiant tyrants. It is hard to balance means and ends. It is hard to temper predilections and prejudices. It is hard to gauge the reactions of people one knows little about. It is hard to master our fears, discipline our power, and curb our hubris. However tempting it is to level criticism at President Bush and his advisers—and we most definitely should—we need to recognize, collectively, that the exercise of prudence and the judicious use of power have not, historically, been among our finest qualities as Americans. We must improve.

ACKNOWLEDGMENTS

⸻⬦⬦⬦⸺

This book would not have been written without the help and encouragement of two people: Eric Edelman and Seth Center. As I note in my Preface, Eric connected me to many key officials in the Bush administration. As I completed chapters, Eric read each one, offered incisive comments, and provided additional information. Although we still disagree on many issues of interpretation, his thoughtfulness and knowledge have enriched my understanding of the complexities of decision-making inside the Bush administration.

Seth was a graduate student at the University of Virginia whose work I supervised. He assisted me with some research when I began writing about the Bush administration. Subsequently, he went to work in the Historical Office of the Department of State and convinced its leaders to do a special project on the Iraq War. For several years, Seth conducted research and assembled documents. He shared none of this with me. His involvement, however, sustained my own interest, and his queries and comments constantly moved me forward. When I wavered in my conviction to write a book, he hassled and prodded. I suspect he will not agree with aspects of this volume, but he made it come to fruition. I am indebted to him.

Over the years, many graduate students at the University of Virginia served as research assistants and wrote papers that clarified important topics. I especially want to thank Lauren Turek, Stephen Macekura, James Wilson, Evan McCormick, and Christopher Maternowski. Their assistance has been invaluable.

For several years I led an undergraduate seminar on "9/11 and American Foreign Policy." Students wrote research papers on every conceivable topic, and many were superb. I especially want to thank Melanie Weismuller. Her analysis of the initial months of occupation and her identification of key sources enriched my own understanding of this critical period.

When I was unable to secure the declassification of many of the documents I hoped to see, I put this project on a back-burner. I did not think I would get back to it. However, during the onset of the pandemic, my wife, Phyllis, encouraged me to use my time to write an article summing up my research and thinking. That article turned out to be about 70 pages and 250 footnotes—impossible to publish in any journal. Several friends were kind enough to read it and offer suggestions on what I should do. My own inclination was to put it aside and move on with my life. But Will Hitchcock, Richard Immerman, Philip Zelikow, and Brian Balogh convinced me that I should turn it into a book. So did two esteemed scholars—Bob Jervis and Marty Sherwin—who subsequently lost their battles with cancer. While I was uncertain whether I had the wherewithal to write another monograph, their encouragement and constructive criticism inspired me to dig in, and David McBride at Oxford University Press embraced the project and made it possible. I am grateful to all of them for their gift of time and advice.

Over the course of my career the Woodrow Wilson International Center has been a second home. When I first got started on this project, Christian Ostermann welcomed me back as a Visiting Scholar. I am grateful for his support, and for that of Sam Wells and Rob Littwak.

For many years, the University of Virginia's Miller Center for Public Policy served as a congenial base for much of my work. Its directors— Philip Zelikow, Gerry Baliles, and Bill Antholis—generously supported my research, convened conferences, hosted speakers, and nurtured dialogue. Philip also spent many hours with me discussing policymaking inside the Bush administration, and offered helpful suggestions. My other colleagues at the Miller Center—Marc Selversone, Brian Balogh,

Will Hitchcock, and Jeff Legro—were wonderful collaborators. Anne Mulligan, Stefanie Abbott, Sheila Blackford, and Mike Greco provided expert assistance and made certain that more things got accomplished than I could have imagined.

I want to offer special thanks to Frank Costigliola and Raj Menon, two of my oldest professional friends. Frank has commented on everything I have written for almost fifty years. Raj and I have been discussing US foreign policy since my early days as a young professor at Vanderbilt University. They both read this manuscript with meticulous care, raised important questions, and offered incisive suggestions. We still disagree on many issues, but the book has benefited greatly from their input. I am grateful for their friendship and their wisdom.

As I wrapped up the first draft of this book, I asked Samuel Helfont to read it and offer suggestions. His knowledge of Iraqi sources and of Saddam Hussein's policies helped me to correct some errors and think more deeply about both Iraqi and US goals.

Writing is always a lonely process, especially so in the middle of a pandemic. I am more than fortunate to have a partner, Phyllis, who knows how to encourage and critique in equal measure. Aside from our common historical interests, she has mapped a trajectory of service to community, commitment to friends, and love of family that has enriched my life. This book would not have been completed without her support.

I

Saddam Hussein

WRETCHED WERE THE conditions into which Saddam Hussein was born in April 1937 in the tiny hamlet of Al-Ouja, just a few miles south of Tikrit. He never knew his father, a poor, landless peasant who died or disappeared before Saddam left his mother's womb. His mother, impoverished, could not care for him, and gave infant Saddam to her brother, Khairallah Talfah. Shortly thereafter, Khairallah, an army officer, was imprisoned for his nationalist, anti-British actions, and Saddam was handed back to his mother who by now had remarried her former husband's brother, Hassan al Ibrahim. Hassan despised the child, and often beat him with a stick. Having no job of his own, Hassan did not send his stepson to school, and encouraged the young boy to steal neighbors' chickens and eggs.[1]

In Al-Ouja, Saddam Hussein grew up in a mud hut. There was no running water, no electricity, no toilet, no kitchen. He slept on the floor in a single room. Animals roamed in and out of the hut. Family members, including his three younger half-brothers, ate with their hands from a communal pot. Neighborhood kids played in dirty alleys, formed gangs, fought and feuded. Children mocked Saddam because he had no father. With no real friends, he learned that to survive he had to be tough, cunning, and self-sufficient. His given name, Saddam, meant "one who confronts," and he did so as a young boy—fighting, stealing, lying, and inflicting cruelty on little animals.

In 1947, his uncle, Khairallah, was released from prison. Saddam's mother sent her ten-year-old son back to Tikrit to live with him, his wife, and their two children, Adnan and Sajita. Sacked from the army, Khairallah now became Saddam's teacher and mentor. In the early 1950s, Khairallah moved his family to Baghdad and took Saddam with him. They settled in Al Kharkh, a section of the city inhabited by poor Sunni and Shi'a. Khairallah taught school, socialized with former and active-duty army officers, and indulged in the never-ending political conspiracies. He hated Jews and Persians alike, but his energy was focused on toppling the existing monarchy, upending the Sunni elite, and excising all semblance of British colonial rule. Khairallah kindled his nephew's nationalist fervor, political passions, and social grievance. He registered Saddam in school, demanded hard work and discipline, and whetted his ambitions. He introduced him to his military buddies, among them his cousin, Ahmad Hasan al-Bakr, who would subsequently become a leader of the Ba'th Party and the key to Hussein's ascent in revolutionary Iraq. Khairallah indulged Hussein's penchant for political street-fighting, gangs, and violence. Hussein acquired a gun, intimidated his enemies, and beat up opponents. As an adolescent, Saddam Hussein made a reputation on the streets of Baghdad.

In July 1958, a group of military officers led by Abd al-Karim Qasim overthrew the king in a bloody seizure of power. The new rulers were divided among themselves, some ardent Iraqi nationalists, some with Ba'th sympathies, and some with communist predilections. Hussein hung out with young members of the small Ba'th Party, although not yet a member himself. The Ba'th stood for Unity, Freedom, and Socialism. When Qasim chose a nationalist path over Arab unity, the Ba'th turned against the new government. Hussein joined them—inciting students to protest and riot. Amid the turmoil, he and Khairallah went back to Tikrit to wreak vengeance on a communist who had insulted his uncle. Hussein murdered the man and went to prison for six months. Upon his release, he was recruited for an assassination attempt on Qasim himself. The plot failed, and Hussein escaped, first, to Tikrit, and then crossed the border into Syria. In Damascus, he met the Syrian founder of the Ba'th Party, Michel Aflaq. Hussein impressed Aflaq, and then moved on to Egypt where he finished high school, enrolled briefly in law school, and spent considerable time reading and talking politics. He was a lonely young man, unhappy, with few friends, and no social life. While in Cairo, he agreed that he would marry Khairallah's daughter, his cousin, with whom he had lived many years as a child and teenager. Marrying one's cousin, solidifying family alliances, was what Tikritis did.

In 1963, the Ba'th seized power, killed Qasim, and launched a bloody crackdown on their key opponents, the communists. Hussein returned to Baghdad, after stopping in Syria and conferring again with Aflaq. Hussein may also have garnered support from CIA agents, who were assisting the Ba'th in Baghdad and encouraging them to hunt down and kill Iraqi communist leaders.[2] Hussein joined the mayhem, recruited allies on the streets of Baghdad, and collaborated closely with Nadhim Kazaar, a young Shi'a Ba'thite already notorious for his cruelty and torture. Far more important, Uncle Khairallah convinced his cousin, General Bakr, to take Saddam as a young assistant. With revolver in hand, Saddam served as Bakr's personal bodyguard, and focused on murdering communist foes on the streets of Baghdad. Bakr soon emerged as a leader of the coup and took the post of prime minister. But the victors again splintered, and right-wing military officers pushed Bakr aside. With no real base of popular support, the Ba'th were toppled and again went into opposition.

Hussein smartly positioned himself as an aide to Bakr. The deposed general, now the acknowledged head of the small Ba'th Party, feverishly worked to organize party cells, and Hussein increasingly took charge of the party's security apparatus as well as its dealings with peasants and its contacts with the military. Inveterate conspirator, he participated in another plot to kill the existing military ruler, and was imprisoned again for almost two years. In jail, he rose early, read incessantly, debated other prisoners, and, most important, maintained contact with Bakr, who harnessed Hussein's pragmatism, opportunism, ruthlessness, and ambition to his own schemes to seize power. With the incumbent regime reeling after the humiliating Arab defeat in the 1967 war with Israel, Bakr conspired with yet another small group of disaffected military officers. Hussein supported a tactical alliance: "we should collaborate with them but see they are liquidated immediately, during, or after the revolution. And I volunteer to carry out the task."[3]

And this is what happened. In July 1968, a small group of military officers, with the support of Ba'th leaders, seized power in a bloodless coup. Bakr was designated president of Iraq, but real power rested with the Revolutionary Command Council. Immediately, Hussein went to work orchestrating a plot to deport or kill two key generals who might challenge Bakr's leadership. Daring and shrewd, he succeeded, forcing them into exile. Bakr now quickly consolidated power, and made Saddam his key assistant, the number two person in the party apparatus. "Their aim was to make the nation loyal to the party, and to make the Ba'th malleable to their own designs. Both men were bent on gaining absolute power; neither could achieve this goal on his own."[4]

Hussein had no formal position in the cabinet. He occupied a small office (adjoining Bakr's), and was conspicuously deferential to Iraq's new president. Among party leaders, he garnered little attention over the years as he had joined the party rather late, spurned ideological debates, spoke politely at party gatherings, and presented himself as a loyal, humble assistant to Bakr. Yet Hussein masterfully gathered power as he gained Bakr's confidence and took control of the regime's security apparatus. Recognizing that the party had little popular support, feeling vulnerable and insecure, he ruthlessly eliminated real and imaginary enemies. He concocted plots against the regime, and blamed Israel and the Jews; he imagined subversion among the Shi'a in Basra, and blamed Iran; he alleged communist subversion, and murdered the party's leaders. Just months after the coup, he identified an Israeli spy ring and hanged fourteen people, nine of them Jews. People were invited to celebrate the event, dance around the dangling bodies, and shout, "Death to Israel!" In early 1970, he charged a large group of military officers with collaborating with the CIA and the Shah of Iran, and sentenced thirty-seven to death. Hussein wanted to strike fear in his enemies. His victims might be dropped in buckets of acid; others might be forced to witness the rapes of their wives, daughters, or mothers. Years later, an observer commented: "There is about Saddam Hussein a peculiar ruthlessness, an almost calculated cruelty."[5]

But there was much more to Saddam Hussein. He worked prodigiously hard, prepared thoroughly for meetings, and demanded rigor and precision from others. Gifted with an astounding memory, he studied and grasped complex issues and was cunning and calculating. Maintaining a low profile, as he did in the late 1960s and early 1970s, he could be charming, gracious, and generous, qualities that he used to ingratiate himself to Bakr while amassing more and more power for himself.[6] Hussein had ambitions: solidify the control of the Ba'th Party; repress Kurdish and Shi'a opponents; strengthen Iraq; unify the Arab world; exterminate Zionism from the Middle East; thwart the Shah's Iran; position himself to assume leadership of the regime. Toward these ends, he was pragmatic and opportunistic. He had no strong ideological convictions. Believing that the world was inhabited with enemies, that the seas were infested with sharks, that the Americans, Soviets, and British were calculating whales, he was flexible and malleable—sometimes supporting Arab unity, sometimes not; sometimes supporting a socialist economy, sometimes championing the private sector; sometimes a secularist, yet often ready to harness religious symbolism to enhance support for the regime. Predicting what Hussein would do at any given moment was excruciatingly difficult, but there was little doubt by the mid-1970s that his quest for power was insatiable—personal power, national power.[7]

Like nationalists of all stripes in his country, Hussein understood that Iraq had an indispensable resource, oil. If he could gain control of the revenue, he could use it to modernize Iraq, garner popular support, strengthen the military, and assert Iraqi influence throughout the region. Hussein studied how the Iraq Petroleum Company (IPC) operated, how it managed production and priced oil. To position himself to nationalize its assets and to withstand pressure from the West, he traveled to Moscow. There, he negotiated with Premier Aleksei Kosygin, and, in April 1972, signed a treaty of friendship providing for political, military, economic, and scientific cooperation. He then issued an ultimatum to the IPC and meticulously prepared to take it over, should Western producers seek to strangle Iraqi production. On June 1, 1972, the Iraqi government took over the IPC. Hussein then flew to Paris. Negotiating with French president Georges Pompidou, he sought France's cooperation and agreed to purchase French armaments. His demeanor throughout was polite, respectful, disciplined, methodical. Without furor, he accomplished what few had imagined possible.[8]

Hussein knew what he wanted to do with Iraq's oil wealth, and the Yom Kippur War of 1973 between Israel and the Arab states and the accompanying elevation of oil prices in international markets afforded him a unique opportunity. In 1970, Iraqi oil income was about $784 million; in 1974 it was $6.5 billion; by 1980 it was $26 billion. Hussein used this money to modernize and diversify the economy of Iraq. He launched huge land reclamation and rural electrification projects. He negotiated contracts with the Brazilians to build railroads, with the French to construct factories, with Belgium to design phosphate plants, and with Germany, Japan, and Yugoslavia to share new technology. He promoted dairy and egg farming and he invested in steel, fertilizer, and chemical plants. He invited scientists and technicians from all over the Arab world to flock to Iraq and assist in its development and modernization. The Ba'th preached socialism, and Hussein poured money into building schools and hospitals. He labored to eradicate illiteracy and provide universal medical care. But he also supported private ownership and entrepreneurship.[9]

Hussein wanted to please the Iraqi people so they would support the Ba'th regime. He desired to modernize Iraq, and make it strong and self-sufficient. He yearned to reclaim Iraq's glorious past, unify the Arab world, and dominate the Middle East region. He devoted huge portions of his new revenues to purchase armaments abroad and to develop an arms industry at home. He worked diligently to diversify his suppliers and nurture Iraqi self-sufficiency. He bought tanks and aircraft, with expenditures climbing from $500 million in 1970 to $4.5 billion in 1975.[10] He turned his personal attention to acquiring and developing weapons of mass destruction (WMD)—chemical, biological, and nuclear—and the means to deliver them. He built pesticide plants near Iraqi phosphate deposits. He developed the means to manufacture bacteriological weapons, considering them cheap and deadly. He purchased a bacteriological lab from France, and acquired technology to produce mustard gas as well as nerve agents like Sarin and Tabun. He went to France and talked to Premier Jacques Chirac about a nuclear reactor, consummating a deal in September 1975, after which Chirac paid a return visit to Baghdad (Figure 1.1). Hussein personally took charge of the Iraqi atomic project, chairing meetings of the Iraqi Atomic Energy Commission, asking penetrating questions, and assembling teams of technicians. In 1979, he signed a secret ten-year nuclear cooperation agreement with Brazil, committing the Brazilians to supply large quantities of low-enriched uranium. He and his assistants also signed dozens of contracts with firms in Britain, West Germany, Japan, the Soviet Union, Yugoslavia, and the United States. His aims

Figure 1.1 Saddam Hussein and French premier Jacques Chirac, 1976. As he rose to power, Hussein negotiated commercial and military deals with the French and tried to garner a long-term ally.
Getty Images, https://www.gettyimages.com/detail/news-photo/jacques-chirac-greets-saddam-hussein-news-photo/640492457

and dealings were no secret to intelligence analysts and informed businessmen and scientists. In 1979, he said candidly, "The states that supply us with arms are friendly, but we cannot guarantee that the present will continue indefinitely. The states that supply us do not agree with us in all of our aims, for the boundaries of our aims and ambitions do not lie in Iraq but extend through the whole Arab homeland."[11]

As he moved forward, Hussein maneuvered adroitly. In the early 1970s, Iraq's Kurds struggled for autonomy. Iran's Shah, hoping to achieve domination of the Gulf, deployed two regiments inside Iraq to help the Kurds. Hussein assumed responsibility for handling this explosive issue. After failing to negotiate an agreement with the Kurds and struggling to suppress the uprising, he struck a deal with Iran. In the Algiers agreement (1975), he allowed Iran to control the Shatt al-Arab straits. In return, Iran withdrew its support of the Kurds, allowing Hussein to crush the rebellion. Nonetheless, Hussein's concession loomed large. His biographers write: He had "overestimated his ability to impose his own solution on the Kurds. . . . This proved to be beyond

Iraq's power and the only escape from the dire straits into which he had maneuvered himself, and his country, was to make a humiliating concession to Iran. . . . During this tortuous journey he proved to be anything but a doctrinaire unwilling to bend. Overwhelmingly pragmatic, he displayed a remarkable degree of flexibility, shifting tactics and twisting ideological tenets in accordance with the pressure of events. His rhetoric apart, Saddam's activities reflected a single-mindedness, geared toward one paramount goal: his own political survival."[12]

More than survive, Saddam Hussein flourished. Although still the number two man in the official hierarchy, his office was the focus of power and decision-making inside Iraq. By the mid-1970s, he controlled the security apparatus, expanded the reach of the party, and appointed allies to lead the growing military establishment. He wagered that Iraqis yearned for stability. With full bellies, educational opportunity, medical care, and mounting standards of living, they would turn a blind eye to repression at the top and to restrictions on civil liberties below. In the late 1970s, Hussein crushed the communist party and murdered its leaders. On one occasion, he invited two communist ministers to his office to discuss their promotion. While drinking coffee, he took out his revolver and shot them dead.[13] In 1977 and 1978, he executed leading Shi'i clerics, imprisoned thousands more, and expelled 200,000 to Iran.[14] He also began supporting terrorist groups, including the Kurdish PKK, Syria's Muslim Brotherhood, and Palestinian groups, like Abu Nidal.[15] "As for Palestine," he said to an interviewer in 1979, his goal was clear: extinguish the Zionist state. "We are in favor of any operations, even suicidal ones, that may serve the Palestinian cause, either within the occupied land or outside it." When he witnessed Anwar Sadat, Egypt's leader, reconcile with Israel and sign the Camp David Accords, Hussein saw it as an act of betrayal—warranting death.[16]

Hussein grew unhappy with Bakr's ineffectual efforts to build Iraq's international stature and he grew uneasy when Bakr sought a union with Syria that might erode Hussein's own position.[17] He decided that it was time to remove his mentor. At a meeting of the Ba'th leadership on July 11, 1979, Hussein and his closest allies overrode the opposition of the party's general secretary, Muhle Abdul Hussein Mashhadi, and moved to push Bakr aside. On July 16, President Bakr announced his resignation on Iraqi television, and Hussein took over.

Less than a week later, on July 22, the new president convened an extraordinary meeting of Ba'th leaders from around the country. About 1,000 delegates attended, and Hussein prearranged to film the proceedings. Taha Yassin Ramadan, the commander of the party's militia, and one of Hussein's most loyal minions, opened the meeting saying sadly that he had to convey news of "a painful and atrocious plot." He then commanded everyone's rapt attention when he announced that all the conspirators were present in the room. With the audience hushed and Hussein sitting nonchalantly in front of the room, smoking a cigar, Ramadan invited Mashhadi to come forward and summarize the details. Looking bedraggled, because he had been brutally tortured in preceding days by Hussein's henchmen, Mashhadi acknowledged that since 1975 he had been part of a plot to remove Bakr and Hussein and effectuate a Syrian-Iraqi union. Hussein then took the podium, feigning sadness that his comrades would not talk to him directly about their differences. Using a handkerchief to hide fake tears, he took out a piece of paper and began reciting the names of sixty-six people, including five top members of the party and many close associates. As he named them, guards came into the room and escorted each person away. At the end of the event, the remaining delegates stood and cheered loudly, "Long live Saddam."

The president then arranged for delegates to participate in the "democratic executions" of twenty-two of the worst offenders. The event was scheduled for August 8 in the courtyard of the building where the conference had occurred. Hussein personally handed pistols to the delegates. The condemned men knelt with blindfolds over their eyes and with their hands tied behind their backs. The executioners put a bullet directly into the temple of the accused. If their nerves failed and the shot ran amiss, professional executioners then stepped up to the writhing bodies and finished the grisly task with another bullet to the victim's head. Hussein filmed this entire event as meticulously as he had filmed the conference itself, turning it into a "tribal bonding session," making the collective leadership complicitous with the heinous act. He was cultivating fear, burnishing his brutality, signaling that he would tolerate no opposition. He then purged hundreds of other party members and military officers. Amnesty International reported over 800 political executions between 1978 and 1982.[18]

Hussein now was in control, cultivating his own personality cult. But his fears did not abate and his sense of vulnerability did not fade. The overthrow of the Shah and the Islamic Revolution in Iran worried him. Coupled with growing Shi'a unrest inside Iraq, Hussein feared the appeal of Iran's new leader, Ayatollah Ruhallah Musawi Khomeini, to Iraq's Shi'a majority population.[19] Hussein did not initially want war and hoped to placate the ayatollah. Amid a crackdown, he tried to placate his own Iraqi Shi'a, donating money to Shi'a institutions, donning the Shi'a robe, the abbaya, prohibiting gambling, and linking his own personal ancestry to Caliph Ali. Khomeini, however, detested Hussein, dismissed his overtures, and encouraged Iraqi Shi'a to overthrow their secular dictator. Spurned, Hussein decided to go to war. Despite Iran's huge demographic and economic superiority, he thought he could take momentary advantage of the disarray in Tehran after the revolution to give Khomeini a bloody nose and recoup his own dignity after the humiliating territorial concession he had made to Iran in the Algiers agreement of 1975. With inadequate military planning and vague strategic goals, Hussein attacked on September 22, 1980. After his armies advanced rapidly, he halted the offensive, hoping the ayatollah in Tehran would sue for peace and stop promoting insurrection inside Iraq. He was wrong. Moreover, his hesitations and ambivalence demoralized his own forces and set the stage for an Iranian counteroffensive and a protracted war.[20]

For eight years, 1980–1988, Hussein's Iraq waged war against Iran. The war was a miscalculation, astoundingly costly in terms of lives and treasure. When Iranian troops moved into Iraqi territory, Hussein used the fighting to brandish his credentials as the defiant leader of Arabs battling the Persians, while also seeking to crush the Israelis and liberate Jerusalem. Throughout these war years, he zigged and zagged, seeking aid from whoever would offer it, including the Americans, and harboring his grievance against those who betrayed him, especially the Americans whose secret dealings with Iran in 1986 infuriated him.[21] Although the Israelis bombed his nuclear reactor in June 1981, they did not quench his nuclear ambitions and WMD programs.[22] When Iranians penetrated Iraqi territory and when his dismal tactical decisions presaged defeat, he ordered air attacks on Iranian cities and authorized chemical weapons attacks on Iranian villages. Iraqis themselves acknowledged that they used 1,800 tons of mustard gas, 140 tons of Tabun, and more than 600 tons of Sarin from 1983 to 1988. In May 1987, Hussein employed his chemical weapons against his own Kurds, gassing about twenty villages, and in March 1988, he unleashed these weapons with devastating results in Halabja, killing 3,500 to 5,000 people. He remained proud of their use.[23] Using intelligence shared with him by the CIA and employing weapons acquired from the Soviets and the French, Iraqi armies in the summer of 1988 finally drove the Iranians out of Iraqi territory and crossed into Iran. Khomeini sued for peace. Hussein accepted the overture, and declared victory.[24]

The costs of the war did not chasten Hussein. Over 125,000 Iraqis died, over 250,000 were wounded. The country's gold reserves were extinguished, and the Iraqi government accrued an external debt of $40–50 billion. The great economic and social progress of the 1970s now seemed ephemeral. Nonetheless, Hussein branded the war as a great triumph for Iraq and for the Arab people and ordered the construction of an enormous arc de triomphe in the center of Baghdad.[25] Assuming an air of grandeur and pomp, he constructed more and more palaces for himself and lived more lavishly than ever before. But amid the glory and grandeur, he sensed his unpopularity, narrowly escaping several assassination attempts in 1989 and 1990. Growing more isolated and cruel, he vested authority in relatives and fellow Tikritis and tolerated corruption among family members while he himself engaged in dalliances that disrupted his marriage and convulsed his family. He murdered army officers who represented potential threats, purged party leaders who did not subordinate themselves to his personal will, and killed his cousin, Adnan, who was his defense minister and closest childhood friend, but who foolishly sided with his sister—Saddam's wife—in a family feud over Hussein's infidelity.[26]

Hussein wanted to allay popular discontent, lubricate the private sector, and thwart rising prices, but could not figure out how to reconcile competing priorities. His policies fluctuated, characterized by incoherence, incompetency, and profligacy. While the costs of reconstruction were estimated at $230 billion and annual oil revenues were declining, he nonetheless accelerated his WMD programs and maintained military imports and military spending at almost wartime levels. His prewar aspirations for social change and economic progress flagged, but his commitment to unconventional weapons never ceased. "Before, during and after the war with Iran," writes a well-informed observer, "Saddam always gave this work [WMD] precedence over other programmes and diverted precious money to it at the expense of civilian needs and other military programmes."[27]

Hussein's WMD programs presented a dilemma. They were costly yet appeared indispensable to deter Iran and Israel, control his own Kurds, and maintain leadership in the Arab world. Toward this end, in 1989 and early 1990, he gave more support to the Palestinians, invited the PLO to move its offices to Baghdad, and championed the creation of the Arab Cooperation Council. Believing that Iraq merited more appreciation for the losses incurred during its struggle with Persians and for the vanguard role it was taking against the Zionists, he expected fellow Arabs to cancel his debts and offer more aid.[28] Hussein was not seeking war with the Israelis nor did he want to provoke the Americans, but his requests for financial succor along with his belligerent rhetoric, inconsistent actions, and human rights atrocities sent mixed signals to friends and foes alike. In turn, he grew frustrated when Kuwait and other Arab producers rebuffed his demands to reduce their oil output and raise their prices and when they ignored his requests for debt cancellation and more loans. He believed that the Americans were conspiring with the Kuwaitis to resist his overtures and colluding with the Israelis to initiate another preemptive attack against his nuclear program. Together, the Zionists, Americans, and rich Gulf Arabs were thwarting his ambitions to transcend Iraq's immediate crisis and achieve its glorious destiny.[29]

On July 16, 1990, just two years after the ceasefire with Iran, Hussein's foreign minister, Tariq Aziz, presented a list of demands to Kuwait: hike oil prices to $25 a barrel; stop stealing from Iraq's Rumalia oil field; cede two key islands; return $2.4 billion in stolen property; suspend debt repayments; and, along with other Arab nations, compensate Iraq for losses in the Iran war.[30] At the same time, Hussein sent 30,000 troops toward the border and threatened to annex Kuwait and redress the historic injustice arising from its separation from Iraq by its former colonial master, Great Britain. Summoning the US ambassador to his

Baghdad Palace, Hussein explained to April Glaspie that he hoped for a peaceful settlement, but would need to do something if diplomacy failed. "How can we make them [Kuwait and UAE] understand how deeply we are suffering?" he inquired. Glaspie retorted that the United States grasped Iraq's needs and wanted friendly relations, but believed that disputes had to be settled without resort to force. She did not give Hussein a green light; she did not, as Foreign Minister Tariq Aziz subsequently acknowledged, "say anything that [could] be interpreted as encouraging the invasion." But she did not say the United States would intervene to stop him. The next week Hussein sent his armies to annex Kuwait.[31]

Hussein grew angry when the United States spearheaded UN resolutions that called for the immediate withdrawal of Iraqi troops from Kuwait and imposed embargos on Iraqi exports and imports. "We are ready" to fight America, he had told the Palestinian leader Yassar Arafat a few months before. If necessary, "we will . . . defeat it and kick it out of the whole region. . . . Our missiles," he acknowledged, "do not reach America, but I swear if they did I would strike it." Ruminating, he imagined that he could "send someone who has an explosive belt to reach Washington," or he might target Americans traveling in Greece or elsewhere in the Middle East. "We have to be beasts."[32] More pragmatically, he tried to sunder the coalition that the United States was assembling. He appealed to his old ally, the Soviets, for support, and to his French friends for assistance. His truculence and intransigence, however, undercut their efforts to be helpful.[33]

With his credibility at stake and fearing humiliation before his own people, Hussein still defied America's ultimatum and UN resolutions. Daringly, he seized civilian foreigners inside Iraq, held them hostage, and hoped to use them to deter the bombing of his country. He launched some SCUD missiles into Israel and raided a border town in Saudi Arabia. He mistakenly thought he could champion the cause of the Palestinians, appeal to the Arab "street," and dissuade leaders like Hosni Mubarak, the president of Egypt, from coalescing against him. He also believed that his air defenses and WMD would give the Americans and the Israelis pause. Iraq possessed chemical weapons, he proudly told Arafat, and "would not think twice" about using them. The Americans, he assumed, would respect these capabilities, and would seek to avoid casualties. His newest chemical weapons, he boasted in November 1990, were 200 times more powerful than those he had used against Iran. "Only few in the world come to our level as far as the chemical and germ weapon superiority."[34]

But the United States was not dissuaded or deterred. Washington assembled a coalition of almost forty nations and deployed more than 500,000 of its own troops to the region. On January 16, 1991, US aircraft and cruise missiles struck Iraqi command centers and defense systems as well as the presidential palace, Ba'th Party headquarters, and the defense ministry. Then, the United States systematically destroyed power stations, electricity grids, factories, and refineries. When Hussein still hesitated, when the Iraqi leader refused to meet with the UN general secretary, President George H. W. Bush issued an ultimatum on February 22 that Iraq must withdraw its troops from Kuwait within twenty-four hours or face a direct confrontation with allied armies ready to invade Kuwait and drive out Iraq's forces. Hussein refused, set Kuwaiti oil fields ablaze, and massacred prisoners. During the next few days the United States and its allies routed the Iraqi army and decimated Iraqi troops as they retreated north. In 100 hours, the United States killed somewhere between 10,000–30,000 Iraqis and captured almost 90,000. Having achieved the UN objective of liberating Kuwait and hesitating to engage in a further massacre of Iraqi troops, Bush ordered a ceasefire. He did not send US forces to Baghdad to overthrow Hussein.[35]

Hussein welcomed the ceasefire, and accepted the humiliating terms offered by the United Nations. He agreed to withdraw troops, recognize Kuwaiti sovereignty, restore the war booty, disclose and eliminate his weapons of mass destruction, and accept IAEA (International Atomic Energy Agency) and UN inspectors (UNSCOM) to monitor Iraqi compliance. He did not initially expect the United States to respect the ceasefire and allow his Republican Guard troops to escape unscathed. When it did, he quickly intuited that, as much as the Americans loathed him, as often as the US president and his advisers called for his removal, they did not want to risk the dismantling of the Iraqi state, a Shi'a seizure of power, and a geopolitical gain for the despised ayatollahs in Tehran. Hussein declared victory, and focused on maintaining power and consolidating his rule. "Soon he was laughing and kidding and joking and talking about Bush," noted his director of military intelligence.[36] Believing that Iran was instigating the unrest and seeking to undermine his rule, Hussein took immediate action to crush a Shi'a rebellion in the south and another Kurdish rebellion in the north.[37] His Republican Guard and Army troops killed tens of thousands of insurgents and forced many hundreds of thousands to flee to Turkey and Iran.[38] When the United States and the United Kingdom instituted no-fly zones in the northern part of the country (and subsequently in the south) to enforce the UN mandate barring Hussein from mistreating his own people, he relented but never assented. He proudly noted that while he remained ensconced in his Baghdad palaces, President Bush lost the US election in 1992 and had to vacate the White House. In his mind, he had bested the American president.[39] When Bush visited Kuwait in 1993, he tried to assassinate him.[40]

Hussein still had to deal with inspectors from the United Nations and the IAEA who insisted that he disclose and destroy his WMD and long-range missiles. They entered Iraq in May 1991 and immediately faced obstruction. Hussein created a concealment committee. After the inspectors found kilos of enriched uranium and documents confirming the existence of an advanced nuclear project, Hussein made modest concessions and destroyed some of his chemical and bacteriological weapons. At the same time, he tried to hide his bacteriological programs, preserve capabilities to produce chemical weapons, and harbor the core ingredients and intellectual know-how to resume his atomic ambitions.[41] He deemed these weapons to be vital to the survival of the regime, the fulfillment of his goals, and the affirmation of his power. In his view, he had employed chemical weapons effectively to repress the Kurds, subdue the Shi'a, punish the Iranians, and deter the Israelis. Even with a small nuclear arsenal, Hussein thought he could affect the behavior of foes and friends and redraw the map of the region. Possession of these weapons could neutralize the arsenals of more powerful adversaries, like the United States and Israel, and allow him to pursue his goals with diplomatic bravado, conventional weapons, and terrorist tactics. Even small numbers provided a shield that could permit greater aggressive activity with less risk of escalatory reactions by more powerful foes. He hoped Iraq might produce about twenty bombs per year. WMD afforded Hussein the means to survive, deter, and blackmail. They were indispensable.[42]

Saddam destroyed some of his chemical weapons and biological agents and allowed IAEA inspectors to remove all weapon-usable nuclear material from Iraq, but refused to cooperate fully and lied about the full extent of his programs.[43] Insisting that the embargos and sanctions were violations of Iraqi sovereignty, he rebuffed UN proposals that permitted limited exports of oil in exchange for the import of food and medicine. The sanctions stymied postwar reconstruction and inflicted even greater pain on the Iraqi people. Inflation skyrocketed and per capita income plummeted from about $2,000 in 1989 to about $609 in 1992. Children went hungry, and child mortality soared. Sewage and water purification systems broke down, and disease spread. Electrical grids could not be repaired, and industrial production stagnated. Unemployment grew, and engineers and technicians fled the country. Incomes stagnated, marriages were delayed, divorce rates increased, and middle-class lifestyles ended. Prostitution, crime, and corruption proliferated. By punishing the Iraqi people for allowing their evil dictator to exist, Americans hoped that disaffected officers would overthrow Hussein. They couldn't. They didn't.[44]

Hussein survived and prevailed. He acted expediently, granting Kurdish autonomy, making cosmetic changes to liberalize the constitution, offering pay hikes to his military officers and security chiefs, and working hard to restore water and electricity.[45] He jettisoned the secular ideology of the party and embraced religious symbolism and rhetoric to placate his majority, restless and angry Shi'a subjects.[46] Mostly, however, he grew more oppressive, corrupt, and erratic. He shifted control from the party to his family and tribal allies. He added layers to his security apparatus and military organs and appointed sons, cousins, and in-laws to head them. He now monopolized decision-making on all important issues. Associates dared not contradict him lest they be killed.[47]

Rightly suspecting attempts on his own life, his paranoia mounted. He moved from palace to palace (there were five palaces in Baghdad alone). He worked in a small office in a sealed corner of the presidential complex. Iraqis were no longer allowed near his residence. Visitors, blindfolded, were taken to see him in official cars so they could not identify his location. His meals were tasted by his cook's son to guarantee against poisoning. When he traveled, there were always decoy motorcades. When he wanted sex, his aides procured women, often young and blond. If they did not satisfy him, their lives were at risk. His cruelty increased along with his isolation. He executed top generals and religious leaders. Escaping assassination attempts and knowing the CIA was targeting him, he tortured and killed imagined suspects and proven plotters. An air force commander was captured, and his fingers cut off one by one before being shot. The following year, Hussein exploited divisions among the Kurds, sent his forces back to Kurdistan, and captured and executed scores of CIA assets cooperating with the opposition group, the Iraq National Congress.[48]

Hussein had the most difficulty controlling his own family. His two sons, Uday and Qusay, feuded with his two sons-in-law, the brothers Hussein Kamil and Saddam Kamil. Hussein Kamil, married to the dictator's oldest daughter, was also minister in charge of military industrialization, with broad authority over scientific research and weapons of mass destruction. Uday loathed Hussein Kamil, suspecting that he was garnering his father's favor. Hussein Kamil, fearing for his life, convinced his younger brother and their wives—Saddam Hussein's daughters—to flee to Jordan. In Jordan, Hussein Kamil agreed to talk to American intelligence analysts about Iraq's WMD programs. He provided information on bacteriological agents that had never been acknowledged and atomic programs that had never been revealed. UN inspectors then hunted down new documents on a chicken farm in Iraq owned by Kamil that confirmed the disingenuousness of the regime and the chronic lying of its ruthless leader.[49] Saddam Hussein had weaponized his biological weapons, developed a more advanced missile program than he had disclosed, and produced more chemical weapons than he had admitted. Most ominously, the UN inspectors learned that he had initiated a crash program in 1990 to acquire a nuclear weapon in less than a year.[50]

Hussein knew he was cornered. He did not contest the accuracy of the new information, but insisted that he had destroyed the weapons and would put an end to the remaining programs, some of which he claimed he did not know about. Although inspectors could not account for all chemical equipment and bacteriological agents that had been identified, they did record progress in the destruction of forbidden weapons. UN officials also were gratified when Hussein in late 1995 and early 1996 finally agreed to an oil-for-food resolution that allowed Iraq to export $1 billion of oil every ninety days and use much of the revenue to purchase food and medicine. Hussein expected that his compliance and goodwill would convince the Security Council—the French, Russians, and Chinese, in particular—to end the inspections. Consequently, he rebuffed the demands to investigate the grounds of his palaces and remonstrated about the mounting evidence that the CIA had infiltrated the inspection teams. In December 1998, believing that he had complied with UN resolutions and that Washington would be satisfied with nothing less than regime change, he abruptly threw out the inspectors (who still maintained that Iraq had not destroyed all its bacteriological agents, disclosed all its chemical programs, or renounced its atomic ambitions). The Americans and British then launched over 400 cruise missiles and sent B-52 and B-1 bombers to strike suspected chemical weapons sites, command-and-control centers, and police and security headquarters. They did so without UN authorization.[51]

Weathering these blows, Hussein calculated that he had managed to rid himself of intrusive inspectors and could now focus on terminating the entire sanctions regime. Shrewdly exploiting the divisions among the permanent members of the UN Security Council and capitalizing on worldwide revulsion of the suffering of the Iraqi people, he negotiated a new oil-for-food agreement. As a result, oil production jumped from about 580,000 barrels per day in 1996 to more than 2.5 million in 2000, and Iraqi revenues (from multiple sources) climbed from $4.2 billion in 1997 to $17.87 billion in 2000.[52] Once oil started flowing, Hussein masterfully orchestrated smuggling schemes and illicit trade arrangements with Jordan, Turkey, Syria, and other governments. Revenue from oil smuggling and illegal surcharges between 1997 and 2001 generated about $6.6 billion.[53] Hussein used some of this money to procure more food, buy medicine, stimulate housing construction, repair infrastructure, and support local manufacturing. Iraq's gross domestic product (in constant 2010 dollars) increased from around $52 billion in 1996 to almost $101 billion in 2000, and GDP per capita rose from about $2,506 to $4,322 during the late 1990s. Despite the shattered infrastructure and incomplete recovery, Iraqis were finally enjoying improving standards of living for the first time since the war with Iran began in 1980.[54]

Better living conditions did not diminish Hussein's paranoia. When his two sons-in-law foolishly decided to return to Iraq, Hussein murdered both of them and sent his daughters and their children into isolation.[55] When Shi'a discontent rose again in 1998, he ordered the killing of Ayatollah Muhammad Sadiq al-Sadr and his two sons.[56] In Abu Ghreib and other prisons, Hussein's minions executed several thousand army officers who were charged with treason. Although the northern Kurdish part of the country was now beyond his control (because of the no-fly zones), his forces nevertheless continued to displace ethnic Kurds, Turkmen, and other non-Arab minorities from around the oil city of Kirkuk.[57] Hussein also turned greater attention to disrupting exile groups and tried to assassinate their leaders, like Ahmad Chalabi. His intelligence service recruited volunteers for these suicide missions and then trained these "martyrs" for operations conducted out of Iraqi embassies in foreign capitals, especially London. Captured Iraqi documents suggest that by 1998 "the scheduling of suicide volunteers was routine enough to warrant . . . a formal schedule."[58]

At the end of the 1990s, Hussein also used substantial parts of his growing oil revenue to build up his military capabilities, revamp Iraq's power, and position himself to realize his regional ambitions. He increased the budget of his Military-Industrial Commission more than forty-fold, from 15.5 billion Iraqi dinars in 1996 to several hundred billion in the following years. He accelerated technical military research projects at Iraqi universities and expanded the military civilian workforce by over 50 percent in three years beginning in 1999.[59] He used secret protocols and trade agreements to evade import restrictions, buy conventional arms, and acquire dual-use equipment for prospective WMD programs.[60] He increasingly challenged British and American planes enforcing the no-fly zones.[61] His support of terrorist actions proliferated. Captured Iraqi documents indicate that he now used terrorism as standard practice, viewing "international terrorist organizations in terms of what they could do to further his historic mission." Always the opportunist, always seeking to shift "the regional balance of power favorably towards Iraq," he had no trouble dealing with Islamic groups so long as they appeared to serve his long-term goals. "Whether attempting to overthrow the Egyptian government or the Kuwait royal family, the vision was always about the centrality of Saddam and his pan-Arab vision."[62]

In 2001, Saddam Hussein's goals had not wavered much since 1979: he wanted "personal greatness" and a "powerful Iraq that could dominate the Middle East and project influence on the world stage."[63] In pursuit of his immediate goal to get the United Nations to lift all sanctions, he did destroy or remove almost all of his WMD programs, but he kept these actions secret lest adversaries take advantage of the country's vulnerabilities.[64] UN inspectors could not vouch that he had destroyed his biological weapons, disclosed all his chemical weapons, or renounced his nuclear ambitions.[65] Most of his advisers and associates were convinced that he would restart these programs as soon as the sanctions regime ended. In 1999, for example, Hussein told his top nuclear scientists that he intended to support them fully when circumstances were propitious. In the same year, he inquired about the length of time it would take to build a production line for chemical warfare agents.[66] Nobody, though, could really predict what he would do should he restart these programs nor how he would behave in pursuit of his long-term ambitions. Fear of Iran and hostility toward Israel pulsated through his veins, but otherwise he was opportunistic, pragmatic, and inconsistent.[67] Despite all the setbacks he had encountered, despite all the miscalculations he had made, Hussein still seemed convinced he could achieve his goals: that nobody "possessed the ruthlessness, competence, or ability to thwart his aims over the long run."[68]

But what, precisely, were these aims, other than ending the hated sanctions? How threatening or dangerous were these goals? Might he seek again to annex Kuwait? Might he try to destroy the Zionist state he despised? Might he appeal to the Arab "street," foment unrest in Egypt, or Syria, or Jordan, and try to remove the leaders he hated? Might he seek to gain leverage over the region's petroleum pricing and shape world oil markets? Might he resume his efforts to unite the Arab world under his tutelage and excise the United States from the region? Might he coordinate with terrorist groups who were seeking their own WMD and hoping to kill Americans, challenge American power, and expel the United States from the Middle East?

The future was unknown, contingent. Even Hussein's attitude toward the United States, although contemptuous, was malleable. While sneering at its hyperpower and convinced it was a paper tiger, he professed a readiness to collaborate when it served Iraq's interests.[69] He could not foresee the attack that would take place on 9/11, nor appreciate how it might reshape America's tolerance of his own risk-taking and erratic behavior. He was certain of only two things: Iraq had a unique place in history—"it will never die"—and he had a singular role to shape that history.[70] He was part of a long, epic struggle to regain Iraq's past glory, aspiring to be remembered as a ruler who was as significant to Iraq as Hammurabi, Nebuchadnezzar, and Saladin.[71] In his view, writes one historian, the Arab world was "a stage on which the Iraqi state, constructed as an emanation of his will, should play the leading role, for the benefit of himself and those who sustained his rule in Iraq."[72] Could others live with the vision he had for himself? Could they feel safe in such a world?

2

George W. Bush

SADDAM HUSSEIN AND George W. Bush: the trajectories of two human beings to national leadership could hardly have been more different. They were born about ten years apart, Bush in 1946. While Hussein slept on the floor of a mud hut, roamed the alleys of Al Ouja, and stole chickens and eggs, Bush was born into a life of comfort, affluence, and status. When Hussein in the mid-1950s was hustling on the streets of Baghdad and cheering the revolutionary nationalist regime of Gamal Abdul Nasser in Egypt, Bush was growing up in Midland, Texas, a small, dusty town in the oil heartland of the Lone Star State where he joined the Cub Scouts, played baseball with friends, went to football games on Friday nights, and attended church with his family on Sundays. When Hussein joined the Ba'th Party in the late 1950s, battled with political foes, and engaged in his first assassination attempt, Bush and his family moved to Houston where he attended a fine private school and then faced his greatest challenge before running for the presidency: adjusting to life at Andover, an elite boarding school in Massachusetts. While Hussein sat in prison in the mid-1960s after another failed assassination, Bush went to Yale, studied some history, eschewed politics, and sneered at the antiwar elitist intellectuals who dominated campus life. While Hussein helped orchestrate the Ba'th seizure of power in 1968, took over the security apparatus, and systematically eliminated foes of the new regime, Bush graduated Yale, joined the Texas Air National Guard, and then decided to attend Harvard Business School. While Hussein nationalized the oil resources of his country and used them to modernize the Iraqi economy and build up Iraq's military power, Bush returned to Midland, Texas, got married, and struggled in the oil business. While Hussein pushed aside his mentor, assumed the presidency of Iraq, murdered his opponents, went to war with Iran, and used chemical weapons to crush the rebellion of his own Kurdish citizens, Bush returned to Washington, DC, to help his father, then vice president, win the presidency.[1]

George W. Bush liked to say that the defining aspect of his character was the unconditional love of his parents.[2] His dad, George Herbert Walker Bush, came from a wealthy, distinguished family. His dad's dad, Prescott Bush, was a Wall Street banker and US senator from Connecticut. Prescott Bush had married Dorothy Walker, whose father, George Herbert Walker, was an even more successful investment banker and competitive entrepreneur. From the Bush line of his father's family, W. inherited a tradition of service, modesty, frugality, discipline, and benevolent paternalism; from the Walker side of his father's family, W. inherited a tradition of competitiveness, swagger, affluence, and luxury; and from his mother's family—the Pierces, an illustrious lineage of its own—W. derived his wit, bluntness, and irreverence. George W. Bush knew that family counted, a family infused with love and commitment, high expectations, rigorous standards, resilience, ambition, and money.[3]

W. was a brash, sassy, charming, good-looking, undisciplined kid who often disappointed Mom and Pop, but they loved him nonetheless. He performed modestly at school, but his family name and connections got him into Yale. He cared little about his academic subjects, but he enjoyed Yale's social life, made friends easily, and was a natural leader. After graduation, W. went back to Texas, joined the Air National Guard and helped his dad in his campaign for the US Senate in 1970. His dad lost yet wound up with high positions in the Nixon administration. W., rather aimless, pondered law school. Rejected, he applied to Harvard Business School and was accepted. There, he learned that it was important to define goals, set priorities, hire able subordinates, accord them responsibility, and hold them accountable, but he garnered attention mostly by wearing cowboy boots and chewing tobacco. After Harvard, W. returned to Midland, Texas, to try his luck in the booming oil business, an industry in which his dad previously had made a small fortune. But W. floundered, perhaps because he drank a bit too much and partied a bit too hard.[4]

W.'s life began to change in 1977 when he was thirty-one years old. At a friend's house, he met Laura Welch, a young woman from his hometown in Midland who was working as a librarian in Austin. W. found her smart, witty, practical, supportive—the perfect wife. Four years later, after fearing they might not have children of their own, they had twin daughters. But W.'s business struggled as oil prices plummeted in the mid-1980s. These "were gloomy years in Midland," he later wrote, "and many were searching for purpose." At his parents' summer home in Kennebunkport, Maine, in the summer of 1985 he met the renowned evangelist Billy Graham. "He had a powerful presence," wrote W., "full of kindness and grace, and a keen mind." Graham inspired him, and deepened his understanding of faith. "Self-improvement," W. recognized, "is not really the point of the Bible. The center of Christianity is not the self. It is Christ."[5]

The encounter with Graham did not immediately change Bush's life. But it inspired introspection and re-examination. At the time, his drinking and restless nature were unnerving him, embarrassing his family, and agitating his wife. "I started asking myself," he later recalled, "if this was really the way I wanted to live my life." After a rousing evening of celebration and drinks on his fortieth birthday at the Broadmoor Hotel in Colorado Springs, he arose the next morning with a terrible hangover. That was it: he decided that very day to give up alcohol. "I realized that alcohol was beginning to crowd out my energies and could crowd, eventually, my affections for other people." W.'s growing faith and his weekly Bible study with friends strengthened his determination and inspired more self-awareness. He never had another drink. Instead, he slowly grew more disciplined and more religious. Not without doubts—"the notion of a living God was a big leap," he acknowledged. But prayer nourished him, steadied him, and helped him become "a better person," a person with whom he was more comfortable. Thereafter, religion and prayer profoundly shaped his sensibilities, rhetoric, and beliefs.[6]

A few months after quitting alcohol in the summer of 1986, W. sold his oil business and moved to Washington to assist his father's campaign for the presidency. W. had lived in his father's shadow as the elder Bush served as ambassador to the United Nations, chairman of the Republican National Committee, director of the CIA, envoy to China, and Ronald Reagan's vice president. Escaping the shadow consumed part of W.'s psyche, but love and loyalty consumed another part. More than anything else, interest and ambition inspired W. to leave Midland and change careers. He always had been interested in politics; it appealed to his competitive nature. He had helped his father, worked in other political campaigns, and himself ran for Congress in 1977–1978. Since the late 1970s he stayed in contact with a young, aggressive political consultant named Karl Rove. In the summer of 1986, his father introduced him to Lee Atwater, his campaign manager. Atwater—a fierce, innovative, no-holds-barred political consultant—invited W. to work in his office and learn the political consulting business. W. did so until victory was achieved and then headed back to Texas to take advantage of a new business opportunity—organizing a consortium of investors to buy the Major League Baseball team, the Texas Rangers. For the next five years, Bush helped manage the organization, market the team, and orchestrate a scheme to build a new stadium. Meanwhile, he cultivated networks of media, business, and political contacts.[7]

W. wanted to run for political office, yet waited for the right opportunity. He dismissed advice to run for governor in 1990 and invested his energy in his dad's re-election campaign in 1992. When Bill Clinton won, W.'s "initial disappointment . . . gave way to a sense of liberation." Now, he could champion his own policies without having to defend his father's. "I wouldn't have to worry that my decisions would disrupt his presidency. I was free to run on my own."[8]

And run he did, for governor of Texas. He asked Karl Rove to plot his political strategy, recruited Karen Hughes, a former television correspondent, to manage his communications team, and hired Joe Allbaugh, a former chief of staff to the governor of Oklahoma, to oversee the entire campaign organization. Against the odds, he defeated Ann Richards, the incumbent governor. Bush focused on four issues: education, welfare, juvenile crime, and tort reform. He preached local control and personal responsibility. He wanted to slash state spending and cut taxes. Recognizing Mexico's importance to the Texas economy, Bush also advocated improved relations, more trade, and moderate immigration policies. Once elected, he worked hard to collaborate with

Democrats and secured the aid of the powerful Democratic lieutenant governor, Bob Bullock, to implement his policies. They successfully pushed Bush's agenda through the legislature. Texas prospered; Bush's popularity soared. In 1996, he turned his attention to using the state surplus to cut property taxes and increase spending on education. He also started to emphasize faith-based initiatives. "Our laws in Texas should encourage people of faith to help people get off and stay off welfare. Our society faces many tough problems. It is time to seek, not shun, divine help."[9]

These rhetorical tropes presaged a new direction in Bush's young political career, tropes that appealed to evangelical voters and garnered him more and more national attention. When he ran for re-election in 1998, he doubled down on his support for tax cuts and for voluntary faith-based initiatives. He wanted "to enlist faith in our battle against drugs and crime and poverty and illegitimacy."[10] In his view, public welfare had failed. Government should empower faith-based organizations—churches and synagogues.[11] He won re-election with almost 70 percent of the popular vote.

In his quest for the presidency in 1999 and 2000, he harnessed the themes that served him so well as governor. He stressed the fissures in American culture and the efficacy of voluntary organizations to ameliorate social woes. Limited government, however, did not mean a "disdain for government."[12] He wanted to support public education and to bolster Medicare with new prescription drug coverage.[13] His trademark became compassionate conservatism, a conservatism that sought to reconcile personal freedom with individual responsibility by stressing the golden rule—love your neighbor as thyself; a conservatism that tried to reconcile limited government with effective government; a conservatism that sought to acknowledge societal ills and catalyze faith-based organizations to tackle those problems. Increasingly, he invoked his own religious conversion to appeal to evangelical voters.[14]

Bush did not know much about foreign policy when he launched his campaign for the presidency. He recognized that he needed to learn a lot more about international affairs. His father introduced him to Condoleezza Rice. She had worked as a Russian expert on the staff of Brent Scowcroft, the former president's national security adviser. Rice then spent much of the decade of the 1990s as the first Black provost of

Stanford University, but maintained her contact with the former president, whom she deeply admired. Rice and W. immediately hit it off. He found her smart, relaxed, and fun-loving. She simplified complex issues. She also loved sports and exercise, traits that endeared her to W. She initially regaled him with stories of Willie Mays, Bush's favorite baseball player, who had been a student in her mother's high school class in Birmingham, Alabama. Rice also liked Bush. He seemed smart, witty, incisive, eager to learn, and disciplined. His compassionate conservatism appealed to her own personal and political predilections.[15]

Rice assembled a team of experts to tutor Bush and help draft his foreign policy speeches. They called themselves the Vulcans, after the Roman God of fire and iron, and a symbol of Rice's home city of Birmingham. Many of them had worked in the administrations of Ronald Reagan and W.'s father. They included Paul Wolfowitz, a prominent neoconservative, who had held important positions in the State and Defense departments and who was then dean of the School of Advanced International Studies at Johns Hopkins University; Richard Perle, a former under secretary of defense and renowned defense hawk; Dov Zakheim, another Reagan defense official with a doctorate in economics and politics from Oxford; Robert Zoellick, a high-ranking, brilliant aide to James Baker, the former secretary of the treasury and secretary of state; Robert Blackwill, a tough-minded realist who had been Rice's boss on Scowcroft's staff; Stephen Hadley, a Yale-trained lawyer who had worked for Wolfowitz in the Bush 41 department of defense; and Richard Armitage, a former naval officer and Vietnam veteran, with extensive experience in the Defense and State departments. Although they often have been treated as a unified group espousing a militant, hegemonic, and missionary role for the United States, they in fact had different interests and proffered diverse advice.

For the most part, they were pragmatists who wanted to sustain the country's military superiority, strengthen its alliances, promote open and free trade, and nurture better relations with America's neighbors in the Western Hemisphere, especially Mexico—something the presidential candidate cared a lot about. Although many of them had signed a letter to President Bill Clinton in 1998 calling for regime change in Iraq, this was not a topic that consumed their attention. "To my knowledge," recalled Zakheim, "the notion of going to war to unseat

Saddam was never debated among the Vulcans." In their sessions with Governor Bush, they placed little emphasis on values or ideals or democracy-promotion or human rights or regime change. These were "second-order" issues. Rice considered herself a realist; power mattered. Interests came first; values would follow. Foreign policy was not social work.[16]

Rice made it clear to the other Vulcans that she was their liaison to the presidential candidate. The other Vulcans recognized that she had established a very special relationship with the candidate.[17] They also were surprised by Bush himself. Few of them knew him before they journeyed to Austin. They found him to be sharp, incisive, and witty. They found a man who was disciplined and patient, direct and courteous, confident and unpretentious. He asked good questions, listened carefully, and possessed an uncanny way to get to the heart of a problem. He conveyed a restless energy, a distaste for jargon, a lust for clarity, perhaps at the expense of curiosity and complexity. He was personable in small groups, and poked fun at himself. He was outgoing, funny, and honest. People who met George Bush invariably liked him.[18]

Bush delivered two major foreign policy speeches as he campaigned for the Republican nomination. They were thoughtful, inspiring, and wide-ranging yet replete with contradictions, ambiguities, and omissions. The United States, he insisted, must not withdraw from the world and must not drift. It must be strong and purposeful. It must pursue its values and its interests. He called this a distinctly "American internationalism. Idealism, without illusions. Confidence, without conceit. Realism in the service of American ideals." Choosing values or interests was a false choice. Together, freedom and democracy meant peace and security; free trade and open markets meant prosperity and individual economic well-being. But engagement did not mean empire; engagement did not mean domination. In a lovely turn of phrase, Bush exclaimed on the steps of the Reagan Library: "Let us not dominate others with our power—or betray them with our indifference. And let us have an American foreign policy that reflects American character. The modesty of true strength. The humility of real greatness."[19]

These appealing platitudes were repeated throughout the campaign. His speechwriter, Michael Gerson, noted that Bush's foreign policy views were entirely conventional, but he was trying to reconcile Bush's penchant for realism and pragmatism with his affinity for the language of idealism and the rhetorical tropes of freedom.[20] Bush talked nobly about a "democratic peace," but emphasized "evil remains." In defense of the nation, he insisted, "a president must be a clear-eyed realist." He stated his priorities: "We must protect our homeland and our allies against missiles and terror and blackmail." "We must restore the morale of the military . . . with better training, better treatment, and better pay." "And we must master the new technology of war." With these overriding goals in mind, Bush explained that he would pursue a "democratic peace" by concentrating on "enduring national interests": collaborating with strong democratic allies in Europe and Asia; "promoting a democratic Western Hemisphere, bound together by free trade"; advancing "interests" in the Persian Gulf and peace in the Middle East, "based upon a secure Israel"; combating the spread of weapons of mass destruction (WMD); and "promoting a world that trades in freedom."[21]

To Bush, evil lurked and freedom beckoned. To Bush, ideals and interests could be rhetorically reconciled in the verbiage of a "new American internationalism." To Bush, military power, free trade, and strong alliances sufficed to run a campaign in which his domestic programs and initiatives appeared far more consequential than his foreign policy agenda. But his priority was clear: "I will defend the American people against missiles and terror." He emphasized: "Once a strategic afterthought, homeland defense has become an urgent duty." To protect the homeland and deter rogue states and great power competitors, the United States needed a ballistic missile defense system.[22]

In these speeches at the Citadel in South Carolina and the Reagan Library in California, there was little focus on Iraq, no mention of Afghanistan, and no reference to the terrorist group of Islamic fundamentalists known as al Qaeda. In an interview Gerson acknowledged that he knew almost nothing about al Qaeda before the attacks on 9/11. When asked on the campaign trail about the Taliban, Bush did not seem to know who they were. Nor did Rice and her Vulcans focus much attention on the terrorist group, or its leader Osama bin Laden. Although Bush spoke vaguely and emphatically about terror and technology, Afghanistan was simply not on his or the Vulcans' "radar screen" in 1999 and 2000.[23]

But Iraq was on Bush's radar screen. In his major speeches, he said little about Iraq, but in the debates with his Democratic foe, Al Gore, he referred to Saddam Hussein more than any other foreign leader. Bush knew that the coalition that his father had put together in 1990— and that Clinton had tried to sustain—was falling apart.[24] He emphasized that sanctions were faltering, and the inspectors were gone. He acknowledged that he did not know whether Saddam Hussein was still developing weapons of mass destruction, but Bush warned that there would be serious consequences if he were doing so. The Middle East, he emphasized, was a part of the globe that was important to the United States. The United States had "friends" there. The region was also important because there was an energy crisis in the United States, and "a lot of the energy is produced from the Middle East." Hussein, he said, "is a danger. We don't want him fishing in troubled waters in the Middle East." Bush acknowledged it would be difficult to revitalize the coalition. "One of the reasons why I think it's important for this nation to develop an anti-missile system [is] . . . to be able to say to the Saddam Husseins of the world or the Iranians, don't dare threaten our friends."[25]

Yet there is no evidence that Iraq was a major preoccupation of the presidential candidate. When John McLaughlin, the deputy director of the CIA, went to Texas to give the Republican presidential candidate his first briefing, Bush listened attentively while McLaughlin discussed, among other topics, Hussein's history with weapons of mass destruction. McLaughlin told him the inspectors were gone and the agency did not have a clear idea of what Hussein was doing. When CIA analyst Michael Morell began to give Bush his daily intelligence briefings in the weeks before he took office, Morell emphasized that the analysts had missed Hussein's nuclear weapons program in the 1980s. By the time they discovered it, the Iraqi dictator was only a year away from posing a real threat. Bush absorbed this information, but was not overly concerned. "My view," said Morell, "from the first day briefing him," was that "he had no preoccupation with Iraq. It was very clear to me that he didn't harbor a particular animosity toward Saddam either because of the unfinished business of the Gulf War or because of the assassination attempt on his father's life."[26] When the British ambassador, Christopher Meyer, went down to Austin to talk to Bush, he found that neither the Middle East nor Iraq was among the candidate's top concerns; ballistic missile defense was. Iraq seemed like a "grumbling appendix."[27]

Nor was Iraq very high on the agenda of Dick Cheney, Bush's choice for vice president on the Republican ticket. Cheney was not a neocon; he was a conservative nationalist. He did not take office advocating regime change or democracy promotion in Iraq. He did have a deep interest in military and intelligence matters, and Bush wanted him to play an outsize role in three areas: homeland security, energy, and government reorganization. But Iraq was just one of many issues on his busy agenda as he prepared to take office, and not high among them.[28]

Cheney grew up in Wyoming, and had a checkered career as a student at Yale and the University of Wisconsin. Deeply conservative, very intelligent, hard-working, and taciturn, he went to Washington as a young man and wound up working for Donald Rumsfeld, a former Illinois congressman and ambitious young Republican politician, in the Office of Economic Opportunity. Subsequently, Cheney followed Rumsfeld to the White House when Rumsfeld became chief of staff to President Gerald Ford. And when Ford asked Rumsfeld to be secretary of defense, Cheney took the position of Ford's chief of staff at age thirty-five. After Ford lost the 1976 election, Cheney returned to Wyoming, ran for Congress, and rose quickly in the ranks of House Republicans. Bush's father asked Cheney to be his secretary of defense in 1989 after his first candidate for the position was forced to step aside. Cheney never got very close to W.'s father, but his service was deeply appreciated and Bush 41 encouraged his son to include Cheney among his mentors when he prepared to run for the presidency. W. liked Cheney, respected his advice, and asked Cheney to help vet candidates for the vice presidency. Watching him operate, appreciating his carefulness, efficiency, and tact, and knowing that Cheney had no aspirations to be president himself, he eventually asked Cheney to join him on the ticket.[29]

Cheney's role in the early years of the Bush administration has been dwelled upon in many accounts, but, as we shall see, it has often been overemphasized particularly in relationship to decisions regarding

Iraq. The misunderstanding is not surprising because the vice president did have a special relationship with the president. He met with Bush frequently—sometimes several times a day. Cheney rarely conveyed his views to other advisers or even his subordinates, yet expressed them directly and privately to the one man who counted, his boss, the president of the United States. Bush respected Cheney, relied on his experience, and trusted him. He felt confident that Cheney would defer when they disagreed. Cheney "knew I was in charge," Bush wrote in his memoir. One of the biggest myths about the administration, said Lewis "Scooter" Libby, Cheney's chief of staff, was that the vice president ran the administration. It is just an "urban legend" that Bush was the pawn of the vice president, emphasized Richard Clarke, the counterterrorism expert.[30]

Once the election took place and the Supreme Court ruled on the ballot-counting controversy in Florida, Bush named his other top advisers. He chose Colin Powell, the former chairman of the Joint Chiefs of Staff during his father's administration, to be the first African-American to serve as secretary of state. Listening to Dick Cheney, Bush selected Donald Rumsfeld to be secretary of defense. The president-elect then asked George Tenet, Clinton's CIA director, to stay in his position. Given the trust and rapport they had established during the preceding eighteen months, Bush selected Condi Rice to be his national security adviser. Many of the Vulcans then filled out other top positions in the administration. After Rumsfeld rejected Armitage as his deputy secretary, Powell asked him—his very close friend—to fill the number two spot in the State Department. Wolfowitz then passed muster with Rumsfeld, who selected him to be his deputy in the Pentagon. Rice chose Hadley to be her principal assistant, and the president asked Zoellick to be the US trade representative.

Given the stature and close ties among many of these advisers, Bush had reason to assume that they would work well together. His intent was to set goals and priorities and then delegate responsibility to competent subordinates who would run their departments. He liked to think of himself as a tough-minded chief executive who knew how to make decisions. He expected Rice to coordinate policy. She quickly learned that rather than constituting a harmonious team of top managers, they started feuding with one another and disrespecting the process that she and Hadley hoped to institute. Initially, the brewing discord did not have much of an impact because Bush focused his attention on his domestic agenda, and his foreign policy advisers did not challenge his priorities.[31]

In his inaugural address on January 20, 2001, Bush crisply stated his key goals: improving America's schools, reforming Social Security and Medicare, and cutting taxes. He framed his agenda in the language of compassionate conservatism. "Our public interest depends on private character, on civic duty and family bonds and basic fairness, on uncounted, unhonored acts of decency, which give direction to our freedom."[32] His administration quickly formulated proposals to slash taxes, support educational reform, and nurture faith-based voluntarism. He won major legislative victories, notwithstanding a small majority in the House and a split Senate.

Bush, of course, did not ignore foreign policy. In his inaugural address, he echoed themes of his campaign: "We will build our defense beyond challenge lest weakness invite challenge. We will confront weapons of mass destruction so that a new century is spared new horrors. The enemies of liberty and our country should make no mistake: America remains engaged in the world, by history and by choice, shaping a balance of power that favors freedom."[33]

What these words meant, of course, was yet to be determined. But, after consulting with Cheney, Rumsfeld, and Powell, Rice submitted a memorandum to Bush three weeks before inauguration day setting forth a "blueprint and a calendar" for the first six months of his tenure. The aim was "to renew America's leadership in the world." This could be done by "boosting military readiness and morale," transforming "defense structure and strategy," and focusing on restoring the nation's "leadership with our Allies," especially in economic and political military affairs. Nothing was more important than defending "America's interests in the Persian Gulf and furthering peace in the Middle East, based on a secure Israel." Rather than "play defense," Rice wanted "to develop policies that are active on Iraq, . . . and are more deliberate on the peace process" between Israelis and Palestinians. While little could be achieved immediately in the bloody struggle between Palestinians and Israelis, Rice stressed that UN sanctions against Iraq "had reached a dead-end." Moreover, the "episodic bombing of Iraq" only made things worse. She thought a "more aggressive policy toward Saddam Hussein" made sense, "but it would cause serious problems in our relations with NATO Allies and the moderate Arab world." This caveat was important because Rice also wanted to strengthen America's alliances, support Russia's stable democratic development, and channel China's rise "into peaceful and pluralist directions."

The memorandum said nothing about Afghanistan or al Qaeda, yet it did highlight the importance of checking the spread of WMD and introducing new measures to combat terrorism. Rice acknowledged that "despite our best efforts, WMD will likely become more accessible and widespread." "Intelligence," she emphasized, was "the first, best line of defense against both WMD and terrorism," and it was imperative to augment US capabilities. Knowing that nonproliferation and counterterrorism measures "may fail in some cases, we must prepare urgently to defend the American homeland from these threats."[34]

Nonetheless, Rice did not feel the sense of urgency that pulsated among her counterterrorism experts and those in the CIA and the National Security Agency (NSA). She retained Dick Clarke on her staff. He had coordinated counterterrorism initiatives during the latter years of the Clinton administration and often sat with other "principal" officeholders—the secretary of defense, the secretary of state, and the national security adviser, among others—when they discussed salient issues. Clarke gave her a memorandum on January 25, 2001, calling "urgently" for a principals meeting to assess the danger posed by the al Qaeda network. In his view, the threat was grave, representing a transnational challenge that required a multiregional policy. He explained that al Qaeda was an "organized major force that is using a distorted version of Islam" to drive the United States out of the Muslim world and to supplant friendly, moderate regimes with theocracies. He wanted the principals to agree on a strategy to end the al Qaeda sanctuary in Afghanistan. He proposed aid to the Northern Alliance in Afghanistan, an amalgam of ethnic warriors who were fighting to overthrow the Taliban government in Kabul. He advocated support for anti–al Qaeda operations from North Africa to Southeast Asia and specifically called for assistance to Uzbekistan. He attached a strategy paper that he and his associates had prepared in December 2000. That paper enumerated the many terrorist groups "sponsored" by al Qaeda.

The organization recently had expanded its contacts with Palestinian rejectionist groups, like Hamas and the Palestine Islamic Jihad. It had "substantial" cells in Morocco, Tunisia, Saudi Arabia, Pakistan, and Algeria. It had additional offshoots in Canada, England, Ireland, Israel, Italy, Spain, Germany, Belgium, Thailand, and Turkey. It had been involved in "a series of high profile attacks on the US in early 1990s." It still had supporters in the United States and worked with collaborators to smuggle bombs across its borders. Categorically, the memorandum stated, "al Qida is present in the United States." Even more worrisome were the reports "that al Qida is attempting to develop or acquire chemical or radiological weapons."[35]

Rice did not share Clarke's assessment of the al Qaeda threat. Like many other officials joining the Bush administration, she regarded Clarke as a bureaucratic self-promoter seeking more staff and more funding to deal with the issues that he oversaw. She downgraded his status, and assigned the issue to a group of deputy secretaries, including Clarke.[36] Her own attention gravitated to North Korea, the Palestinian-Israeli conflict, and the means to deal with Beijing after a Chinese jet fighter collided with an American espionage plane. These were the foreign policy matters that gained visibility in the press and commanded the president's attention during his initial months in office. Behind the scenes, however, Clarke and the deputy secretaries labored diligently to design a workable long-term strategy to deal with al Qaeda.

President Bush made no effort during these early months to design an overall national security strategy. He met only once with his full National Security Council, on January 30, and announced that Rice, not Cheney, would run future meetings, thereby resolving a simmering dispute between the folks working for the vice president and those working for Rice.[37] Rice's own inclination was to eschew any operational role, allow the Department of Defense to make defense strategy, and empower the Department of State to conduct foreign policy. Secretary of State Powell, for his part, wanted to quell the intifada inside Israel and mediate the Palestinian-Israeli conflict. Deputy Secretary Armitage hoped to diffuse the incendiary controversies in South Asia between Pakistan and India. Other State Department officials labored to strengthen relations with NATO allies, thwart North Korea's nuclear ambitions, and tamp down the acrimony with China. On some of these issues, they clashed with their counterparts in the offices of the vice president or the secretary of defense; on others, like the re-nunciation of the anti-ballistic missile treaty with Russia, they worked harmoniously. Rice sought consensus, yet disputes occasionally forced the president to intervene, sometimes supporting Powell, oftentimes not. But Bush never met with his full national security team during the spring and summer of 2001.[38]

Rice, Powell, Rumsfeld, and Cheney—the key "principals"—did meet numerous times in these early months to discuss Iraq policy. They wrestled over defining US goals. Acknowledging that there was little chance to topple Hussein and that his foes in exile were weak and di-vided, they did not dwell on regime change. They wanted to thwart his weapons of mass destruction programs and contain the threat he posed to neighbors. They focused on the faltering sanctions regime and the dangers American pilots increasingly faced conducting operations in the no-fly zones. In February 2001, the Iraqis launched fourteen surface-to-air missiles and used anti-aircraft fire fifty-one times against American and British planes. On February 15, the United States retal-iated above the 33rd parallel, hitting targets outside the no-fly zone, triggering demonstrations in many capitals, and disrupting the first bilateral meeting between Bush and Mexican president Vicente Fox.[39]

When Bush met with British prime minister Tony Blair on February 23, he and Secretary of State Powell outlined US concerns. "I want to develop a realistic policy on Iraq," said Bush at the very onset of the discussion. Arab friends, he continued, did not think US policy was working. They thought sanctions were hurting Iraqi children, and roiling popular sentiment in their own countries. Powell then elabo-rated on the administration's thinking. Iraq was much weaker than a decade ago. "But there are problems," he said. "Saddam is still there. And he is using his oil wealth not to benefit his people but to develop weapons of mass destruction. His nuclear programs did not amount to much, but his chemical and biological problems raised 'big questions.'" "Controlling Saddam's arms must be a priority. He must come into compliance with the inspections regime. . . . If he did so, we could sus-pend sanctions and eventually eliminate them." Bush then emphasized his concerns with the no-fly zones. They "scare me." He believed that Iraqi anti-aircraft fire would bring down an American plane and lead to the loss of American lives. If action were taken, Bush wanted no "pin pricks"; "we should strike to hurt him, not chase our tail." Bush wanted fewer missions, "more erratic, hard to predict missions." Bush's distaste for Hussein was palpable: "He does not accept our values and understands only force." But he stated his goal clearly: "isolate Saddam, and make him less of an actor on the world scene." The British left the meeting understanding that the president was not advocating regime change.[40]

Ballistic missile defense and overall defense strategy—not Iraq—were the issues that most consumed the attention of Secretary of Defense Rumsfeld and Deputy Secretary Wolfowitz. Rumsfeld had chaired a commission on missile defense in 1998. What he learned during that experience shaped his approach to military strategy. In a world of smaller, but more deadly threats, the United States had to be able to defend itself and its friends "against attacks by missiles and other terror weapons." This was essential "to protect our freedom to act in a crisis." Adversaries, he insisted, must be denied "the opportunity and benefits from the threat or use of weapons of mass destruction." Wolfowitz, like Rumsfeld, dwelled on the need to transform US armed forces to deal with looming threats, and he did not even mention Iraq during his confirmation hearing. "We need a deterrence," Wolfowitz insisted, that will "deny our adversaries the opportunity and benefits that come from the use of weapons of mass destruction." In simple terms, this meant that counterproliferation initiatives were imperative to deny foes the chance to blackmail the United States. The United States must not be self-deterred by fears that adversaries possessed and might use weapons of mass destruction in future crises.[41]

Rumsfeld and Wolfowitz were not worried about an imminent threat. On June 21, Rumsfeld told the Senate Armed Services Committee, "Today America is strong; we face no immediate threat to our existence as a nation or our way of life." This position afforded the United States a unique opportunity to transform its military establishment and its strategy to meet new challenges. Warning that "complacency can kill," Rumsfeld dwelled on the threat posed by rogue states with weapons of mass destruction. "Imagine," he said to the Senate committee, "what might happen if a rogue state demonstrated the capability to attack the US or European populations with nuclear, chemical or biological weapons of mass destruction? A policy of intentional vulnerability by the Western nations could give rogue states the power to hold our people hostage to nuclear blackmail—in an effort to prevent us from projecting force to stop aggression." Old-fashioned deterrence could not work with leaders like Saddam Hussein and Kim Jong-il, the leader of North Korea. No one could be certain how they will react in a crisis. "We know from experience that they have already demonstrated a willingness to use these weapons." But Rumsfeld was less worried about their use in wartime than in peacetime. "The regimes seeking ballistic missiles and nuclear, chemical and biological weapons see them not only as weapons to use in war, but as tools of coercion—means by which they can intimidate their neighbors and prevent others from projecting force to defend against aggression. . . . [T]hey are doing it because they believe that they can use these weapons to deter us from acting in ways contrary to their interests."42

From the moment he entered the Pentagon, Rumsfeld pushed relentlessly to shake things up, transform its bureaucratic processes, and orchestrate a new strategy. He brought in Steve Cambone, who had run the missile defense commission, as his closest aide. They disdained and distrusted many of the civilian bureaucrats who ran key parts of the Pentagon and also many of the general officers on the joint staff and elsewhere in the department. They brought in their own consultants to work on the Quadrennial Defense Review. Their actions alienated many of their subordinates and infuriated some military officers. Rumsfeld was tough, relentless, demanding, and often contemptuous. He remonstrated against all the constraints he faced, often not realizing how his own attitude and behavior reinforced opponents of change. People respected his intelligence and his drive, but they often abhorred his manner. General Hugh Shelton, the chairman of the Joint Chiefs of Staff, detested Rumsfeld. Shelton's assistant, Douglas Lute, noted Rumsfeld's "caustic style, a dismissive style that did not promote a sense of being in this together, a sense of teamwork." Other officers despised Cambone. Christopher Lamb, a high-level civilian official who supported the objectives of his new bosses, nonetheless recounted a general telling him that if "he had just one bullet left in his gun he would save it for Cambone." "In my entire professional career," said Lamb, "I've never been in an environment that was so politically charged or just filled with animosity."[43]

The new strategy Rumsfeld and Wolfowitz championed was a "capabilities-based strategy." It was "premised on the idea that to be effective abroad, America must be safe at home." It was geared to a new era of uncertainty when many nations and non-state actors were seeking WMD and developing asymmetric capabilities to strike the United States, but officials could not identify the most likely source of threat. "It is possible, however, to anticipate the capabilities that an adversary might employ to coerce its neighbors, deter the United States from acting in defense of its allies and friends, or directly attack the United States or its deployed forces." This strategy, Rumsfeld and Wolfowitz stressed, also afforded the United States the opportunity to capitalize on its advanced technologies and capabilities, but it depended on huge new investments and a willingness of military leaders to discard traditional thinking and antiquated weapons systems and embrace strategies that emphasized information, mobility, and flexibility.[44]

The president embraced this approach, and so did Dick Cheney. In May 2001, Bush asked Cheney to oversee homeland security. This assignment appealed to Cheney who, as a former secretary of defense, cared deeply about strategy, security, and intelligence. His specific charge was to ensure the homeland would be protected from—and able to recover after—an attack with weapons of mass destruction. Cheney asked Scooter Libby, his chief of staff, to take charge of this matter, a responsibility that Libby deemed important and challenging. Cheney and Libby talked frequently to Tenet at the CIA and to Clarke on Rice's staff. Libby assembled a team of experts to review past studies, ponder new initiatives, and make recommendations. He and Cheney were very worried about a prospective attack on the American homeland with biological or chemical weapons. They arranged to participate in the "Dark Winter" bioterrorism exercise at Andrews Air Force Base on June 22 and 23, 2001. Arranged by the Center for Strategic and International Studies and the Johns Hopkins Center for Civilian Biodefense, the exercise aimed to improve decision-making should a bioterrorist attack, like smallpox, occur simultaneously with portentous international developments. The core scenario involved a prospective attack by Iraq on Kuwait in the aftermath of the lifting of sanctions and the termination of the no-fly zones.[45]

Libby and his colleagues agreed that not much progress was made on homeland defense during their first months in office, partly because Cheney's own attention was diverted by an energy task force that the president asked him to chair. With blackouts plaguing California, hurting the economy, and capturing public attention, officials knew they had to address this matter. The secrecy of the commission's work engendered much controversy, as did Cheney's indifference to carbon emissions and his opposition to the Kyoto Treaty, an international agreement to deal with global warming. Cheney's commission highlighted the need to increase supplies, exploit new technologies, enhance efficiency, promote conservation, and diversify sources. It did not focus attention on Iraq and Iran. Noting the importance of OPEC and Persian Gulf oil resources to the global economy, the study urged the administration to open up Saudi Arabia, Kuwait, Qatar, Algeria, and the United Arab Emirates to foreign investment and to integrate the US, Canadian, and Mexican energy sectors. But it also emphasized that "measures to enhance US energy security . . . [must] begin at home."[46]

While Cheney labored on this comprehensive energy study, Scooter Libby and Eric Edelman, his foreign policy adviser, lamented the absence of a coherent, overall international strategy. They felt policy was drifting. Their uneasiness grew in May and June when warnings of a terrorist attack from al Qaeda escalated. Although Rice and Hadley tried to design a comprehensive approach to the region—including Afghanistan, Pakistan, and India—Edelman and Libby felt the regional approach was insufficient. In their view, the administration needed a comprehensive strategy that integrated and reconciled the pursuit of interests in different parts of the globe, something like the Defense Policy Guidance they had worked on in 1992. They were "struggling" with lots of discrete issues, "one-offs," ruminated Edelman.[47]

The intelligence analysts and counterterrorism experts, however, thought action—not study—was imperative. "The threat from terrorism is real, it is immediate, and it is evolving," CIA director George Tenet told the Senate Armed Services Committee in March 2001.[48]

As the danger mounted in May, Tenet and his deputy director, John McLaughlin, anguished. "From every nook and cranny of the planet," Tenet subsequently wrote, information poured in of an impending spectacular attack. "We are going to get hit," Tenet told Rumsfeld's aide, Steve Cambone. Morell, the president's daily briefer, conveyed the news to Bush. Rarely in Morell's career had he seen such ominous information, warnings of a "history-changing" strike. The president kept asking where the attack would occur and when. Tenet and Morell said they did not know, but they were certain of its eventuality. Could it take place inside the United States? Bush pressed. Morell gave the same answer, again and again: "There is nothing in the intelligence to indicate that [it would take place in the United States], but this guy, Bin Laden," said Morell, "would like nothing more than to bring the fight here and he has the capability to do that."[49]

Bush's queries prompted Morell to ask his colleagues to prepare a special briefing for the president on the al Qaeda threat to the United States. By the time Morell presented it on August 6, the warnings had waned. Bush was then at his Crawford, Texas, ranch for several weeks of vacation. Morell still briefed him every day, but there was nothing new to report. "Between mid-July and September 11, it is virtual radio silence," Morell recollected. The president seemed reassured that, if an attack occurred, it would more likely emanate outside the United States than inside. Nonetheless, Cofer Black, the director of the counterterrorism center, urged his colleagues to go on a war footing. Nothing of that sort happened. Nobody, noted Morell—a great admirer of the president—grabbed the reins and said, "Let's sit down and make sure the entire US government is focused on a strategy." They just "waddled along," said Armitage.[50]

During his August stint on his ranch in Crawford, Bush nevertheless had reason to reflect favorably on his first nine months in office. He had secured his tax cuts, garnered legislative support for his education bill, and created a faith-based office in the White House. He had wrestled with the issue of whether the federal government should support stem cell research and had decided to sustain work on existing stem cells but not support additional initiatives. His domestic agenda was proceeding nicely, and his polling numbers were in the mid-50s approval range.

But his foreign policy was floundering. There was no clear direction to it. In July, Rice turned some attention to writing a national strategy paper, and secured assistance from the Policy Planning Staff in the Department of State. Her draft was entirely conventional, a statement that could have been written with only slight permutations by anyone in the foreign policy establishment at the time, Democrat or Republican. It began, "This is a time of opportunity." No "hostile global rival" could challenge American power. The opportunity should be exploited to create an open, free, law-abiding international order. Only three impediments threatened this goal: discord among the advanced democracies; renewal of great power security competition; "and tyranny, corruption, ignorance, poverty, and disease." The United States should overcome these obstacles "not by acting unilaterally," or seeking "hegemony." There was little of "lasting consequence" that could be achieved "without the sustained cooperation of the European allies." Prudence dictated that the administration be wary of the rise of China, the resurgence of Russia, and the potential of India, but it should seek to develop cooperative relationships based on free markets, respect for human rights, and democratic freedoms. Regarding those few countries still afflicted with "outright despotism," like North Korea and Iraq, the United States had to deal with them "firmly and without illusions as to their legitimacy." The "external threats" they posed had to be contained, while the administration labored to "alleviate the internal suffering of their people." Overall, the United States must nurture its own economic base, support education, and reinvigorate trade. The draft eschewed unilateralist impulses, although the administration's rejection of the Kyoto Treaty and the International Criminal Court, among other actions, already had roiled many of its traditional allies.[51]

Rice's paper then turned its attention to US military capabilities and defense strategy. For the most part it echoed the work going on in the Department of Defense. The country had no rivals. "The threat of nuclear war had decreased dramatically." Yet danger lurked from "asymmetric threats—weapons of mass destruction, cyber-war, anti-satellite weapons." The United States had "to prepare for the unexpected." To do so, the United States had to discard its Cold War strategy; downsize its reliance on tanks, cruisers, and bombers; and build a "force structure that is altogether more mobile, stealthy, and lethal." The goal was to reassure allies, dissuade potential adversaries, deter hostile acts, and defeat attacks if dissuasion and deterrence failed. "We must be able to defend at home—against terrorists and asymmetric threats—in order that we may confidently defend abroad."[52]

During the late summer, when the threat from a terrorist attack seemed to abate, attention gravitated back to Iraq. Most top policymakers thought that Iraq was contained—for the immediate future. Even Bush's more hawkish advisers—Cheney, Libby, Rumsfeld, and Wolfowitz—thought that Hussein, for the time being, could be kept in his box.[53] But there was little doubt, even among Bush's more dovish advisers, that he was a looming threat. New information suggested that Hussein might be acquiring aluminum tubes to revive his nuclear program. At the same time, reports from a new source—an Iraqi scientist in exile in Germany, code-named Curveball—highlighted Hussein's chemical warfare capabilities. Carl Ford, the head of intelligence and research in the State Department, wrote Powell a memorandum, "Iraq—Saddam Riding Higher than Ever." According to Ford, Hussein was "buoyed by his gains over the past year." He had consolidated his hold on power, reduced his diplomatic isolation, and further eroded sanctions. Emboldened, "Saddam is preparing to push back hard against any efforts by us to restrict him." William Burns, Powell's assistant secretary for Near Eastern Affairs, saw things much the same way: "Saddam Hussein continues to garner support for lifting sanctions against Iraq and to link his cause to the Arab-Israeli conflict via fiery rhetoric and aid for Palestinian victims." Hussein was "in his jail cell" for the time being, but might break out if sanctions collapsed and enforcement of no-fly zones ended.[54]

Defense Department officials were not enthusiastic about Powell's desire for "smart sanctions"—sanctions earmarked to limit the import of items with military capabilities. At meetings, Wolfowitz advocated a long-term policy designed to topple Hussein and bring about regime change. But he was not supporting a military invasion, or the deployment of US ground forces. He wanted to arm the Iraqi opposition, enforce a safe-haven zone in Shi'a-dominated southern Iraq, and recognize a provisional government in areas outside of Hussein's control. Wolfowitz abhorred Hussein, the repressive tyrant, but he was not driven by a desire to promote democracy in that beleaguered country. In testimony to the Senate Armed Services Committee on July 12, he explained precisely what was on his mind: a rogue state with a genocidal dictator might engage in aggression and threaten to use missiles armed with weapons of mass destruction. The short-range missile threat, Wolfowitz insisted, arrived a decade ago; the intermediate-range missile threat now existed; and the long-range threat to American cities "is just over the horizon." Countries like Iraq were developing these capabilities to check Washington's ability to project force to stop their acts of aggression. They wanted to "hold our people hostage to blackmail and terror." They aimed to "force us into a truly isolationist posture," to self-deter. "And they would not even have to use the weapons in their possession to affect our behavior and achieve their ends." Wolfowitz finished his testimony in behalf of new resources for missile defense, not by focusing on Iraq, but by specifying the threats from Iran and North Korea.[55]

Rumsfeld totally supported Wolfowitz's ideas about missile defense; they were his—Rumsfeld's—ideas. But the defense secretary was conflicted about regime change. On July 27, he submitted a memo to Rice, with copies to Cheney and Powell. Sanctions were weakening, and Hussein's air defenses were improving, making US protection of the no-fly zones more and more dangerous. But rather than focus on sanctions and no fly zones, Rumsfeld wanted his colleagues to grapple with overall policy. He outlined three options. The United States "could roll up its tents and end the no-fly zones before someone is killed or captured." Washington could then monitor Hussein's behavior from a distance. This would end "the pretense" that prevailing policy was "keeping Saddam in the box" when we know he has crawled a good distance out of the box" and will "ultimately" endanger his neighbors and our interests. This option seemed to have little appeal because it was evident that Hussein was still developing his weapons of mass destruction and the means to deliver them. In light of this, Rumsfeld posed a second option: trying to get America's moderate Arab friends to support a policy of regime change. He knew those friends would have strong reservations, but he noted that "the risks of a serious regime-change policy must be weighed against the certainty of an increasingly bold and nuclear-armed Saddam in the future." A third option "is to take a crack at initiating contact with Saddam Hussein." He might respond positively. "Opening a dialogue with Saddam would be an astonishing departure for the USG, although I did it for President Reagan." Although it would garner some praise, Rumsfeld added, it might cause friends, "especially those in the region, to question our strength, steadiness, and judgment." And, in any case, Hussein was not likely to accommodate US interests over the long run.

Rumsfeld refused to say, as often was the case, what he favored. He noted that "Saddam's options will increase with time, while ours could decrease." Iraq policy, moreover, needed to be considered in conjunction with the Arab-Israeli situation. "A major success with Iraq would enhance US credibility and influence throughout the region." In conclusion, he said: "why don't we get some smart people to take this memo, rip it apart, and refashion it into an appropriate paper for discussion at an early Principal Committee meeting?"[56]

Zalmay Khalilzad, the Afghan-born national security expert on Rice's staff, was doing just that. Khalilzad had grown up in Kabul, spent a year in California as a high school exchange student, and then studied for his doctoral degree in political science at the University of Chicago with the renowned strategist Albert Wohlstetter. After teaching for ten years at Columbia University, Khalilzad served in the Ronald Reagan and George H. W. Bush administrations. In May 2001, Rice and Hadley asked him to be their senior director for the Persian Gulf and Southwest Asia. Khalilzad spent a good part of the summer re-examining policy toward Iraq. Starting with the fact that it was the declared policy of the United States under the Clinton administration to support regime change, he laid out a series of options to enhance sanctions, promote fissures within the regime, and support Hussein's foes at home and abroad.[57]

At a principals meeting in early August—the vice president linked in from Wyoming, and Rumsfeld and others were in the Situation Room in the White House—they thrashed through the issues yet again. Edelman described the meeting vividly. Powell and other people "were pissing all over poor Zal's paper. They were discussing all the usual stuff—assistance to opposition groups, tightening sanctions, doing this, doing that. So everyone is crapping on the paper." Then, suddenly, with a flair for the dramatic, Rumsfeld picked up the paper and threw it in the middle of the table, "You know what? You guys are right. This is a piece of crap. . . . This is a crappy policy; it is the crappiest Iraq policy I can imagine except compared to all the rest. . . . I mean none of these things are going to be completely free of problems. No matter what we do this is a messy problem, that's why we're discussing it. . . . This is what we get paid for," Rumsfeld concluded in an exasperated tone.[58]

There was a lot of laughter. But nothing was resolved. As Khalilzad wrote in his own memoir, "The document laid out a series of options short of a full-scale invasion that the president could consider if he decided to topple Saddam's regime."[59] But the principals did not resolve their differences and the president did not have to decide anything. There were no orders to update war plans. Nor did President Bush throw strong support behind the State Department's desire for smart sanctions.[60] Nobody felt satisfied with the prevailing policy toward Iraq, but they could not agree on how to fix it. Their concern, however, was not democracy promotion; they were worried about the eroding sanctions, the absence of inspections, the risks to pilots enforcing the no-fly zones, new WMD initiatives, and the stability and peace of the region. Looming over the horizon was Hussein's Iraq, an Iraq armed with intermediate-range missiles and presumed chemical and biological weapons that might empower his aggression and paralyze American counter-measures in a regional crisis. If he were in a box for the time being, or not, he seemed likely to break out of it in the future—and then what?[61]

While high-level officials could not agree on a policy toward Iraq—and Bush displayed no great concern about it—they did resolve their differences and agree on a policy toward Afghanistan and al Qaeda. On August 13, the deputies approved Hadley's draft proposals to provide more assistance to anti-Taliban groups in Afghanistan and additional aid to Uzbekistan. The plan also called for diplomatic pressure on the Taliban government to disperse al Qaeda jihadists from their training camps, and for covert actions to topple it, if the leaders in Kabul refused to do so. Planning action over a three-year period, the recommendations also envisioned possible direct US military intervention. Powell, Cheney, Rumsfeld, and Rice were scheduled to discuss this plan in early September. Before the meeting, Clarke wrote Rice a blistering memorandum remonstrating against the procrastination of the last nine months. It was imperative, insisted Clarke, to decide whether al Qaeda represented "an existential threat to the American way of life," or did not. There was "no in-between," and the principals should ponder how they will feel, and what they would have wished they had done, when hundreds of Americans were killed. When Cheney, Powell, Rumsfeld, and their colleagues actually did meet on September 4, they quickly agreed on the proposed plan. Many specifics, however, still needed to be worked out regarding the financing and arming of Predator drones, the details of the covert initiatives, and the methods of direct US military intervention. Nonetheless, the National Security Policy Directive was sent to the president on September 10, and awaited his signature.[62]

President Bush displayed no alarm. He did not participate in the meeting on September 4, nor did he highlight the al Qaeda threat in previous weeks. He subsequently acknowledged, "I didn't feel that sense of urgency. My blood was not nearly as boiling."[63] In one cryptic meeting with Rice in the spring, he told her that he was "tired of swatting flies. I'm tired of playing defense. I want to take the fight to the terrorists."[64] But he did not follow up; the issue did not sustain his attention. He spent little time asking about the sources and motives of the terrorist group called al Qaeda. On one occasion, when Morell reiterated the salience of the al Qaeda threat, the president kiddingly told him, okay, Mike, "you've covered your ass." When Bush talked publicly about foreign policy in the days and weeks before 9/11, his focus was on missile defense. He spoke to Rice, Tenet, and Cheney almost every day and he heard a lot about the al Qaeda threat, but he did not communicate to the public any concerns about a prospective domestic attack.[65]

Nor did the threat of domestic terrorism command the sustained attention of any of his top advisers. Powell subsequently told the 9/11 Commission staff that the administration had taken a long list of actions to thwart the threat, but in an interview he conceded that he did not assign enough importance to this matter. His closest friend in the State Department, Richard Armitage, and his closest aide, William Smullen, acknowledged that the administration did not take the threat seriously enough.[66] Nor did Rumsfeld. When he listed dangerous surprises that he needed to think about, an al Qaeda attack was not among them. His subordinates, including Cambone and Wolfowitz, thought the reports of an impending attack might be disinformation.[67] They were frustrated that the intelligence community could not identify the nature or location of the threat, nor offer precise guidance on what to do.

Rice and Hadley adhered to the president's strategic priority— missile defense—while they worked diligently, albeit not urgently, to design a long-term regional strategy to deal with al Qaeda. They did not think the United States was a likely target. "The homeland threat was simply not sufficiently on anyone's radar screen at the national level before 9/11," Rice wrote.[68] That statement was not literally true because Cheney and Libby were very concerned with homeland security and they took Tenet's warnings seriously, but they did little to prepare domestic agencies to thwart the threat.[69] Nor did John Ashcroft, the attorney general, or the leaders of the FBI. The 9/11 Commission subsequently wrote, "domestic agencies never mobilized in response to the threat. They did not have direction, and they did not have a plan to institute. The borders were not hardened. Transportation systems were not fortified. Electronic surveillance was not targeted against a domestic threat."[70]

Nobody was ready for the attack on 9/11. It was not because administration officials were focused on Iraq and Saddam Hussein. It was because the president had not assigned significant importance to homeland security, had not spent much time on it, and had not catalyzed much action. Bush's priorities were domestic—taxes, education, and faith-based initiatives. His advisers did not contest those priorities. They believed the United States was in a preponderant position, and rather invulnerable to any immediate threats.

On September 10, 2001, President Bush prepared to fly to Florida to highlight one of his signature domestic priorities, the No Child Left Behind Act. Many of Rumsfeld's assistants were in Russia laying the groundwork for the renunciation of the anti-ballistic missile treaty and the furtherance of their plans for missile defense. Rumsfeld, on September 10, delivered a stunning address at the Pentagon, signifying what he cared most about. "The topic today," he announced, "is an adversary that poses a threat, a serious threat, to the security of the United

States of America. This adversary . . . attempts to impose its demands across time zones, continents, oceans and beyond. With brutal consistency, it stifles free thought and crushes new ideas. It disrupts the defense of the United States and places the lives of men and women in uniform at risk. . . . It's the Pentagon bureaucracy."[71]

3

9/11

AT 8:46 A.M. on September 11, 2001, American Airlines flight 11 crashed into the North Tower of New York City's World Trade Center, somewhere between the 94th and 98th floors. Traveling at a speed of 440 miles per hour, all eighty-one passengers and nine flight attendants on the plane died instantly. Tons of jet fuel spilled onto the floors of the building and into elevator shafts, spawning enormous fires and suffocating smoke. More than a thousand workers and visitors above the 98th floor had no chance of escape. Scores jumped from windows to certain death, several holding hands. A total of 1,466 visitors and employees perished.

About fifteen minutes later, at 9:03 A.M., United Airlines flight 175 smashed into the South Tower of the World Trade Center between the 77th and 85th floors. Millions of Americans, having heard of the first crash, were now watching news on television as the Boeing 767, traveling at a speed of 587 miles per hour, hit the building and erupted into a huge fireball. Hundreds of people died instantly, but many more on the lower floors descended steps, seeking to escape the inferno enveloping them. If they were able to make it to the plaza below, it was littered with furniture, computers, clothing, shoes, airplane seats, and parts of bodies. After waving gently for several minutes, at 9:59 A.M., the South Tower collapsed, with 110 stories of concrete, steel beams, glass, and wires plummeting to the earth, creating massive piles of black ash and asphyxiating smoke. About thirty minutes later, the North Tower also collapsed, killing everyone above the 91st floor as well as about 200 firefighters who had entered the building seeking to rescue people. The rubble on the ground rose to about 100 feet (Figure 3.1).

Meanwhile, at 9:38 A.M., American Airlines flight 77, scheduled to fly from Dulles Airport outside of Washington, DC, to Los Angeles, crashed into the Pentagon. Flying at maximum speed, the Boeing 757 with fifty-eight passengers ignited an immense explosion on the ground floor of the E-ring. The plane penetrated about 200 feet through brick and concrete, killed about 125 people inside the building, and ignited fires with intense heat, heavy smoke, and cascading flames. Although the damage was mostly limited to this one specific part of the Pentagon, more than 100 additional workers were injured.

Twenty-five minutes after AA flight 77 hit the Pentagon, United Airlines flight 93 crashed into the ground near Shanksville, Pennsylvania, instantly killing the thirty-seven passengers on the Boeing 757. The hijacked plane was probably bound for the Capitol Building when passengers tried, yet failed, to enter the cockpit and seize control of the plane, just twenty minutes away from its target in Washington, DC.[1]

Figure 3.1 The attacks on the World Trade Center and the Pentagon on 9/11 shocked the nation and catalyzed the Bush administration's global war on terror.
Getty Images, https://www.gettyimages.com/detail/news-photo/view-through-a-broken-out-office-win dow-shows-the-wreckage-news-photo/51514042

On that morning, September 11, 2001, as President George W. Bush entered Emma E. Booker Elementary School in Sarasota, Florida, just before 9 A.M., aides informed him that a plane had flown into the World Trade Center. He called Condoleezza Rice, his national security adviser. She told him that they had no real information on what happened, and he proceeded into the classroom for his publicity event, highlighting his commitment to education. While he sat in front of the room and the second graders read aloud from the book *The Pet Goat*, his chief of staff, Andrew Card, quietly approached him and whispered that a second plane had crashed into the South Tower. The president sat still for a few additional minutes, stared vacantly, and then politely asked to be forgiven for not delivering his prepared remarks. As he was whisked into his limo and driven to Air Force One, he spoke to Rice on the phone and she told him about the third jet striking the Pentagon.

"We're at war," the president declared quietly to Card and Karl Rove, two of his closest aides who were with him in Florida.[2] "My blood was boiling," President Bush subsequently wrote in his memoir, but to his aides he seemed focused, "preternaturally calm." He wanted to return to Washington immediately, but the Secret Service, Vice President Dick Cheney, and Rice warned him that it was unsafe. Angered, grudgingly, he flew to Barksdale Air Force Base in Louisiana. During the flight, communication back to Washington was difficult, but on the plane's television screen the president and his closest aides could see people climbing out the windows of the North Tower and grasping the ledges before leaping to their deaths. "I felt their agony and despair," the president later wrote. "I was certain I had just watched more Americans die than any president in history."[3]

Amid the confusing information he kept receiving, amid grief and anger, Bush still did not know the extent of the attack or its source. Even after the fourth plane went down in Shanksville, he did not know if the day's assaults were over. "There was a real fear," wrote Rove, that "the terrorists wanted to decapitate the government by killing its leaders, starting with President Bush."[4] On the plane to Barksdale, the president asked Michael Morell, his CIA briefer, "who did it?" Morell said it could be Iran or Iraq, but neither had reason to do something so risky. "I would bet everything I have, including my children's future, that the trail will lead to bin Laden and al Qaeda."[5] A few hours later, after the president flew to Offutt Air Force Base in Nebraska, CIA director George Tenet informed him on a videoconference call that three of the hijackers could now be linked to al Qaeda. Worse yet, more attacks were likely. Bush declared, "We are at war against terror, and from this day forward, this is the new priority of our administration."[6]

The attack on 9/11 by nineteen Islamic fundamentalist jihadists shocked, embarrassed, and infuriated Bush and his advisers. "I saw him transform," said Morell. "I saw him transform from a president who really didn't have a strong agenda, didn't really have a clear path that he was on, that quite frankly was struggling. . . . I saw him transform from that to commander-in-chief and to somebody who almost instantaneously" knew he had a mission "to protect the country from this happening again; I saw that right in front of me." From the president's first words on Air Force One, wrote Rove, his assistants knew Bush regarded the moment as a turning point in history.[7]

Bush said he "wanted to kick ass," and a few days later he told legislators, "fuck diplomacy."[8] But Morell, Rove, and others describe him as "calm, collected, determined."[9] The president disregarded the advice of Cheney and Rice and decided to return to the White House and address the nation. As Air Force One flew from Offutt back to the nation's capital in the late afternoon, the lights in the plane dimmed and several advisers fell asleep, but Bush wandered back into the staff compartment. Morell stood up and quietly asked him if he was okay. Morell could not recollect Bush's precise response, but the president's tone was unforgettable. "It wasn't the words," Morell reported, the words were banal, something like, "'I'm fine, Michael; thanks for asking.' But it was the tone that spoke volumes about his determination and his focus." His tone impressed Rove and others as well. Bush conveyed a new sense of purpose, of destiny. Morell attributed the transformation to the president's faith, a conviction that "he was made president to get the country through this and to make sure that this never happened again."[10]

When he returned to the White House in the early evening, the nation's capital was transformed. Driving into the city to help prepare his evening address, Karen Hughes, his confidante and communications director, described the stark new reality: "There was nothing: no one on the sidewalks; no one in the streets; no people, no cars, no signs of life in the nation's capital. From a distance, I saw something too bizarre to contemplate: men dressed in black brandishing machine guns. It felt like a scene from some foreign capital after a coup. . . . It was the most chilling image of the day: downtown Washington, the home of freedom and democracy, suddenly turned into an armed camp, the only sign of life, men in black holding instruments of death."[11]

Hughes reviewed the speech with the president. It was brief. Its goals were to provide reassurance and resolve. But in a few short paragraphs, Bush communicated his grasp of the situation, and his approach to the challenges ahead. The terrorist attack, he told the American people, was an assault on "our way of life," on our freedom. The "acts of mass murder" were intended to intimidate Americans, to catalyze "chaos and retreat." But that would not happen. His first priority, he declared, was to help the injured and protect the innocent. His administration would then identify the assailants and bring them to justice. Appealing for unity in "the war against terrorism," he declared, "We will make no distinction between the terrorists who committed these acts and those who harbor them." And he finished solemnly, asking for prayers to comfort those who grieve, and quoting Psalm 23, "Even though I walk through the valley of death, I fear no evil, for You are with me." "None of us," he concluded, "will ever forget this day. Yet we go forward to defend freedom and all that is good and just in the world."[12]

After his address, he met briefly with his top national security advisers (Figure 3.2), received confirmation that al Qaeda conducted the attack, and emphatically declared that nothing must interfere with waging the war on terror. "Nothing else matters. . . . This is our only agenda."[13] He then decided to go to sleep in his usual bedroom, ignoring pleas from the Secret Service that he and his wife, Laura, spend the night in the much safer bunker and operations room beneath the White House. As he tossed and turned, ruminating over the horrific and portentous events of the day, he was startled by shouts that the White House was under attack. In their nightclothes and bare feet, the president and his wife (carrying Barney, their Scottish terrier) were hustled down to the underground shelter. A few minutes later they were told it was a false alarm, that the fighter jet approaching the White House "was one of ours."[14]

Figure 3.2 Bush takes command, 9/11.
George W. Bush Library (LP-GWB), courtesy of the National Archives Catalog [National Archives identifier 5997259].

Fear of impending attacks pulsated through Washington as Bush prepared to meet with his national security team on the morning of September 12. Driving to the White House over the 14th Street Bridge, Michael Gerson smelled the Pentagon burning. Washington seemed transformed, the streets empty.[15] "I wondered how many sleeper cells there were in the United States," wrote Dick Clarke, the chief counterterrorism guru whose warnings had not been taken as seriously as they should have been by Rice, Secretary of Defense Donald Rumsfeld, and Under Secretary of Defense Paul Wolfowitz.[16] Before the formal meeting began, the president met with his closest aides in the Oval Office. Karen Hughes recalled that the president cut her off, and exclaimed, "Let's get the big picture. A faceless enemy has declared war on the United States, so we are at war. We are going to wage this war; it requires a strategy, a plan, a vision, a diplomatic effort and the understanding of the American people." This would now be the focus of his administration, he declared. "We have to explain it to the American people. We have to prepare for another attack, perhaps a much worse one." The likelihood "is that somebody's going to get blown up today," he muttered later that day.[17]

When all of his top advisers then assembled for the larger meeting, many topics needed to be addressed. Who was responsible for the attack? How could the military respond? What information had been collected about domestic threats? How to handle air traffic? How to protect power plants and nuclear reactors? And many more. But before Rumsfeld and General Hugh Shelton, the outgoing chairman of the Joint Chiefs of Staff, could begin a discussion of military options, Bush interceded and insisted on an assessment of all the tools at his disposal to wage war against terrorist groups: diplomatic, economic, financial, and political. Some participants felt the discussion turned chaotic; Stephen Hadley, his deputy national security adviser, believed the president catalyzed a careful assessment of grand strategy, an analysis that continued in the afternoon and that produced the global war on terror (GWOT).[18]

Discussing goals, the president and his advisers determined that the United States could not destroy al Qaeda. Their objective, explained Hadley, was to eliminate al Qaeda as a threat "to our way of life"—"to get to the point where it doesn't change how we live, the openness of our society." Nor would the United States wage war against all terrorist groups—not, for example, against the Basque separatists or FARC in Colombia; the United States needed to focus on those "with a global reach." If governments harbored terrorists, Bush insisted, they too would be treated accordingly. During the next few days, the president defined his priority. He repeatedly rejected suggestions from Rumsfeld and Wolfowitz that Iraq become a target for initial action. "We'll get to Iraq at the appropriate time," he declared. Although pressing Clarke for information about Iraq, the president did not think Saddam Hussein was the source of the attack. In Hadley's words, this was "not about Iraq, this is Afghanistan. Debate over."[19] When Wolfowitz tried to refocus attention on Iraq at meetings at Camp David—the presidential retreat—over the weekend of September 15 and 16, Bush shunted his advice aside.[20] Rather than hold Iraq accountable for the attack, he sent a shrill message to Hussein through the Iraqi representative at the United Nations that he had better not take advantage of America's preoccupation with Afghanistan.[21] The global war on terror would start by dislodging the Taliban from power in Afghanistan and eliminating the al Qaeda presence in that country. It would not end there; but that is where it would begin.

President Bush communicated his strategy to the American people in an address to Congress on September 20, nine days after the attack. He framed the challenge in rhetorical tropes that pitted freedom against tyranny, good against evil. He explained to the American people who attacked them—"a collection of loosely affiliated terrorist organizations known as al Qaeda." They practiced "a fringe form of Islamic extremism." They aimed to "kill Christians and Jews, to kill all Americans," and they made no distinctions between civilians and military. They had been responsible for previous attacks on American embassies and warships in the Persian Gulf. Their leader was Osama bin Laden. He was linked to terrorist organizations in more than sixty countries. Bin Laden and al Qaeda, Bush proclaimed, want "to overthrow existing governments in many Muslim countries." They want to "drive Israel out of the Middle East. They want to drive Christians and Jews out of vast areas of Asia and Africa."

Bush went on to explain that the Taliban government in Afghanistan welcomed al Qaeda and provided a safe haven and training grounds. The Taliban, Bush said, embodied the same values as al Qaeda. They "brutalized" their own people, oppressed women, jailed critics, and demanded religious conformity. The first goal of the United States, therefore, was to demand that the Taliban hand over the leaders of al Qaeda, destroy their training grounds, relinquish all foreign nationals unjustly imprisoned, and allow Americans access to certify that terrorists no longer operated in their country. These were non-negotiable demands, Bush insisted. Should the Taliban reject them, their leaders would share the same fate as the terrorists.

Bush then clarified for the American people the larger struggle in which they were now engaged. "Our war on terror begins with al Qaeda, but it does not end there. It will not end until every terrorist of global reach has been found, stopped, and defeated." It would be a long struggle, Bush said. It would be waged on many fronts: financial, diplomatic, and military. "We will pursue nations that provide aid or safe haven to terrorism. Every nation, in every region now has a decision to make: either you are with us, or you are with the terrorists. From this day forward, any nation that continues to harbor or support terrorism will be regarded by the United States as a hostile regime."

The mission could be no less, he explained, because the terrorists "hate our freedoms—our freedom of religion, our freedom of speech, our freedom to vote and assemble." They aimed to "disrupt and end" the American way of life. They desired to intimidate and sow fear; they wanted America to forsake its friends and retreat from the world. That was not going to happen, Bush declared. He intended to mobilize US military capabilities for a civilizational struggle, and he welcomed aid from America's friends abroad. But in fighting this battle, Bush told Americans, they must not forget their values. "We are in a fight for our principles, and our first responsibility is to live by them. No one should be singled out for unfair treatment or unkind words because of their ethnic background or religious faith."[22]

It is worth pausing here and reflecting on what the president was saying and doing. He was announcing a global war on terror. He was framing the struggle as a civilizational battle over a way of life. Like many of his advisers, Bush felt keenly that "our way of life" really was at stake. "We must rid our world of terrorists so our children and grandchildren can grow up in freedom," he declared.[23] "By sowing fear," Rumsfeld wrote, "terrorists seek to change our behavior and alter our values. Through their attacks, they trigger defensive reactions that could cause us to make our society less open, our civil liberties less expansive, and our official practices less democratic—effectively to nudge us closer to the totalitarianism they favor."[24] This was an updated iteration of the fear of the garrison state, a concern that had inspired the struggles against Nazism and communism. One is struck by how keenly the proponents of the global war on terror felt this way, and how, instinctively, they fell back on rhetorical tropes that resonated deeply in the American psyche. "This is a war against our way of life," ruminated Rumsfeld in one of his "snowflake" memoranda. "Victory is for our children to be able to go out of the house, play in the yard, and go to school without our fearing for their lives." Paradoxically, these advisers were not so much yearning to promote democracy abroad as they were seeking to preserve it at home. "If we don't want our way of life to be fundamentally altered," Wolfowitz explained in an interview on September 13, "we have got to go after the terrorists and get rid of them. That is why the stakes are so high."[25]

The president shared these views, and he was the key decision maker. Almost all participants comment favorably on the way he conducted himself during these first days: angry yet calm; determined yet dignified; empathetic yet vengeful; reassuring and inspiring. In the literature, however, Bush's role in the onset of the global war on terror is often obscured by the emphasis on Cheney, Rumsfeld, Wolfowitz, and Scooter Libby, the vice president's chief of staff—by their alleged obsession with Iraq.[26] This is wrong: Bush ordered the global war on terror; he insisted on going after state sponsors as well as the terrorists themselves; he placed the focus on Afghanistan; he relegated Iraq; he demanded employment of diverse tools; he insisted on projecting strength—boots on the ground. Nobody around him thought anyone but he was calling the signals in the immediate aftermath of 9/11. "He was absolutely in charge," Tenet recalled. He was "confident, determined, forceful," acknowledged Dick Clarke; "focused, straightforward, and tough," thought Alberto Gonzales, the White House counsel and friend of Bush. "In those critical moments for the country," wrote Rumsfeld, "he was somber, purposeful, and determined to act. He was deeply saddened, . . . but not distracted by his sorrow." While others around him were shaken, his clarity and calm inspired confidence. He "steadied me," confessed Rice.[27] And the public response was overwhelmingly positive. Bush's approval ratings soared into the 90 percent range, the highest in Gallup polling history.[28] On September 18, Congress authorized him to use military force against those responsible for the attack by a vote of 98–0 in the Senate and 420–1 in the House.

Yet it is important to recognize that Bush's global war on terror was not a surprising response to 9/11. Bush's predecessor, Bill Clinton, also placed terrorism "at the top of the diplomatic agenda," and had announced a similar policy. Clinton's 1998 national strategy paper declared: "As long as terrorists continue to target American citizens, we reserve the right to act in self-defense by striking at their bases and those who sponsor, assist or actively support them."[29] By the time Bush took office in January 2001 a variety of studies and reports had focused on the worldwide terrorist threat, on al Qaeda, on weapons of mass destruction, on rogue states and state sponsors. The National Commission

on Terrorism conducted its work in 1999, identified twenty-eight organizations on the State Department's terrorist list, and called for more
aggressive action to thwart their efforts and pressure their sponsors.
The terrorist groups, emphasized the commission, had become more
lethal, more focused on Americans, and more political in nature. Five
of the seven nations identified by the United States as state sponsors of
terrorism already had programs to develop weapons of mass destruction. The report then stated:

> Al-Qaida is the best known transnational terrorist organization.
> In addition to pursuing its own terrorist campaign, it calls on nu-
> merous militant groups that share some of its ideological beliefs to
> support its violent campaign against the United States. But neither
> al-Qaida's extremist political-religious beliefs nor its leader, Usama
> bin Ladin, is unique. If al-Qaida and Usama bin Ladin were to dis-
> appear tomorrow, the United States would still face potential ter-
> rorist threats from a growing number of groups opposed to perceived
> American hegemony. Moreover, new terrorist threats can suddenly
> emerge from isolated conspiracies or obscure cults with no previous
> history of violence.[30]

Analysts and officials dealing with counterterrorism stressed that
the terrorist threat was growing, multidimensional, and elusive. "The
threat from terrorism is real, it is immediate, and it is evolving," warned
Tenet in March 2001.[31] Admiral Thomas R. Wilson, the head of the
Defense Intelligence Agency (DIA), testified at the same time that he
worried most about a major terrorist attack, "either here or abroad," with
weapons designed "to produce mass casualties."[32] In early September,
the chairman of the JCS acknowledged that "a domestic terrorist attack could occur at any time."[33] General Tommy Franks, commander-
in-chief of US Central Command (CENTCOM), ruminated about a
catastrophic internal attack, but he emphasized that he was most concerned about the unprecedented cooperation between known and ob-
scure terrorist groups in the region under his command—the Middle
East, Persian Gulf, and Southwest Asia. Al Qaeda was indisputably
the greatest threat, particularly portentous and elusive because it was
a coalition of factions of radical Islamic groups operating in dozens

of countries in his region of command, and beyond, including the Philippines and Indonesia.[34]

When Bush and his advisers declared a global war on terror, dwelled on terrorist networks and their sponsors, and launched their assault on Afghanistan, their overriding goal was to prevent another attack on American citizens, the United States, and its allies. They stated this again and again in their policy memoranda, in their memoirs, and in their interviews. "Keep the terrorists from striking again," was Bush's number one goal. "Preventing the next attack," Cheney emphasized, should be "our top priority." Our "principal motivation," said Rumsfeld, should be self-defense, "not vengeance, retaliation, or punishment."[35] They agreed that defense meant going on the offensive: destroying the terrorists and persuading or intimidating the states that provided a safe haven or assistance to change course. In a memorandum to the president, Rumsfeld stated the goal simply and starkly, "We are after terrorists and the regimes that support them." Wolfowitz stated it publicly: "We have got to root out the terrorist networks. And we have got to end the support that they get from a number of states."[36]

These officials believed that weakness invited aggression. They embraced the paradox: the United States had become the most powerful nation in the world yet it also had become more vulnerable to terrorists, rogue states, and asymmetric threats.[37] State Department reports on global terrorism catalogued the number of terrorist attacks each year: 304 in 1997, 274 in 1998, 395 in 1999, 426 in 2000, and 348 in 2001. Twenty-five Americans died in 1996, six in 1997, twelve in 1998, five in 1999, twenty-three in 2000. In 2001, there were 219 attacks against US facilities and citizens. The portentous nature of the attacks also mounted: the New York World Trade Center in 1993, US and coalition troops stationed at Khobar Towers in Saudi Arabia in 1996, the American embassies in Kenya and Tanzania in 1998, and the Navy guided-missile destroyer USS *Cole* in Yemen's Aden harbor in 2000. If previously hesitant, Bush and his advisers now felt they had to reshape the global security environment that permitted terrorist networks to fester and flourish. The terrorists, Bush believed, "interpreted our lack of a serious response as a sign of weakness and an invitation to attempt more brazen attacks." His aims were clear: thwart attacks from any terrorist group with global reach, not just al Qaeda, and either topple the regimes or reshape the behavior of any state that provided assistance or training to these terrorist groups.[38]

Bush sought security. "Few understand," wrote Tenet, "the palpable sense of uncertainty and fear" that gripped policymakers. CIA analysts were "absolutely convinced" that another attack was coming, and "scared to death" they would not be able to thwart it. Morell went to the Oval Office almost every day with Tenet to brief the president, often "wondering if we're going to get hit today." "We assumed another attack was imminent," Rice recalled. The pressure was "unspeakable." She asked Steve Hadley, her friend and deputy, "Are you afraid?" "Not for myself," Hadley said, "But I can't bear the thought that something might happen to my daughters." The president remained calm, noted Gerson, while a "brooding sense of threat" gripped the White House. According to Rove, "Nerves were jangled, emotions high, and safety concerns real." "I had to confront my own mortality," remembered Hughes, "Every day for those first several days, we expected another strike." "I was nervous, I was anxious," Laura Bush subsequently admitted. There was "pitifully little information," remembered Attorney General Ashcroft, about "how severely vulnerable [we were] to terrorists inside our country." Believing another attack was imminent, the Treasury Department, adjacent to the White House, made plans about what to do if the building was "wiped out." "It's coming," reflected General Peter Pace, the vice chairman of the JCS, "there is no way to prevent it forever."[39]

But Bush was focused on doing just that. On September 12 at the end of an NSC meeting, he turned to John Ashcroft, his attorney general, and bluntly said, "Don't ever let this happen again." "Every day since has been September 12," Rice recollected. "We all had the overwhelming sense that we were still one step behind the terrorists and in danger of another successful attack."[40]

Amid the fear and worry, Bush and his advisers felt a keen sense of responsibility for having "let the country down." Most Americans, wrote Rove, experienced 9/11 through terrifying pictures on their television screens. But when President Bush went to New York on September 14, he met directly with the bereaved families (Figure 3.3). Listening to their despair, their faces racked with grief, he too grieved.[41] Meeting with reporters on the morning of September 14, asked about the prayers

Figure 3.3 Bush consoling families of victims and feeling responsible to thwart future attacks.
George W. Bush Library (LP-GWB), courtesy of the National Archives Catalog [National Archives identifier 5997309].

he was offering and the emotions he was feeling, the president conveyed a sense of what it meant to be in charge at such a time. Fighting back tears, he said he was trying "not to think about myself right now. I think about the families, the children. I am a loving guy, and I am also someone, however, who has got a job to do. And this is a terrible moment."[42]

It was terrible because they had failed to protect the American people, and they knew they could not afford to fail again. "I was not on point," Bush acknowledged. "I didn't feel that sense of urgency."[43] "We missed it," Cheney bluntly stated. The vice president and his staff—tasked by the president in May 2001 to prepare for an attack with weapons of mass destruction—felt an abiding responsibility to prevent another devastating assault. There was a feeling, explained Seth Carus, a bioterrorist expert on Cheney's staff, "that we'd screwed up big time. Government had failed the American people." We were all "traumatized," recalled Eric Edelman, Cheney's national security adviser. Everybody felt a sense of responsibility, "not again on our watch."[44] Carl Ford, the head of intelligence at the State Department, remembered the same feelings: "The president, his advisers, and members of Congress were traumatized by 9/11. It happened on their watch. They swore to protect the nation from all threats, foreign and domestic. They failed."[45] If another attack occurred, acknowledged Doug Feith, the under secretary of defense, "the government could be seen as violating the social contract—as failing to fulfill its most basic duty, which is to provide security."[46] Bush agreed. Meeting with the president almost every day, Morell intuited his feelings. From "my gut, listening to him, hearing him talk, hearing his questions, . . . [Bush] came to believe that the fundamental responsibility of a president of the United States is to protect the country, protect American citizens. That is the paramount responsibility of the president."[47]

Mixed with a keen sense of responsibility were feelings of guilt and worries about the political repercussions, should they fail again. After all, in their pre-9/11 strategy report, defense officials had defined homeland security as the framework for their new strategy—but they had failed to provide it. Cheney and Libby had been tasked to improve intelligence and preparedness and to "defend against the harm [weapons of mass destruction] can inflict," and now were uncertain if they could succeed.[48] "Haunted" by 9/11, "the White House was obsessed with preventing the harsh blame that would come after the next attack," wrote Jack Goldsmith, a former top official in the Justice Department.[49] Rice acknowledged that she "could not have forgiven" herself if there had been another attack. "And had that happened," people would want to know, "why did you not do everything in your power to keep it from happening again?"[50] President Bush grasped the basic reality: public opinion would be shaped "by whether there was another attack."[51]

Bush and his advisers had good reason to suspect that they might have much to explain if all the facts leading up to 9/11 were made public. When a commission subsequently examined the events of 9/11 and when the CIA inspector general conducted a thorough investigation of his agency, they noted deeply embarrassing evidence that would have been devastating politically, should another attack occur. The president had never discussed the threat emanating from al Qaeda publicly nor had he met with Dick Clarke, his counterterrorism expert, or offered specific instructions to address the challenge. Nor had Powell and Rumsfeld invested themselves in the counterterrorism mission prior to 9/11 despite many warnings of impending attacks. Even Tenet, while exhorting that lights were flashing red, had hesitated to reallocate resources within the CIA to deal with the danger he was underscoring. And though most warnings focused on attacks abroad, there were plenty of signs of al Qaeda infiltration into the United States and aspirations to strike domestically.[52]

Bush and his advisers believed they could not have done anything to prevent the attack on 9/11. Nonetheless, they knew they were deeply vulnerable politically should a second attack occur. "The recriminations would flow like water from a fire hose," thought Clarke.[53] Rove, the president's friend and political strategist, grasped the situation yet hoped to use the war on terrorism to retain control of the House and take back the Senate in the 2002 elections. "We can go to the American people on this issue of winning the war . . . because they trust the Republican Party to do a better job of . . . protecting America." But what if they failed? What if the American people learned that the president had information that might have been used to prevent the 9/11 attacks, yet did nothing? What if there were another attack?[54]

Fear, guilt, anger, political expediency, a deep sense of responsibility, and a yearning for revenge inspired Bush's determination to wage a global war on terror. He made the decision to focus initially on Afghanistan where al Qaeda's base was located and where jihadists from around the globe gathered to train for missions abroad.[55] He wanted decisive action, but he was stymied when the Taliban government ignored his diplomatic demands to hand over bin Laden and when he realized that his military advisers were not ready to wage war. In fact, they were confused and divided. The Pentagon had no plan, no model for military action in Afghanistan, and no good targets to strike. When General Franks, the CENTCOM commander, came to Washington to present his ideas, he was hammered by the Joint Chiefs of Staff and exasperated by Rumsfeld's incessant questioning. He threatened to resign.[56] Meanwhile, Tenet and Rumsfeld sparred with one another, each seeking to cast primary responsibility for the plans in Afghanistan onto the other. Bush wanted a small footprint and bold action. He was furious about the delays. He ordered Rice to get OSD and CIA to agree. She went home "praying" that they would be able to reach accord the following day. Finally, they did—a plan, partly designed by Tenet's subordinates, and partly conceived by Wolfowitz's aides, that linked American Special Forces and CIA operatives with those of the so-called Northern Alliance, a coalition of ethnic minority groups that had been battling the Taliban for years. The first CIA operatives entered Afghanistan on September 26.[57]

Progress was slow. Linking up with Tajik and Uzbek warlords took time, even though contacts had been established over the last few years. Moreover, the leader of the Northern Alliance had been murdered by al Qaeda operatives on the eve of 9/11, making it more difficult to agree on a battle plan. Tribal leaders in the north needed supplies, not just arms, but horse feed, saddles, medicines, and food—and they wanted cash. Coordinating with the CIA, the military air-dropped supplies and started bombing enemy targets on October 7; intelligence operatives arrived with briefcases filled with millions of dollars. But for several weeks the warlords remained uncertain of the American commitment and unimpressed by the magnitude of aid. US intelligence analysts and officials got bogged down in a stultifying debate about whether they should establish contacts with Pashtun leaders in the south before the Northern Alliance launched its major offensive in the north. General Franks wanted additional time to think through these issues and avert a new civil war inside Afghanistan, but Rumsfeld impatiently, sometimes angrily, insisted on bolder, quicker initiatives. He argued that dramatic action was necessary to take Kabul, remove the Taliban from power, and, most of all, demonstrate to other state-supporters of terrorism that they might be the next targets if they did not change their ways.[58]

Rumsfeld's impatience boiled over in a memorandum to the chairman and vice chairman of the Joint Chiefs of Staff on October 10. His strategic aim was "to disrupt the terrorist networks and to make life unacceptably difficult for nations harboring, facilitating, financing and/or tolerating those networks." But DoD was doing pitifully little to fulfill this aim. "I am seeing next to nothing," Rumsfeld lectured his top commanders, "that is thoughtful, creative or actionable." There was "a complete disconnect" between his aspirations and his subordinates' performance.[59]

As military planners and intelligence operators struggled to design a workable plan, fears of another attack inside the United States mounted. The CIA started presenting a "threat matrix" to the president, a daily summary of potential attacks on the homeland. The list, a compilation of threats that analysts collected during the prior twenty-four hours, ran forty to fifty pages a day. It was a "God-awful idea," reflected Morell. But at the time, it was absolutely "hair-raising," indicating more than 400 threats per month, and often forcing the president himself to ruminate about or determine the most salient threats.[60] Every day, at a 5 P.M. meeting at the CIA, top officials met to discuss the items on the matrix. "[W]e were scared to death we would not be able to prevent the next attack," remembered John McLaughlin, deputy director of the CIA, "and we were absolutely convinced more attacks were coming." "Always," wrote Tenet, "there was a palpable fear in the room that the United States was about to be hit again—either here or our interests abroad. No one thought there was a minute to waste."[61]

On September 18, even before US boots hit the ground in Afghanistan, amid the chaos and anxiety, letters containing anthrax began circulating in the US mail. On October 5, Bob Stevens, a reporter in Florida, died after inhaling anthrax. Three days later, anthrax was found in the offices of American Media in Boca Raton, Florida, where Stephens worked. On October 9, more letters laced with anthrax were discovered. One of the letters read: "You cannot stop us. We have this anthrax. You die now. Are you afraid? Death to America. Death to Israel. Allah is great."[62]

Anxieties grew. On October 18, anthrax turned up in the Senate office building of Tom Daschle, the Senate majority leader (Figure 3.4). On that same day, sensors detected the presence of a botulinum toxin in the White House, a deadly substance that, if dispersed, could kill large numbers of people. Bush, Cheney, Rice, and other top staffers might have been exposed. Cheney conveyed this information to the president by videoconference while Bush was in Shanghai. The vice president looked shaken as he prepared to attend a formal dinner. "His face was as white as his tie," commented Bush. It turned out to be a false alarm, but high-ranking civilian and military officials started taking the antibiotic Cipro to protect themselves. The contamination shut down five House and Senate office buildings and the Supreme Court.[63]

The anthrax scare raised the specter of catastrophic terrorism with weapons of mass destruction. It "wreaked fear and near panic in the

Figure 3.4 Searching for anthrax at Senate Hart Office Building, November 18, 2001.
Getty Images, https://www.gettyimages.com/detail/news-photo/hazardous-materials-experts-enter-the-hart-building-of-the-news-photo/119747503

capital," remembered Alberto Gonzales. Intelligence analysts and policymakers riveted their attention on the prospect of an attack with biological and chemical weapons. "The threat reporting about additional attacks on the homeland was off the charts," Morell emphasized in an interview. "Al Qaeda's interest in anthrax was real." Seth Carus, one of three bioterrorist experts on Cheney's staff, labored with colleagues to determine whether the spores were of domestic or of foreign origin. The uncertainty compounded the anxiety. It "confirmed everybody's view that there were going to be these follow-on attacks," said Carus. "We were concerned," recalled General George Casey, "about some type of chemical weapon deployed, either in a US city, or brought in, in a container, on a boat. I just remember we were wargaming and scaring ourselves to death about how ill-prepared we were to do it." The president was deeply affected by the anthrax scare, wrote his press aide, Scott McClellan. Nobody then, or since, could definitely figure out the source of the anthrax spores.[64]

At the time, CIA director George Tenet asked the counterterrorism center to review all its materials to determine whether al Qaeda or other terrorists might be seeking to develop weapons of mass destruction. "What we discovered stunned us all," recollected Tenet. "The threats were real." Evidence suggested that bin Laden had been seeking WMD for several years and new information revealed that several of his most trusted subordinates were talking to Pakistani scientists about acquiring biological, chemical, and radiological/nuclear weapons, "to possess not as a deterrent but to cause mass casualties in the United States." Tenet assembled a new team, under Rolf Mowatt-Larssen, to work on al Qaeda's quest for WMD: "You have to be out in front of the threat, thinking the unthinkable, anticipating what they're planning," he told Mowatt-Larssen. "Terrorists with WMD is one thing we can't get wrong," Tenet continued. "If it turns out al Qaeda doesn't have WMD, great, then the immediate threat might pass. But we need to build a long-term capacity to prevent groups from acquiring WMD. Our old world is gone." As Mowatt-Larssen began making the rounds at intelligence headquarters, talking to scientists, experts, and collectors of information, he concluded that the probability of terrorists developing "improvised nuclear devices" (IND) was small, "but if it were to ever happen, it would change the world."[65] Bush was so worried that he personally called the Pakistani president twice and asked him to count his nuclear warheads and make certain none had been stolen.[66]

Amid the anxieties aroused by the circulation of anthrax letters and the information emanating about al Qaeda's WMD ambitions, policymakers felt an urgent need to enhance the ways the government gathered and shared information. Well aware that they had missed key signals in the months and years leading up to 9/11, recognizing that government agencies had failed to share evidence and collaborate with one another, and assuming that sleeper cells existed in the country, they wanted more freedom to monitor phone calls and communications, including e-mails, from inside the country to those abroad. The prevailing process of going through the Foreign Intelligence Surveillance Court seemed laborious and antiquated. Robert Mueller, the new head of the FBI, shocked Bush at the end of September when he told the president that the agency had reports of over 300 potential terrorists inside the United States. These reports—their number and intensity—alarmed intelligence officials. Tenet worked with General Michael Hayden, the head of the National Security Agency (NSA), and with

Cheney and his top assistants, Scooter Libby and David Addington, to craft a new executive order that allowed the administration, without securing a warrant, to eavesdrop on private communications. They also labored with Alberto Gonzales and with John Ashcroft to write the USA PATRIOT Act. This legislation, passed on October 26, reduced the barriers between the nation's foreign and domestic intelligence agencies. It also augmented the legal authority of the government to surveil its citizens.[67]

Nonetheless, the sense of danger continued to mount. On October 23, Bush told the military chiefs that bin Laden might have a nuclear device that could destroy half of Washington. Tenet gave more specific warnings of an attack on October 30 or 31. Bush instructed Cheney to leave for an undisclosed location—Camp David. From there, Cheney participated in a videoconference call to General Franks on November 2. He prodded Franks to accelerate his campaign in Afghanistan. Another attack seemed "imminent," Cheney told Franks, and it might be more devastating than the first one. "Time is not on our side." Reflecting the portentous warnings, Joseph Hagin, the White House chief of staff for operations, kept a cadre of 70 to 150 senior managers from across the executive branch on twenty-four-hour bunker duty in a mountain hideout not far from Washington. He explained: "In the case of the use of a weapon of mass destruction, the federal government would be able to do its job and continue to provide key services and respond." At the same time, David Chu, the under secretary of defense for personnel and readiness, outlined the steps being taken to protect the Pentagon from a chemical or biological attack.[68]

In early November, the tide of war inside Afghanistan suddenly changed. The Northern Alliance, accompanied by US special forces and supported by devastating US air power, took the key northern town of Mazar-e-Sharif on November 9. On November 11, Herat—in western Afghanistan—fell. After much debate inside the administration about whether the United States should support the takeover of Kabul, the Northern Alliance moved on the capital and seized it with little resistance on November 13. In the south, the United States threw its support behind Hamid Karzai, a Pashtun leader who had been living in Pakistan, but had crossed into Afghanistan to galvanize anti-Taliban forces in the region. In early December, Karzai took the city of Kandahar without much of a battle. Rumsfeld estimated that 8,000 to 12,000 Taliban and al Qaeda fighters were killed, but many also fled into the mountains and across the borders into Pakistan and Iran.[69]

"I was overjoyed by the scenes of liberation," wrote Bush. His spirits buoyed—after his critics had been carping for weeks that the administration was becoming enveloped in another Vietnam-type quagmire— the president did not think for a moment that victory had been achieved. Afghanistan was simply the initial battle in a global struggle against terrorists and their state sponsors. "Everyone must have a sense of progression," Bush told his military chiefs.[70]

This was easier said than done. Lamenting the difficulty of devising adequate tactics, Rumsfeld exhorted his subordinates to "figure out a way to get the job done: We must put pressure on the terrorist networks and their supporters fast. . . . [W]e must push them off balance, increase their costs, and, over time, they will run out of money, be frightened, recruits will decline, defections will rise and their supporters will fall away." The aim, Rumsfeld emphasized, was not vengeance or retaliation; the goal was to prevent another attack. The United States had to eviscerate terrorist networks. It had "to aid local peoples to rid themselves of terrorists and free themselves of regimes that support terrorism." Rumsfeld adamantly opposed the idea of incorporating the Taliban in a new Afghan government. If the war on terrorism did not "significantly change the world's political map," Rumsfeld wrote the president, the United States would not have achieved its aim.[71] The administration had "to pursue al Qaeda terrorists around the world— as well as terrorists from other significant groups," explained Douglas Feith, the under secretary of defense. He and his colleagues had to devise strategies "to handle each of the key states in the global terrorist network, especially those with nuclear, biological, and chemical weapons ambitions."[72]

Iraq was referenced in some of these memos and conversations, but Saddam Hussein was not a key preoccupation. Feith and General Peter Pace, the vice chairman of the JCS, examined which state supporters of terrorism "might be manageable through diplomacy or other nonmilitary means, and which might require the President to use military means, though not necessarily to launch a war." The aim, said Rumsfeld, "was to fight smart, rather than simply use direct force." Not even Wolfowitz, who was most committed to regime change in Baghdad, wanted to use American troops to invade the country. Repeatedly, Wolfowitz emphasized what was most on his mind: preventing another attack. "We're dealing with something that is much more than just one individual or one organization. . . . We have got to root out the terrorist networks. And we have got to end the support that they get from a number of states. . . . Remember, there are a number of these networks. They interact with one another." They "extend even into our own country." Pressed whether Saddam Hussein was on his target list, Wolfowitz said, yes, "He is one of the problems. Osama bin Laden is one of the problems. These are networks, including not only Osama bin Laden's network, but other radical anti-American networks. We are going to have this as a campaign and treat the problem as a whole." It required more than military action; it required the use of all the nation's instruments of power—its intelligence services, its financial wherewithal. "We have economic resources that the whole world begs for."[73]

Bush agreed that all the nation's considerable assets had to be employed in the global struggle against terror. He did not envision a "conventional war," focused on military operations. He wanted to deploy resources in different ways—for intelligence gathering, diplomacy, humanitarian aid, and financial pressure.[74] In these first days and weeks after 9/11, he and his advisers assigned far more importance to Pakistan than to Iraq. On day two, September 12, Deputy Secretary of State Armitage met with the Pakistani chief of intelligence, General Mehmood Ahmad. He was visiting Washington at the time of the attack. Armitage had worked closely with Pakistani intelligence officials in the 1980s, and felt he could speak bluntly. Pakistan, he stressed, must cease support of the Taliban and al Qaeda and must allow US access to bases. In return, Armitage promised that the administration would lift the prevailing sanctions and provide financial assistance. The next day, Secretary of State Powell called Pakistani president Pervez Musharraf and reiterated US demands. Subsequently, Armitage flew to Islamabad to speak directly to Musharraf, as did Rumsfeld, Powell, and Tenet. Bush talked with the Pakistani president on September 15 and then dined with him in New York at the residence of the US permanent representative to the United Nations. He pressed Musharraf to join the battle against al Qaeda.[75]

Bush emphasized that the global war on terror was not against Muslims. Welcoming Indonesian president Megawatni Sukarnoputri to Washington a week after 9/11, Bush told the leader of the world's most populous Muslim nation, "the war against terrorism is not a war against Muslims, nor is it a war against Arabs. It's a war against evil people who conduct crimes against innocent people." It was a war against Muslim jihadists and Islamic fundamentalist terrorists. Their views were "antithetical to those of most Muslims." The American global war on terror, the president and his advisers insisted, was not a religious crusade; it was a civilizational struggle, an ideological battle— "good versus evil."[76]

Bush tried to understand the motives of the jihadists. He invited Zalmay Khalilzad, the Afghan-American Sunni Muslim on Rice's staff, to spend time with him at Camp David. For hours they discussed "the history of Afghanistan and the wider Muslim world." "The president asked the overarching question on his mind. What had gone wrong in the Islamic world? Why the rise of terrorist groups like al Qaeda?" In Khalilzad's view, it was a failure of modernization: "from Syria to Iraq, modernist leaders largely failed to deliver progress or restore greatness."[77] The president did not probe deeply; he did not ask if his country had done anything to arouse so much anti-Americanism— to inspire so much hate. With utmost sincerity, he naively ruminated, "I'm amazed that there is such misunderstanding of what our country is about, that people would hate us . . . like most Americans I just can't believe it, because I know how good we are, and we've got to do a better job of making our case. We've got to do a better job of explaining to the people in the Middle East . . . that we're [not fighting] a war against Islam or Muslims. . . . We're fighting evil."[78]

President Bush wanted to garner the assistance of friendly Muslim governments and hoped to destroy the terrorist networks that existed in their lands. For example, he and his advisers worried about the links between al Qaeda and the Abu Sayyaf Group (ASG) in the southern Philippine islands. This group had been involved in scores of terrorist attacks during the 1990s. It had plotted to blow up US airliners and assassinate the pope, and had kidnapped three American citizens in May 2001. More worrisome, ASG had links to a group which was soon identified as Jemaah Islamiya (JI). JI had roots in Indonesia and sought to establish a caliphate throughout the southeast Asian region, including Malaysia, Singapore, Thailand, the Philippines, and Indonesia.[79] Bush wanted to crush these jihadists, deny them safe havens, and garner the support of the Indonesian and Filipino governments in the war on terrorism. With the Pentagon still smoldering a week after the attack, Bush asked the Indonesian president to condemn the terrorist assault and promised hundreds of millions of dollars in aid. When she returned to Jakarta and faced overwhelming anti-American sentiment, she backtracked on her support. Nevertheless, the administration redoubled its efforts to garner Indonesian assistance in the war on terror, selling munitions for counterterrorism and launching a broad-based public relations campaign.[80]

There was a dark side to the global war on terror. As US Special Forces and CIA operatives moved into Afghanistan, they started capturing Taliban soldiers and al Qaeda terrorists, many of them Arabs from distant lands who had been training there. They learned that dozens of Pakistan's best scientists, along with top army officers and nuclear engineers, had formed a consortium, Ummah Tameer-E-Nau, or UTN. This organization offered its services to the Taliban, Libya, and al Qaeda. Vice President Cheney, charged with the mission to safeguard the nation from domestic sabotage with weapons of mass destruction, waged a tenacious campaign inside the administration to deny captives the rights guaranteed them by the Geneva Convention. He believed they should not be treated as prisoners of war, nor as criminals, but tried by specially created military commissions where their ability to defend themselves would be significantly circumscribed. Amid unsubstantiated rumors from "several reliable foreign intelligence services" that a small nuclear device had been smuggled into New York City, Cheney deemed it imperative to extract intelligence from captured prisoners. He insisted that the administration use every means at its disposal to achieve its objectives. He urged the president not only to create these military commissions, but also to permit the rendition and torturous interrogation of enemy captives in CIA prisons abroad. The administration knew far too little about al Qaeda, Hadley explained; it desperately needed to know more. Bush agreed: "For me," he wrote, "the lesson of 9/11 was simple: don't take chances."[81]

Whether abandoning American values, practices, and legal obligations led to actionable intelligence is still disputed, but there can be no doubt that the president was consumed with worry about another attack inside the United States. "We're in a window of vulnerability," he told the directors of the FBI and CIA. "Remember that al Qaeda was in America for years before 9/11, and we didn't find them. We didn't stop them from flying planes into the WTC and the Pentagon. Keep looking. Be skeptical . . . . Come back with your thoughts. . . . We've got a long way to go to secure the homeland."[82]

With the nation grieving and seeking revenge, with news arriving of impending new attacks, the president again and again cast the perpetrators of 9/11 as "evildoers." They yearned to kill Americans and extinguish their freedoms. They had "no justification for their actions. . . . The[ir] only motivation is evil." The president vowed that he would not forget the wound inflicted on the country, nor those who inflicted it. "I will not yield; I will not rest; I will not relent in waging this struggle for freedom and security for the American people."[83]

By rooting his reaction in the rhetorical tropes of freedom and branding his policy as a "global war on terror," the president obfuscated as much as he illuminated. Terror, after all, is a tactic, not an enemy. Jihadist fury, moreover, did not emanate from hatred of American values. Nor were all terrorists focused on America; many had local objectives.[84] Bin Laden, his al Qaeda followers, and other radical Islamists were inspired by grievances deeply felt and widely shared among Arabs throughout the Middle East: their loathing of Israel, their outrage over the hardships suffered by their Iraqi brethren, their scorn for the apostate regimes in the region, their contempt for American hegemony, and their revulsion at the presence of American troops near Mecca. They were assailing American deeds, not its freedoms.[85]

However misleading was his rhetoric and branding, Bush's invocation of "freedom" to justify a "global war on terror" appealed to many Americans. His words reflected American fears, underscored American values, and conveyed some fundamental truths. Osama bin Laden had declared war on the United States. His fatwa was evil, calling upon Muslims to kill Americans and their allies.[86] He was contemptuous, telling his followers time and again that the United States looked strong but was weak and cowardly.[87] Nor was the president wrong when he framed the struggle in global terms and focused on jihadist networks. Terrorist groups were metastasizing, and al Qaeda did have links to many that aimed to inflict harm on Americans and their country. And the president made sense again when he chose to assign priority to Afghanistan because the regime in Kabul did provide safe haven to bin Laden and to thousands of trainees who flocked to al Qaeda camps for instruction, indoctrination, and empowerment.

Most Americans in the fall of 2001 applauded Bush's efforts. He aimed to destroy the terrorists who had murdered almost 4,000 Americans—terrorists who had wreaked havoc in America's capital and most renowned city, who had assailed the symbols of American power and wealth, and who had inspired fear and a lust for revenge. So far, there had not been any follow-up attacks in the United States despite overwhelming information that al Qaeda yearned to inflict more harm. The president's first steps appeared effective and popular. His approval ratings hovered between 85 and 90 percent. More than three-quarters of the American people approved of his actions in Afghanistan.[88] Foreign leaders trekked to Washington, expressing sympathy, seeking aid, and offering assistance.

Bush's self-confidence mounted. Spurred by his faith in God and American values, confident he was fighting evil, certain he was engaged in a protracted struggle with a tenacious foe, he believed there was much still to be done. "The best defense is a good offense," Bush told his top intelligence officials. "Take the fight to the enemy overseas, where we can operate with impunity. Once they get to the homeland, the odds of success tilt toward the terrorists."[89]

4

Iraq

ON THE AFTERNOON of 9/11, with the fires still burning and ambulances blaring, Secretary of Defense Donald Rumsfeld returned from the smoke-filled courtyard to his office in the Pentagon. His closest aide, Under Secretary Stephen Cambone, cryptically recorded the secretary's thinking: "Hit S.H. [Saddam Hussein] @same time; Not only UBL [Osama bin Laden]; near term target needs—go massive—sweep it all up—need to do so to hit anything useful."[1]

The president did not agree. That night, when George W. Bush returned to Washington, his focus was on reassuring the nation, relieving the suffering, and inspiring hope. Informed that al Qaeda was most likely responsible for the attack, he did not focus on Iraq. The next day, at meetings of the National Security Council (NSC), Rumsfeld and Deputy Secretary of Defense Paul Wolfowitz again advocated action against Saddam Hussein. With no good targets in Afghanistan and with no war plans to dislodge the Taliban, defense officials thought Iraq might be a better target to demonstrate American resolve and resilience. Their arguments did not resonate with anyone present.[2]

The next evening, however, President Bush encountered Richard Clarke and several other aides outside the Situation Room in the White House. According to Clarke, his outgoing counterterrorism expert, the president said, "I know you have a lot to do and all . . . but I want you, as soon as you can, to go back over everything, everything. See if Saddam did this. See, if he's linked in any way." Clarke assured the president that they would reassess, but stressed that Hussein had nothing to do with the carnage; it was al Qaeda, Clarke insisted. Then, he muttered to his assistants, "Wolfowitz got to him."[3]

But there is no real evidence that Wolfowitz did get to Bush. The president may have talked about attacking Iraq in a conversation with Prime Minister Tony Blair on Friday, September 14. But when Wolfowitz raised the issue anew at the meetings at Camp David over the weekend, Bush made it clear that he was embarked on a global war on terror, and that Afghanistan was priority number one.[4] The president did not think that Hussein was linked to 9/11. George Tenet, the director of the CIA, and Michael Morell, his daily intelligence briefer, told him that Iraq had nothing to do with the attack; Condoleezza Rice and Steve Hadley, his top national security advisers, told him the same thing.[5] Vice President Dick Cheney and his top aide, Scooter Libby, did not want to assign priority to Iraq.[6] In his key speeches during the first week after 9/11, the president did not focus on Iraq.[7] Michael Gerson, his most influential speechwriter, said Bush did not believe that Hussein was linked to 9/11.[8] On September 19, when reporters asked him if he had a special message for Saddam Hussein, the president spoke generically: "anybody who harbors terrorists needs to fear the United States. . . . The message to every country is, there will be a campaign against terrorist activity, a worldwide campaign."[9] When General Tommy Franks, the commander of American forces in the region, suggested to Bush that he begin military planning against Iraq, the president instructed him not to do so.[10]

On September 26, the president asked Rumsfeld to come to the Oval Office for a private conversation. Bush invited Rumsfeld to assess the "shape of our military plans on Iraq." He was concerned about prospective Iraqi attacks on American planes in the no-fly zones. Rumsfeld clarified that this was no longer a priority. As they conversed, Rumsfeld "did not get the impression" that the president had resolved to topple Saddam Hussein's regime. After Rumsfeld said he would talk to Franks about reviewing the existing plans, Bush went on to discuss the real agenda item: news of Rumsfeld's son's drug addiction. "Are you doing okay?" the president inquired.[11]

Rumsfeld was not okay. He was deeply affected by his son's recurrent crises, disappearances, and failed treatments. But Rumsfeld would not allow himself to be distracted from the president's overriding mission: to prevent another attack. He fervently believed that the best strategy was to aid "local peoples to rid themselves of terrorists and to free themselves of regimes that support terrorism." He did not want to rely heavily on direct aerial attacks. "We should avoid as much as possible creating images of Americans killing Moslems." But it was essential to act promptly to bring about new regimes in Afghanistan and other key states that supported terrorism.[12] He was eager to back "a potential coup or insurrection" in Iraq, should circumstances be propitious.[13] But circumstances were not propitious.[14]

Neither Rumsfeld nor his top subordinates, Wolfowitz and Feith, favored a full-scale military invasion to overthrow Saddam Hussein. They wanted to get rid of a "regime that engages in and supports terrorism and otherwise threatens US vital interests." They wanted to do so without a significant deployment of US forces. Wolfowitz explained that he was not championing a march to Baghdad; he was amplifying the ideas he had been discussing for years—supporting a Shi'a rebellion in the south, establishing an enclave or a liberation zone for the organization of a provisional government, and, if successful, denying the Iraqi dictator control over the oil resources of the region. He was not "in favor of invading and occupying the whole country." "[I]f we're capable of mounting an Afghan resistance against the Soviets," Wolfowitz thought, "we could have been capable of mounting an Arab resistance."[15] Bush was not disinterested in this approach, and it comported with Rumsfeld's strategic vision that Washington should assist local peoples to overthrow regimes that supported terrorism. But neither Rumsfeld nor Wolfowitz could convince the president to divert his attention from Afghanistan and the broader war on terror.

The civilian proponents of regime change inside the Pentagon were not fantasizing about or even discussing democracy-promotion or nation-building. Their purpose, Wolfowitz stressed in an article in 2009, "was to remove a threat to national and international security. Whether the Iraq War was right or wrong, it was not about imposing democracy." His statements and memoranda in the fall of 2001, as well as those of Under Secretary of Defense Douglas Feith, do not have an ideological or idealistic edge, as is often asserted. Wolfowitz's focus was on preventing another attack and securing the homeland and empowering the United States. In interviews, Wolfowitz explained again and again that he was not concerned with retaliating for 9/11; he was consumed with the urgency of thwarting the next attack. "The objective now was to eliminate any global terrorist networks and any state support for terrorism." In testimony to the Senate Armed Services Committee on October 4, 2001, as well as in his public statements at the time, Wolfowitz stressed that Americans had to recognize that they had entered a new era of vulnerability. "September 11th caught us by surprise. We must prepare ourselves for the virtual certainty we will be surprised again."[16]

Wolfowitz deferred to Bush's priority. He helped devise the strategy to have Special Forces and CIA operatives link up with the Northern Alliance to topple the Taliban. But he and Feith and their civilian colleagues inside the Pentagon did not relinquish the idea of regime change in Iraq. They were convinced that Hussein was dangerous. They were incensed by his gloating over the 9/11 attack. There "was only one world leader who praised the attacks and that was Saddam Hussein," Wolfowitz explained. The Iraqi dictator seemed to be saying, "This is what you have coming to you and there will be more if you don't change your policies."[17] There is little evidence that Hussein actually said those words, but Wolfowitz and his colleagues were revolted by a series of Iraqi statements after 9/11 that illustrated the dictator's nefarious outlook. September 11 "was God's punishment," said one Iraqi government-controlled newspaper on the very day of the attack. "The United States reaps the thorns its rulers have planted in the world," said another. More ominous, on September 20, as anthrax spores began circulating in Florida, *Babil*, another state-controlled newspaper, observed, "It is possible to turn to biological attack, where a small can, not bigger than the size of a hand, can be used to release viruses that affect everything." And on October 8, three days after the first American died from inhaling anthrax, *Babil* ominously reported, "The United States must get a taste of its own poison."[18]

Bush's focus gravitated to Iraq as fears of an attack with weapons of mass destruction mounted in October 2001. Those who worked with him on a daily basis did not feel that he had a sense of unfinished business with the Iraqi dictator as a result of the failure to topple him in 1991, as did Wolfowitz. Nor was Bush seeking to get even for the dictator's effort to assassinate his father in 1993.[19] Bush's contempt for

Hussein, nonetheless, was visceral. "There's no question that the leader of Iraq is an evil man," he told reporters on October 11. "After all, he gassed his own people."[20] Hussein's record of brutality, his defiance, his arrogance had "real purchase" with Bush.[21] "The American people don't like him," Bush bluntly told British prime minister Tony Blair. "He does not accept our values and understands only force."[22]

What helped to solidify Bush's relationship with Blair was their shared disgust for Hussein, bin Laden, and other jihadists who attacked innocent civilians. At the press conference after their first extensive conversation at Camp David in February 2001, Blair sounded even more determined than Bush to deal with Hussein. The Iraqi dictator had "a record on these issues"—he had murdered thousands of his own people, attacked Iran, and tried to annex Kuwait. If given a chance, "his infatuation with WMD" would resume.[23] The specter of Hussein with WMD haunted Blair and Bush after 9/11. Their common sense of victimhood, their zealotry about the basic values at stake, and their fear that Hussein might disseminate weapons of mass destruction to terrorists brought the two men together. They believed that they were engaged in an "existential" struggle with fanatics who were seeking to capture "the mind, the heart, and the soul of Islam." They found that they not only liked one another, but shared deep-seated religious convictions and a faith in the civilizational struggle that beset them.[24]

Time and again at press conferences in the weeks and months after 9/11, President Bush talked about the Iraqi dictator. He stated his views clearly: he could not tolerate Hussein's possession of weapons of mass destruction at a time when it was becoming clearer that terrorists were seeking such weapons. When Helen Thomas, a probing reporter from the Hearst newspaper chain, questioned whether the American people would support an expansion of the war on terror into Iraq, Bush retorted, "Our focus is on Afghanistan." But his aim was to eliminate terrorist cells wherever they existed, and "to bring to justice" not only the terrorists, but also the host governments that supported them. With regard to Iraq, Bush continued, he knew Hussein was "evil" and he knew what Hussein had done in the past. "We know he's been developing weapons of mass destruction. And I think it's in his advantage to allow inspectors back in his country to make sure that he's conforming to the agreement he made, after he was soundly trounced in the Gulf

War. And so we're watching him very carefully. We're watching him very carefully."[25]

What Bush and his advisers saw troubled them. In the spring and summer of 2001—before 9/11—the reporting became more worrisome as analysts in various agencies began debating the meaning of Iraq's acquisition of aluminum tubes and re-examining their assessments of Hussein's WMD intentions.[26] In the fall of 2001 came additional reports from Curveball—the Iraqi defector in Germany—about Iraqi work on biological weapons. Senior policymakers were told that Hussein had established mobile biological warfare production plants and now possessed "BW capabilities surpassing the pre–Gulf War era."[27] This information circulated as reports about al Qaeda's interest in weapons of mass destruction mounted. In Afghanistan, CIA collectors found letters indicating that al Qaeda leaders had a deep interest in developing biological weapons, especially anthrax, for a mass casualty attack in the United States.[28] They learned this as they struggled to determine the source of the anthrax spores that killed Americans in late September and early October. The challenge, explained Seth Carus, a bioterrorist expert on Cheney's staff, was how to interpret the limited information they had. Libby was inclined to believe the origins were external, probably Iraq; Cheney was not so certain. The information was partial, elusive, yet portentous. It was "like seeing an iceberg," said Carus; "you don't know how much of the iceberg you're seeing. There clearly were parts of it we weren't seeing."[29]

Tenet and Morell conveyed the information to the president day by day in meetings filled with anxiety. Morell would go to sleep in the early evening and get up at 11:30 P.M. to be at work at 12:30 A.M. He would review the threat matrix with colleagues at CIA headquarters. He would then meet Tenet at the Old Executive Office Building and they would walk over to the Oval Office to brief Bush at 8 A.M., often ruminating about whether they would get "hit" that day given the amount of threat reporting they were seeing. The president would then ask about threat number 5 or 6 or 17 or 46.[30]

Among other challenges, they struggled to make sense of the limited information they had about Hussein's interest in and possession of weapons of mass destruction. The Iraqi dictator had expelled international inspectors in 1998, and, subsequently, the CIA had been unable to penetrate and collect valuable information. Assessing what was happening in Iraq was tough, confusing, and worrisome. If you "put all that stuff on the table," Morell reflected, "and if you took a week and went through it all, you would come to the conclusion that he had a chemical weapons capability, that he had chemical weapons stockpiled, that he had a biological weapons production capability and he was restarting a nuclear program. Today you would come to that judgment based on what was on that table." But what was on the table, Morell acknowledged, was circumstantial, flimsy, and suspect, much of it coming from Iraqi Kurdish foes of the regime. We should have said, "Mr. President, here is what we think: A, B, C, and D. But what you really need to know is that we have low confidence in that judgment and here is why." But, instead, Morell was telling the president that Hussein "had a chemical weapons program. He's got a biological weapons production capability."[31]

Although poorly assessed, the information that Morell conveyed in the fall of 2001 did not determine the views of President Bush and his top advisers. They were already predisposed to think that Hussein had weapons of mass destruction. This was not simply true of the hawks in the administration, like Rumsfeld, Wolfowitz, Feith, Cheney, and Libby. Secretary of State Colin Powell and Deputy Secretary of State Richard Armitage thought Hussein had WMD.[32] Rice and Hadley believed he possessed WMD.[33] State Department intelligence analysts as well as NSA and CIA counterparts shared the same view.[34] They argued over the purpose of aluminum tubes and the import of uranium yellowcake, and they were aware that Iraq would need five to seven years to develop a nuclear weapon once reconstitution got underway. Nonetheless, they thought they knew that Iraq had biological and chemical weapons, or could develop them quickly, and that Hussein aspired to reconstitute a nuclear program. Foreign intelligence partners concurred. Tony Blair and his most trusted advisers felt the same way. Nobody told Bush that Hussein did not have WMD.[35] Subsequently, some US analysts said they conveyed the views that officials wanted them to deliver.[36] But in the fall of 2001 it is not at all clear that policymakers were seeking incriminating evidence, nor evident that analysts felt political pressure. What preoccupied them—analysts and policymakers alike—was knowledge that they had previously underestimated Hussein's penchant to cheat. What they knew from their own lived experience—from recent history—was that Hussein had developed and used weapons of mass destruction. Analysts knew, Morell explained, "that he once had the stuff and actually used it." They knew that he once "was very, very close to getting a nuclear weapon, much closer than we thought." They knew, said Morell—Bush knew, Cheney knew—that Iraq once "had a weapons program that we completely missed."[37]

These beliefs and predilections weighed heavily on Bush and his advisers as additional information flowed into Washington about Hussein's links to terrorists. Previously, the Department of State had identified Iraq as a state sponsor of terrorism. Although Hussein's regime had not engaged in anti-Western terrorist acts since 1993, it did wage a campaign to murder dissidents living abroad and it did welcome Palestinian resistance organizations to Baghdad as well as an Iranian terrorist group. After 9/11, the State Department noted that Iraq "was the only Arab Muslim country that did not condemn the attack." Even Iran, the world's most ardent supporter of international terrorism, denounced the 9/11 attack and expressed condolences. But not Baghdad. Meanwhile, Iraq continued to support the Palestinian intifada against Israel.[38] More worrisome were new intelligence reports suggesting that Iraqis were training terrorists for hijacking and demolition operations against US naval vessels. Al Qaeda, some analysts speculated, might be receiving "support" from Iraqi special services and from "access" to Iraqi embassies and diplomatic posts.[39] These reports were not "finally evaluated intelligence," but could not be ignored. Their possible salience mounted when Czech intelligence informed the CIA that Mohammad Atta, one of the 9/11 hijackers, had met with an Iraqi intelligence officer in Prague on April 9, 2001. This news, supported by a fuzzy photo of the alleged meeting, sparked Cheney's interest and prompted many queries from the president himself.[40]

In daily briefings to the president, Morell stressed that "there was no Iraq involvement in 9/11 . . . zero; zippo; nothing." Nonetheless, he told Bush that Iraq was a terrorist state. "They conduct their own terrorism. Their intelligence service conducts terrorism [in] places around the world and they . . . give money, training, to a bunch of Palestinian groups. So they were to some extent in bed with terrorism, not al Qaeda, but with their own terrorism and support of terrorism."

In Morell's view, Bush turned his attention toward Iraq because he was ruminating, "what if this guy [uses] this stuff . . . against us or what if he were to give this stuff to one of these groups that he supports and they were to use it against us? I would have failed in my final responsibility." There was "no doubt" in Morell's mind "that those links to terrorism . . . shaped the president's thinking."[41]

Those possible links heightened the threat perception of many people around Bush. Eric Edelman, Cheney's national security expert, put it this way: civilian policymakers thought Saddam had WMD; al Qaeda wanted WMD; Saddam celebrated 9/11: hence, attention naturally gravitated to Iraq.[42] Bush's top military leaders thought precisely the same way. Many were not eager for war with Iraq. Many believed that Saddam was in his box. But they agreed, in the words of General Franks, "Any power that could provide al Qaeda with nerve agents or anthrax was a major strategic concern."[43] In the "angst of the moment," explained General Peter Pace, the vice chairman of the Joint Chiefs of Staff, Iraq commanded attention because military analysts asked:

> What else don't we know? We didn't see 9/11 coming. . . . What might hurt us really, really badly? Then you start thinking about Saddam Hussein, and you say, Ok, he's got chemical weapons. We know that because he has used them on his own people, he has used them on his neighbors, so he's got that for sure. He has a nuclear program that the Israelis blew apart, but we know about the part they blew apart above the ground; we don't know if he's got anything underground. If chemical weapons were to get in the hands of the terrorists, which is possible, what might that lead to? So, . . . I'm thinking to myself, Hmn, OK, this is certainly a place from which the next attack could emanate. This guy is obviously a bad guy.

Hussein sometimes pretended to be our friend, Pace continued, but he really wasn't. General Richard Myers agreed: "With the United States still reeling from the shock of the earlier anthrax attacks, [Iraq] was a threat no one could ignore."[44]

Focusing on Iraq did not mean that policymakers thought Hussein was an imminent threat. Not even Bush's hawkish advisers thought that. "I wasn't worried," Wolfowitz explained, "about what he would do in 2001; I was worried about what he would do in 2010 if the existing containment . . . collapsed." Wolfowitz continued: "It wasn't a matter of thinking he was an immediate danger, as much as thinking if we didn't find a better way of dealing with him than we had he could become quite dangerous over a ten-year time frame." Wolfowitz wanted to eliminate global terrorist networks and their state supporters when there was an opportunity to do so, and that time was now. It was not a matter "of retaliating for this attack [on 9/11]; it is the matter of preventing the next one and the one after that." Wolfowitz acknowledged that Iran, too, was a state supporter of terrorism, perhaps even more so than Iraq. But he thought that Iraq could be pressured to make concessions. "I thought there was more chance that Saddam could be backed down by a threat. . . . I think if we had put together a reasonable list of demands on Saddam that he might have been frightened enough to comply."[45]

Feith agreed. Saddam Hussein was a "gathering threat," not an imminent threat. The Middle East, Feith believed, was boiling with anger. Hussein yearned to exploit the unrest to expand Iraqi power. In these circumstances Bush could not allow the Iraqi tyrant to reignite his WMD programs when sanctions failed, and Feith was sure they were failing. The administration needed to apply pressure now, when it could.[46] Wolfowitz's and Feith's friends in the vice president's office concurred. Seth Carus, Libby's subordinate, explained: "Iraq was going to be a problem in the future and it was better to deal with it now when they were weak than wait for the future after the sanctions come off and Saddam resumes all his weapons programs and he is strong."[47]

These hawkish advisers who wanted a policy of regime change now—not full-scale war—were worried about Hussein's prospective ability to blackmail the United States and constrain the exercise of American power. Wolfowitz stated this clearly to the Senate Armed Services Committee on October 4. "By holding our people hostage to terror and fear, their intention is for America to be intimidated into withdrawal and inaction—leaving them free to impose their will on their peoples and neighbors unmolested by America's military might." Feith explained it in a book he subsequently published: "Catastrophic weapons in Iraq's hands were a threat not just because Saddam might decide one fine day to use them to hit the United States. A likelier problem was that they would affect our willingness to defend US interests," like the protection of Kuwait, Saudi Arabia, and Israel.[48]

Fear of an attack inside the United States was juxtaposed with concerns over the projection of American power abroad. Rumsfeld felt that the United States invited attack because Washington appeared weak, feckless. Cheney and Libby believed that irresolution wrought contempt among the jihadists and America's adversaries. Washington had failed to demonstrate strength or retaliate effectively after the bombing of the World Trade Center in 1993, the assassination attempt on the president's father in 1993, and the sequential attacks on Khobar Towers in 1996, American embassies in Tanzania and Kenya in 1998, and the USS *Cole* in 2000. Adversaries had learned "that the US, if tweaked would flinch." Shocked by the events of 9/11, fearing another attack, feeling vulnerable, seeking revenge, Rumsfeld and his hawkish colleagues were not advocating full-scale war against Iraq in the fall of 2001. Nonetheless, they yearned to get rid of Hussein, demonstrate American resolve, protect US interests, and thwart the resurgence of Iraqi power when they had an opportunity to do so.[49]

Other advisers inside the administration felt differently. They shared the hawks' contempt for Hussein, but they believed he was contained. "He was in a box," Powell recalled. These advisers believed that Iraqi capabilities had been seriously degraded since 1991, and the United States should focus on creating "a sense of geopolitical order that would deprive extremists of oxygen." State Department officials worried less about Iraqi military capabilities than about Iraqi propaganda alleging American responsibility for the starvation of millions of Iraqi children. In their view, Hussein "was a nuisance, not a mortal threat."[50] Many military officers concurred. General Myers thought Iraqi military capabilities had shrunk by more than 50 percent since 1991. His predecessor, General Shelton, believed "Iraq was in a complete state of containment." Shelton's military assistant, General Douglas Lute, thought that "Saddam was essentially neutered in terms of the threat to the region."[51]

Hussein had been seriously weakened by sanctions and the presence of inspectors. But now the latter were gone, and the former were eroding. Consequently, his future behavior was uncertain, and troubling even to Bush's more dovish advisers. If Hussein extricated Iraq from the sanctions regime, he could then augment his conventional capabilities and revive his WMD programs. Carl Ford, the head of intelligence at the State Department, informed Powell that the Iraqi dictator would use illegal revenues—now amounting to about $3 billion annually—"to consolidate his power base and to rebuild his military (including WMD) programs."[52] Powell and Armitage wanted to thwart Hussein's ambitions by instituting "smart sanctions," sanctions that applied solely to the import of military items. But it was hard to get members of the UN Security Council to agree, and effective implementation was unlikely. Sanctions, reflected Kofi Annan, secretary-general of the United Nations, "could never be made smart enough to spare the Iraqi people from continued suffering; nor . . . robust enough to ensure . . . that Baghdad wasn't [rearming] in contravention of [its] obligations to the Security Council."[53]

The conundrum facing US policymakers was how to contain Hussein if the sanctions regime ended and if UN monitors did not return. Could the United States tolerate such a situation?[54] General Franks, the CENTCOM commander, outlined the challenges to the Senate Armed Services Committee. Despite Hussein's degraded military capabilities, he could still project power and Iraq continued to shoot at US and UK aircraft enforcing the no-fly zones. Hussein circumvented existing sanctions and felt little pressure to readmit inspectors. He remained a threat to his neighbors. "Our regional partners," emphasized Franks, "do not yet possess the capability to deter Iraqi aggression without our assistance."[55]

Vice Admiral Thomas R. Wilson, the head of the DIA, concurred. For the time being, he told the same Senate committee, Hussein's "options are constrained." But challenges ahead loomed large: Hussein wanted "to reassert sovereignty over all of Iraq, end Baghdad's international isolation, and, eventually, have Iraq reemerge as the dominant regional power." CIA director Tenet said much the same thing: Hussein's power was now circumscribed. But what would happen if the United States and the United Kingdom stopped enforcing the no-fly zones and his isolation ended? "Our most serious concern," said Tenet, "was the likelihood that he [would] seek a renewed WMD capability both for credibility and because every other strong regime in the region either has it or is pursuing it."[56]

Other advisers did not fret greatly about these scenarios. State Department officials did not want the president to divert attention from Afghanistan. Along with some military officers and counter-terrorism experts, these policymakers did not think Hussein had any significant links to terrorists, none to al Qaeda, and no likelihood of acquiring nuclear capabilities in the near future. Dick Clarke expressed their views clearly: "Even if Iraq still had WMD stockpiles, possession of weapons of mass destruction is not in and of itself a threat to the United States. . . . Never did I think the Iraqi chemical and biological weapons were an imminent threat. . . . Nothing in 2002 indicated Saddam intended to build nukes, much less use them, and certainly not imminently." The White House and the CIA should have known there was no "imminent threat" to the United States, insisted Clarke.[57]

Bush was not so certain. For him, the risk calculus had changed dramatically after 9/11. He, the president of the United States, was charged with the responsibility to protect the American people from another attack. Among his advisers, all of them, there was certainty that such an attack would occur, certainty that the jihadists yearned to inflict more harm, and certainty that Saddam Hussein was a monstrous tyrant seeking to garner revenge after his 1991 defeat. But was he opportunistic enough to assist jihadist enemies of the United States? The president kept hearing discordant views. Military officers, like Shelton, and State Department officials, like Armitage, thought Iraq had few ties to terrorists. General Franks, on the other hand, believed that Hussein had such links, and Shelton's successor, Richard Myers, had been worrying for years "that terrorists would somehow acquire Iraq's WMD."[58] Although few officials thought Hussein had a role in the 9/11 attacks, advisers like Rumsfeld and Cheney, as well as Wolfowitz, Feith, and Libby, suspected that he might have links to the terrorist networks that were metastasizing, that were portentous, and that quested for state support. "My belief," said Wolfowitz, "was that he had the capacity to hand off biological agents to terrorists. It was a very serious concern." Rice, Hadley, and Morell, among others, considered such fears to be entirely reasonable. If nineteen Saudis with boxcutters could do what they did on 9/11, Hadley said, "think about Saddam Hussein who's developing WMD and supports terror—what he could do, and what he could give the terrorists, and what they could do with it." Rice explained her thinking this way: "We'd failed to connect the dots on September 10, and never imagined the use of civilian airliners as missiles against the World Trade Center and the Pentagon; that an unconstrained Saddam might aid a terrorist in an attack on the United States did not seem far-fetched."[59]

In early October, Tony Blair advised Bush to proceed slowly. Blair agreed that Hussein was a wicked tyrant and looming danger. Sanctions were failing, and Hussein's penchant for WMD could not be ignored. Although the British prime minister's intelligence officials were telling him that Hussein had no role in 9/11 and did not actively cooperate with al Qaeda, they were also conveying confusing and ambiguous messages. The threat of "WMD terrorism" from Iraq, they said, was slight—"because of the risk of US retaliation." But Hussein had not given up on terrorism as a policy tool. "Saddam is an opportunist. We judge he would be willing to use terrorism if he thought he could gain advantage or exact revenge on his enemies without attracting disproportionate retaliation. Saddam has miscalculated in the past and he could again misread the response his actions would attract."[60]

"I have no doubt we need to deal with Saddam," Blair wrote Bush. But for the time being, the two leaders must "leave all options open." If we "hit Iraq now," Blair warned, "we would lose the Arab world, Russia, probably half the EU and my fear is the impact on Pakistan." Far better to deliberate quietly and avoid public debate "until we know exactly what we want to do; and how we can do it."[61]

President Bush was inclined to agree, and wait. He had no doubt that the United States needed to deal with Hussein. Condi Rice stated the administration's position succinctly at a press conference on November 8: "the United States does not intend to let the Iraqis threaten their own people, threaten their neighbors, or threaten our interests by acquiring weapons of mass destruction." But she did not say what the United States would do or what it specifically desired, except for the return of UN weapons inspectors.[62]

Bush, as Blair advised, wanted to keep his options open. He was deeply conflicted because short-term and long-term risk assessments were so challenging, so perplexing. He was told that Iraq was not linked to 9/11 and that Hussein's relations with al Qaeda were probably spasmodic and opportunist, yet he was receiving information that those ties might be more extensive than previously realized and that al Qaeda's quest for weapons of mass destruction more earnest than anticipated. He was told that Hussein's links to terror did not pose a threat to the United States, yet he was also being informed that the Iraqi dictator used those links to encourage terror against Israel and spread opposition to America's friends in the region, especially Saudi Arabia. He was told that Hussein possessed biological and chemical weapons capabilities and would probably not hand such weapons off to terrorists, but he was also hearing that al Qaeda's tentacles were spreading, terrorist networks proliferating, and their animus toward the West intensifying. He was told that Hussein had no existing nukes; this might have been reassuring except that he was also being told that the Iraqi dictator would resume his programs as soon as he escaped from the sanctions regime. Some advisers emphasized that Hussein was in his box so long as the United States remained in the region, sustained smart sanctions, and maintained the capacity to respond militarily. But he was also told that the sanctions regime was eroding, that it wrought starvation and misery upon the Iraqi people, that it inspired anti-Americanism and jihadism throughout the region, and that, therefore, it had to be terminated. He was told that containment would work so long as the United States kept a forward presence in the region, but he was also told that that forward presence, especially the stationing of troops in Saudi Arabia, wrought anger throughout the Middle East and augmented the number of jihadists. He was told that Iraq was not an imminent danger and he should do nothing, yet would become a long-term threat and should be dealt with now.[63]

The president reckoned with very tough trade-offs. Bush liked to say that he was a patient man. If he wanted to mobilize public opinion for a war against Iraq in behalf of regime change, he would have had little difficulty in November and December 2001. His favorable ratings in the polls were in the mid-80s, and surveys indicated that about 75 percent of the American people were in favor of going to war against Iraq.[64] Yet Bush made no effort to catalyze support for such a war, nor did he dwell publicly on regime change.

Ruminating about Iraq, he focused on Afghanistan. Until the second week in November that war did not proceed well, and the president weathered some sharp criticism. Subsequently, he acknowledged that he was nervous about the strategy, uncertain of the progress. But he remained calm, projected confidence, traits commented upon again and again in memoirs and interviews.[65] Then, suddenly, Taliban forces collapsed. "Within days," Bush wrote in his memoir, "almost every major city in the north fell. The Taliban fled Kabul for mountain hideouts, in the east and south. Women came out of their homes. Children flew kites. Men shaved off their beards and danced in the streets." "We are free," they shouted.[66]

"I was overjoyed by the success of liberation," he wrote.[67] Bush and his advisers were buoyed by their success. They triumphed against heavy odds, beyond their expectations. A sense of their own power now mixed with their ongoing dread of another attack.[68] Fear and power were surely an intoxicating, dangerous brew. Temptation mixed with anxiety, stirred by pride and hubris. General Myers waxed euphoric about images of "our Special Forces on horseback, charging across the dry grass slopes of the Hindu Kush foothills with their Northern Alliance partners. . . . This was [military] transformation made tangible. . . . We had developed a new way to fight wars . . . [and] we had dared to use it." In three months, Myers exclaimed, "we had overthrown the Taliban and liberated millions of Afghans."[69] The Americans "were fueled by the belief that they had done something very important in Afghanistan," commented David Manning, Blair's national security adviser, with whom Rice spoke frequently.[70]

Bush thought so, too. "I was feeling more comfortable as commander-in-chief," he commented.[71] On November 21, in the shadows of anthrax and the cheers of liberation, Bush quietly took Rumsfeld aside after an NSC meeting. "Where do we stand on the Iraq planning?" he inquired.[72]

Nothing much had been done since the initiation of the Global War on Terror. The hawks in the administration had spent almost no time dealing with Iraq. There were too many other things to worry about. Cheney, however, now encouraged the president to update the war plan for Iraq. Bush agreed.[73]

Yet President Bush still had not decided on going to war. "I want to know what the options are," Bush told Rumsfeld. "Frustrated with the military's lack of readiness prior to the invasion of Afghanistan," Rice noted, the president "sought an early outline of the Iraqi battle plan if it ultimately proved necessary." Bush subsequently explained, "A president cannot decide and make rational decisions unless [he understands] the feasibility of that which may have to happen." He meant to be saying to his secretary of defense: "show me what you have in place in case something were to happen."[74]

Seeking options made sense, but also revealed uncertainty about the road ahead. At the time, Rumsfeld did not think that Bush had made up his mind to go to war. Nor did Rice, or Hadley, or Myers.[75] The president knew that the sanctions against Iraq were faltering. He said publicly that they were like Swiss cheese. Hussein was garnering illegal revenues in the billions of dollars and using that money to augment his conventional capabilities and support his terrorist networks and suicide missions.[76] Secretary of State Powell and Deputy Secretary Armitage hoped that a new regime of smart sanctions would constrain Hussein's military ambitions while mitigating the suffering of the Iraqi people. Bush showed little enthusiasm for smart sanctions, frustrating the secretary of state and his aides who believed that containment rested on sanctions and monitoring, both of which were faltering.[77] But neither did Bush settle on an alternative approach to deal with Saddam Hussein's Iraq.

Nor did he do much to quell the simmering feuds among his top advisers. Different policy predilections over Korea, China, Israel/ Palestine, the Kyoto climate accord, and military commissions rankled, but personality conflicts and bureaucratic infighting mattered greatly. Rumsfeld was crotchety, overworked, dogged, and inscrutable. He returned from a trip to Central Asia in early October tired and irritable. He started complaining to Rice about the way she was controlling access to meetings, about too many meetings. He wasn't allowed to bring enough aides. "I am like a one-armed paperhanger," he wrote her in December. "I have to have help. I cannot function efficiently trying to do as much as we are doing."[78] Aside from his disdain for Rice, Rumsfeld antagonized other colleagues needlessly, perhaps inadvertently. He alienated Shelton, who was chairman of the joint chiefs.[79] From day one, he embittered Armitage when he interviewed him to be his deputy and treated him with condescension. In turn, Armitage infuriated Wolfowitz with his alleged leaks and nasty infighting.[80] More important, Rumsfeld irked Powell on a trip to Australia with little

digs and caustic comments. Powell, accustomed to respect and defer-
ence, did not feel he was part of the team Bush was putting together.
"There was a significant personality difference between me and the
president and me and the others," Powell later reflected. He felt apart,
alone in a locker room, where the boys snapped their towels playfully
while he sat in a corner.[81] This analogy hardly applied to Cheney, who
often remained quiet at meetings and who impressed many with his
intelligence, memory, and thoughtful questioning.[82] But the efforts
of Cheney's staff to play a key role in foreign policymaking agitated
State Department officials and made life more challenging for Rice
and Hadley, Bush's national security advisers.[83] From the outset,
there was no Bush team, even though everyone, including Powell and
Armitage, found the president gracious and respectful, albeit inscrutable in his own way. "I cannot tell you," Powell said to interviewers
in 2017, "and I don't think anybody can tell you why and when and
what actually moved him to decide that Iraq had become the number
one issue."[84]

This uncertainty was not surprising. A few days after telling Rumsfeld
he wanted an update on war planning for Iraq, Bush remained opaque.
He was asked by reporters, "What is your thinking about taking the
war to Iraq?" He reiterated what he had been saying for the last two
months: "Afghanistan is still just the beginning. If anyone harbors a
terrorist, they're a terrorist. If they fund a terrorist, they're a terrorist.
If they house terrorists, they're terrorists. . . . If they develop weapons
of mass destruction that will be used to terrorize nations, they will be
held accountable. And as for Mr. Saddam Hussein, he needs to let inspectors in his country to show us that he is not developing weapons of
mass destruction."[85]

Hussein was not doing much to allay American fears or assuage
the sensibilities of US policymakers. His foreign minister, Tariq Aziz,
floated some letters suggesting a willingness to open negotiations.[86]
But these overtures were not followed with any concrete actions signaling a readiness to allow inspections to resume or to resolve contested
matters. Hussein continued to treat the UN restrictions with disdain.
Talks held between Iraqi and UN officials went nowhere, and Hans
Blix, executive chairman of the UN Monitoring, Verification and
Inspection Commission (UNMOVIC), said the documents submitted

by the Iraqi government contained scant data that could resolve out-standing disputes.[87]

Instead, the Iraqi dictator continued to mix manipulation with contempt. Iraqi scientists continued to design missile systems "with the assumption that sanctioned material would be readily available." Hussein used his oil revenues to leverage support from France, China, and Russia to end UN sanctions. At the same time, he invested his growing financial reserves in strengthening Iraq's military-industrial complex and acquiring dual-use items and materials that might be used for chemical and biological weapons.[88] Hussein also accelerated or sustained Iraqi support for terrorist activity in Kuwait and Saudi Arabia, including the targeting of American aid workers. Although US intelligence analysts knew that he was financing the activities of several Palestinian terrorist groups, they were not aware of his growing support for Hamas's activities, in return for which, according to captured Iraqi documents, Hamas seemed "willing to do Saddam's bidding." Some US officials, like Wolfowitz, suspected that Hussein was making common cause with Islamic radicals, but they did not really know that it was indeed happening.[89] What they did know was that the dictator's atrocious behavior showed no signs of abating. Amnesty International, Human Rights Watch, the UN Commission on Human Rights, as well as the State Department, continued to report on his "all-pervasive repression and oppression," his arbitrary executions, his expulsion of Kurds and Turkmen from their homes in Kirkuk, Tuz, and Khormatu, his murder of Shi'a clerics, and his affinity for torture, like cutting out the tongues of regime critics and raping the wives and daughters of men suspected of disloyalty.[90]

Yet Bush averted talk of regime change or democracy promotion in his public comments. The Iraqi dictator was "evil," brutish, repressive, and aggressive, but neither Bush nor his advisers were animated by hopes of creating a freedom-loving Iraq. That was not part of the president's "original calculus," wrote Rumsfeld.[91] Even when the president talked about his goals in Afghanistan during these weeks, his words were measured, stressing that he wanted a "stable form of government after we leave."[92] As for Iraq, attention gravitated there for obvious reasons, explained Cheney: "if you had to identify somebody who was likely to provide a connection between terrorism on the one hand and weapons of mass destruction on the other, who is a more likely prospect than Saddam Hussein?"[93]

Hawkish advisers like Rumsfeld, Cheney, and Libby and their neoconservative friends, like Wolfowitz and Feith, were not inspired by missionary fervor or idealistic impulses. Their motives were more pedestrian and more compelling, ones they have emphasized again and again in their memoirs and their interviews. They were seeking to safeguard the country from another attack, save American lives, avoid the opprobrium that would come from another assault, and preserve the country's ability to exercise its power in the future in behalf of its interests. There is no reason to doubt the veracity of these claims (despite scores of books and articles that argue otherwise). They comport with contemporary documentation. Examine, for example, Feith's advice on September 18, or Rumsfeld's strategic thinking on September 30, or the defense secretary's October 30 revision of Feith's memorandum of October 16, or Wolfowitz's press comments on September 13 and 14, or his extensive Senate testimony on October 4. If the president authorized a campaign for regime change in Iraq, Feith wrote, its purpose would be "to eliminate a regime that engages in and supports terrorism and otherwise threatens US vital interests." The motive was simple: "self-defense." Whether a good or a bad idea, there was little idealism here; not much missionary fervor.[94]

The president and his advisers focused on Saddam Hussein because they perceived a menace in Baghdad, a tyrant who murdered his opponents, gassed his minorities, embraced weapons of mass destruction, committed unwarranted aggression, encouraged terrorists, sponsored suicide missions, defied American power, and in the future could endanger US interests. To deal with this man, the president wanted to examine an updated war plan. Whether Bush would employ it was another matter.

5

Coercive Diplomacy

"DICK, THE PRESIDENT wants to know what kind of operations plan we have for Iraq," Secretary of Defense Donald Rumsfeld said to General Richard Myers, the chairman of the Joint Chiefs of Staff.[1]

The date was November 21, 2001. The Taliban government in Afghanistan was collapsing and al Qaeda jihadists were fleeing their training camps. President George W. Bush wanted to ponder next steps in the global war on terror, and Rumsfeld aimed to have the Pentagon ready to offer concrete options should the president choose to take military action against Iraq. The secretary of defense had been frustrated, indeed angry, over the absence of military plans to deal with al Qaeda in Afghanistan. That was not going to happen again.

Rumsfeld knew the existing war plan for Iraq was out of date. It was "frozen in time"—"stale, slow-building," and totally inconsistent with his determination to transform military thinking, tactics, and procedures. General Myers, his newly installed chairman of the Joint Chiefs, agreed. Myers recognized that Iraqi military capabilities had declined since 1991 when the United States had led an international coalition to expel Iraqi troops from Kuwait. New precision-guided weapons in the American arsenal and improvements in communication meant that planners could more effectively coordinate US troop movements—day or night, in good or bad weather—and they could more precisely surveil, target, and destroy the enemy. Soldiers could maneuver more quickly and fewer of them would be required. How many, and how fast, would be debated for the next year.[2]

On November 26, Rumsfeld flew to Tampa, Florida, the head-quarters of Central Command, to speak to Tommy Franks, its top-ranking officer. Publicly, the visit appeared as a victory lap, the two men affirming how well things were evolving in Afghanistan and mocking the idea of a quagmire. Privately, the secretary of defense engaged Franks in a sustained discussion of Iraq policy. He believed Saddam Hussein's regime was brittle. He wanted US plans to exploit the dictator's vulnerabilities, heighten his paranoia, and strip away his supporters. "Focus on WMD," Rumsfeld's talking points began. He then dwelled on what it would take to build "momentum for re-gime change." He wanted Franks's planners to identify targets for cap-ture, destruction, or sabotage: WMD sites, offensive missile locations, Republican Guard headquarters, and oil fields. Rumsfeld then enu-merated prospective military operations, like seizing the western de-sert, securing the Jordanian border, cutting off Baghdad, thwarting the movement of WMD materials, and protecting a provisional gov-ernment that might be set up in the south, or north, or both. Finally, Rumsfeld's bullet points highlighted "regime change," "decapitation of government," and "how start." His overriding theme: "Surprise, speed, shock, and risk." The defense secretary urged Franks to jettison the old paradigm, employ few troops, act swiftly, and take risks.[3]

The next day, Myers flew to Tampa to speak to Franks. Together, they videoconferenced with Rumsfeld. Franks agreed that the existing plan for Iraq was outdated. He said he had learned a lot in Afghanistan. He now grasped the efficacy of his precision-guided weapons and the utility of Special Forces. Rumsfeld crisply concluded, "Fine, General, Please dust off your plan and get back to me next week."[4]

One week was an incredibly short time span, but Franks had be-come accustomed to Rumsfeld's grueling demands, incessant probing, and intrusive meddling. After initial exasperation, he had grown ac-customed to dealing with him. In fact, Franks was delighted that the secretary of defense was relying on CENTCOM, on him, rather than the joint staff in Washington. The Pentagon bureaucracy and the chiefs of staff often infuriated him more than did Rumsfeld. Franks was a folksy, driven, disciplined, able, and foul-mouthed soldier from Midland, Texas, the same town and the same high school of Laura Bush, the president's wife. He was at the apex of his career, struggling to bring the Afghan campaign to a triumphant end and, now, tasked to plan a new approach to dealing with Iraq. He knew he had to please Rumsfeld and satisfy the president; he also knew he did not want to be hassled by a mob of "mother-fuckers" in Washington, the generals and admirals who headed their services inside the Pentagon.[5]

Before he could do much, on December 1, Franks received another missive from Rumsfeld. The secretary of defense wanted a "commander's estimate" of what it would take to structure an Iraq war plan. According to Bob Woodward, the renowned journalist who has examined the leaked document, "Rumsfeld wanted to know how Franks would conduct military operations to remove Saddam from power, eliminate the threat of any possible weapons of mass destruction, and choke off his suspected support for terrorism." The general was instructed to report to Washington in three days.[6]

On December 4, Franks appeared at the Pentagon for a confidential meeting with Rumsfeld, Under Secretary of Defense Douglas Feith, General Myers, and Peter Pace, the vice chairman of the JCS. Initially, they focused on "assumptions," assumptions about the objectives of the war. Unlike 1990, when the objective was to excise Iraqi troops from Kuwait, this time the goal was "to remove the regime of Saddam Hussein." Rumsfeld concurred, and emphasized, "The President will ultimately make that decision." The general continued with his second assumption: if war occurred, the mission was to ensure that Iraq could no longer threaten its neighbors with either conventional forces or weapons of mass destruction. In short, the goals were straightforward: "regime change and WMD removal."[7] It would require 400,000 troops, Franks speculated, about a 20 percent reduction from previous estimates. Rumsfeld thought the number was too large, a relic of old thinking. He wanted Franks to return in a week for another iteration of his thinking. They met again on December 12 and December 19. Franks and his planners kept recalibrating to meet Rumsfeld's desires for a smaller, more robust force that could be mobilized more quickly and achieve goals more swiftly.[8]

The sessions at the Pentagon with Rumsfeld were designed to hone Franks's thinking for a presentation to the president. Rumsfeld wanted Bush to get to know Franks and gain confidence that he could rely on the Defense Department, rather than the Central Intelligence

Agency (CIA), to take action and execute plans. On December 27, Franks flew to Texas to meet the president at his ranch at Crawford during the Christmas holidays (Figure 5.1). The next day, December 28, in a secure videoconference room at the ranch, the general took out twenty-six slides and outlined his planning. Attending the meeting— on screens—were Rumsfeld at his home in Taos, Vice President Dick Cheney at his ranch in Wyoming, and in the White House Situation Room were Secretary of State Colin Powell, National Security Adviser Condi Rice, and CIA director George Tenet. Franks explained that his plans were tentative, preliminary, hardly plans at all, actually concepts of how to deal with Saddam Hussein, given the lessons learned in Afghanistan and the advances in US capabilities. He focused on the "slices" of the regime that could be targeted and the vulnerabilities of Hussein's dictatorship that the United States could exploit. He clarified the time it would take to prepare for action, the basing requirements, the actions that could be initiated before the war began, and the scope

Figure 5.1 General Tommy Franks visits Bush at his ranch in Crawford, Texas, to discuss contingency plans for war in Iraq, December 28, 2001.
Getty Images, https://www.gettyimages.com/detail/news-photo/president-george-w-bush-with-general-tommy-franks-commander-news-photo/51708738

and nature of the attack. He talked about employing Special Forces, as had been done in Afghanistan, mobilizing exile groups, and capitalizing on Kurdish and Shi'a hatred of the regime. The general was eager to begin conversations with the Gulf states to secure basing rights and assistance; he wanted to place CIA operatives into Iraq; he desired to move pre-positioned equipment from Qatar to Kuwait, much closer to the Iraqi border. Much of the planning could be segmented into "influencing" operations, actions designed to intimidate Hussein, foment internal opposition, and nurture distrust among regime leaders. If really effective, these steps might obviate the need for military action altogether. Concluding, Franks said that he knew it was premature to assume that war would occur. Nonetheless, taking some initial steps would enable the president to expedite whatever campaign he might decide upon.[9]

Franks's presentation catalyzed an important discussion. Rumsfeld thought the general's troop numbers—105,000 to start the war, and about 230,000 to finish it—were just estimates, and probably excessive. Tenet emphasized that the agency did not have the contacts and capabilities in Iraq that it had accumulated over decades in Afghanistan. Cheney worried about Iraqi employment of weapons of mass destruction. Rice wondered what the United States could do if Hussein pulled forces back to Baghdad and fortified himself inside the capital.[10]

The president, overall, was impressed. Keep working on it, he instructed Rumsfeld and Franks. We'll keep at it, said Rumsfeld, "but we're not recommending war or war timing—just prudent preparatory steps." The president concurred. He was not set on war. "We should remain optimistic," he said, "that diplomacy and international pressure will succeed in disarming the regime." But he also stressed that he needed options, should Hussein prove recalcitrant.[11]

Franks spent the rest of the morning driving around the ranch with Bush, before declining lunch and heading back to Tampa. He did not feel any sense of urgency. "I never got the sense," Franks told interviewers in 2014, "that Bush wanted to do this [go to war]. 'By gosh, I'm going to do this, and sooner is better than later.' That was never communicated to me." The general left the ranch, thinking "It was not certain that America would go to war in Iraq. But it was certain that we would set conditions in the region, and improve the military infrastructure that would allow us to launch a decisive campaign, should the president order us to do so."[12]

Franks's advice and planning were welcomed by Bush because they very closely coincided with what British prime minister Tony Blair was proposing. Officials in London worried that Washington, emboldened by success in Afghanistan, might quickly go to war against Iraq. Blair's advisers thought such action would backfire. They despised Hussein as much as did Bush, but they did not assume that Hussein could be removed easily from power. They did not think they could orchestrate a coup, and they did not believe that Iraqi exiles constituted a viable force to overthrow the Iraqi dictator. Hussein was too entrenched in power and opposition groups too thoroughly infiltrated by his intelligence services. Overt military action, moreover, would reverberate badly throughout the Middle East and Persian Gulf, adding to Hussein's popularity and risking a war with weapons of mass destruction.[13]

Instead of military action, Blair advocated "a strategy for regime change that builds over time." In a "UK/US Eyes Only" paper, he laid out his thinking: "We draw attention to Saddam's breach of UN resolutions; we say regime change is 'desirable' (although not yet setting it as a military objective); we signal willingness to support opposition groups and build a regional coalition against Saddam; we demand weapons inspectors to go back in; and without specifying that we will take military action if the demand is not met, we let it be clearly seen that nothing is ruled out. But our time frame is deliberately vague." The aim, thought Blair, was to unsettle Hussein, "possibly forcing concessions out of him; and giving ourselves room to manoeuvre."[14]

David Manning, Blair's national security adviser, brought this paper to Washington during the first week of December 2001, at the same time that Franks and his planners were carving up their slices and matching them to US capabilities. Manning talked to Rice, with whom he was forging a close relationship. He reported back to Blair that she assured him that the administration had not determined to resort to military action.[15]

British strategy and Franks's planning were attractive to Bush because they comported with his inclination to use American power to elicit concessions from the Iraqi dictator. "President Bush believed," Rumsfeld subsequently wrote, "that the key to successful diplomacy with Saddam was a credible threat of military action. We hoped that the process of moving an increasing number of American forces into a position where they could attack Iraq might convince the Iraqis to end their defiance." The administration thought that building a military force would affect Hussein's calculations, said Hadley. "We thought it would coerce him . . . to do what the international community asked, which is either destroy the WMD or show us that you destroyed it. That was it. Either do it, or if you've already done it, show it, prove it."[16]

Bush wanted to intimidate Hussein. He wanted to use the threat of force to remove the Iraqi dictator from power. He also wanted to use the threat of force to resume inspections and gain confidence that Iraq did not possess weapons of mass destruction. He did not really know which of these two goals had priority. They were distinct, yet often conflated. He sometimes wanted Hussein's removal in order to feel assured there was no threat of WMD falling into the hands of terrorists; at other times, he wanted to use the threat—the demand for inspections—as a ruse to justify military invasion in order to overthrow him. These conflicting, overlapping impulses coursed through Bush's mind for the next year. He never clearly sorted them out, yet each would become more and more compelling.

Bush and his advisers remained focused on Hussein's regime because they were wrapping up military operations in Afghanistan and pondering what to do next in the global war on terror. They were exhilarated by the downfall of the Taliban government, the liberation of key cities, and the spirit of cooperation among allies in forming a new government in Kabul. They felt good that they were bringing key jihadists "to justice." But they were frustrated that many jihadists were escaping from Franks's troops and the Northern Alliance. They suspected that bin Laden was alive, holed up in a cave somewhere, and aspiring to inflict new wounds on Americans. How do I know this? the president rhetorically asked journalists on the day he met with General Franks at his Texas ranch. "I receive intelligence reports on a daily basis that indicate that that's his desires."[17]

The threat of terrorism did not abate. An al Qaeda terrorist with explosives was arrested on a plane in Michigan in December 2001. On December 13, 2001, two militant organizations allied with al Qaeda in Pakistan—Lashkar-e Taiba and Jaish-e-Muhammad—tried to blow up India's parliament and kill its leaders. Hamas suicide bombers killed twenty-six Israelis in Jerusalem and Haifa. Intelligence analysts tracked these developments. US officials tried to mediate the rancor between Pakistan and India and modulate the Israeli reaction. Most of all, they aimed to protect the American homeland from another shocking assault. "Militant Islamic terrorism's reach was more extensive than we realized," wrote one of the CIA's top analysts. Although the United States and its partners "were methodically attriting the al-Qaeda organization," militant extremism was spreading and bin Laden's global jihad "was becoming a reality."[18]

No threat worried Bush and his advisers more than the prospect of terrorists getting their hands on weapons of mass destruction. Yet this specter mounted. As US soldiers and intelligence analysts explored the disbanded terrorist camps in Afghanistan, they were discovering hard drives, documents, and information. They learned that Ayman al-Zawahiri, the number two man in the al Qaeda leadership, was intensely interested in the development of biological and chemical weapons, especially anthrax, and aspired to employ such weapons for a mass casualty attack in the United States. Cheney was informed, and so was the president, and analysts were instructed to pursue all their leads. Eventually, they discovered that bin Laden had had two close associates in Khartoum in the 1990s, a Syrian nuclear scientist named Mohammad Luray Bayazid, also known as Abu Rida al-Suri, and an Iraqi agronomist named Mubarek al-Duri. The latter was tracked down in Sudan in the spring of 2002. Interrogated—not tortured—al-Duri blurted out his repressed fury: "I do not deny it. If we could kill millions of Americans, it would be justifiable for all the harm they have done in the world." Rolf Mowatt-Larssen, the CIA official questioning al-Duri, along with Sudanese intelligence officers, commented, "There was hatred in my target's eyes. It was a hatred many others shared for everything the West stood for." Mowatt-Larssen then reflected, "When I began my work, I was skeptical that men in caves were capable of carrying out a WMD attack. No more. There was no doubt in my mind that the threat of WMD terrorism was real." Succinctly, CIA director Tenet noted, "Our fears of imminent attack did not go away as 2001 slid into 2002."[19]

The relationship of Iraq to these developments remained enigmatic. Thousands of jihadists fled Afghanistan to find new sanctuaries, and news circulated that some were entering northeastern Iraq. Secretary of State Powell inquired whether Hussein might be offering Iraq as a safe haven for bin Laden. Carl Ford, the head of Intelligence at the State Department, reported that bin Laden might have reached out to the Iraqi dictator, but it was unlikely that Hussein would allow Islamic fundamentalists to establish a base in Iraq lest they mount a threat to his own rule. Yet there was plentiful evidence that al Qaeda loyalists were moving into an area of northeastern Iraq outside of Hussein's control. Was he aware of it? Probably. Was he welcoming it? Uncertain. The CIA concluded: "it would be difficult for al-Qaida to maintain an active, long-term presence in Iraq without alerting the authorities or obtaining their acquiescence."[20] Yet neither the DIA nor the CIA thought that Hussein had anything to do with 9/11; nor did they believe that any formal collaborative relationship existed between the Iraqi regime and al Qaeda. But they also acknowledged that "mutual antipathy . . . would not prevent tactical, limited cooperation."[21] At the end of the year, the State Department report on terrorism starkly concluded: "Iraq planned and sponsored international terrorism in 2002." "Throughout the year, the Iraqi Intelligence Service [IIS] laid the ground work for possible attacks against civilian and military targets in the United States and other Western countries."[22]

Such thinking and reporting, sometimes uncertain and often inconsistent, sustained apprehensions inside the White House. No scenario could be worse than a terrorist attack with weapons of mass destruction. Some new evidence, however wrongheaded, accelerated anxieties, such as claims that Iraq sought uranium from Niger.[23] When leaked to the news media, these allegations aroused much controversy, but they did not affect fundamental beliefs. What did not change was the certainty that Iraq had biological weapons and chemical programs. What did not change was the assumption that Hussein would reignite his nuclear programs when sanctions were lifted and conditions were more propitious. Succinctly summarizing what they thought they knew, Carl Ford informed Powell, "Saddam Hussein will exploit any opportunity to advance his WMD and ballistic missile programs."[24]

Assessors, like Ford, did not hype the nuclear threat; it would take Iraq five to seven years, they said, to develop a weapon unless Hussein somehow acquired fissile material more swiftly. But few analysts minimized the threat emanating from Iraq's biological and chemical programs. "Baghdad probably has reconstituted its offensive BW program to pre–Gulf War levels in well-concealed, underground, or mobile facilities," Ford told Powell. It was expanding its biotech infrastructure. It posed a "credible CW threat," although it still lacked the infrastructure for a "robust" CW program. At the end of February, the DIA concluded that "The Iraqi regime maintains covert offensive chemical and biological weapons programs, despite claims that such programs have been eliminated." European intelligence agencies, Secretary of State Powell was told, concurred with these findings, even though their governments opposed action to bomb Iraq: "There is no argument that Iraqi WMD capabilities pose a significant threat." In March 2002, Ford reiterated to Deputy Secretary of State Armitage, "all Allies believe Iraq has exploited the current lack of UN inspectors to develop covertly an offensive WMD capability."[25]

British analysts were saying the same things. "There is real reason for concern about Iraq's WMD programmes, principally CBW and long-range missiles," wrote the British foreign minister's private secretary to David Manning. According to British intelligence, the Iraqis were concealing information about 31,000 chemical munitions, 4,000 tons of precursor chemicals for chemical weapons, 610 tons of precursor chemicals for the nerve agent VX, and very large quantities of growth media acquired for the production of biological weapons. They had restored chemical and biological weapons facilities, and reignited some CW- and BW-relevant activity.[26] Such assessments did not cease during the winter of 2002, even though British intelligence thought Hussein feared a US military attack. "Iraq continues to pursue its WMD programmes," concluded the British Joint Intelligence Committee in February. "If it has not already done so, Iraq could produce significant quantities of biological warfare agents within days and chemical warfare agents within weeks of a decision to do so."[27]

Bush wanted to remove Saddam from power, and he wanted inspectors to return to Iraq, but he did not know if he wanted to go to war to achieve one or another of these objectives, or both. On January

3, he met with Tenet, along with the deputy chief of the CIA's Near East division and its head of Iraqi operations. They told Bush and Vice President Cheney that covert actions would not work to overthrow Hussein. The United States, they explained, was deeply distrusted by the Kurds in the north and the Shi'a in the south because Washington had betrayed them in the past and left them exposed to Hussein's revenge. They would not rise up unless they were absolutely convinced of US determination to get rid of the despised dictator. The CIA could not recruit sources unless the agency could say convincingly to dissidents inside Iraq that military action was imminent. In short, they told Bush that "the bifurcated policy of trying to contain with one hand and trying to overthrow with the other wasn't going to work. The only way to succeed was for the CIA to support a full military invasion of Iraq." Bush was disappointed. Nonetheless, he decided to persevere with the bifurcated policy. Not yet ready to choose between containment and regime change, he would live a while longer with "dissonance and inconsistencies."[28]

In January 2002, Bush's principal advisers and their deputies spent a great deal of time discussing next steps toward Iraq. "The issue," according to Eric Edelman, Cheney's national security expert who often attended the meetings of deputies, "was how do we deal with Saddam? Can we get him to give up his WMD? What would we want him to do to demonstrate that he has abandoned these programs. . . . If he did not give up his WMD what tools of coercion did we have?"[29] The principals and deputies pondered whether containment could be strengthened through the application of smart sanctions or the reconfiguration of the rules governing the no-fly zones. They reexamined the prospects for regime change through covert actions or the operations of exile groups and expatriates. They discussed whether they could pressure Hussein to relinquish power, or whether they could use force to overthrow him. Their deliberations were inconclusive. They could not resolve what to do. "Yet no one," wrote Rice, "believed that Saddam would give up power peacefully, and overthrowing him using . . . the Iraqi National Congress seemed highly unlikely. We were really down to two options if we wanted to change course: increasing international pressure to make him give up his WMD or overthrowing him by force."[30]

Bush's inclination was to mobilize international pressure. "I expect Saddam Hussein to let inspectors back into the country," he told journalists on January 16, 2002. "We want to know whether he's developing weapons of mass destruction. He claims he's not; let the world in to see," declared Bush. "And if he doesn't we'll have to deal with him at the appropriate time."[31]

The president ratcheted up the pressure. On January 29, 2002, in his State of the Union message, Bush explained that "what we have found in Afghanistan confirms that, far from ending there, our war against terror is only beginning." Terrorist camps, he said, still existed in at least a dozen countries. "A terrorist underworld, including groups like Hamas, Hizballah, Islamic Jihad, Jais-e-Mohammed, operates in remote jungles and deserts and hides in the centers of large cities." US military initiatives, he acknowledged, were taking place in Bosnia, the Philippines, and Somalia. But this was not enough. The United States had "to prevent regimes that sponsor terror from threatening America or our friends and allies with weapons of mass destruction." North Korea "is a regime arming with missiles and weapons of mass destruction. . . . Iran aggressively pursues these weapons and exports terror." But the president's longest passage focused on Iraq. That country "continued to flaunt its hostility toward America and to support terror." It "had plotted to develop anthrax and nerve gas and nuclear weapons over a decade." It was "a regime that agreed to international inspections, then kicked out the inspectors. This is a regime that has something to hide from the civilized world." Together, these three states, Bush declared, "constitute an axis of evil, arming to threaten the peace of the world."[32]

Those words, "axis of evil," captured the attention of the world. They were not the words of Cheney, Rumsfeld, Wolfowitz, or Libby.[33] They represented Bush's mindset, words scripted by Michael Gerson, his chief speechwriter, on the basis of a memorandum written by one of his assistants, David Frum. Gerson explained that Bush could not abide brutal dictators, like Saddam Hussein, who abused their own people, supported terrorism, possessed chemical and bacteriological agents for warfare, wanted to develop nuclear weapons, and desired to thwart the power of, or blackmail, the United States. But this did not mean that Bush favored military action, Gerson emphasized; in fact, the president wanted to avoid war. He hoped pressure would work.[34]

But pressure was not likely to work without the threat of force. Bush pondered how he could compel Hussein to live up to his obligations and get rid of his WMD. "All he cares about," Bush ruminated, "is staying in power. Maybe if he thinks we'll overthrow him, he'll change." Rice, a former professor, told the president that, among academics, that was called "coercive diplomacy." The president loved that terminology.[35] He was not alone in thinking this way. At almost this precise time, the British Joint Intelligence Committee concluded that, although Hussein's diplomats were "nominally" re-engaging with the United Nations and employing a "charm offensive," Hussein offered nothing new. Only the threat of "large-scale military action" might persuade him to change his mind and permit the return of weapons inspectors.[36] "The best way to get Saddam to come into compliance with UN demands," said Cheney, "was to convince him we would use force."[37]

Leading Democrats did not disagree. In early February, Senator Joseph Biden, the Democratic chairman of the Foreign Relations Committee, held hearings dealing with the State Department's budget request for fiscal 2003. Secretary of State Powell emphasized that the war on terrorism was his number one priority. Biden was fully supportive, but gravitated to another subject. Talking about an "axis of evil," he said, confused friends and angered allies. Powell retorted that the president was simply trying to explain that "even if we finished with al-Qaeda in Afghanistan, even if we got al-Qaeda everywhere that is in the 50-odd countries that it is located, we still have a problem, the civilized world has a problem." There were regimes, Powell emphasized, that not only supported terror but were developing WMD. They "could provide the wherewithal to terrorist organizations to use these sorts of things against us." Biden queried whether this meant that the president was announcing a new policy of preemption, as allies feared he was doing. After Powell denied this allegation, Biden proclaimed his own fears about the proliferation of weapons of mass destruction and especially about Iraq. "I happen to be one that thinks that one way or another Saddam has got to go and it is likely to be required to have U.S. force to have him go and the question is how to do it in my view, not if to do it."[38]

Two days later, Biden held another set of hearings, "What's Next in the War on Terrorism?" Sandy Berger, President Bill Clinton's national security adviser, testified. He agreed with Bush that each alleged member of the axis of evil posed "unmistakable dangers." He then went on to say, "Saddam was, is and continues to be a menace to his people, to the region, and to us. He cannot be accommodated. Our goal should be regime change. The question is not whether, but how and when." Biden agreed with Berger, insisting that Hussein "had to go." Like former president Bill Clinton and secretary of state Madeleine Albright, many prominent Democrats "could not question the goal of ousting Saddam Hussein." But the question was how, and with whom? Who would follow him? What vision did the administration have?[39]

Bush did not have the answers to these questions, but he decided that he would ratchet up the pressure. Meeting with the press on February 13, he was asked about regime change in Iraq. "One of the worst things that can happen in the world," he said, "is terrorist organizations mating up with nations which have had a bad history and nations which develop weapons of mass destruction." He would not permit such nations "to hold America hostage and/or harm Americans and/or our friends and allies." He wanted "to work with the world to bring pressure on those nations to change their behavior." They had a choice to make. "And I'll keep all options available if they don't make the choice."[40]

A few days later Bush signed a directive to the CIA to plan for regime change in Iraq, a decision consistent with the Iraq Liberation Act of 1998, a bill signed by Clinton, passed in the House of Representatives by 360–38, and approved by unanimous consent in the US Senate. Bush now authorized the agency to support opposition groups and conduct sabotage operations inside Iraq. It could work to disrupt regime revenues and thwart Iraq's illicit procurement of goods that had been sanctioned by the United Nations. Bush instructed the agency to conduct information campaigns to undermine the regime and to confuse its military and intelligence officials about US intentions. Soon thereafter, Tenet met with Kurdish leaders to discuss these plans. The CIA director assured them that this time the United States was serious; this time Hussein was "going down"; this time the US military would back up its covert operations. "Of course," he subsequently acknowledged, "he did not know if what he was saying was true, whether war was going to happen." But without intimidation and threats, there was no prospect that Hussein would change his behavior.[41]

Bush authorized an intelligence operation that could complement military planning. The latter was proceeding, but not refined. Franks updated his concepts with Rumsfeld on February 1, and with the full national security team on February 7. His plan—called Generated Start—envisioned three key phases, ninety days of force preparation, forty-five days of bombing and covert operations, and then ninety days of combat operations, involving about 300,000 troops. Bush asked numerous questions about the timing, noting that he could not be sure when the attack would occur, or if it would occur. Rumsfeld again indicated his desire for the plan to involve more firepower and quicker pacing, "shock and awe." Franks emphasized that his ideas were evolving concepts. Bush appeared satisfied. So was Secretary of State Powell: "No one seemed trigger happy."[42] Rumsfeld reminded Franks, "Remember, there's a fine balance between thorough preparation and triggering a war, and the President has not decided to go to war."[43]

In fact, many planners at CENTCOM did not believe their plans would ever be executed. They were stunned by the frequent leaks of highly classified materials at the Pentagon. The leaks themselves reflected the acrimonious climate among high-level military and civilian officials serving under Secretary of Defense Rumsfeld. His attempt to exclude the service chiefs from the planning process was infuriating, confusing, and counterproductive, reinforcing the poisonous atmosphere that he had nurtured since his first months in office.[44] But the planners at CENTCOM also hated the constant interference of Under Secretary of Defense Feith and his subordinates. As nerves frayed and leaks proliferated, rumors circulated that some high-ranking officers opposed going to war. Others believed that the leaks were purposeful, "part of an elaborate information campaign to put pressure on the Iraqi government in order to compel compliance with Washington's demands to cooperate with WMD inspectors."[45] This was not simply gossip among mid-level planners at Tampa. Both General Myers, the chairman of the JCS, and General George Casey, head of strategic planning on the joint staff, believed that the planning was designed to support Bush's coercive diplomacy—"to make sure that he had a viable war plan to back up his diplomacy." They did not think the president had decided to go to war.[46]

The acrimony within the military establishment mirrored the friction that was mounting among members of the national security bureaucracy. In late December, as Franks was flying to Texas to meet with Bush, Rumsfeld wrote a cryptic note to Condi Rice: "I notice you are starting to send out memos saying, 'If no objections are raised, the NSC paper will be considered as approved.' . . . Please change your procedure so that you need to hear back from me before you can assume that something is approved." Four days later, as the new year approached, he reminded her again: "having silence mean assent is a poor policy"; it misleads people.[47]

Rice and Hadley, of course, were not trying to mislead anyone. They were working tenaciously to tackle momentous issues in an environment fraught with tension and uncertainty. In fact, on 9/11, Rice, Cheney, Rumsfeld, and Powell had dinner together at Camp David. At a wrenching moment, they wanted to patch up wounds and begin collaborating. "We'd do that on a number of occasions," Cheney subsequently recalled, "or we'd have lunch over at the Pentagon, but it just never clicked the way you would like to have had it work."[48] The greatest shortcoming of Rice and Hadley, in the view of most participants in the NSC process, was their quest to garner consensus. This was exceedingly difficult to achieve when Defense officials "treated the interagency process with an abiding animosity."[49] Issues festered; endless wrangling ensued. Meetings were "strange," said John McLaughlin; nothing seemed to get resolved. Perhaps that was because Rumsfeld forbade action without his assent, and he did not allow his subordinates to speak for him. And when he spoke he questioned and queried rather than clarified.[50]

The friction was mounting in February 2002 when the president agreed that Cheney should go to the Middle East and Persian Gulf. Rumsfeld told his subordinates to figure out what they wanted the vice president to accomplish on his trip. He planned to visit Jordan, Egypt, Oman, Saudi Arabia, Qatar, Bahrain, the UAE, Kuwait, Israel, Turkey, and Yemen. As a former secretary of defense and prominent oil executive, Cheney knew many of the leaders of these states. Defense officials wanted Cheney to underscore that, although no policy had been determined, the United States regarded Hussein as a continuing threat to the entire region. He was to explore, however delicately, the assistance they might offer should the United States engage in combat operations to overthrow the Iraqi dictator.[51]

State Department officials were uneasy about Cheney's trip. Bill Burns, the assistant secretary of state for Near East Affairs, went along on the trip with Cheney and his assistants, Scooter Libby, Eric Edelman, and John Hannah. "Getting into Iraq," Burns wrote Secretary Powell, "will be a lot easier than getting out. . . . Regional stakeholders worry that we will come in, create a mess, and then leave them to deal with the consequences." Although Arab governments "would like to see Saddam gone," they made the "cold calculation that the risks posed by the uncertainties of regime change outweigh the current threat from Saddam. They believe a UN arms control regime and a continued US military presence (at roughly current levels) would more than keep the peace." They were far more concerned, Burns wrote, with Israeli-Palestinian relations. The United States, he insisted, needed "to put the MEPP [Middle East Peace Process] on a more even keel and increase our credibility. Otherwise, most regional publics will view any action against Iraq in light of a US double-standard and as a continuing campaign against Muslims and Arabs."[52]

During their trip to the region, from March 10–20, Burns urged Cheney to meet with Yasser Arafat, the Palestinian leader, who was holed up in his compound in Ramallah and was surrounded by Israeli troops threatening to seize or kill him. In the midst of the Intifada against Israeli occupation, suicide bombings convulsed Israeli society, portending a dramatic escalation of hostilities.[53] In London, and then in the region, British and Arab heads of state told Cheney that they agreed Hussein had to go, but dealing with Iraq required a comprehensive effort to quell the incendiary atmosphere in Palestine/Israel. Cheney acknowledged the volatility of the Palestinian-Israeli controversy and was willing to meet with Arafat but only if the Palestinian leader agreed to renounce terror publicly. Arafat did not do so, and Cheney left the region without seeing him and with emotions at fever pitch. In early April, after another suicide bombing at a Passover seder killed scores of Israelis, Prime Minister Ariel Sharon launched a massive military offensive to reoccupy key cities in the West Bank.[54]

Regarding Iraq, the vice president felt he had advanced under-standing of the US position. Everywhere, he stated that the admin-istration had not resolved what it would do. But "he signaled our seriousness of purpose," Burns wrote, emphasizing that Hussein posed a great danger to the region and the world, "especially because he al-ready possesses biological and chemical weapons and is pursuing nu-clear weapons." Cheney said the United States was determined to stop Iraq from continuing its programs or acquiring new weapons. "The vice president's interlocutors," Burns reported, "raised no objections. . . . No one rejected the point that the US must do what it can to protect itself and its friends from a Saddam regime armed with weapons of mass destruction."[55]

Cheney reported back on his mission, and the president and vice president met with the Cabinet and talked to the press. Everyone in the region, Cheney said, grasped the seriousness of the situa-tion. They recognized the menace posed by Hussein's biological and chemical weapons and his nuclear ambitions. They understood, Bush said, that Americans were resolved to fight the war on terror relentlessly.[56]

But as to precise action, Bush conveyed mixed messages, filled with purposeful innuendos to intimidate Hussein, yet fraught with ambi-guities. On March 22, he said "no military action against Saddam was imminent." But he emphasized that Hussein was a dreadful leader who gassed his own people and possessed the world's most frightening weapons. He could hand them off to some terrorist organization, cre-ating a true "nightmare scenario." And, yes, the president went on to say, he supported regime change. It had been his predecessor's position and his own since his inauguration as president. There was no ambi-guity about his commitment to regime change—until he ended his remarks by stressing something else: "And I hope, of course, he allows inspectors to go into the country, like he promised he would do, not for the sake of letting inspectors in but to showing [sic] the world that he has no weapons of mass destruction."[57]

The president wanted to focus on the global war on terror and on Iraq, but his attention was deflected by the terrorist suicide bombings in Israel and the Israeli military reaction. While Powell, Rumsfeld, and Cheney wrestled with one another on whether the United States should pressure Israel to end its military operation or intensify its efforts to mediate a peace settlement, Bush decided to give a major speech outlining his views. On April 4, he called on Arafat to renounce terror, and emphasized that Israel had a right to defend itself. But he also stressed that Israel should stop its military offensive, end its settlement activity, terminate the occupation, and withdraw to secure boundaries consistent with the United Nations. The Palestinians had a right to their own state, he declared, and Israel had a right to its security. Although seeking to sound impartial, he could not conceal his visceral hatred of Arafat and his loathing of terrorism. He called on Palestinian leaders to do "everything possible in their power to stop terrorist activities, to disrupt terrorist financing, and to stop inciting violence by glorifying terror . . . [and] telling suicide bombers they are martyrs. They're not martyrs. They're murderers. And they undermine the cause of the Palestinian people." Although he endorsed a recent peace initiative proposed by Saudi Arabia, Bush offered nothing of his own. Instead, he sent Secretary of State Powell back to the region to help negotiate an end to the fighting and to ascertain a basis for long-term peacemaking.[58]

In Bush's mind, the Israeli quest to crush Palestinian terrorist attacks resembled his own quest to wage a global war on terror. Terrorists were killers, he told Trevor McDonald, a British journalist, in a long interview following the speech. Killing innocent people was beyond the pale, an intolerable affront to human decency. "There must be a world effort to stop the suicide and the killers," he declared. And, no, he told McDonald, the war on terror was not stalemated. The struggle required patience, determination, tenacity, and resolve. He had these qualities; so did the American people. "We're going to do whatever it takes to rout out these terrorist organizations." Asked if this would include an attack on Iraq, Bush replied that Hussein was a dangerous man who possessed weapons of mass destruction and who was not unwilling to use them. Although the president said he had "no immediate plans" to conduct military operations, it remained an option.

Have you made up your mind that Iraq must be attacked? McDonald queried. "I made up my mind that Saddam needs to go," Bush succinctly stated. "That's all I'm willing to share with you. The policy of my government is that he goes. . . . The worst thing that could happen would be to allow a nation like Iraq, run by Saddam Hussein, to develop weapons of mass destruction and then team up with terrorist organizations so they can blackmail the world. I'm not going to let that happen." Asked whether he thought he could assemble a coalition to attack Iraq, the president gravitated back to inspections. He said a "coalition can be assembled to demand that Iraq let inspectors back in, like he agreed to after the Gulf War. I don't know why the man won't let inspectors in. He's probably got something to hide, don't you think?" McDonald pressed, "What you really want Saddam to do is to let the inspectors back in." Of course, said Bush. But it is not so much an issue of inspectors, as it was "upholding his word." McDonald pressed again: so you will attack anyway, even if he allows inspectors back in? Bush, irritated by the probing, pushed back. He said he had no plans to attack "on his desk." The "policy of my Government is Saddam not to be in office. . . . [I]t's in the interests of the free world that he not be allowed to develop weapons of mass destruction. And the first thing he must show us [is] whether or not he has weapons of mass destruction, just like he promised he would do."[59]

The interview revealed the ambiguities of coercive diplomacy. The language was purposefully threatening, instrumental in intent, seeking to prompt Hussein to flee or to open up his country. But the interview also highlighted the conflated notions of regime change and weapons inspections. If the president were satisfied with the latter, might he relent on the former? Bush wanted both, and, even more, he wanted proof that Iraq did not have WMD. To achieve this clarity, coercive diplomacy required diplomacy. Yet the president still had not developed a diplomatic strategy to implement his notional grasp of coercive diplomacy, nor had he resolved which of his goals had priority. But coercive diplomacy involved military intimidation and vested the credibility of the president and the nation in delivering a satisfactory outcome, however ambiguous it was.

Bush did grasp that his global war on terror required more than military threats and regime removals. "History has given us an opportunity," the president told McDonald, "to fight for freedom, and we will fight for freedom." Motivated by fear of another attack, Bush increasingly recognized the need to communicate a vision of what he wanted to accomplish, not only in Iraq, but elsewhere. The global war on terror required a positive purpose. Whereas Hussein was "a pariah who was guilty of grave atrocities against humanity," the president had to offer a vision of a more peaceful, better world to come, a vision of human freedom and individual dignity. Bush knew that; he said it; he acted upon it.[60]

In March 2002, at the same time that he was reviewing the results of Vice President's Cheney's trip to the Middle East, the president gave a talk at the Inter-American Development Bank in Washington, DC, and then delivered a major speech in Monterrey, Mexico, to a UN Financing for Development conference. "We are at a moment of hope," he declared, "in an age-old struggle against world poverty." The United States "wanted to bring hope and opportunity to the world's poorest people and to call for a new compact—for development defined by greater accountability for rich and poor nations alike." Elegantly, and eloquently, he tied this struggle against poverty to the war on terror. "We fight against poverty because hope is an answer to terror. We fight against poverty because opportunity is a fundamental right to human dignity. We fight against poverty because faith requires it and conscience demands it. We fight against poverty with a growing conviction that major progress is within our grasp." He understood that "persistent poverty and oppression can lead to hopelessness and despair. And when governments fail to meet the most basic needs of their people, these failed states can become havens for terror."

His administration, he announced, would increase its core development assistance by 50 percent over the next three years, meaning an annual increase of about $5 billion. The money would be invested in a new Millennium Challenge Account that would be allocated to nations "that govern justly, invest in their own people, and encourage economic freedom." The president said his administration would reward nations that open their markets, fight corruption, and curtail bureaucratic impediments to investment and trade. His aim was to double the size of the world's poorest economies within a decade. "We cannot leave behind half of humanity as we seek a better future for ourselves. We cannot accept permanent poverty in a world of progress. There are no second-class citizens in the human race. I carry this commitment in my soul. . . . As the civilized world mobilizes against the forces of terror, we must also embrace the forces of good."[61]

Saddam Hussein now loomed as the exemplar of the forces of evil in the world and enabler of the forces of terror. During these critical months after the downfall of the Taliban government when the Bush administration was reconfiguring its war on terror, Hussein did little to allay US fears and assuage Bush's sensibilities. He glorified Palestinian suicide bombers and reveled in his financial support to Palestinian terrorists—actions that revolted Bush.[62] The Iraqi dictator recognized the sovereignty of Kuwait and opened discussions with UN officials, but refused to allow inspectors to return. His truculence and intransigence even exasperated his Russian supporters.[63] At the same time, he continued to use his permissible oil exports to leverage support at the United Nations to end the sanctions regime. He allocated illicit revenues from the Oil-for-Food Program to augment funding for many proscribed activities, including support of the Iraq Atomic Energy Commission.[64] Defying another set of prohibitions, he authorized the production of short-range ballistic missiles.[65] Although reports of his past links to al Qaeda remained contentious and inconclusive, ominous evidence filtered into Washington in April. Al Qaeda operatives were leaving Iran and entering northeastern Iraq, and some were even showing up in Baghdad.[66] Meanwhile, Hussein did nothing to ameliorate his image as one of the world's worst abusers of human rights. The UN Human Rights Commission denounced his regime and condemned it anew for its "all-pervasive repression and oppression sustained by broad-based discrimination and widespread terror."[67]

President Bush posed his resolve against Hussein's defiance. Coercive diplomacy was his antidote to Hussein's intransigence, duplicity, and belligerence. The president, however, still struggled to clarify what coercive diplomacy could achieve and how it could be implemented. He wanted to be rid of Saddam Hussein, but he was not sure what he would do if the dictator relented, invited back inspectors, and made an honest effort to confirm what Iraqi diplomats proclaimed—that the regime had no weapons of mass destruction. Might the president then be satisfied with less than regime change? Probably, he did not know; his own advisers remained uncertain about their boss's intentions.[68] But

Bush was certain of one thing: his adversary would not be dissuaded from his despicable and frightening behavior unless confronted with the threat of force.

His new friend, Tony Blair, felt the same way, and they were scheduled to meet at the end of the first week in April.

6

A Special Relationship

PRIME MINISTER TONY Blair wanted a special relationship with the president of the United States. He had nurtured one with Bill Clinton, but wondered whether the head of Britain's Labour Party could replicate the same rapport with the leader of America's more conservative, business-oriented Republican Party. Happily, in his first meetings with George W. Bush, he was pleasantly surprised to see how well they got along. Nonetheless, Blair knew that his country and his Cabinet were not eager to go to war to remove Saddam Hussein. Although Hussein was a despicable dictator, that fact alone did not make it legal, ethical, or wise to wage war to be rid of him. How to consummate that special relationship with the American president while furthering British interests and preserving the peace was a daunting challenge.[1]

British diplomats watched developments in Washington closely. "The administration appears to be gearing up for a decision on removing Saddam, but are not quite there yet," wrote the British ambassador, Christopher Meyer, on February 13, 2002. He thought the hawks in the Pentagon and the Office of the Vice President were eager to act, and much of the American media judged war to be inevitable. But the military planning remained rudimentary. What also remained unclear was "how the US will handle the UN track, above all the inspection regime." "Our objective," Meyer emphasized, "is to persuade the US" to show its desire to implement the UN resolutions in order to garner worldwide understanding of its actions should Saddam fail to comply.[2]

In London, British officials pondered how to handle Washington's desire for regime change. Labour Party officials agreed with their Republican counterparts in Washington on certain fundamentals. They believed that the Iraqi regime's "continued development of weapons of mass destruction" made it a "demonstrable threat" to the stability of the region. They concurred that Hussein had an "appalling human rights record" and that he engaged "in the widespread use of torture and mass execution of political detainees." They acknowledged that Iraq was violating UN resolutions that had been designed to modulate the regime's threatening behavior to neighboring countries and to constrain its weapons programs. Removing him, however, would not be easy. Nor would it be easy to replace him with a benign successor. One paper concluded: "A US attempt to create a more equitable long-term distribution of power in Iraq would require a massive and lengthy commitment. . . . Ten years seems a not unrealistic time span for such a project."[3]

So, what to do? The British Cabinet discussed policy toward Iraq at a meeting on March 7, 2002. Foreign Secretary Jack Straw explained that the sanctions regime was about to be modified, making it easier for Iraq to import food and medicines. These changes, he hoped, would undercut Hussein's heretofore successful efforts to win sympathy on the Arab "street." Nonetheless, he insisted that Iraq still had to comply with UN resolutions and must eliminate all its weapons of mass destruction [WMD] before relations could be normalized and sanctions terminated. "No decision," he emphasized, "had been made on launching further military action against the Iraqi regime but it was important to ensure that the British public and international opinion understood the true nature of the threat posed by the regime and the need to respond effectively."[4]

Some Cabinet officials emphasized that it was important to distinguish between the campaign to thwart international terrorism and the efforts to end Hussein's WMD programs. Others stressed that military action must not take place without a legal basis and without domestic support and international approval. Some insisted that the Iraqi dictator had to be convinced "that military action would ensue if he failed to comply with United Nations Security Council resolutions." But international approval, they agreed, especially among Arab nations, could not be obtained without serious parallel efforts to settle the Israel/Palestine problem.[5]

Blair deftly summed up the reservations he was hearing and the anxieties he was sensing. He said it was important that the United States not act unilaterally and that it was critical to reinvigorate the Middle East Peace Process (MEPP). Nonetheless, it was imprudent to ignore the threat posed by Saddam Hussein and his WMD programs. "The right strategy was to engage closely with the Government of the United States in order to be in a position to shape policy and its presentation. . . . No decision to launch military action had been taken and any action taken," Blair said, "would be in accordance with international law."[6]

Blair's advisers prepared an "Options Paper." Their current objectives were to preserve "peace and stability" in the Persian Gulf and ensure "energy security." They wanted to reintegrate "a law-abiding Iraq," which did not possess WMD and which did not threaten its neighbors, into the international community. Embracing "the least worst option, we have supported containment of Iraq, by constraining Saddam's ability to rearm or build up his WMD and threaten his neighbours." Containment had been partially successful, but it was now faltering. Although intelligence was poor, Iraq continued "to develop weapons of mass destruction" and to sustain its biological weapons (BW) and chemical weapons (CW) programs. If it had not already done so, it "could produce significant quantities of BW agents within days and CW agents within weeks of a decision to do so."

Consequently, there were now two broad options: toughen the existing containment policy, or "regime change by military means." Toughening containment required the reinsertion of UN inspectors. "Our aim should be to tell Saddam to admit inspectors or face the risk of military action." But this demand was not likely to produce satisfactory results. "Saddam is only likely to permit the return of inspectors if he believes the threat of large-scale military action is imminent and that such concessions would prevent the US from acting decisively. Playing for time, he would then embark on a renewed policy of non-cooperation." Meanwhile, even the renewed, more sophisticated regime of smart sanctions "would collapse in the long-term."

Regime change seemed like a more desirable goal. But effectuating regime change without full combat operations and a land war was unlikely. The groups in exile were divided and weak; internal foes were impotent. Neither covert operations nor a limited air campaign to support the Kurds in the north or the Shi'a in the south was likely to be effective. Nor would a Sunni "autocrat" successor be much better. "Even a representative government could seek to acquire WMD and build up its conventional forces, so long as Iran and Israel retain their WMD and conventional armouries." Nonetheless, if regime change was the chosen strategy, the best tactic for overthrowing Hussein was a land campaign, but that, too, was fraught with danger, logistical impediments, and worrisome unintended consequences. Moreover, the memorandum pointed out, "regime change has no basis in international law." At this stage, the options memorandum concluded, "we need to wait to see which option or combination of options may be favoured by the US government."[7]

Blair sent his national security adviser, David Manning, to Washington in early March to ascertain what the Americans were thinking. Manning met with members of Condoleezza Rice's national security team and also dined with her in the evening. The talks went well; they were frank and cordial, especially when he was alone with Rice. Her "enthusiasm for regime change," he wrote Blair, "is undimmed." Yet she recognized that the administration did not have answers to the big issues: how to garner international support; how to assess the value of the various exile groups seeking to overthrow Hussein; how to link up with the Iraqi dictator's internal foes; and how to conceptualize an effective postwar program.[8] A record of their conversation does not seem to exist, but Manning subsequently explained that at the time he did not believe the key goal should be regime change. He did not think Hussein could be overthrown by an internal coup, and he deemed war illegal, unpopular, and ill-advised. Manning's aim was to avoid a land war; the means of doing so was to get inspectors back into Iraq. If they could make the UN process work and persuade Hussein to accept inspections, the Americans and the British could gain confidence that Iraq had been disarmed, and they could claim that the regime had changed.[9]

Manning informed Blair that Rice and the president were earnestly interested in British views. They had not yet resolved what they would do. They nonetheless grasped that if the Iraqi dictator were offered new proposals for inspection and if he rejected them, that refusal would constitute a powerful argument justifying military action.[10]

Blair did not have a "game plan" of his own. He favored regime change, but knew it was unpopular. "Public opinion is fragile," he wrote. "International opinion is pretty skeptical." These attitudes among his fellow Labourites baffled him. "From a centre-left perspective," he wrote, "the case should be obvious. Saddam's regime is a brutal, oppressive military dictatorship. He kills his opponents, has wrecked his country's economy and is a source of instability and danger in the region." Blair could grasp how Tories hostile to nation-building and conscious mostly of "national interest" might oppose regime change, but kindred spirits on the Left "should be gung-ho on Saddam." His friends opposed, he thought, because they believed he was simply toadying up to Washington, and they assumed the Americans were mostly intent on settling "old scores." Moreover, they didn't think the WMD problem was worse than it had been. Blair thought they could make the case for regime change most persuasively by focusing on the evil nature of the regime itself and by convincing friends that they were pursuing British, not American, interests.[11]

Figuring out British interests was a daunting challenge; deciding on a game plan even more difficult. Blair's senior advisers offered ideas before their prime minister traveled to Crawford to meet President Bush. "The key strategic problem," wrote Gordon Hoon, the minister of defense, "is the spread of WMD—of which Saddam is only one unpleasant dimension." Hoon stressed that it was a serious problem, yet Iran might be even more culpable than Iraq, and any Iraqi leader, Hoon pointed out, might "seek to achieve a balance of forces with Iran." "Before any decision to commit British forces, we ought to know that the US has a militarily plausible plan with a reasonable prospect of success compared to the risks and within the framework of international law." Hoon did not offer anything more precise, but hoped Blair would persuade Bush to allow the British to participate in the military planning.[12]

Foreign Secretary Jack Straw was more worried. "The rewards from your trip to Crawford will be few," he wrote Blair. "The risks are high, both for you and the Government. I judge that there is at present no majority inside the PLP [Parliamentary Labour Party] for any military action against Iraq. . . . Colleagues know that Saddam and the Iraqi regime are bad. Making that case is easy." Considerably more difficult was persuading them that the threat from Iraq had grown, that it was qualitatively different from the Iranian or North Korean threat, that military action was legal, and that the results "would be a compliant law-abiding replacement government." Although he believed that Iraq had absolutely nothing to do with 9/11, Straw knew that Iraq was different than other rogue states: Iraq had invaded its neighbors, used WMD, and breached UN resolutions. Eliminating Iraqi weapons of mass destruction, therefore, was a desirable goal. But "regime change per se is no justification for military action," he emphasized. Iraq was a looming danger, not an imminent threat. Since the new sanctions were not likely to be effective, regime change might be desirable as part of an overall strategy to eliminate Iraq's WMD capacity, but not as a goal itself. Straw urged Blair to seek "the unfettered readmission of weapons inspectors." To achieve this goal, military pressure might be necessary, but he remained wary of military action. He reminded the prime minister that it was the perception of threat that had changed, not the threat itself. There was no guarantee that a replacement regime would be any better than Hussein's. "Iraq has no history of democracy," he concluded.[13]

Blair listened. He was most concerned with Iraq's WMD programs.[14] He did not think that Hussein had had anything to do with 9/11. But he thought that Hussein was a "profoundly wicked" and "psychopathic man"; his sons were even worse. Regime-type mattered to him. The Iraqi dictator had killed thousands with chemical weapons. Without inspections and with sanctions eroding, he would become more menacing as he developed more such capabilities. Blair worried that the "porous" nature of the regime might allow biological or chemical agents to get into the hands of terrorists. The Iraqi dictator was a looming threat and must be dealt with now. 9/11 was an attack "on us," Blair believed, and he wanted "to stand shoulder to shoulder" with the Americans.[15]

At Crawford, during the first weekend in April, he said this directly to President Bush. If there was no other way to deal with Hussein except through military action, Britain would stand side by side with America. If there was no other way of dealing with the threat, "we were going to remove him." But Blair used the meeting at Crawford to discuss the larger dimensions of the problem. He believed they were confronting "a new threat that was based, not on political ideology, but on religious fanaticism. It was a complete perversion of the proper faith of Islam, but it was real and active." To thwart the appeal of Islamic fundamentalist terrorists, who wanted "to kill very large numbers of us," the American and British governments needed to tackle the underlying problems; they had to focus on the Palestinian struggle with Israel—that was "absolutely fundamental." According to Manning, who was with Blair in Crawford, the two leaders spent more time talking broadly about the Middle East than about Iraq.[16]

Blair did not regard Iraq as the overriding issue, but he grasped Bush's preoccupation with the Iraqi dictator and wanted to shape the direction of the American president's policy. He pressed the case for inspections through a UN process. Bush pushed back. He told the prime minister "that the policy of my Government is the removal of Saddam and that all options are on the table." Yet he appreciated Blair's sensibilities. Afterward, Bush told the press "that he really liked" Blair; that it was "refreshing" to work with a leader who possessed moral clarity, who recognized Saddam for the brutal, evil man he was.[17] Yet Blair explained to Bush that the key objective was to get inspectors back into the country. If Saddam refused, Blair said he was ready to collaborate with Bush to remove him. But if Saddam agreed to inspections, "we are going to have to take yes for an answer." Bush was dubious of the UN route because he didn't "believe that Saddam would ever, in good faith, give up his WMD ambitions or programmes." Nonetheless, he agreed that the United States must build a coalition for dealing with Iraq "whatever 'Right wing kooks' might be saying." The American president also conceded to Blair that "America would have to adjust policy if Saddam let the inspectors back in and the inspectors were able to function properly." President Bush, Blair subsequently recounted, "made it clear to me that, if the UN route worked, then it worked. We would have to take yes for an answer."[18]

The British left Texas "reassured that it was quite possible to persuade Bush to use the international system," rather than to bypass it. At Crawford, Jonathan Powell, Blair's political adviser, noted: We were trying to say to the Americans: Don't rush! Build a coalition. Take the UN route. Avoid unilateral action. Bush listened. A British diplomatic telegram summed up the meeting:

> The Prime Minister came away convinced that President Bush would act in a calm, measured and sensible but firm way. There was no question of precipitate action. But they agreed that Iraq's WMD programmes were a major threat to the international community, particularly when coupled with Saddam's proven track record on using these weapons. Letting the programme continue was not an option. The President and the Prime Minister agreed that action in the UN was the priority. It was essential to get the weapons inspectors deployed to begin to assess the extent of Iraqi WMD programmes. The Prime Minister had been tough in his demands that Saddam must let the inspectors back in "any one, any time, any place that the international community demands."[19]

In the weeks after Crawford, Bush's attention gravitated to the Palestinian/Israeli fratricide in the West Bank of the Jordan River. He sent Secretary of State Powell back to the Middle East. Powell's job was to persuade the Israelis to end their military offensive, get Arafat to stop the suicide terrorist attacks, and orchestrate the basis for a more enduring settlement. In Washington, Cheney insisted that the time was not ripe for a peace conference. He did not think Arafat could be trusted. Bush was caught in a crossfire between his vice president and his secretary of state. The president despised Arafat and did not want to deal with him, yet believed that Palestinians deserved a state of their own. Bush also sympathized with the Israelis' preoccupation with their security, their vulnerability to suicide attacks, and their right to defend themselves. He infuriated Palestinians by calling Israeli prime minister Ariel Sharon a "man of peace," and he incensed Powell when he instructed the secretary of state to withhold any statement referencing a peace conference. "I had rarely seen Powell so angry," wrote Assistant Secretary of State Bill Burns, who was traveling with him at the time.

"He slammed the phone down, his jaw clenched and eyes flashing, and said 'Goddamn it. They never stop undercutting me.' "[20]

Bush was not seeking to undermine his secretary of state. He was listening to conflicting advice and forming his own views, somewhere between Powell, who wished to talk to all sides and reignite a comprehensive peace process, and Cheney, who preferred to shun Arafat and postpone any action altogether.[21] But the acrimony over the Palestinian/Israeli conflict spilled over to other issues and worsened relations among the NSC principals and their deputies when they discussed next steps regarding Iraq. Secretary of Defense Donald Rumsfeld, Deputy Secretary Paul Wolfowitz, and Under Secretary Douglas Feith were eager to use the 1998 Iraq Liberation Act as a means to fund and train Iraqi exiles to help liberate Iraq and shape its postwar governance. State Department officials like Bill Burns had profound misgivings about the legitimacy and credibility of these exile groups inside Iraq, especially Ahmed Chalabi's organization, the Iraqi National Congress (INC). Although resolving this issue would be critical if military action were undertaken and Hussein overthrown, the principals kept deferring action on this matter. The president did nothing to hasten a decision.[22]

The procrastination reflected the tortuous path of the military planning. It proceeded slowly, becoming more and more contentious as civilian officials in OSD relentlessly pressed the military planners at CENTCOM for smaller forces and swifter action.[23] When a leading UK defense official visited the Pentagon in May and spoke to Feith and Peter Rodman, the assistant secretary of defense for international security affairs, he reported to his colleague at the foreign ministry that "there was a distinct feel that momentum had flagged."[24] The French, too, thought the Americans had been chastened since Cheney's visit to the region. They were hoping that American pressure might eventually induce Iraqi acceptance of UN inspections—the indispensable precondition for avoiding military action. "[I]f the fear of US intervention receded," the French believed, "there would be no co-operation at all from the Iraqis."[25] Threatening military action to secure Iraqi compliance, however, meant preparing war plans, configuring forces, and deploying troops—matters of great complexity and even greater consequence, if Hussein remained recalcitrant and war came.

These complexities were glaringly apparent at meetings at the White House during the second week of May. On May 11, General Franks presented an update of his war plans to the president and his principal advisers. He dwelled on a new alternative to the former plan, "Generated Start," that previously had been discussed. The new plan, "Running Start," strongly desired by Rumsfeld and his civilian officials in OSD, called for a much smaller coalition force and much more rapid execution of the air and land offensive, leading to the swift capitulation of the Iraqi regime. These were still concepts, Franks emphasized, still theories; there were no concrete plans to execute, he said. Secretary of State Powell—a former chairman of the Joint Chiefs of Staff—listened respectfully and then pointed out various problems with Franks's new war concept, also stressing that it would be difficult to garner international support. Cheney, too, raised various issues, wondering how the United States would respond if the Iraqis employed weapons of mass destruction. Surprisingly, he gravitated into a discussion of inspection issues. Could they be made effective? Could US members serve on the UN teams?[26]

Even more surprising, at an NSC meeting three days later, Cheney was the first "to challenge the justification for military action." What was the case? he asked. Was it strong enough to justify the employment of military force? Was it strong enough to get allies to join us? According to his chief of staff, Scooter Libby, the vice president still wanted to think hard about alternatives to war. Cheney, of course, was not against going to war, but he was not yet resolved that it made the most sense. Acknowledging publicly that there was no evidence linking Hussein to 9/11, he still believed the Iraqi dictator remained a looming threat. Cheney worried that the sanctions regime would end, and Hussein would use his mounting oil revenues to advance his WMD programs. Worse yet, he might share those weapons with terrorists. "And there is no doubting," he added, that terrorists yearned to strike again with the deadliest of weapons.[27] Now was the time to deal with Hussein—to remove this threat. The question was how.

Reinstituting the inspection regime could be regarded as a means to remove the threat, if Hussein agreed, or as a step to war—a casus belli—if he did not comply. Deputy Secretary of State Richard Armitage wanted to restart inspections and bolster the authority of the UN monitoring organization (UNMOVIC). Feith was against this course of action. Bush decided in favor of the State Department position. He determined that the administration should "support initiation of UNMOVIC inspections."[28] Thereafter, Rumsfeld and Feith worked hard to emphasize that the goal of US policy was not inspections, but disarmament. They worried that, under the threat of military pressure, Hussein might agree to inspections, as he had in the past, and then impede the ability of the inspectors to do their job effectively. The United States and the rest of the world might then be faced with both an ineffectual inspection process and a failing sanctions regime, leaving Hussein free to resume his WMD programs and his bellicose behavior. He might then threaten his neighbors, like Kuwait, Saudi Arabia, and Israel, and seek to blackmail their protectors, adumbrating the failure of containment.[29]

Bush struggled to define his priorities—inspections, disarmament, containment, regime change. He often stated categorically that his goal was regime change.[30] He did not have much faith in the new sanctions regime and he saw few signs that Hussein was changing his behavior or re-evaluating his attitude toward inspections. In April, the National Command of the Iraqi Ba'th Party assailed the United States for protecting its Zionist protégé and called for strikes against US interests in the Arab homeland.[31] In early May, the talks between Iraqi diplomats and UN disarmament officials went nowhere. According to Hans Blix, the head of UNMOVIC, the Iraqis put unnecessary roadblocks in the negotiations by seeking to limit the scope of the inquiry and demanding assurances that there would be no military action.[32]

Given prevailing circumstances, Bush thought containment made little sense. "The word 'contain,'" he said, "doesn't work if someone's got the capacity to deliver a weapon of mass destruction." Ignoring much of the history of the Cold War and conflating state and nonstate actors, he wondered, "How can you contain somebody when they've got the ability to blackmail or launch a weapon?" Every day, he explained, he was informed of new plots to kill Americans or threaten allies. Every day he sorted through warnings of impending attacks. After 9/11, no one in his position—no one tasked with defending American lives and sovereignty—could be anything but alarmed. But he was not resolved to wage war to remove Saddam. What he wanted, he said, was for "the Iraq Government [to] allow full and open and unfettered inspections. . . . [T]he world ought to ask, why won't you allow for inspections?"[33]

The president did not hear news that eased his anxieties. In late May, intelligence analysts reported that al Qaeda operatives were moving into Baghdad. "We have noted an increased al-Qaida presence in Iraq in recent weeks. Most recently, senior operational planner Abu Mu'sab al Zarqawi arrived in Baghdad, ostensibly for medical treatment. Other individuals associated with al-Qaida are operating in Baghdad and are in contact with colleagues who, in turn, may be more directly involved in attack planning" (Figure 6.1).[34]

Since 9/11 there had been little al Qaeda activity in Iraq, and regional analysts and counterterrorism experts disagreed with one another about the nature of the relationship between the Iraqi dictator and Osama bin Laden. Bush and his principal advisers were aware of the

Figure 6.1 A Jordanian police photo of the jihadist Abu Mu'sab al-Zarqawi, whose plotting and actions in Kurdish Iraq inspired fear and worry in administration circles.
Getty Images, https://www.gettyimages.com/detail/news-photo/ahmed-fadheel-khalayleh-a-jordanian-fugitive-also-known-as-news-photo/1687949

dispute. Hardly anyone thought Iraq had anything to do with 9/11 and few claimed any active collaboration. Nonetheless, there were "a dozen or so reports of varying reliability mentioning the involvement of Iraq or Iraqi nationals in al Qaeda's efforts to obtain CBW training." The Intelligence Community (IC) summarized the relationship as "murky," but this new information about Zarqawi in Iraq sounded ominous. He was a terrorist, a Jordanian jihadist who had fought in Afghanistan, conspired against the monarchy in Jordan, plotted to blow up the Radisson hotel in Amman, met with bin Laden, and managed his own training camps in Herat. He was already celebrated for his toughness, radicalism, and barbarity. He lusted to wreak revenge on Americans.[35]

Reports of Zarqawi's whereabouts in Iraq arrived at about the same time that policymakers received secret information about an Iraqi procurement agent in Australia. Allegedly, he was seeking to buy GPS mapping software of American cities, fueling more anxiety among intelligence analysts in Washington. Might the Iraqi dictator be seeking to plot a mass casualty event inside the United States with his chemical or biological weapons? Might that explain his interest in developing unmanned aerial vehicles?[36]

Although such scenarios might seem like flights of fantasy, they were more than imaginaries for the policymakers who, on their watch, had seen nineteen men with boxcutters highjack jet planes, destroy the Twin Towers in New York, and hit the Pentagon right outside the nation's capital. If officials were being criticized for not imagining and preparing for an attack like the one on 9/11—as they were in a recent speech by Senator Hillary Clinton[37]—they now drove themselves to prepare for worst-case contingencies. Cheney and Libby, for example, traveled to Atlanta to the Centers for Disease Control to garner more information about the nation's readiness to deal with smallpox or anthrax attacks.[38] Leaked information about Iraqi acquisition of aluminum tubes and uranium yellowcake captivated public attention and triggered controversy about Iraq's nuclear capabilities, but US officials were far more worried about Iraq's biological and chemical weapons programs. In May, the US Intelligence Community assessed that Iraq's biological weapons program posed "a credible but elusive threat." Lacking "smoking gun evidence," the IC nonetheless judged that Baghdad probably had "reconstituted its offensive BW program to pre–Gulf War levels in well-concealed underground or mobile facilities." Iraq's chemical warfare programs were not nearly so advanced, but the regime, according to intelligence analysts, was "making intensive efforts to rebuild its chemical infrastructure." Regarding Hussein's nuclear programs, "all agencies agree that Iraq does not now possess a nuclear weapon, the means to produce weapons-grade fissile material, or a stockpile of such material. . . . [But] given the prolonged absence of UN inspectors—hitherto a vital deterrent—opportunities for nuclear reconstitution once again exist, and it has become difficult to prove Iraq has not restarted its program."[39]

Bush said again and again that his most compelling fear was the prospect of terrorists acquiring weapons of mass destruction from rogue regimes who were developing them and inclined to proliferate.[40] On June 1, he ratcheted up the pressure on such regimes with his graduation speech at West Point. He did not focus on Iraq. He spoke more generically, emphasizing that the country faced "a threat without precedent." The grave new danger to freedom "lies at the crossroads of radicalism and technology. When the spread of chemical and biological and nuclear weapons, along with ballistic missile technology—when that occurs, even weak states and small groups could attain a catastrophic power to strike great nations." America's enemies, Bush warned, wanted "the capability to blackmail us or to harm us or to harm our friends." He would not allow this to happen. New threats required new thinking. Because deterrence and containment might no longer apply, the United States needed to consider preemptive action "to defend our liberty and to defend our lives." He did not say that he was committed to such action. Outlining how difficult it was "to uncover terror cells in 60 or more countries," he stressed that his administration would use every tool at its disposal: diplomatic, financial, military. The purpose was clear: "we must oppose proliferation and confront regimes that sponsor terror." Facing evil, the United States had to maintain its moral clarity. "Moral truth is the same in every culture. . . . Targeting innocent civilians for murder is always and everywhere wrong. Brutality against women is always and everywhere wrong." But he was not pessimistic. Crises offered opportunities. "We have a great opportunity to extend a just peace by replacing poverty, repression and resentment around the world with hope of a better day." The twentieth century had ended "with a single surviving model of human progress" based on the rule of law, limits on the power of the state, respect for women, religious tolerance, free speech, equal justice, and "nonnegotiable demands of human dignity." Inspired by the need to fight terror, the United States could aspire to a more hopeful future based on those same values that Bush and his advisers felt had prevailed in the long twilight Cold War with Soviet communism.[41]

This was not mere rhetoric. At this very time, Bush launched a massive effort to fight HIV/AIDS. On June 19—the same day he heard another report from General Franks about his evolving war plans—he announced that his administration would allocate $500 million to prevent mother-to-child transmission of HIV/AIDS in twelve African and Caribbean nations where the disease was most prevalent. He regarded this initiative as an integral part of his global war on terror: the need to remove the despair and poverty on which he believed terrorism thrived. After the public press conference, Joshua Bolten, his deputy chief of staff, told a small group of leading scientists that this was just a beginning. "Think big," Bolten told Anthony Fauci, the director of the US National Institute of Allergy and Infectious Diseases.[42]

A few days later, Bush also gave a major speech on the Middle East. "I call on the Palestinian people," Bush declared, "to elect new leaders, not compromised by terror." Bush was appalled by the suicide attacks on June 18 and June 19, killing 26 Israelis and wounding 124. Rumsfeld and Cheney did not want him to give the speech. Powell wanted him to lay out the conditions for peace and talk more constructively about borders and the future of Jerusalem. Bush charted his own path, delivering a speech that reflected his own values and beliefs. To the Palestinians, he said: stop the terror, stop the corruption, build representative institutions and a democracy. To the Israelis, he implored: stop the settlements, end the occupation, support a Palestinian state. To Americans, he said the United States must stay engaged, provide aid and leadership, and offer a vision of a better world based on American values. He concluded his speech: "This moment is both an opportunity and a test. . . . The Bible says: 'I have set before you life and death; therefore, choose life.' The time has arrived for everyone in this conflict to choose, peace, and hope, and life."[43]

Bush envisioned the speech as an even-handed, earnest approach to break the deadlock and project a new path toward a better future. But his demand that the Palestinians get rid of Arafat and choose new leaders, while pleasing Israelis, shocked most leaders around the world. State Department officials immediately grasped the need to design a more "practical roadmap" and "to create a better balance of responsibilities." Too many tasks had been heaped on the Palestinians, Bill Burns wrote Secretary of State Powell, too few on the Israelis.[44] When Bush traveled to Canada for a G-8 meeting following the speech, he encountered much displeasure. Bush thought he was championing new initiatives aimed at fighting worldwide poverty, tackling disease and malnutrition, supporting economic growth and development, and paving the way for an Israeli-Palestinian rapprochement. Not many leaders saw things as he did.[45]

Instead of seeing developments as Bush hoped they would, the British were growing alarmed by US planning for war in Iraq. A British defense ministry team visited Washington in late June and Admiral Michael Boyce, the chief of British defense forces, met with General Myers, the chairman of the American Joint Chiefs of Staff, in Brussels. The British said they wanted to participate in US planning, although they made clear to their American interlocuters that their prime minister had made no political decision to join the United States in waging war. What they learned worried them. They voiced their concerns to the prime minister's national security adviser, and Manning, in turn, advised Blair that his key ministers must address developments. The Americans, Manning wrote, "were thinking big," and moving fast. They were envisioning a commitment of 250,000 troops, costing perhaps $70 billion. They could activate their plans in the fall after the congressional elections. Their thinking, however, was fraught with problems. They had not worked through their basing requirements or the logistical hurdles. They did not know where the Iraqis were hiding their weapons of mass destruction. They had not decided what assistance they wanted from London. Most of all, there was "a total policy void in which the military planning has taken place." Military planners in the Pentagon and at CENTCOM in Tampa were working in "splendid isolation—without an overarching campaign strategy for dealing with Iraq." Nothing had been resolved regarding a successor government to Hussein's. Not much thinking had yet been focused on how to garner international support or present a legal basis. Foreign Secretary Jack Straw urged Blair to get more involved. "The key point is how to get through to the Americans that the success of any military operation against Iraq—and protection of our fundamental interests in the region—depends on devising in advance a coherent strategy which assesses the political and economic as well as military implications."[46]

In the available British records, however, there is scant reference to the key Iraq issue consuming the attention of US officials from about mid-June to mid-August. Bush and his top advisers were now focused on whether or not to take military action against Zarqawi, the terrorist leader who had met with bin Laden in Afghanistan and had moved, first, to Iran, and then to Iraq. Zarqawi was now collaborating with Ansar al-Islam, the fundamentalist Islamic group in northeastern Iraq that was battling a mainline Kurdish Party for control of the region. The CIA, in fact, had infiltrated a small team into the region. In July, team leaders reported the existence of 200 al Qaeda terrorists and over 700 Ansar al-Islam fighters. The al Qaeda loyalists, seemingly under the leadership of Zarqawi, had located in the village of Sargat, not far from the town of Khurmal. There, Zarqawi took over a building and began experimenting with biological and chemical agents that terrorists could put in ventilating systems for mass casualties. According to one of the CIA agents, "they were full bore on biological and chemical warfare. . . . They were doing a lot of testing on donkeys, rabbits, mice, and other animals." The CIA agents had no doubts that they were al Qaeda fighters, trained in Afghanistan, but saw no evidence that they were linked to Hussein. Nor were there indications that the Iraqi dictator had hidden his own WMD in the region. But the American covert operators were confounded by the fact that every single person with whom they spoke believed Saddam had WMD: "nobody believed that Saddam had gotten rid of these weapons."[47]

In Washington, the Joint Chiefs of Staff favored action against Khurmal. So did Cheney, Rumsfeld, and Wolfowitz. These hawkish advisers could not believe that al Qaeda was in Iraq—even a part not controlled by Hussein—without the dictator's complicity. Their suspicions grew when information placed Zarqawi himself or other al Qaeda fighters in Baghdad. For Wolfowitz, it defied reality to think these developments could be occurring without Saddam's support or forbearance. The dots could be connected. Zarqawi was a barbarous terrorist; he was experimenting with biological weapons; he was in Baghdad; he yearned to conduct mass casualty events in Western Europe and the United States. He needed to be taken out, and his alleged protector, Hussein, needed to be removed. But immediate military action against Zarqawi in Khurmal might complicate efforts to orchestrate international support for removing Hussein and for deploying more substantial forces to the region to crush his armies.[48]

From mid-July to mid-August, the principal NSC advisers discussed these matters almost daily, often conflating the immediate concern with Zarqawi with the larger goals of toppling Hussein and gaining control over his presumed WMD. Cheney now became the leading proponent for war. Two high-ranking State Department officials, Bill Burns and Richard Haass, warned against the prospective repercussions of military action. Secretary of State Powell talked frequently with Jack Straw and shared the British foreign secretary's view that precipitous action was unnecessary and could prove countereffective. At meetings with the president's other top advisers, Powell insisted that regime change could not justify war. Like Straw, he emphasized that diplomacy might still work to muster international approval, or to intimidate Hussein to change his behavior, or to encourage his foes to topple him. Bush participated in some of these discussions, posed thoughtful questions, did not clarify his own position, and bided time. He resisted the advice of Cheney, Rumsfeld, and his military chiefs to take immediate military action. He told Franks that he was pleased that CENTCOM was quietly pre-positioning forces should he need to take precipitous action. Yet again he reminded his top general that these steps did not constitute "a commitment on my part to use military."[49]

While these deliberations were occurring among Bush's principal advisers, Richard Dearlove, the chief of the British Secret Intelligence Service (MI6), and Kevin Tebbit, the permanent under secretary in the ministry of defense, went back to Washington. American views were firming up, they reported. "The principal conclusion to be drawn," Tebbit wrote Manning, "is that the Administration as a whole is increasingly united in the view that military action will be taken against Iraq to bring about regime change and remove WMD risks." Tebbit was struck "with the air of unreality, given the enormity of what is envisaged and the absence of planning detail or policy framework to credibly make it happen." Dearlove met with Rice on July 19, and also gathered the impression that a decision had been made. Rice felt that evidence confirmed Hussein's possession of WMD and his "links to terrorists [in Iraq] stoking fears of a repeat 9/11 with WMD." That insertion "in Iraq" may well have been a veiled reference to the ongoing discussions regarding Zarqawi, but it is not clear. Manning brought Dearlove's assessment directly to Blair's attention and commented: "Not much doubt here that the Administration is bent on action soon. . . . Our views on links between Iraq, terrorism, and development of WMD are different from Condi's: not proven at best."[50]

As he prepared for a major Cabinet meeting to discuss policy toward Iraq, Blair knew that his ministers were profoundly worried about the drift of American policy and Blair's support of it. In the defense ministry, most officials acknowledged that Hussein had attacked his neighbors in the past and still was developing weapons of mass destruction. But they did not think he posed an imminent threat. He was not currently threatening anyone; his WMD programs were not as worrisome as Libya's and Iran's; and his links to al Qaeda were unproven. "Saddam is being contained. There is no objective justification for a preemptive attack on Iraq now or in the immediate future." Straw shared many of these views, worrying that military action in Iraq would hurt alliance relations, exacerbate relations with Arab nations, and lead to a prolonged occupation.[51]

At the Cabinet meeting on July 23, Blair listened to his ministers' reservations. They seemed sure that the United States was heading toward war. They worried that Bush and his advisers had "fixed" the intelligence to support military action and failed to make a legal case to justify such action. The Americans had not thought through their military plans, and, worst of all, had not assessed the prospective consequences. Blair took note of their concerns. He thought popular support could be mobilized. It would make "a big difference," he maintained, "if Saddam refused to allow in the UN inspectors. Regime change and WMD were linked in the sense that it was the regime that was producing the WMD. . . . If the political context were right, people would support regime change." John Scarlett, head of Britain's

Joint Intelligence Committee, noted that "Saddam would allow the inspectors back in only when he thought the threat of military action was real." Straw agreed with Scarlett's observation, but had his doubts about the prime minister's confidence that he could mobilize popular support by issuing an ultimatum calling for inspections. Perhaps, Straw suggested, the Americans should proceed on their own. Blair shot down that idea, saying it would be the "biggest shift in foreign policy for fifty years, and I'm not sure it's very wise." Harangued by reservations and skepticism, the prime minister interjected, "It's worse than you think. I actually believe in doing this."[52]

What Blair believed was what Bush believed: they were dealing with a profoundly evil man who possessed weapons of mass destruction, who could not be trusted, and who might deal with terrorists, even if heretofore he had little to do with al Qaeda. What Blair believed was what Bush believed: Hussein had to be confronted now. He had to be challenged to adhere to his promises and abide by UN resolutions. He needed to invite back the inspectors, and they had to confirm the absence of weapons of mass destruction and/or destroy those that existed. If the United States and the United Kingdom did not challenge Hussein now, when they had the opportunity and justification to do so, "we would have to deal with him eventually and in tougher circumstances." By then, Blair feared, "we would have lost our nerve."[53]

The Cabinet discussion ended with no firm conclusions, but with the "assumption" that for the time being the United Kingdom "would take part in any military action." Blair had not catalyzed a rebellion against his leadership, but he recognized the opposition he faced inside his own administration, his Labour Party, and his country. He needed a game plan of his own. He decided to write a personal note to President Bush, and to have David Manning deliver it to the White House. "I will be with you, whatever," the note began. "But this is the moment to assess bluntly the difficulties." The military part, he acknowledged, was "hazardous," but he would dwell on the political context. "Getting rid of Saddam is the right thing to do. He is a potential threat. He could be contained. But containment, as we found with al Qaeda, is always risky. His departure would free up the region. And his regime is probably, with the possible exception of North Korea, the most brutal and inhumane in the world."

Blair stressed the desirability of establishing a political coalition, if not a military one. To mobilize such a coalition, he wrote Bush, they needed UN authority. Public support in key nations, like France and Germany, could not be garnered if they did not act under the auspices of the United Nations. "My real point," Blair emphasized, "is that opinion in the US is quite simply on a different planet from opinion here, in Europe, or in the Arab world." People elsewhere simply didn't "have the same sense of urgency post 9/11 as people in the US; they suspect—and are told by populist politicians—that it's all to do with 43 settling the score with the enemy of 41." Bush and Blair, therefore, had to design a strategy to achieve a coalition. They needed to present Hussein with an ultimatum, as Bush had presented to the Taliban the previous September. We should state, said Blair, that Hussein "must let the inspectors back in unconditionally and do so now." There would be no negotiations, no new talks with UN Secretary-General Annan: "take it or leave it." In Blair's view, this procedure would "neutralize opposition around the UN issue." If Hussein did say yes, "we continue the build-up and we send teams over and the moment he obstructs, we say: he's back to his games. That's it." Blair thought Hussein would probably screw up or procrastinate, providing a casus belli for the United States and Britain to move ahead militarily.

But they also needed to make a public case, Blair explained. They had to expose the evidence demonstrating Hussein's possession of WMD and his links to terrorists. They must illuminate "the abhorrent nature of the regime." They also had to tackle the Middle East imbroglio between Israelis and Palestinians and launch new initiatives to make regime change in Afghanistan look like a success. They needed, moreover, to work toward some democratic endgame in Iraq, as hard as that would be. "Just swapping one dictator for another seems inconsistent with our values."[54]

Manning delivered this note to the White House on July 29. He met with Rice and explained to her that Blair could not go to war in behalf of regime change. Political realities, he said, made it imperative to garner UN approval. The overriding goal of the United Kingdom was disarmament. If inspectors returned and Hussein was disarmed, containment might work and the regime might be considered changed.

Blair wanted to get rid of the Iraqi tyrant, but it was imperative to plan strategy carefully and weigh the consequences of removing him.

Rice was so impressed with Manning's presentation that she arranged for him to see the president the next morning. Manning repeated what he had told Rice, and said that if the United States wanted Britain as an ally, it was imperative to take the issue back to the United Nations and secure a new resolution calling upon Iraq to comply with inspections and monitoring. If Hussein remained recalcitrant, then the international community could be relied upon to support military action to remove him and thereby gain control of his presumed weapons of mass destruction.[55]

Manning and Rice arranged for their bosses to have a secret phone conversation on July 31. Blair urged Bush to revive the issue of inspections, take the matter to the United Nations, and secure accord on an ultimatum to Hussein. Blair did not think the Iraqi dictator would comply and he was eager for regime change, but he told Bush "repeatedly" that if Hussein complied with UN resolutions, there would not be an invasion. As in April, Bush grudgingly agreed. Blair later recalled, "I knew at that moment that George had not decided. He had . . . a conceptual framework in which the pivotal concept was that Saddam had to come fully into compliance and disarm but he had taken no final decision."[56]

Neither Blair nor Bush was eager to go to war. They were wrestling with what they regarded as a profoundly difficult challenge. They were building a special relationship on their shared abhorrence of an "evil" leader who had used weapons of mass destruction in the past and who could not be trusted with their possession in the future. "The primary consideration for me," said Blair, "was to send an absolutely powerful, clear and unremitting message that, after September 11, if you were a regime engaged in WMD, you had to stop." This was not a matter of morality, insisted Blair, it was self-interest.[57] "After September 11," Blair explained in his memoir, "the thinking was this: if these terrorist groups could acquire WMD capability, would they use it? On the evidence of September 11, yes. So how do we shut the trade down? How do we send a sufficiently clear and vivid signal to nations that are developing, or might develop, such capability to desist? How do we make it indisputable that continued defiance of the will of the international community will no longer be tolerated?"[58]

Blair believed, correctly, that Bush would no longer tolerate the persistence of this looming threat. Blair knew, correctly, that Bush was heading to war if he could not gain assurance that Hussein was not developing and/or possessing WMD. The question was whether Bush would be satisfied with anything less than regime change. The answer seemed uncertain because Bush himself probably did not know. Inspections, Bush realized, could ease Blair's mission to stand shoulder to shoulder with him if Hussein persisted in his defiance and if Bush went to war.

But what would happen if the Iraqi dictator complied and cooperated with the UN inspectors? The answer seemed unclear, but almost all policymakers and intelligence analysts agreed on one critical factor: Hussein would not make any concessions, and would not open his country to inspectors, unless confronted with the threat of force.[59] If threatened, he might then still prevaricate, and war might ensue. But if he complied and acted in good faith, might that suffice to alter the trajectory to war? However unlikely, Blair hoped so. Hence he built his special relationship with the American president on the foundational issue of inspections. "Had Saddam welcomed inspectors and fully co-operated," Blair maintained, "action would have been avoided. I made this clear to President Bush and he agreed."[60] The "single" most important development in the whole decision-making process, Blair insisted, was the president's decision to demand another round of UN inspections. In the prime minister's view that represented a "huge compromise on his part and a huge opportunity for the international community to get its act together."[61]

Bush was not certain if demanding inspections would change the risk equation and alter his trajectory. But he appreciated Blair's support, respected his political courage, and felt a kindred spirit who grasped the nature of "evil." "America has got no better friend," he said (Figure 6.2).[62] Like Blair, his overriding fear was the prospect that weapons of mass destruction would make their way into the hands of terrorists. Like Blair, he knew that the Iraqi dictator had no nuclear weapons, and was not responsible for the 9/11 attack. But the president had every reason to believe, based on the intelligence he was receiving, that Hussein possessed biological weapons, could develop chemical weapons rapidly, and aspired to restart his nuclear programs. He had every reason to

Figure 6.2 Bush and British prime minister Tony Blair shared a view of the evil and danger of Saddam Hussein's tyrannical rule. As they developed mutual respect and a cordial relationship, Blair influenced Bush's pursuit of coercive diplomacy. Getty Images, https://www.gettyimages.com/detail/news-photo/president-george-w-bush-and-british-prime-minister-tony-news-photo/71532088

worry about Hussein's dealings with terrorists, regardless of whether or not the Iraqi dictator had a collaborative relationship with bin Laden. With Palestinian "martyrs" killing Israelis, with Pakistani terrorists targeting Indian legislators, with al Qaeda jihadists seeking the world's most destructive weapons, with Hussein supporting Palestinian suicide bombers, and with Zarqawi hiding in Iraq and showing up in Baghdad, Bush wanted to reduce risk. He had not paid enough attention before 9/11. He was not going to make that mistake again. Moreover, he knew he had the power to topple Hussein. Yet he also recognized the dangers that came with war. Might Hussein use weapons of mass destruction? Might the United States become ensnared in a nation-building quagmire? Might war precipitate tumult throughout the Arab world, acrimony among his closest allies, and disgrace for his newest friend, Tony Blair? Fear, power, and hubris led toward war. Prudence and uncertainty led toward inspections.

On July 31, Bush told Blair that he had not yet decided on war; that he might opt to give the Iraqi dictator one more chance to comply with his promises. Where this would lead was not certain because no one really knew how Hussein might react to an ultimatum backed by force. Bush's hawkish advisers would soon push back, but their influence, they knew, might not prevail. "Everyone else can debate and assume," Blair wrote, "only one person decides." Blair was confident that Bush had not yet decided.[63]

7

Deciding

NOT MANY OF President George W. Bush's top advisers, other than Condoleezza Rice, knew of his phone conversation with Tony Blair. They continued to focus intently on Abu Musah al-Zarqawi's ongoing actions in northeastern Iraq. At a meeting of the president's principal advisers on August 2 that included Secretary of State Colin Powell, Vice President Dick Cheney, Secretary of Defense Donald Rumsfeld, and National Security Adviser Rice, the CIA reported that it had identified a chemical factory in the town of Khurmal that was probably being used to make and test ricin and cyanide. The agency had no doubt that al Qaeda terrorists were located in and around the town. Saddam Hussein, it believed, had to know about these developments. According to Alberto Gonzales, the president's friend and White House counsel who attended the meeting, "this was the clearest evidence yet that al Qaeda was in Iraq, making poison and planning on killing people."[1]

The principals debated what to do. Meeting on almost a daily basis, they studied new intelligence that was both murky and ominous. Briefings suggested that Hussein was enhancing the infrastructure for WMD production and seeking to develop anthrax, aflatoxin, and ricin. Cheney, Rumsfeld, George Tenet, the CIA director, and General Richard Myers, the chairman of the Joint Chiefs of Staff, discussed various tactical options to knock out the chemical plant in Khurmal, including a B-2 airstrike, Tomahawk missiles, or a covert raid. They asked Gonzales for legal guidance on whether the information they possessed justified military action on the basis of humanitarian concerns or legitimate self-defense. Powell was concerned but cautious. He argued that military action would be regarded "as a unilateral start to the war in Iraq" and could complicate diplomatic efforts both to secure a UN resolution and to garner Turkey's cooperation in a future war effort. President Bush weighed the conflicting advice. Again, he deferred action. He was skeptical of the evidence and not eager to act militarily against the chemical facility near Khurmal, an area outside of Hussein's control, although Cheney and Rumsfeld urged him to do so.[2]

But he was not sanguine about the situation. Believing that "Iraq was a serious threat growing more dangerous by the day," he put his imprimatur on a new version of the war plan that General Tommy Franks brought to the White House on August 5. Franks explained that previous concepts had now been refined and integrated into a real plan— a "Hybrid" plan that incorporated elements from previous iterations, "Generated Start" and "Running Start." The time required to prepare for the attack, once the president so ordered, was narrowed to about two weeks, during which troops, aircraft, and war materiel would flow to the region. Then, a sixteen-day air campaign would begin. While key targets and infrastructure were devastated, about 20,000 to 30,000 Army and Marine troops would deploy to Kuwait. They would spearhead the ground campaign, taking place just a little over a month after the president made his initial decision. While land combat would begin with this small contingent of troops, reinforcements would pour into Iraq with the intention of completing the fighting in 125 days with no more than 200,000 soldiers. Phase IV operations would then begin aimed at stabilization and reconstruction. The quick start to the ground campaign, Franks hoped, might trigger a coup to topple Hussein, one of the overriding goals of the war itself.[3]

Bush approved this plan. But war planning did not mean war. Many key aspects still needed to be worked out. The president bluntly told Franks, "We're not going to war unless we have to."[4] He did not think the war plan was entirely satisfactory. He was not sure the United States should attack. His secretary of state—a former chairman of the Joint Chiefs of Staff—was warning him to think through the consequences of a military invasion. Hussein might employ his weapons of mass destruction, Powell told the president. Battlefield success might not mean victory. The United States could become ensnared in a messy, turbulent, postwar quagmire.[5]

This conversation took place on the very evening that Franks presented his Hybrid war plan, just before Bush's departure to Crawford, Texas, for a month's respite on his ranch. Powell had asked Rice to arrange the meeting, a long dinner, followed by more talk in the president's private living quarters. The secretary of state did not often seek such meetings and did not often converse with the president alone, or just with Rice. But he had been pondering the pros and cons of military intervention, especially as the news from Khurmal became increasingly worrisome. His conversation with the president was based on a memorandum that William Burns, his assistant secretary of state for Near Eastern Affairs, had prepared in his office. The memo, entitled "Iraq: The Perfect Storm," enumerated the many things that could go wrong: pre–regime change, during regime change, post–regime change. Each section contained a laundry list of possibilities, with no effort to assess the likelihood of any specific scenario.

Pre–regime change, the Iraqis might "play an inspection card at last minute," thereby shattering the unity of the permanent members of the UN Security Council, or the Iraqis might extend their terrorist actions beyond Israel and hit US targets, or the Jordanians might take their own preemptive action to restore Hashemite rule inside Iraq.

During the process of regime change, the Israelis might strike Iraq, or vice versa, or the Iranians and Syrians might maneuver to exploit the situation, or Hizballah might attack northern Israel, or the Turks might seize Mosul, or a Sunni general might topple Saddam and garner Saudi support.

Regarding the postwar situation, the prospective scenarios were far more complex depending on whether the United States would seek to install a new regime and withdraw quickly, or decide to stay and effectuate structural change and representative government. Each of these scenarios had its own pitfalls, "but the point is that immediately after liberation a powerful dynamic will begin mixing US military, media, new Iraqi authorities, paroxysm of revenge, recriminations and angling for power by key constituencies." Confronted with "inchoate and escalating disorder in the provinces," administration officials would face "an agonizing decision: step up more direct security role, or devolve power to local leaders." This meant that "we need to think now about a very big and expensive commitment. This is a five- or ten-year job, not a fast in and out."

But the memorandum did not make the case that ominous scenarios should deter action. It did not assess the pros and cons of going to war. In fact, it began with an acknowledgment that war and regime change—if done right—"could be a tremendous boon to the future of the region, and to US national security interests."[6] Nor did Powell—on that evening of August 5—try to persuade Bush that military action was unwarranted, or that he opposed it. Powell's aim was to outline the many uncertainties that inhered in military action. If the United States proceeded alone, he told the president, it would have to deal with the broken china, as in a Pottery Barn store. Sensing Powell's passion, more than he normally displayed at meetings of the National Security Council, the president listened attentively. Bush asked, what might he do to deal with the menace that Hussein represented. Like Prime Minister Tony Blair, Powell said the president should take the matter to the United Nations and seek to reinvigorate the inspection process. By so doing, the United States could recruit allies, internationalize the problem, and place the onus of responsibility for war on Hussein, should the latter continue his defiance. Powell hoped the United Nations would disarm the Iraqi dictator and avoid war. He did not think this would happen, but he explicitly told the president that the scenario he outlined might leave Hussein in power. If he unexpectedly complied, Powell stressed, the United States would have to live with him. According to Powell, Bush "squirmed," yet said he could tolerate such an outcome, although he would not be happy with it.[7]

"I listened carefully and shared Colin's concern," Bush later wrote in his memoir. "It was another reason I hoped diplomacy would work."[8] The president then went off to Crawford the next day, still not sure how the United Nations would fit into his plans, whether he would authorize military action, or which of his concerns—inspection, disarmament, containment, or regime change—were of utmost importance.

Rather than sort through these issues and discuss the pros and cons of going to war, or the advantages or liabilities of embracing a new UN process, his national security advisers locked themselves in debates over the "goals" of military action, should it occur, and the role of

Iraqi exiles in the liberation and future composition of an Iraqi provisional government. Rice presented a paper on "liberation strategy" to her colleagues on August 6. When the administration moved to bring about change in Iraq, she wrote, it wanted to "create a democratic, unified Iraq that can be a model of good governance for the region and a strategic partner of the United States. . . . We do not want the world to view US actions in Iraq as a new colonial occupation." According to Douglas Feith, the under secretary of defense, Rumsfeld "bristled" at the framing of the memorandum and its disregard of US interests. The aim of US policy, Rumsfeld exhorted, was not democracy promotion; it was safeguarding US interests: thwarting terrorism, eliminating weapons of mass destruction, discouraging Hussein's regional adventurism, and eradicating a tyrannical regime. "We should be clear," Feith argued, "we were not starting a war to spread democracy. . . . Would anybody be thinking about using military power in Iraq in order to do a political experiment in Iraq in the hope that it would have positive political spillover effects throughout the region? The answer is no."[9]

Subsequent papers moved in the direction preferred by OSD officials. Basically, Bush's top advisers were sorting through their own thinking and predilections and debating with one another without resolving concrete issues. This was most apparent in the ongoing arguments over the role Iraqi exile groups should play in the process of regime change. Rumsfeld and Cheney, along with Feith and Scooter Libby, were ardent champions of training, funding, and employing these groups in the "liberation" of Iraq and its postwar governance. On August 12, for example, Rumsfeld sent a memo to General Richard Myers, the JCS chairman, requesting "a plan to recruit, train, and equip armed opposition elements to enable them to be prepared to participate in operations aimed at replacing the Saddam Hussein regime."[10] State Department officials opposed the thrust of these ideas and did all they could to delay such actions. They thought the Iraqi exile groups lacked indigenous support and were hopelessly divided among themselves. They argued that US troops would need to remain and assume responsibility for the governance of Iraq during a transition phase of unknown duration. They informed Deputy Secretary Richard Armitage that it was imperative "to have a uniform/fully coordinated idea of what would constitute an acceptable outcome before taking action against Iraq."[11]

Rice and Hadley seemed unable or unwilling to overcome divergent views, and the president did not intercede and resolve the disputed issues.[12] He may not have been aware of the growing concerns that General Franks was not paying enough attention to what would happen after the fighting. In their meetings, Franks and Rumsfeld spent most of their time discussing combat operations. Rumsfeld kept probing Franks, asking hard questions, and pressing for more rapid action. Feith recognized that CENTCOM was not focused on Phase IV—the reconstruction and stabilization period—but his relations with Franks were so fraught that he could not make headway. Other military officers on the Joint Staff, like General George Casey, then the director of Strategic Plans and Policy, watched developments with growing alarm. The operational plans, he explained, were "so difficult and so complex, and the outcome . . . so uncertain" that the combat phase "became all-consuming and there was precious little intellectual and emotional energy left to say, 'okay, let's put the plan together for the postwar.'" Casey did assemble a small group of military officers on the Joint Staff to assist CENTCOM and to serve as liaison between the Pentagon, the State Department, and the NSC. But Franks, in the words of General Casey, "never embraced the postwar mission" and Rumsfeld never encouraged him to do so. "I don't think there was any doubt that Secretary Rumsfeld did not want to be involved in the postwar reconstruction of Iraq. He wanted to be out of there as fast as he could." Nonetheless, Casey, who had had extensive experience in the Balkans in the late 1990s, struggled to garner the attention of Hadley, Feith, and State Department officials like Marc Grossman and Ryan Crocker. If the administration was going to war—and Casey was not sure that was the case—postwar security and reconstruction merited far more attention than they were receiving in July and August 2002.[13]

Throughout the summer of 2002 public talk of impending war mounted. On August 15, 2002, in the midst of the national debate, General Brent Scowcroft published an article in the *Wall Street Journal* expressing his reservations about the march to war. Scowcroft had been national security adviser to Bush's father as well as to President Gerald Ford in the 1970s. He was much esteemed among national security professionals of both parties. He argued that Hussein had nothing to do with the attacks on 9/11, maintained meager relations with terrorists, and was not an immediate nuclear threat. Seeking to remove him from power forcefully, Scowcroft stressed, would inflame the entire Middle East region and alienate allies. Rather than attack Iraq, Scowcroft argued that the administration should press the UN Security Council "to insist on an effective no-notice inspection regime in Iraq."[14]

Scowcroft's article, appearing at the same time that other prominent Republicans, like Henry Kissinger, Dick Armey, and James Baker, were expressing reservations about the trajectory of Bush's Iraq policy, angered some of Bush's closest aides, including Rice. The president was irked that Scowcroft raised his concerns publicly rather than privately. Yet Bush did not dismiss Scowcroft's views. Not yet committed to going to war, and influenced by the advice of Blair and Powell, Bush discussed the UN route the very next day on a videoconference call with his national security advisers. They agreed with Powell's recommendation that they pursue a "new strategy" through the United Nations. Yet they clarified neither the substance of the new strategy nor the content of the president's prospective message to the UN General Assembly.[15]

The president did not explain whether the aim of his new strategy was regime change or effective inspections and Iraqi disarmament. In the State Department, many officials thought war was inevitable. Friction now was so intense between OSD and the State Department, and between Cheney and Powell, and between Libby and Armitage, that Marc Grossman, the number three ranking officer at Foggy Bottom, called his old colleague Eric Edelman, who now worked for Libby. They met discreetly at the Corcoran Gallery of Art. Grossman asked, had the president decided on war? Edelman said he did not think so. Nor did Cheney, Rumsfeld, or the top generals at the Pentagon.[16]

In fact, Bush's decisions to reject the recommendations of Cheney and Rumsfeld to bomb Khurmal and to embrace the advice of Blair and Powell to secure a new UN resolution ignited intense anxiety among hawkish advisers in the Pentagon and the vice president's office. Annoyed by Scowcroft's interference, Cheney decided to respond. On August 26, before the annual convention of the Veterans of Foreign Wars, he argued the case for preemptive action to remove Hussein. Making lots of assumptions about Iraq's tyrant and ignoring some of the lessons of the Cold War, he declared: "Containment is not possible when dictators obtain weapons of mass destruction, and are prepared to share them with terrorists who intend to inflict catastrophic casualties on the United States." Saddam Hussein, Cheney insisted, was "a sworn enemy." He had promised to end his nuclear weapons program and to destroy his chemical and biological weapons. But he had not done so. Instead, he lied, cheated, killed his foes at home, and threatened his neighbors abroad. Getting inspectors back into Iraq, Cheney stressed, was no solution. Hussein would evade their efforts and continue to pursue his nefarious ambitions. There was no doubt that he already had weapons of mass destruction and yearned to acquire and develop more of them. "Armed with an arsenal of these weapons, and seated atop ten percent of the world's oil reserves, Saddam Hussein would then be expected to seek domination of the entire Middle East, take control of a great portion of the world's energy supplies, directly threaten America's friends, and subject the United States or any other nation to nuclear blackmail."[17]

Cheney's speech reflected the anxieties among Bush's hawkish advisers that pursuing a new UN inspection regime might leave Hussein in power and the Iraqi threat intact. During the next few weeks they conducted a systematic campaign to highlight the links between al Qaeda and the Iraqi regime. They wanted Bush to act militarily and remove Hussein, not request a UN resolution for a reinvigorated inspection process. Zarqawi's operations inside Iraq, they thought, were proof of the regime's complicity. Wolfowitz and Feith, and Cheney and Libby studied the raw intelligence and increasingly challenged CIA and DIA estimates that there were few links between al Qaeda and Iraq. Even if al Qaeda terrorists were in a part of Iraq not controlled by Hussein, they asked, could not the Iraqi dictator put an end to their presence if he wanted to do so? Did not Zarqawi's presence in Baghdad signal that Saddam was complicit in Zarqawi's operations, or acquiescent? Would it not be irresponsible to permit the manufacture of chemical and biological agents in northeastern Iraq if they were intended to hit targets in Western Europe and perhaps the United States? Why should the administration trust the CIA's judgment that the secular and religious differences between Hussein and bin Laden would preclude their prospective collaboration against a common enemy—the United States? And why should US policymakers deem the relationship between Hussein and al Qaeda to be the most salient issue? Could not, might not, the Iraqi dictator collaborate with or transfer his biological and chemical weapons to other terrorist groups with whom he clearly was dealing? Or might Hussein's own intelligence service go after American targets? The intelligence was murky, and administration hawks thought they were using their imagination—exactly what they had been accused of not using prior to 9/11—to envision worst-case scenarios. "This isn't about revenge or retaliation," Feith argued, "but about self-defense." This wasn't about coordination or control; it was about the possibility that Hussein might provide a safe haven for, or training or financing of terrorist actions that would endanger the United States or its allies.[18]

For the most part, intelligence analysts were not bullied or intimidated by this offensive, as often has been argued.[19] Nor was the president persuaded of a connection between the Iraqi regime and the events of 9/11, or of Hussein's existing links to al Qaeda's operations in Khurmal, or elsewhere. After one unusual session in the Oval Office during which Libby made a powerful case for an ongoing relationship between the Iraqi regime and the al Qaeda terrorists, the president remained unconvinced and simply said: "Keep on digging."[20] And, of course, Libby and Feith did keep on digging, but intelligence analysts in the CIA and DIA were not cowed. Inside the defense establishment, the DIA again and again pointed out that the case for a collaborative relationship between Iraq and al Qaeda was thin. "Compelling evidence demonstrating direct cooperation between the government of Iraq and al-Qaida has not been established, despite a large body of anecdotal information."[21]

At the top of the intelligence establishment, George Tenet, the director of the CIA, John McLaughlin, the deputy director, and Michael Hayden, the head of the National Security Agency, were harried by these incessant queries and heated arguments between some of the president's most influential advisers and the analysts in their own agencies (who sometimes differed among themselves). They acknowledged that Cheney, Libby, and Feith studied the evidence carefully and asked salient questions. Their relentless probing impelled a reconsideration of previous estimates. As the CIA scrutinized its own data in August and September 2002, Tenet came to see that his analysts had underestimated the links between al Qaeda and Iraq, but they still did not amount to the conclusions that Feith and Libby wanted—that there was active coordination between Hussein and al Qaeda. "The general pattern that emerges," judged the CIA, "is of al-Qaeda's enduring interest in acquiring chemical, biological, radiological and nuclear (CBRN) expertise from Iraq."[22]

That mattered greatly because the president, as Rice explained, and Michael Morell, his CIA briefer, reaffirmed, was not focused on the connection between Hussein and September 11. What he cared about was "the potential link between Iraq's WMD and terrorism going forward."[23] And it was not just a matter of Hussein deciding to hand off his biological or chemical weapons to terrorists, a prospect the president did worry about. But he and his top advisers were equally concerned, perhaps more concerned, that Iraq's possession of these weapons would blunt the use of American power. They were not afraid that Hussein would use nuclear weapons "to hit the United States. A likelier problem," explained Feith, "was that they would affect our willingness to defend US interests." In other words, as Hussein amassed more biological and chemical weapons and pursued Iraq's nuclear ambitions, he would be emboldened while his adversaries might hesitate to deter and contain him. Our job, said Cheney, would become "infinitely more difficult in the face of a nuclear-armed Saddam Hussein."[24] For Cheney and Libby, for Wolfowitz and Feith, it made sense to act before the looming threat matured—to act while there was opportunity to safeguard Americans at home and US friends and interests abroad.

While Bush remained in Crawford, these hawkish advisers in the administration prepared the case for prospective action against Iraq, should the president so decide. In the office of the secretary of defense, Feith prepared a study justifying anticipatory self-defense. He and his colleagues also prepared classified and unclassified memoranda spelling out "The Case against Iraq."[25] The State Department labored on another document, "A Decade of Deception and Defiance," emphasizing the Iraqi dictator's long history of recalcitrance and prevarication.[26] Condi Rice and her team put the finishing touches on a new national strategy statement that, when published in September, attracted worldwide attention. The gist of all these documents was to highlight the new and unprecedented threat stemming from the nexus of weapons of mass destruction, terrorists, and rogue states with tyrannical and unpredictable rulers, like Iraq. In this new environment, traditional concepts of deterrence and containment might not suffice to protect the United States. Officials had to be prepared to take preemptive action against "emerging threats before they are fully formed."[27]

Bush said he would act with "deliberation," "using the best intelligence." The reality, however, was that the intelligence was murky, leading to contentious assessments, conflicting judgments, worrisome contingencies, and uncertain recommendations. There was little doubt that al Qaeda wanted weapons of mass destruction, but much doubt about whether the Iraqi regime would share its knowledge or its weapons. There was little doubt that Iraq either possessed biological and chemical weapons or could produce them quickly, but much doubt about their location, magnitude, and employability. There was little doubt that Hussein aspired to restart his nuclear programs, but much doubt about whether he had done anything concrete to realize that aspiration in recent years. There was little doubt that Hussein supported, even extolled, Palestinian suicide bombers and had many contacts with other terrorist groups, but much doubt about the nature of his ties with al Qaeda. There was also little doubt that Iraq was weaker than it had been a decade earlier, but considerable certainty that the regime was maneuvering successfully to evade sanctions and regain influence. There was little doubt that containment had worked in the past, but uncertainty about whether it could work in the future if sanctions eroded, inspectors did not return, and US-UK enforcement of the no-fly zones ended—all of which were possibilities. There was little doubt that other rogue regimes, like Iran, Libya, and North Korea, also yearned to possess weapons of mass destruction, but even less doubt that Iraq constituted a unique case because it had employed its chemical weapons, murdered thousands of Iranians and Kurds, and defiantly violated one UN resolution after another for more than a decade. Beyond doubt was Hussein's reputation for brutality and ruthlessness.

There were no easy solutions to the Iraq problem, and that contributed to the disarray within an administration that was now beset with intense bureaucratic and personal feuding. "Weigh the risks of doing something, and then think carefully of the risks of not doing anything," advised Rumsfeld.[28] Yet, ironically, that was exactly what he and his colleagues were not doing in any systematic fashion. Shortly, Rumsfeld himself would submit a "parade of horribles," another laundry list of things that could go awry.[29] Yet, akin to Bill Burns's "perfect storm" memorandum, Rice and Hadley did not use these warnings to frame papers or structure debates about the most fundamental questions of all: Did the advantages of military action outweigh the prospective liabilities of military action? Should the United States go to war to ensure effective inspections and Iraqi compliance with UN disarmament resolutions? Should the United States employ force to remove Hussein from power? Alternatively, should the United States sustain its policy of containment? Senior NSC staff members, like Steve Biegun, Franklin Miller, and Elliott Abrams, recognized that major issues were not being discussed, or when discussed, not resolved. They seemingly did little to redirect attention to fundamental issues.[30]

President Bush did not demand examination of these matters yet nonetheless resisted the pressure from the hawks. He decided to see if he could accomplish his key objectives—disarming Iraq and removing Saddam—without war. He disapproved of Cheney's speech to the Veterans of Foreign Wars. "Call Dick and tell him I haven't made a decision," he instructed Rice. Cheney's speech, according to Steve Biegun, the executive secretary of the NSC staff, was totally out of sync with the president's desires.[31] Although Cheney may have discussed the "tenor" of the speech with the president, it did not go through the normal vetting process.[32] Bush, in fact, called Blair while the British prime minister was vacationing in France. He said he was frustrated "that everyone assumed we had made up our mind and that the march to war was inexorable." After Blair returned to London, they talked again. Bush reminded Blair that they must not forget that the goal was disarmament, not simply inspections. If Hussein cooperated, his compliance would signal that the nature of the regime had changed, allowing him to stay in power while no longer constituting the specter he appeared to be. Neither Bush nor Blair expected compliance, but the choice would be Hussein's.[33]

Meanwhile, Powell and Straw were talking to one another frequently (as were Manning and Rice) and beginning to plan their strategy to achieve a UN resolution calling for inspections, monitoring, disarmament, and potential military action if Hussein breached his promises.

Straw visited Powell on August 22 while the American secretary of state was on vacation on Long Island. If Hussein accepted a "hard-edged ultimatum," Straw said, "the case for military action would be ended for the time being." A key question they had to face "was whether they could live with a Saddam Hussein who had fulfilled the UN mandate." Powell believed that "if WMD were dealt with," the president would not insist on regime change.[34] That Powell was correctly interpreting Bush's thinking was made clear a few days later when Rice told Manning that if Saddam accepted "wide-ranging disarmament measures," which she did not expect, this meant that "Saddam would be forced to run Iraq in a completely different way." In a note to Blair, Manning commented, "The fact that the Administration is conceptualizing this thought, rather than reiterating its commitment to regime change irrespective of Saddam's behavior, is significant."[35]

Bush returned to Washington in early September and began preparing for key meetings with his national security advisers and with Blair, who was scheduled to visit on September 7. Manning was now talking to Rice almost every day about a prospective UN resolution. Rice stated Bush's goal clearly: Saddam "must forswear WMD." If Saddam complied, "it would bring about a new openness, and a new domestic political situation."[36] At the NSC meeting on September 7, Bush deflected the arguments of Cheney and Rumsfeld, and resolved to take the issue to the United Nations. He would ask for a new resolution demanding inspections, disarmament, and enforcement. Everyone in the room, Rice subsequently wrote, "heard the President say, either he will come clean about his weapons, or there will be war."[37] But the president was not keen to take military action. "To me," wrote George Tenet, "the president still appeared less inclined to go to war than many of his senior aides."[38]

After the NSC meeting, Bush met with Blair and told him that he was seeking "to remove the threat in Iraq without war."[39] There was no doubt that Bush wanted to get rid of Hussein, but he was grudgingly ready to accept less. Manning later said, "Certainly Condi Rice is saying at this point privately to me she accepts that it would be a changed regime" if Saddam accepted the UN monitors and disarmed. It is not what the Americans most wanted, Manning added, but they grasped the logic of their decisions. If Hussein complied, the Americans knew they would have to live with him, said the British ambassador to Washington.[40] At a meeting of NSC principals following the president's meeting with Blair, Rice said emphatically, "The president is not anxious to go to war. War is the last resort." Rumsfeld understood. Frustrated, he penned a memorandum to Rice: "The President has not recommended invading Iraq. Therefore, I do not think I should go up [to the Hill and testify to congressional committees] and make the case for invading Iraq." Bush acknowledged publicly that there were many ways to effectuate regime change, a goal he was not abandoning, but which might be accomplished if Hussein lived up to his obligations and disarmed.[41] "If Saddam at this point had genuinely changed," Blair recalled, "had he welcomed inspectors and cooperated, action would have been avoided."[42]

Neither Blair nor Bush, neither Straw nor Powell, neither Manning nor Rice anticipated that Hussein would change unless threatened by military action. Indeed, almost every observer thought this was the case. When Powell and Straw met in New York on September 16, they agreed "that we will only get a peaceful solution if we prepare for war." "The paradox with respect to Iraq," said Straw, "was that diplomacy had a chance of success only if it was combined with the clearest possible prospect that force would be used if diplomacy failed."[43] The British minister of defense emphasized the same point: "The clearer we are that we would use force, the likelier it may be that we don't have to."[44] Hans Blix, the Swedish head of UNMOVIC, agreed. Hussein will "not move without forceful, sustained pressure," Blix said to Secretary of State Powell. He repeated this axiom to Blair, and Blair said much the same to French president Jacques Chirac and Russian president Vladimir Putin. They agreed.[45]

According to Rice, Bush was pursuing the policy of "coercive diplomacy." The president hoped Hussein would yield to "the united pressure of the international community, and the buildup of US forces would make that pressure credible." "Either Saddam would comply or Saddam would leave," explained Hadley.[46] But there remained ambiguity whether that pressure was designed primarily to make Hussein disarm, to make him depart, or to spark a coup to overthrow him. News of unrest inside the Iraqi military and rumors of another assassination attempt on Hussein's life sparked new hopes of a coup.[47]

Rice imagined that military pressure might trigger regime collapse. Rumsfeld wanted to ascertain if Arab leaders might arrange his exile. Powell and Haass, Edelman speculated, probably hoped that Hussein's regime would crack under pressure and "some Ba'thist general would put a bullet in Saddam's head."[48]

On September 12, Bush stood before the UN General Assembly and presented the US position. UN principles, he emphasized, were now challenged by "outlaw groups" and immoral governments with "violent ambitions." "In one place—in one regime—we find all these dangers in their most lethal and aggressive forms." The American president then catalogued Iraq's transgressions over the last decade, and declared that the United States could no longer tolerate Hussein's defiance. He called upon the United Nations to pass a new resolution that stipulated the conditions that Iraq must meet. But war could be avoided and peace preserved if the Iraqi regime "immediately and unconditionally" disclosed, removed, or destroyed all its weapons of mass destruction and long-range missiles; if it ended all support for terrorism; if it ceased persecuting its own people; if it stopped circumventing economic sanctions; and if it provided information about all Gulf War personnel whose fate was still unknown. Then, in words that resonated with his conversations with Blair, Bush declared that "if all these steps are taken, it will signal a new openness and accountability in Iraq." Tacitly—perhaps too tacitly—he was signaling that Hussein might remain in power. But if Iraq did not comply—if it continued its attempts to acquire and deploy "the most terrible weapons"—options would narrow. An "emboldened" regime might then supply these weapons to terrorist allies seeking to inflict even greater horror than that witnessed on September 11. "We cannot stand by and do nothing while danger gathers," Bush concluded.[49]

The speech was met with stony silence, but it catalyzed a round of intense diplomacy in the UN Security Council. During the six weeks that followed, Bush talked constantly with Blair, Powell with Straw, and Manning with Rice. The administration wanted a tough resolution that would require Hussein to clarify the present state of his armaments, resolve the ambiguities that remained about his chemical and biological weapons and his nuclear program, and open the country to comprehensive and rigorous inspection. Moreover, Bush wanted any defiance, any misstatements, any obstruction to justify the use of military force. If the Americans had their way, military action would ensue automatically from any transgressions without requiring additional UN resolutions. But French and Russian opposition, and British reservations about many details, impelled Bush and Powell to constantly modify the American position. Bush voiced his frustration repeatedly, yet grudgingly conceded.[50] After talking briefly with the president at the White House, Blix felt that Bush was trying to say that "at least for the time being," the United States was "sincerely trying to advance in step with the UN. It was an affirmation that, despite all the negative things that Mr. Cheney and others in the administration had said about the UN and about inspection, the US was with us for now."[51]

Bush's decision to support a UN resolution and his willingness to make concessions to garner approval inside the UN Security Council signified his desire to achieve his goals without war. "We were giving Saddam one final choice," explained the British prime minister. If Hussein welcomed the inspectors and complied, "action would have been avoided. I made this clear to President Bush and he agreed." The Americans knew perfectly well, Manning subsequently noted, that "we had given Saddam a get out of jail card if he chose to use it."[52] Bush sidelined the Pentagon and the Office of the Vice President and put Rice and Powell in control of the administration's management of coercive diplomacy. At the United Nations, US Ambassador John D. Negroponte and his aides negotiated the details under the watchful eyes of Rice and her staff.[53] The positive inducement that coercive diplomacy required seemed to be the president's willingness to allow Hussein to remain in power if he opened up Iraq, welcomed inspectors, and either relinquished his WMD or demonstrated he did not possess any.[54]

President Bush believed "his hand would be strengthened with the international community and with Saddam" if Congress approved the use of military force.[55] He worked hard to mobilize public support for possible preemptive action, should coercive diplomacy fail.[56] In September, he issued the administration's national security strategy statement. Although the document recapitulated many traditional features of US national security doctrine—support for military superiority, alliances, open trade, and poverty eradication, "a balance of power in favor of freedom"—it highlighted the new threats of the post-9/11 environment. The conjoining of radicalism, terrorism, and technology demanded new thinking. Deterrence and containment might no longer be suitable for the threats of a post–Cold War world, and preemptive action—anticipatory self-defense—might be necessary.[57]

The rhetorical onslaught was designed to get Congress to pass a resolution authorizing the president to use military force in Iraq if he deemed it necessary to protect US security interests. Bowing to legislators' requests for information justifying such a resolution, the administration assembled a National Intelligence Estimate (NIE) on Iraq's weapons of mass destruction and declassified most of it. The NIE judged "that Iraq has continued its weapons of mass destruction programs in defiance of UN resolutions. Baghdad has chemical and biological weapons as well as missiles with ranges in excess of UN restrictions; if left unchecked, it probably will have a nuclear weapon during this decade. . . . Since inspections ended in 1998, Iraq has maintained its chemical weapons effort, energized its missile program, and invested more heavily in biological weapons; in the view of most agencies, Baghdad is reconstituting its nuclear weapons program." The NIE went on to say that Iraq for the time being "appears to be drawing a line short of conducting terrorist attacks . . . against the United States." But Hussein might assist Islamic terrorists to launch such attacks with chemical or biological weapons if he felt "sufficiently desperate."[58]

The NIE judgments did not affect the perceptions or policy predilections of key officials. The conclusions represented the aggregation of much of the information policymakers had been seeing in daily and weekly intelligence assessments. Indeed, the daily intelligence that appeared in presidential briefs was probably more worrisome than that conveyed in the NIE.[59] The purpose of the NIE was to influence the public debate and congressional voting, not to inform the policy process. Requested by Democratic senators, it made it more difficult for them and for thoughtful skeptics of both parties to oppose the resolution. Although its judgments were terribly flawed and grossly exaggerated Baghdad's capabilities, they reflected what most analysts believed at the time. This thinking of course was skewed by inadequate collection, poor tradecraft, unreliable sources, and, most of all, inferences drawn from past experience and history.[60]

Analysts had doubts about many of their own claims, but they were doubts, not certainties. Carl Ford, the head of intelligence in the State Department, informed Powell at the end of August that many of the WMD reports he received were "based on speculation rather than hard evidence." For example, the aluminum tubes, cited by the CIA and DIA as indications of Hussein's intent to restart his nuclear programs, were acquired by Iraq for other purposes, according to Ford's own analysts and those of the Department of Energy. But Ford did not dispute the overall thrust of the NIE.[61] Neither his analysts nor those in other agencies were purposefully distorting evidence to build a case for war. They struggled—poorly and ineffectively—with difficult issues of collection and assessment. DIA analysts, for example, continued to highlight the gaps in their own information and acknowledged that they were not aware "of any current indications that Iraq is actively preparing transnational terrorist operations." Although there was little likelihood that Hussein would use foreign terrorist organizations to accomplish his aims and although the DIA thought most terrorist groups hosted in Iraq were "effectively defunct," the future was uncertain. "At first glance, al-Qaida and the Husayn regime appear to have diametrically opposed interests and ideological orientations, but the possibility exists of limited cooperation against a mutual enemy—the United States."[62]

Ambiguous conclusions, along with uncertain scenarios, did not unsettle Bush's senior advisers. Cheney, Rumsfeld, Libby, Wolfowitz, Feith, Powell, Armitage, and their subordinates were experienced officials, fully cognizant that the "intelligence" they received was always incomplete and imprecise.[63] Rumsfeld, in fact, asked his director of intelligence on the Joint Staff to assess the accuracy of what they knew about Iraq's weapons of mass destruction. "We've struggled to estimate the unknowns," wrote General Glen D. Shafer. "Our assessments rely heavily on analytic assumptions and judgment rather than hard evidence." Shafer's subordinates thought the Iraqis had a viable nuclear weapons design, but they did not know the status of Iraqi enrichment capabilities. Their knowledge of the Iraqi nuclear weapons program was "based largely—perhaps 90%—on analysis of imprecise intelligence." With regard to biological weapons, they knew Iraq had "the knowledge needed to build biological weapons without external expertise." They "knew" the Iraqis had produced anthrax, ricin toxin, botulinum toxin, and gas gangrene. Their knowledge of the biological weapons Iraq could produce was "nearly complete," but their "knowledge of how and where they are produced is probably up to 90% incomplete." With regard to chemical weapons, the status report continued, "We know Iraq has the knowledge needed to build chemical weapons without external expertise. . . . Our overall knowledge of the Iraqi CW program is primarily limited to infrastructure and doctrine. The specific agent and facility knowledge is 60–70 percent incomplete." Appealing to Rumsfeld's predilections and idiosyncrasies, the report concluded, "We don't know with any precision how much we don't know."[64]

"This is big," Rumsfeld wrote his chairman of the Joint Chiefs of Staff after he read the assessment.[65] But the secretary of defense did not forward this status report, as he sent many other "snowflakes," to Rice, Cheney, and Powell. Uncertain, incomplete, tentative "intelligence" did not shake Rumsfeld's conviction that Iraq had weapons of mass destruction. Nor did it shake anyone else's assumptions. If they had probed more deeply, if they could have stepped back and interrogated their assumptions, they might have been able to see the flaws, the gaps, the ambiguities, and the inconsistencies that subsequently became so obvious not only to their critics, but also to them.[66] At the time, however, the conclusions in the NIE did not catalyze any rethinking because they seemed so plausible; so consistent with Hussein's past conduct; so much more sensible than alternative explanations of Hussein's behavior, recalcitrance, and deceit.[67]

Nobody in the policymaking community, moreover, was arguing the opposite case; nobody was claiming that Hussein did not have weapons of mass destruction. "Not once in all my meetings in all my years in government," wrote Richard Haass, the director of the Policy Planning Staff in the State Department, "did an intelligence analyst or anyone else for that matter argue openly or take me aside and say privately that Iraq possessed nothing in the way of weapons of mass destruction. If the emperor had no clothes, no one thought so or was prepared to say so." Franklin Miller, who coordinated aspects of Iraqi military and political policy for Rice and who had been studying intelligence reports for more than a decade, said much the same thing. Bush had scant reason to think that Hussein had gotten rid of his WMD. "When we moved troops into Iraq in March of 2003," General Franks recounted in an interview, "there was not a doubt in my mind [that Iraq had weapons of mass destruction]. Because of my talking to Bush, I can guarantee you there was not a doubt in his mind." Middle East leaders repeatedly told Franks that the Iraqi dictator possessed such weapons and would use them if attacked. "General," Egyptian president Hosni Mubarak said to Franks, "I tell you the truth. Saddam, he has the WMD. He told me he will use it on you."[68]

During these critical months in the late summer and early fall of 2002, Hussein did little to nurture a more benign view of his intentions or his character. In his annual speech on August 8, commemorating his "great victory" in the Iran war, he warned that the new "forces of evil will carry their coffins on their backs." He was not averse, he said, to equitable dialogue with Americans or to international law, but he would not be intimidated. He did not believe that US or coalition forces would ever reach Baghdad. Tariq Aziz, his deputy prime minister, remonstrated against the return of weapons inspectors and Iraqi vice president Taha Yassin Ramadan called Hans Blix, the head of the UN inspection agency, a spy.[69] Nonetheless, sensing the tide of events after President Bush's speech to the United Nations on September 12, Hussein said Iraq would accept the return of inspectors unconditionally. But when Blix set forth the conditions for their return in a letter dated October 8, there was no response from the Iraqi government.[70] "Saddam determined to retain Iraq's WMD," concluded the British Joint Intelligence Committee in early October.[71] And meanwhile, Iraq intermittently fired anti-aircraft artillery and surface-to-air missiles at US and UK aircraft in the southern no-fly zone.[72] This action was particularly ill-suited to nurture goodwill because OSD officials already had delineated "behavior with respect to coalition aircraft" as one of the two most important "early tests" of the regime's "good faith."[73]

Nor did the overall environment abroad and at home inspire confidence that the American homeland was now secure from another attack. On September 18, a suicide bombing at a bus stop in Israel killed a policeman and wounded three people. The next day, a terrorist bombing in Tel Aviv killed six and wounded nineteen. On September 25, two terrorists belonging to the Jaish-e-Mohammed group raided the Akshardham temple complex in Ahmedabad, India, killing thirty people and injuring scores of other bystanders. On October 12, a bombing in Bali, Indonesia killed 202 people, mostly Western tourists. In Russia, on October 19, a car bomb outside a McDonald's restaurant in Moscow killed one person and wounded five. In the United States, in September, the FBI arrested six Yemeni terrorists trained by al Qaeda in Afghanistan. In early October, sniper attacks around the Washington beltway killed ten people. In late October, Laurence Foley, an American diplomat, was assassinated outside his home in Amman, Jordan. The Department of State reported that over 3,000 al Qaeda operatives or associates had been detained in over 100 countries. Al Qaeda "is still planning attacks," the State Department warned. Iraq, it judged, remained among the states providing "a safe haven, transit point, and operational base for terrorist organizations that included al Qaida." A new stream of very secret "intelligence," moreover, suggested that Hussein might be interested in attacking the United States. These reports turned out to be inaccurate but were very worrisome at the time, explained Michael Morell, Bush's former CIA daily briefer.[74]

Amid turmoil and uncertainty, with congressional elections looming, with Hussein procrastinating and still defiant, and with negotiators at the United Nations locked in a tedious debate over the wording of a new resolution, Bush continued to cultivate support for a resolution authorizing him to use force. In a major speech in Cincinnati on October 7, he again explained why he was so concerned with Iraq: "On any given day, Iraq could decide . . . to provide biological or chemical weapons to a terrorist group or individual terrorists." Quoting a former weapons inspector, Bush declared: "Saddam Hussein is a homicidal dictator who is addicted to weapons of mass destruction." He must be confronted. "Failure to act would embolden other tyrants, allow terrorists access to new weapons and new resources, and make blackmail a permanent feature of world events." He concluded, "We refuse to live in fear."[75]

The president, however, was not declaring war. He was summoning support for congressional action and for the UN resolution. According to his speechwriter, Michael Gerson, his press secretary, Ari Fleischer, and Rice, his national security adviser, the president was still practicing coercive diplomacy. He threatened war, yet emphasized that military action was not imminent or inevitable. Hussein, the president said, could choose to disarm or be disarmed. The UN resolution would require him to accept inspectors, allow them access to any site at any time, and permit them to interview Iraqi scientists abroad where they and their families would be safe from revenge or retaliation. The Iraqi dictator, Bush insisted, must dismantle or relinquish his WMD, cease his support for terrorism, and stop repressing his own people. Using language whose full significance was probably understood only by his closest advisers and their British counterparts, he said, "Taking these steps would also change the nature of the Iraqi regime, itself. America hopes the regime will make that choice." But it would only make that choice if Congress and the United Nations sent the right message, only if Saddam grasped that he faced the military power of the United States and the international community.[76]

Emphasizing the threat that Hussein represented and stressing disarmament—illuminating the tyrant that he was yet avoiding talk of regime change—the president wanted to secure support in Congress for the resolution authorizing him to use force. At the same time, he hoped to catalyze a consensus among the members of the UN Security Council to approve a tough resolution ensuring inspections, disarmament, and enforcement. He wanted to strengthen his diplomatic hand and buttress his coercive diplomacy. But he was also practicing smart politics. Most Americans—roughly 53 to 60 percent—favored the overthrow of Hussein, but public opinion polls indicated that many more people would accept military action in support of regime change if they witnessed the Iraqi dictator's continued defiance regarding inspections.[77] But that choice was Hussein's.

Tough talk to protect the nation's security was good politics as the congressional elections approached and the domestic economic situation still remained grim in the aftermath of the 9/11 attack. Some observers thought public opinion regarding military action to topple Hussein was softening and needed to be firmed up. But Republican leaders were not overly worried about their ability to garner support for a war to oust the Iraqi dictator. Most Democrats hesitated to speak out against the war because they grasped the popularity of Bush's position on this issue and because they wanted to concentrate on jobs and the economy.[78] What most worried Republicans was the prospect that Democrats would assail them for unpreparedness on 9/11. On September 19, for example, during a joint House and Senate Intelligence inquiry, administration officials faced such accusations and grasped the implications. "Are you saying," Congresswoman Nancy Pelosi asked Paul Wolfowitz, "that September 11th happened because it included neglect of responsibility?" Wolfowitz, of course, denied saying anything of the sort. But just a few minutes before Pelosi's insinuation, Deputy Secretary of State Armitage acknowledged to the committee that he and Wolfowitz had spent the previous evening pondering what kind of hearing they would be having "if a terrible event happened from Iraq," and "we hadn't done something."[79] Inside the White House, there was no such speculation. "The American people would never forgive us," mused Alberto Gonzales, if "we suspected Saddam might be dangerous but ignored the threat."[80]

Bush scorned such political talk, but he knew that his administration and his legacy depended on preventing another attack.[81] Although he had not resolved whether his priority was to disarm or dispel the Iraqi dictator, he labored successfully to mobilize public and congressional support behind his policies. During the second week of October, the House approved the resolution authorizing him to use military force by a vote of 296–133, and the Senate did the same, 77–23. The president's party then went on to achieve dramatic success in the 2002 elections. The Republicans picked up two seats in the Senate and gained control of the upper chamber while they added eight members in the House, increasing their majority, a very rare outcome for an incumbent administration.

The president did not gloat over his victory. In a press conference on November 7, he did not take personal credit for his party's success. Nor did he claim that it was a mandate to go to war or take preemptive action against Iraq. When reporters assailed him with questions about his future plans, he emphasized that the dictator must disarm. "I am insistent upon one thing about Iraq, and that is that Saddam Hussein disarm. . . . If he's not going to disarm, we'll disarm him." And although Bush was often justly criticized for hyping the nuclear threat, he was remarkably candid: "And by the way, we don't know how close he is to a nuclear weapon right now. We know he wants one. But we don't know. We know he was close to one at one point in time. We have no idea today. Imagine Saddam Hussein with a nuclear weapon. Imagine how the Israeli citizens would feel. Imagine how the citizens of Saudi Arabia would feel. Imagine how the world would change, how he could alter diplomacy by the very presence of a nuclear weapon."[82] The president was seeking to imagine things he had not imagined before 9/11.

Throughout these months Bush rarely engaged in idealistic talk about democracy-promotion. If he took military action to enforce Iraq's compliance with UN resolutions, he hoped that regime change would lift the shackles on the Iraqi people and nurture freedom throughout the region. But he was motivated by his perception of threat, not by dreams of a democratic Iraq. He worried that, in the long run, a defiant, repressive dictator with weapons of mass destruction could check the exercise of American power in a critical region of the world or, in the short term, collude with terrorists who hated the United States and its allies. He was concerned with America's vulnerability to another attack after 9/11, knowing there were groups who yearned to inflict more harm on the country. He was inspired by a sense that America's superior values—its freedoms—were being reviled, challenged, and endangered by ruthless, barbaric networks of terrorists whom Saddam Hussein tolerated or championed.

Sometimes the president overstated the evidence he had—Hussein's a threat, Bush said, "because he is dealing with al Qaeda." That was an exaggeration. But the president did know that Zarqawi was in Iraq and had been in Baghdad. He knew Zarqawi had links to al Qaeda and was experimenting with biological and chemical weapons. And he knew that the Iraqi dictator supported suicide bombings and celebrated the martyrs. When Bush said he could not tolerate al Qaeda–type networks who might be trained and armed by Hussein, he was addressing this ambient threat. "To ignore these threats," he warned, "is to encourage them, and when they have fully materialized, it may be too late to protect ourselves and our allies. By then, the Iraqi dictator will have had the means to terrorize and dominate the region, and each passing day could be the one on which the Iraqi regime gives anthrax or VX nerve gas or, someday, a nuclear weapon to a terrorist group."[83]

Employing such rhetoric the president and his advisers often exaggerated the "intelligence" they had about Iraqi nuclear programs and the regime's links to al Qaeda. They conflated their sincere convictions that Iraq constituted a looming threat, or a gathering threat, with apprehensions that Hussein was an imminent threat, justifying pre-emptive action. Bush was pitting his resolve against Hussein's defiance. Again and again, he declared that he was a patient, deliberate man, but he would not be toyed with. His credibility was on the line. America's credibility was on the line. "I think it is very important that when the United States speaks, we do what we say, for our credibility and for the sake of peace. I told the world loud and clear, if you harbor a terrorist, if you feed a terrorist, if you hide a terrorist, you're just as guilty as the killers who came to America."[84]

Bush's sense of victimhood and his unreflective hubris shone forth. He often repeated, "out of the evil done to America," good would emerge.[85] He wanted vindication for himself, his country, and the values he cherished. He talked passionately about the freedoms he loved and the goodness of the American people—all of which were endangered by terrorist actions, rogue dictators, and weapons of mass destruction. In the midst of waging his global war against Islamic jihadists, Bush took time to honor Muslim Americans. They share our grief and our values, he said. "Bigotry is not part of our soul. It's not going to be part of our future." To fight evil, he declared, you need to love your neighbor.[86]

Bush decided that he must confront Hussein—meaning the Iraqi dictator must disarm, or face removal. On November 18, the UN Security Council finally passed Resolution 1441. It was not as tough and stringent as Bush had hoped it would be. To secure unanimity, he allowed it to be watered down. It did not guarantee military action should Hussein continue to lie and defy. But it did lay down a set of expectations, a demand for information, an inspection process, a rigorous timetable, and a reminder that the regime already was in material breach of past resolutions, thereby providing justification for the United States to take unilateral action if it chose to do so.[87]

What was uncertain was whether Hussein would comply. The intent, Rumsfeld reminded Bush, was "to confront Saddam with a clear choice: either he decides to continue to defy the United Nations and to maintain its WMD programs, or he cooperates fully with a disarmament regime as the only way to stay in power."[88] Nobody thought he would do the latter, if not threatened. To threaten—to support diplomacy and to prepare for action should diplomacy fail—Bush authorized General Franks to start implementing his military plan. In October, key components of the command moved to Camp Doha, Kuwait. Franks reshuffled his commanding officers, placing David McKiernan in charge.[89] A looming threat, Bush decided, would be matched by a looming invasion. Hussein would need to choose.

But Bush did not assess whether the costs of the looming invasion, should it occur, were commensurate with the threat that existed. He met with Franks many times to examine the military campaign. They discussed what it would take to defeat Iraq's armies, gain control of its weapons of mass destruction (although their location was unknown), and remove its dictator. The president told his commanding general that he worried about a bloodbath in Baghdad and the prospective use of WMD. Rice expressed her concerns about the plan's unfulfilled base requirements. Secretary of State Powell questioned whether Franks was underestimating the requisite troop numbers.[90] Focused mostly on tactical matters regarding the combat phase of the operation, the president and his principal advisers did not spend much time examining the overall risks of their policies. Bush had decided to practice coercive diplomacy—to deploy his troops and intimidate his adversary—hoping to achieve his goals (the disarmament of Iraq and the removal of its dictator, or both) without using force. If his foe proved recalcitrant, however, the president's credibility, America's credibility, would be at risk. Coercive diplomacy would end with a military intervention, yet the prospective costs of that intervention had not been calculated.

This mattered because President Bush did want a free, democratic Iraq to emerge if he resorted to military action. But so far he had spent little time discussing the institutions, policies, and expenditures that would be required to translate the liberation of Iraq into a better life for its citizens. In his meeting with Franks on September 6, he asked his commanding general, "Can we win"? "Yes sir," said Franks. "Can we get rid of Saddam?" the president asked again. "Yes, sir," said his general.[91]

The president did not ask, "What then?"

8

Resolve

IN HIS BRIEF radio address to the nation on Saturday morning, November 9, 2002, President George W. Bush praised the UN Security Council for the passage of Resolution 1441. It meant, Bush declared, that "the Iraqi regime had to declare and destroy all weapons of mass destruction or face the consequences." The resolution, he explained, "presents the Iraqi regime with a test, a final test. Iraq must now, without delay or negotiations, give up its weapons of mass destruction, welcome full inspections, and fundamentally change the approach it has taken for more than a decade. The regime must allow immediate and unrestricted access to every site, every document, and every person identified by inspectors." The old game of "cheat-and-retreat" was over. The president would no longer tolerate acts of defiance. "If Iraq fails to fully comply with the UN resolution, the United States, in coalition with other nations, will disarm Saddam Hussein."[1]

The Iraqi regime remained opaque and conflicted. In a speech sent to the Iraqi National Assembly, Saddam Hussein's powerful son, Uday, denounced UN Security Council Resolution 1441. On November 12, the members of the National Assembly voted unanimously to reject it and sent their recommendation to the governing Revolutionary Command Council over which his father presided. Sadoun Sammadi, the speaker for the National Assembly, said the resolution was simply a pretext for US aggression. Foreign Minister Naji Sabri called on the Arab League to help his country thwart colonial aggression. But on November 13, in a letter to UN Secretary-General Kofi Annan, Sabri reversed himself.

Iraq would welcome the inspectors and cooperate with them. Once they affirmed that no weapons of mass destruction existed, the Iraqi regime assumed sanctions would be lifted. The lies and manipulations of the British and American governments—their history of "injustice and destruction"—would be exposed to all humanity.[2]

The Iraqi dictator himself was cagey, secretive, opportunistic, and manipulative. He thought he could outsmart and defy the Americans. He did not think the Bush administration would use force to remove his regime. Believing that Washington had no good reason to invade Iraq—the United States, in his view, already had a position of preponderance in the region and he was sure they knew he had no weapons of mass destruction—he calculated that the Americans were playing a game of bluff with him. They wanted to intimidate and force him to flee, but he was confident they would not invade and risk casualties. Americans were cowardly, he believed; they did not have the stomach for bloody battles, mutilated warriors, and body bags. Hussein ruminated with his lieutenants about how the United States had pulled out of Somalia after only a few soldiers had been killed and how they waged war in the Balkans with air power. In 1991, they did not march to Baghdad because they were afraid he would use chemical weapons, and in 1993, even after he tried to assassinate Bush's father during a post-presidential visit to Kuwait, President Bill Clinton simply blew up his intelligence headquarters. To the Iraqi dictator, this act did not seem bold, but cowardly. It was proof that America was a paper tiger, confirmation that Iraq's stalwart troops, attuned to suffering, would be able to thwart an American attack and inflict enough casualties to impel decision makers in Washington to bargain rather than to force him to flee or to dismantle his regime.[3]

More important, Hussein calculated that Bush would not be able to use the excuse of weapons of mass destruction to assemble a military coalition to overwhelm his regime. He thought he could outfox the Americans, permit the inspectors to return, and make enough symbolic concessions to sever the consensus within the Security Council. He hoped to garner French and Russian support for a face-saving resolution of the crisis and the lifting of sanctions. Tariq Aziz, his deputy prime minister, subsequently told his American inquisitors that Hussein believed that economic self-interest—oil deals, trade, and debts—would impel Moscow and Paris to check Washington's bellicose instincts. The Iraqi ambassador in Moscow assured Aziz in October 2002 that President Vladimir Putin "will not allow the use of force against Iraq."[4]

Hussein's inclination now was to assuage the inspectors, open up Iraq, and order his subordinates to cooperate with the UN monitors. He surprised many of his top advisers when he told them in late November and December 2002 that he had no weapons of mass destruction. Many of his associates did not believe him. They thought he was playing another game. He sometimes hinted that he was playing a game, that he had something up his sleeve. What he wanted to do was buy time—to cooperate just enough to garner a clean bill of health from the UN Monitoring, Verification and Inspection Commission (UNMOVIC) and the International Atomic Energy Administration (IAEA). He might then divide the French and Russians from the Americans and British and make it difficult for Washington to justify a war to remove him from power. With inspectors back in Iraq, moreover, the United States might hesitate to attack. Meanwhile, the inspectors' inability to find WMD would just underscore how wily he was. His adversaries at home and abroad—the Kurds, some Shi'a in the south, the Iranians and the Israelis—would still fear that he possessed such weapons, or could develop them quickly, and deploy them in a crisis.[5]

Hans Blix, the executive director of UNMOVIC, and Mohamed ElBaradei, the head of the IAEA, went to Baghdad immediately after the passage of UN Resolution 1441. For two years Blix and his subordinates had been examining old documents, analyzing new evidence, assembling experts, and preparing for the eventual resumption of inspections. Blix now wanted to iron out the details for the transportation and housing of his inspectors. He met with Iraqi officials and with Foreign Minister Sabri. He talked to them about the sites they wanted to visit and requested lists of all persons who had been engaged in the development of weapons of mass destruction. He warned against the Iraqi habit of assigning too many minders and focusing too much media attention on the inspectors. Noting that the first inspection teams would arrive during the last week in November, Blix emphasized that Iraq must submit a full and accurate declaration of its chemical, biological, and nuclear weapons initiatives as well as its ballistic missiles and other delivery systems, like unmanned aerial vehicles. It must identify all research and development sites, disclose all weapons, and report all former and current programs. Blix warned the Iraqis to avoid the mistakes of the past, of revealing too little too late.[6]

On his way back to New York he stopped in London and told Prime Minister Tony Blair that he was satisfied with the practical arrangements he had worked out, but worried that he saw no change in the Iraqi disposition to give up their commitment to develop and possess weapons of mass destruction. They did not seem ready, for example, to pass legislation prohibiting the involvement of Iraqi citizens in WMD programs. Blair was not surprised to hear that there was no fundamental change in attitude, saying he anticipated that the Iraqis would resume their old "cat-and-mouse game."[7]

The Iraqis were playing a dangerous game because American anxieties were not abating. The CIA noted that the Iraqi Intelligence Service (IIS) "was becoming increasingly aggressive in planning attacks against US interests." More than forty intelligence reports suggested that Iraqis wanted to attack US facilities abroad or to transfer weapons of mass destruction that could abet attacks. Two reports suggested the IIS might target US facilities in Turkey; a State Department cable from Baku indicated that the Iraqis were engaged in similar activities there.[8] Analysts also thought that Iraqi biological and chemical weapons programs were looking more grave. They now judged that Hussein actually possessed biological weapons, maintained chemical warfare stockpiles, restarted chemical warfare production, and was developing an offensive chemical weapons program. In December 2002, CIA's Weapons Intelligence Non Proliferation and Arms Control Center (WINPAC) reiterated that "Iraq retain[ed] an offensive CW program." In February 2003, CIA director George Tenet reported that Iraq was testing missiles and unmanned aerial vehicles that exceeded permissible ranges. Al Qaeda, he told senators and congresspersons on the intelligence committees, was "still dedicated to striking the US homeland," and Iraq, he claimed, had provided training in document forgery, bomb-making, poisons, and gasses to al Qaeda members or their associates. For the most part, British intelligence assessments of Iraqi WMD capabilities—not on Iraqi terrorist links—comported with these estimates.[9] Although subsequent investigations concluded that these judgments were deeply flawed, rarely were top officials informed that some of the reports were tainted by sources who were fabricating evidence; nor were policymakers told about the agency's growing skepticism regarding the credibility of its principal source of information about Iraqi biological programs—Curveball.[10]

In November and December 2002, the Defense Intelligence Agency, the State Department's Office of Intelligence and Research, and British intelligence minimized the likelihood of Hussein's handing off these chemical or biological weapons to other terrorists, but Bush and Cheney remained deeply worried.[11] The vice president thought the Iraqi dictator might employ smallpox as a weapon in a future confrontation. He convinced Bush to support a new research and production effort to be called Project BioShield and to allocate $6 billion to fund it. On December 13, Bush announced that US military personnel and key civilians in high-risk areas of the world would receive smallpox vaccines and he quietly set aside 20 million doses as a strategic reserve.[12]

But the administration's attention now was riveted on the endgame of coercive diplomacy. Secretary of Defense Donald Rumsfeld sent a memorandum to the president shortly after the passage of the UN resolution. Hussein, he emphasized, had two choices: continue the game of cheat and retreat, or disarm completely. Our immediate task, the defense secretary insisted, was to test which choice he was making. "Militarily," Rumsfeld wrote, "we need to continue our preparations— not only to keep up the military pressure that reinforces US/UN diplomacy, but to be prepared to move relatively quickly should Saddam do something that leads you to decide to act." He wanted to be ready to protect the Kurds and seize the oil fields in northern Iraq, to take the port of Basra and control the southern oil fields, and neutralize the SCUD threat against Israel.[13]

Most of all, Rumsfeld had to grapple with General Tommy Franks's request to push ahead with the deployment of almost 300,000 troops to the region. The defense secretary did not respond with alacrity. He knew he had to calibrate deployments to support the president's wishes, and Bush still did not want his options limited. If war occurred, the president intended to destroy Hussein's regime. The dictator would not survive as he had after the first Persian Gulf War in 1991. But Bush was not yet ready to wage war and he wanted deployments to buttress his coercive diplomacy. Rumsfeld, therefore, told Franks "to dribble" out the deployments, even if the practice upset his local commanders, as it did. The goal, said Rumsfeld, "was to keep the pressure on for the diplomacy but not so much to discredit the diplomacy." On December 6, Rumsfeld authorized the first major deployment order; thereafter, it was to be a slow, gradual process. The fact that he was "disaggregating" the process in order to bolster the administration's diplomacy was not widely understood, but Bush and Rice knew exactly what was happening.[14]

The war preparations themselves were not going well, caused in part by the practice of coercive diplomacy. General David McKiernan did not like the Hybrid plan he inherited when he was appointed by Franks in September to direct the land war effort. He recognized that if the Iraqi regime collapsed quickly he would not have enough troops to consolidate control and ensure stability. McKiernan wanted to do away with the sixteen-day air campaign that would precede the land attack, and he requested more troops to capitalize on the initial battlefield successes that he expected. He wanted more soldiers to sustain the attack, march toward Baghdad, and secure hundreds of prospective WMD sites that had still not been identified. His new plan, which came to be called Cobra II, reversed many of the ideas that Rumsfeld and Feith had been insisting on for the previous ten months.[15]

But the new plan could not be finalized without knowing whether the new Turkish government would allow the stationing and deployment of British and American troops, the necessary prerequisite for a pincer movement emanating from north and south. Deputy Secretary of Defense Paul Wolfowitz and Under Secretary of State Marc Grossman went to Ankara during the early days of December to seek Turkish approval. They explained that the president had not determined to go to war, but preparations, deployments, and Turkish collaboration were indispensable to convince Hussein to disarm.[16] When the Turkish government continued to vacillate, British defense officials remonstrated over the ambiguity of the military planning. They believed that the Americans were minimizing the lead times for initiating military operations in order "to allow the maximum time for UN/diplomatic process to unfold." They now estimated that US forces would reach a peak of readiness in February and that Washington would then be under enormous pressure to go to war—"to use it or lose it."[17]

With military plans still evolving and coercive diplomacy still unfolding, officials anxiously awaited the Iraqi declaration. On December 6, Bush asked Tenet if the CIA would be able to judge the accuracy of Iraq's forthcoming submission. Assured that the agency could do so, Bush remained suspicious. The Iraqi attitude, he said, "was grudging and conditional." He thought Hussein might be moving some of his weapons of mass destruction to Syria. He was hearing "in granular detail" that the Iraqis were cheating, and they were still occasionally firing on American and British pilots enforcing the no-fly zones. The Iraqi declaration, he told the American people on December 7, needed to be credible, accurate, and complete. It would take a little time to assess it. If it disappointed, "the Iraqi dictator would have demonstrated to the world once again that he has chosen not to change his behavior." His defiance, the president emphasized, would be met by American resolve.[18]

The Iraqi government submitted its "declaration" on December 8. The main body of the declaration was about 3,000 pages, with an additional 5,000 pages of supporting documents in Arabic. Blix understood that the Iraqis had been asked to do a lot in a short period of time. Nevertheless, he was sorely disappointed. "The declaration," Blix wrote in his memoir, "had certainly not been used as the hoped-for occasion for a fresh start, coming up with long hidden truths. It looked like a repetition of old, unverified data." On December 19, Blix reported to the UN Security Council that the Iraqis "had not provided material or evidence that solved any of the unresolved disarmament issues." Disappointed, he was not prepared to declare Iraqi bad faith. UNMOVIC, he emphasized, needed time to inspect, inquire, clarify, and conclude.[19]

American and British officials were not surprised. The CIA assessed that there were gaping holes in the Iraqi declaration. The State Department's Office of Intelligence and Research thought it "would not resolve any priority issues." British intelligence analysts said much the same: the declaration failed to address any of the outstanding matters. In fact, it confirmed entrenched attitudes about Iraqi duplicity and solidified convictions that the Iraqis were cheating as they had repeatedly done in the past.[20]

At an NSC meeting on December 18, Bush declared: "if there are gaps, it is clear he is not willing to disarm." Secretary of State Powell seemed to agree: "Saddam has put the rope around his own neck. It is up to us how quickly to tighten it." Then, the president suddenly posed the central question: "Is war inevitable?" Rumsfeld and Cheney thought so, but Powell categorically said, "No." Bush retorted that he "was not so sure. I think war is inevitable. Saddam is not going to disarm. The quicker we determine, the better off we are." Rather than resolve the issue with a systematic discussion of the central issues—whether it was desirable to go to war, whether Hussein's intentions and capabilities endangered vital interests—the president stated that the United States should ratchet up the pressure and exhaust all options before declaring war.[21] When the CIA mission manager for Iraq reported (at this same meeting) that his task of recruiting agents was complicated by the mixed messages emanating from Washington—war is inevitable; Bush's diplomacy is for real—Bush, according to the journalist Bob Woodward, retorted: "Yep. . . . I know I have put you in a difficult position. I know that this is hard, but this is the course we're on. And we're going to have to keep doing all of these elements at the same time." Coercive diplomacy, in other words, meant living with contradictions.[22]

Bush and Blair still hoped that Hussein might relent or crack under pressure, and war could be avoided. The underlying British assumption was that the "coercive campaign" required "careful orchestration," and the Iraqi dictator had to be convinced "that his regime will not survive unless he is willing to compromise on WMD." Although Blair preferred to topple Hussein, the British prime minister knew that popular opinion in his country was against going to war; indeed, most of his advisers were against going to war. Only a second UN resolution saying that Hussein was in material breach could provide the legal and political basis for joining the US war effort. "Maximum pressure," Blair thought, might yield a second resolution with an ultimatum. If Saddam caved, or fled, war might be avoided "altogether," or alternatively, there would be a "clear consensus for removing Saddam."[23] Blix supported this approach. As head of the UN monitoring agency, his "gut" told him that Hussein "still engaged in prohibited activities," and more military pressure might induce him to be more forthcoming.[24]

Bush did not believe the United States needed a second resolution to justify war. He was determined to press the issue, to confront Hussein. Yet confronting him was still infused with ambiguity for the president. Did it mean regime change, or did it mean unfettered inspections and enforced disarmament? Bush asked Rice and Hadley to work with the intelligence community to put together a public presentation demonstrating the violations and misbehavior of the Iraqi regime. When the analysts presented the case to the president and his top advisers on December 21, Bush was unimpressed. "Nice try," Bush said. "Joe Public," he continued, would not be persuaded. "I've been told all this intelligence about having WMD," he said to Tenet. Is "this the best we've got?" It is "a slam dunk," Tenet retorted, meaning that the accumulated evidence could be made more convincing. "Needs a lot more work," Bush told Rice. But "make sure no one stretches to make our case."[25]

During the next week, Tenet's subordinates, under the supervision of Deputy Director John McLaughlin, worked feverishly to beef up their case. They met with Rice at the White House on December 28. They reviewed the evidence they could convey to the public, using information that they thought they could extrapolate from the October National Intelligence Estimate (NIE). Again, Rice was sorely disappointed by what she heard. Is this all you have? she exclaimed. "You have gotten the president way out on a limb." Daily briefings had convinced her that the case was much more persuasive than it now seemed.[26]

The president was not so sure of the public case, but he never doubted that the Iraqi dictator had weapons of mass destruction and he greatly feared that Hussein might share them with terrorists. His daily briefings had been much more alarming than the accumulated, verifiable evidence. Subsequently, he acknowledged, "we should have pushed harder on the intelligence and revisited our assumptions."[27] But at the time he was not asking his advisers and analysts about the veracity of the evidence. His beliefs were entrenched based on the "intelligence" he had received over the past two years, the lessons extrapolated from decades of dealing with the Iraqi dictator, and the absence of dissenting voices in high administration circles. Instead of prodding his advisers to re-examine the evidence and reassess their assumptions, he asked them whether they could mobilize the information to persuade the American public and the international community that the Iraqi regime was in material breach of its commitments, justifying the prospective use of military force if Hussein did not flee, reveal what weapons he possessed, or demonstrate convincingly that he no longer had them.

Bush spent the Christmas and New Year holidays struggling, straining. "There was a lot of stress," he confided to the journalist Bob Woodward. "There was a lot of tension."[28] He talked to his father, the former president, about Iraq, something he rarely did. "I told Dad I was praying we could deal with Saddam peacefully but was preparing for the alternative. I walked him through the diplomatic strategy. . . . He shared my hope that diplomacy would succeed," but acknowledged that force must be employed if Hussein did not comply. After the new year began, the president sent a letter to his two daughters, who were away in college, "I pray the man in Iraq will disarm in a peaceful way. We are putting pressure on him to do just that and much of the world is with us."[29]

The gravity of the decision weighed on the president. The advisers, analysts, and speechwriters who were closest to him did not see a man who was eager for war, but they could see a president who was approaching a turning point. On January 3 or 4, he spoke intently to Rice. Coercive diplomacy, he said, was not working. "Saddam was getting smarter about how to deal with Blix." The Iraqi dictator seemed to be up to his old tricks. The inspectors seemed to be finding nothing significant. Bush feared the international consensus was fraying; Hussein was succeeding at concealing his weapons and exploiting the rifts among the great powers. "We're not winning," he told Rice. "We're probably going to have to go to war." She agreed: "You have to follow through on your threat. If you're going to carry out coercive diplomacy, you have to live with that decision."[30] Neither the president nor his national security adviser mentioned the possibility that Hussein might not have the weapons they assumed he had; neither considered positive inducements to elicit Hussein's cooperation, like terminating sanctions or abandoning regime change as official policy. Hussein's record of duplicity and brutality discouraged such thinking.

Bush's decision for war was crystallizing, but he was not yet there, constrained by his grasp of the gravity of the matter before him and by his (fading) hope that Hussein might cave or flee, yet impelled to move forward because he felt so confident of American power and American values. In his view, Hussein was a growing menace, not a waning threat. On January 10, he met with a group of prominent Iraqi émigrés. He inquired about their personal stories of hardship, torture, exile, and opposition. He asked what they knew about life inside Iraq, about the health and education of the people, their loyalty to the regime, and their hopes and aspirations for the future. He was assured that American troops would be greeted "with flowers and sweets." He was characteristically succinct: "I believe in freedom and peace. I believe Saddam Hussein is a threat to America and to the neighborhood. He should disarm but he won't, therefore we will remove him from power. . . . His heart is made of steel." He sounded like his mind was made up, but as they prepared to leave, he said, "We haven't reached conclusions. . . . Maybe one year from now we will be toasting victory and talking about the transition to freedom."[31]

Saddam Hussein was doing rather little to assuage American suspicions. In an Army day speech on January 6, he enveloped his national mission in religious guise, a rhetorical trope he had been employing for the past decade. "When you the valiant people of Iraq, renew your pledge to Allah, to yourselves, to the nation, and to humanity at large, . . . you not only strengthen your adherence to your belief and your sacrifices for the faith . . . but you ensure final victory over the enemies of Allah—your enemies. . . . Our right is a clear right, as clear as [the US] falsehood. . . . Allah shall drown [the US] in shame." Assailing Washington for its collaboration with Israel and for its quest to control the resources of the region, he warned "that the enemy will pay dearly later . . . for its reckless greed and expansionism." He excoriated the inspectors for going beyond the declared objectives of UN Resolution 1441, for seeking to interview Iraqi scientists, and for requesting information they had no right to solicit. He reminded the United States "of the terrible end of all empires" that had committed aggression against Iraq. On January 7, after meeting with advisers, Hussein continued his vitriol: "The enemy thinks it will make us despair with time. In fact, we will make [the enemy] despair with the passage of time." Disparaging the work of inspectors, he again accused them of reconnaissance: "they know these weapons do not exist." Beckoning for Arab unity to resist American imperialism, he and Tariq Aziz denounced American attempts to control Arab oil, weaken Iraq as a regional power, and abet the criminal policies of the Zionists in Palestine.[32]

Meanwhile, UNMOVIC and the IAEA continued their work. By mid-January, over 380 sites had been visited—laboratories, plants, manufacturing facilities—by 250 to 300 inspectors. Blix noted on January 9 that, although inspectors had found "no smoking guns," it was now altogether clear that the Iraqi declaration of December was incomplete. He emphasized Iraq's failure to account for weapons known to exist as a result of previous inspections in the 1990s. He also complained about the reluctance of Iraqi officials to provide the names of scientists, as they were obligated to do. Blix emphasized that Iraq had to account for the import of missile engines, stocks of VX gas, and the ingredients used to produce missile fuel and chemical bombs. If these items had been destroyed, UNMOVIC required proof of their destruction. ElBaradei reported more positive impressions, saying thus far "no evidence of ongoing prohibited nuclear or nuclear-related activities had been detected" and adding that the aluminum tubes that had attracted so much attention were not designed for a nuclear weapons program. More work, of course, needed to be done. "It's true," said Dimitrios Perricos, the head of UNMOVIC inspections inside Iraq, "that the Iraqis are opening doors, but they are opening installations they know we are aware of. The real test will be when we start going to facilities where they will be surprised." Blix and ElBaradei planned to return to Baghdad on January 19–20 to confer with Iraqi officials.[33]

US policymakers were waiting, watching, and acting. On January 11, Cheney asked Rumsfeld to participate in a meeting with the Saudi ambassador, Prince Bandar. As American forces now were moving into the Persian Gulf and plans for an invasion were being refined and finalized, the vice president requested base and overflight rights. Along with General Richard Myers, the chairman of the Joint Chiefs of Staff, the vice president and the secretary of defense explained their war plans to Prince Bandar, who was mightily impressed. Heretofore the Saudis had wavered in their support for war, shaken by memories of Washington's failure to destroy the regime of the Iraqi dictator during the last war and allowing him to achieve heroic status on the "Arab street" for his defiance of America. Bandar now asked whether Hussein would survive. "Once we start," the vice president crisply responded, he will "be toast."[34]

For the first time, Rumsfeld wrote in his memoir, he felt war might be inevitable. But the defense secretary was still operating to support the president's policy of coercive diplomacy. On that same day, he approved the deployment of an additional 35,000 troops to the Persian Gulf, along with accompanying aircraft and warships. "Successful diplomacy," he commented, "required a credible threat of military action." He hoped "that the process of moving an increasing number of American forces into a position where they could attack Iraq might convince the Iraqis to end their defiance." Rumsfeld believed the president was still wrestling with the decision to go to war. Bush, he thought, was moving incrementally, yet reluctantly, to take the final step.[35]

The president was nearing the finish line. On January 13, he arranged to have a short, private conversation with his secretary of state. Bush told Powell, "I really think I'm going to have to take this guy out." He did not ask Powell for his opinion; he asked for his support. Bush said the inspections were floundering, and Hussein was not complying. The secretary of state discreetly prodded the president to think through the consequences of war. In a conversation that lasted about twelve minutes, Bush assured him that he had done so, and repeated that war remained a last resort. Sensing the president's resolve, the secretary of state—a former Army general and chairman of the Joint Chiefs of Staff—was not inclined to argue the pros and cons of going to war. Powell said, "Yes sir, I brought you through the diplomatic process [at the UN from September to November]; I can't walk away now."[36]

But from Powell's perspective, the game was not yet over. The inspections were still ongoing. The French, Russians, and Germans had not yet abandoned the unified effort to squeeze the Iraqi tyrant, and Hussein might still be convinced of his imminent downfall if he were not more forthcoming. Not least, Powell felt empowered that the president had asked him to present the final brief to a global audience. "I need you," said the president, "to go make the case to the world via the UN. You have the most credibility of the whole team—frankly the only credibility of the whole team." Not yet ready to throw in the towel, Powell replied, "Yes sir." He was still determined "to see if we can find a diplomatic way out of this."[37] If he could make a persuasive case at the United Nations, if he could work harmoniously with the British, if he could keep the French and Russians on the same page, if he could garner another victory inside the Security Council—perhaps Hussein might recalibrate his own strategy to save himself. Perhaps the Iraqi tyrant would acknowledge his past lies, disclose his secret weapons, or, best of all, flee to save his life, if not his regime. Such outcomes were not foreclosed.

Thinking war was still premature, Powell resolved to double down on his efforts to mobilize support for a second resolution that, on the one hand, might finally force Hussein to capitulate or, on the other, would make it a lot easier for Blair and the British to join Bush and the Americans in a military invasion. Powell hoped that Blix's report, scheduled for late January, might help clarify the way forward. On January 14, Rice went to see Blix in New York, and they discussed the inspectors' progress in Iraq. Blix later wrote:

> It did not seem to me that she excluded the possibility that the Iraqi regime would crack under the increasing military pressure and reveal whatever weapons stock it had. This was a possibility I myself was hoping for. At this stage my gut feeling was still that Iraq retained weapons of mass destruction. The early opportunity to declare them regrettably, had been missed in 12,000 pages. Perhaps more military pressure would do the trick. I had nothing against inspection backed by pressure, but how far could the game of chicken go?[38]

Not much further. There were indications that Hussein was reacting to the pressure. He again urged his subordinates to cooperate. The inspectors made progress. They saw few signs of the weapons the regime had sworn to destroy. Yet Iraqi cooperation remained grudging. Among other matters, Blix noted that interviews had not yet been scheduled with key Iraqi scientists, illegal missile engines had been found, eleven empty warheads designed for chemical weapons had been discovered, and a stash of nuclear documents had been located in a private home. More disturbing, the Iraqi dictator chose not to meet with Blix and

ElBaradei when they visited Baghdad. "An opportunity had not been used well," Blix lamented. Moreover, in a letter to Kofi Annan, the UN secretary-general, the Iraqi foreign minister complained bitterly about the inspectors, reinforcing perceptions of the regime's "stridency." Although ElBaradei shared some of Blix's misgivings, he did not think Hussein had restarted his nuclear program. But Blix felt that the Iraqi government still was prevaricating and foot-dragging on many substantive matters. In his view, Hussein still had not made a "strategic" decision to open up and collaborate. But he might if he had more time.[39]

Bush was inclined to give Saddam a little more time, but not much. Some of his analysts and advisers thought that Hussein might yet cave, or flee.[40] On January 22, however, French president Jacques Chirac and Gerhard Schroeder, the German chancellor, stated publicly that they were against a second resolution authorizing the use of military force; war, they said, was a terrible solution to the problems posed by the Iraqi regime. At a time when Bush and Blair hoped to forge a united coalition that might intimidate Hussein, the dissension within the Western community played into his hands and made a satisfactory outcome all the more unlikely. The Iraqi dictator probably was smiling in his palace, mused Alberto Gonzales, the president's legal counsel and friend. Reflecting the thinking in the White House, Gonzales wrote, "the decisions of France and Germany would make war more likely rather than less, since Saddam would have a reduced incentive to cooperate and comply with the UN resolutions." Rumsfeld fully agreed.[41]

However, Bush was not yet ready to terminate the practice of coercive diplomacy and abandon hope for consensus at the United Nations. He did not want to undercut Blair's efforts to secure parliamentary support of military action, which seemed to depend on the passage of a second resolution at the United Nations that would again declare Hussein in material breach and justify war. When Jack Straw, the British foreign secretary, met Cheney on January 23, he pressed for more time, arguing that if Blix and ElBaradei presented a report that underscored Iraqi non-compliance, it would buy time during which they could try to forge an international consensus behind a second resolution that might force the Iraqi dictator to leave. "If the international community was united," Straw said, "then the Arabs could go to Saddam with a strong message that he had either to go or his regime would face destruction."

Arab leaders, Straw told the vice president, "were desperate to get rid of Saddam. A second resolution would embolden them." With the Iraqis "rattled," and the regime "fracturing," the Americans and British might achieve their goals without firing a shot. More time would afford the inspectors an opportunity "to produce compelling evidence of Iraqi deceit," galvanize Arab support, and reshape politics in the United Kingdom, Europe, and the wider world.[42]

Cheney listened intently. He said the administration was still figuring out the next steps, and it might depend on Blix's report to the Security Council on the 27th. Speaking personally, Cheney said he was not against a second resolution. But he was not sure that buying time would serve any purpose. "The burden of proof was on the Iraqis and they were not delivering." He worried about drifting through months of discussion at the United Nations while the troops were waiting in the Persian Gulf. The weather made this undesirable. More important, Cheney worried that delay might erode American credibility in the region. He alluded to the World Trade Center bombing of 1993, the 1998 destruction of US embassies in East Africa, and the attack on the USS *Cole* in 2000. "The US had been struck with apparent impunity. If we backed off now or sat there for months, the Saudis and others would also back off. It would be one more example of bold talk and no action. We would never get them gingered up for action again." Once military operations began, Cheney thought the Iraqi regime would collapse quickly and Iraq's WMD would be discovered promptly. When Straw retorted that military action without a second resolution would divide the international community and embolden Hussein, Cheney agreed that the United Nations could serve to legitimate action. Nonetheless, he worried that the French and Germans would use a debate over a second resolution to belabor the situation, postpone action, and damage American credibility. Decisions, Cheney concluded, would have to await Blair's visit to Washington, already scheduled to take place immediately after Blix's report.[43]

On the same day that Straw and Cheney talked in Washington, Deputy Secretary of Defense Paul Wolfowitz gave a major speech at the Council on Foreign Relations in New York, National Security Adviser Condi Rice penned a widely read op-ed in the *New York Times*, and the White House circulated its brief, "What Does Disarmament Look

Like?" Wolfowitz insisted that Bush's goal was disarmament, not regime change. "There is still hope," Wolfowitz emphasized, that "if Saddam is faced with a serious enough threat . . . he might decide to adopt a fundamentally different course. But time is running out."[44] Rice reinforced Wolfowitz's warning, and accused Hussein of lying. She catalogued the list of American grievances, claiming that the Iraqi declaration was incomplete. The regime, she insisted, concealed information about its possession of anthrax, violated limitations on the range of its ballistic missiles, failed to account for thousands of tons of chemical precursors, spied on the inspectors, and restricted interviews with key scientists and witnesses.[45]

Blix privately remonstrated against Rice's criticisms, but his presentation to the UN Security Council on January 27 underscored many of the issues she had outlined. Carefully avoiding any allegations that Iraq possessed WMD, Blix emphasized that the regime failed to demonstrate it did not have them. Although there had been 300 inspections of 230 different sites, Iraq still had not addressed key issues. UNMOVIC still wanted clarification about the possible weaponization of a VX agent, about chemical bombs, about 8,500 liters of an anthrax agent, about missiles that exceeded the permissible range of 150 km, about casting chambers used to produce solid-fuel missiles, and about the concealment of documents regarding the laser enrichment of uranium. Blix noted that inspectors often could not tell whether ostensible violations were innocuous and accidental, or "whether they were the tip of a submerged iceberg." "When we have urged our Iraqi counterparts to present more evidence," he told members of the Security Council, "we have all too often met the response that there are no more documents." This was unsatisfactory, he concluded, yet he hoped Iraq would make a "strategic" decision to cooperate, something he had not yet seen.[46]

Blix's report did not change assumptions in Washington and London that Hussein was cheating, lying, and maneuvering. According to British intelligence assessments, the Iraqi leader did not yet grasp the seriousness of his position. He was under increasing pressure from the inspectors and the military buildup, but he still did not expect an attack. He still thought he could exploit rifts in the international community, and maneuver both to stay in power and retain his WMD. John Scarlett, chairman of the British Joint Intelligence Committee, wrote Blair's national security adviser that Hussein's control remained "total," yet brittle. Upon military action, the regime would collapse quickly. But thus far, Scarlett emphasized, "I have seen nothing yet to indicate that he sees himself and his regime as finally doomed."[47]

President Bush now resolved to go to war in March unless Hussein unexpectedly changed course. On January 28, at a Cabinet meeting, Bush expounded: "We are the light in a very complex world. We will have allies with us when we attack."[48] In his State of the Union message that very night, he was resolute: the war against terror, he said, "is a contest of will in which perseverance is power." Iraq must "show exactly where it is hiding its banned weapons, lay those weapons out for the world to see, and destroy them as directed." Before 9/11, Bush explained, many observers thought Hussein could be contained. "But chemical agents, lethal viruses, and shadowy terrorist networks are not easily contained. Imagine those 19 hijackers with other weapons and other plans, this time armed by Saddam Hussein." Bush then announced that on February 5, Secretary of State Powell would ask the Security Council "to consider the facts of Iraq's ongoing defiance." "We will consult," Bush proclaimed, but "if Saddam Hussein does not fully disarm, . . . we will lead a coalition to disarm him."[49]

On January 30, the president met with his military commanders and asked if they were now prepared to wage war. They assured him they were. The next day he met with his Cabinet. By the end of the meeting, he seemed as resolved as he could be. "Subject to a dramatic turn of events," he would initiate military action on February 22. The air war would begin on March 10, and ground troops would move into Iraq on the 15th. Henceforth, Bush declared, "the military plan should not be geared for diplomacy; it will be geared to win militarily."[50]

But Bush still hesitated. When British prime minister Blair traveled to Washington on January 31, he told the president that he could not muster parliamentary support for military action without a second UN resolution. He pled for more time. He hoped a new Security Council resolution might alter Hussein's calculations inside Iraq, reshape the attitudes of Iraq's Arab neighbors, and reduce the political impediments he faced in London. Recognizing his friend's tenuous political position and averse to going to war without a key ally, the president responded affirmatively to Blair's request and rejected the advice of Cheney,

Rumsfeld, and Rice. He calculated that his decision to use military force would garner much more public support if he worked through the United Nations and had allies, like the British, joining him.[51]

Appearing at a news conference with the British prime minister, Bush underscored that Tony Blair was his friend—America's friend. "I trust his judgment, and I appreciate his wisdom." Blair praised the president's leadership and expressed satisfaction with their talks. They must continue to work "in every way that we can [to] mobilize international support and the international community to make sure that these twin threats [of terrorism and WMD] that the world faces are dealt with." Bush was prepared to work for a second resolution even though he had little faith that Hussein would change his behavior and even though he believed the United States could act legally without one. The deliberative process at the United Nations, however, must not be protracted—weeks, not months, he insisted. Containment, Bush emphasized, no longer worked. His "vision shifted dramatically after September the 11th," he reminded reporters. "I now realize the stakes. I realize the world has changed. My most important obligation is to protect the American people from further harm. And I will do that."[52]

Yet his advisers grasped that his plans could still change, that there were still "off-ramps." Gonzales, who was attending many of the meetings of principals and the NSC, wondered if Bush would take military action without the British. Rumsfeld, too, was not certain whether "Bush had fully decided." The president's national security advisers, Rice and Hadley, as well as his principal speechwriter, Michael Gerson, still thought the outcome was contingent. "Up until the day of the ultimatum," Gerson recalled, "I remember the president telling me . . . that Blair thought there was a significant chance that Saddam would give in. That was the clear preference. . . . [The president] was not looking for excuses for attacking Iraq." He wanted to set forth "the conditions by which Saddam could back down and still achieve our security objectives there."[53]

Seeking to collaborate with Blair, Bush instructed Powell to make the case against Hussein to the Security Council. If the speech were powerful enough and galvanized the international community behind a second resolution, perhaps, then, the Iraqi dictator would see the handwriting on the wall and relent, or, at least, a second resolution would enhance Blair's case to the British parliament. The preparations for Powell's speech were elaborate and contentious. Powell asked Rice for guidelines for the speech. She and Hadley gave him a long draft that the vice president's office had worked on in the aftermath of McLaughlin's unsuccessful presentations to Bush and Cheney in late December. Libby had seized the initiative to write a more persuasive brief indicting Hussein's regime. Along with his assistants, John Hannah and Eric Edelman, they wrote a comprehensive indictment focusing on Hussein's possession of weapons of mass destruction, violations of past obligations, links to terrorists, and disgraceful record of brutality and ecological degradation. Powell did not like what he read. He hated Libby's account of the Iraqi dictator's links to terrorists and he was not interested in the dictator's human rights abuses. He brought Libby's document over to the CIA. He said he wanted to focus mostly on Hussein's WMD. His own staff and Tenet's analysts thought the OVP draft was "garbage," although much of the material in the draft emanated from classified CIA documents that the vice president had preserved from previous briefings. Powell's assistants then labored for four or five days at the CIA with Tenet's subordinates focusing mainly on reframing the indictment of Hussein's transgressions regarding weapons of mass destruction. Powell had his reasons: the case against Hussein had to rest on his disregard of previous UN resolutions, not on matters that members of the Security Council would regard as interference in the sovereign affairs of member states and not on allegations of terrorist associations that would not be regarded as consequential, or even heinous, to many UN participants. Powell and Tenet believed they developed a persuasive case.[54]

On February 5, 2003, with Tenet sitting behind him, Powell presented the American case against Saddam Hussein (Figure 8.1). The secretary of state displayed satellite photographs of Iraq's alleged subterfuge and concealment. He cited information gleaned from informers, detainees, and intercepts. He insisted that Hussein had violated UN resolutions, failed to cooperate with the inspectors, maintained biological and chemical weapons, and planned to reignite a nuclear program. To a lesser extent, Powell condemned Hussein's support of terrorism, and dwelled on al Qaeda's continuing lust for chemical and biological weapons. He focused on the terrorist Abu Mu'sab Zarqawi, who,

Figure 8.1 Secretary of State Colin Powell delivering his speech at the United Nations and highlighting the evidence of Iraq's alleged possession of weapons of mass destruction, February 5, 2003.
Getty Images, https://www.gettyimages.com/detail/news-photo/secretary-of-state-colin-powell-addresses-the-united-news-photo/97281899

allegedly, had ties to Osama bin Laden. Zarqawi had hid in Iraq, had been seen in Baghdad, had experimented with chemical weapons, and had schemed to launch attacks in Europe, Russia, and elsewhere. Iraq's failure to "disarm and come clean"; its indifference to, or harboring of, terrorists like Zarqawi; and its interactions with al Qaeda operatives, Powell stressed, put it in further "material breach" of its disarmament obligations. The United Nations, proclaimed Powell, had given Iraq one last chance. Hussein was not responding. Members of the international community must not shirk their duties; they must not avoid their responsibility to take action in the face of Iraq's defiance.[55]

Powell's speech, soon to be ridiculed for its many inaccuracies, riveted attention around the world, but did not change attitudes. Representatives of key countries at the United Nations stated that Powell's evidence underscored the need for continued inspections, but did not warrant the immediate use of force. They did not share the Bush administration's sense of threat. Since the outpouring of sympathy after the attack on 9/11, worldwide attitudes toward the United

States had soured. Many people abroad deplored the administration's unilateralist instincts, suspected its motives, and critiqued its judgment. Many people around the globe appreciated the terrorist threat and regarded Hussein's Iraq with contempt, yet they assumed that the United States was motivated by its quest for oil and they believed the preoccupation with Iraq diverted attention from the more important war on terrorism. Huge majorities in France, Germany, and Russia objected to the use of military force against Iraq.[56]

Although failing to convince that Hussein's regime constituted an imminent threat warranting war, Powell's speech focused attention on Iraq's machinations and ratcheted up the pressure for the Iraqi dictator to comply with the inspectors. Blix and ElBaradei went back to Baghdad on February 8 and 9. Blix thought the Iraqis were "genuinely rattled," and were seeking to show progress. ElBaradei was pleased that IAEA inspectors were finding no signs of a nuclear program. Yet, overall, Blix felt they "obtained much less than . . . was needed" and the Iraqis were doing "too little, too late," foolishly obstructing reconnaissance flights, restricting interviews, and delaying passage of legislation outlawing work on WMD. Although Blix no longer was interested in seeing Hussein himself, the Iraqi dictator had ignored ElBaradei's overtures.[57] On February 14, they reported to the Security Council that they had found "no smoking guns," no clear-cut sign of Iraqi weapons of mass destruction, but, regrettably, Blix emphasized that the Iraqi government still had not accounted for many prohibited items. Politely rebutting some of Powell's claims and vexed by American pressure, Blix told council members that the inspectors would need more time to complete their task, not a lot, but more. Although American intelligence analysts were not fully cooperating with UNMOVIC, Blix did not think the United States was impeding his efforts. But he did want more time, and said he would report again at the end of the month.[58]

Bush and his advisers were frustrated by the mid-February reports of Blix and ElBaradei. Rice told Blix that she was tired of the "process game."[59] Yet the president put up with it throughout the month of February. While remonstrating against the delays and asserting that he had decided to move forward with military action, he still worked for a second resolution and hoped that Hussein would crack or flee.[60] What might satisfy him and avert war remained unclear. At a meeting with his top military and civilian advisers on February 5, he agreed with Rumsfeld's declaration that "disarmament means no more Saddam."[61] Rice told Manning that there were now only two possible outcomes: Hussein could leave, or comply and face the consequences (whatever that might mean).[62] But Rice and Hadley thought Bush's overriding preoccupation was ridding Iraq of the prohibited weapons. Bush confided to the British that, although he could not say it publicly, he still preferred a second resolution and disarmament to war and regime change.[63] He warned Hussein not to throw away his last chance, yet offered no inducements or commitments.[64] Visiting Russia, Secretary of State Powell said that peace could still be preserved if Hussein made the "strategic" decision to cooperate.[65] Blix's own impression was that "US leadership was planning for war at full steam ahead, with an option for calling it off in the unlikely event that Iraq cracked."[66]

Blix, like most observers, believed that military pressure remained essential to leverage concessions from Hussein. There were signs that the Iraqi dictator was bowing to the pressure, as many observers thought he would. Hussein said he did not want war. He invited the American broadcaster Dan Rather to Baghdad for an interview. He challenged President Bush to a debate. Most significantly, Hussein allowed the inspectors to blow up some illegal missiles.[67] If Hussein had more time, he might go further, thought Blix. More time might clarify the baffling enigma over whether the Iraqi regime did or did not possess prohibited weapons. Personally, Blix believed that Hussein was concealing WMD—that the Americans and the British were right. He lunched with the European Union heads of mission in New York on February 28 and told them that "there had been no change of heart, just more activity." "Iraq had attempted to conceal things." Nonetheless, he also emphasized that the inspectors had not yet found anything incriminating. Seeking to ascertain the real facts through some innovative approaches to complex technical issues, Blix was exasperated by American timelines. The inspection process, he believed, might work if the Americans would be patient.[68]

On March 1, UNMOVIC issued its quarterly report. It had conducted more than 550 inspections on 350 sites. Of these, 44 sites were new ones. Inspectors collected more than 200 chemical and more than 100 biological samples. Overall, the Iraqis had cooperated on process. They provided access promptly to all sites without advance notice. They facilitated the establishment of UNMOVIC's infrastructure to test and examine evidence. But the Iraqis had been less than forthcoming on "substance." They had not fully cooperated. They restricted access to scientists and responded belatedly and half-heartedly to requests for a presidential decree banning all work on WMD. Iraq "could have made greater efforts to find" proscribed items. "It is hard to understand," UNMOVIC concluded, "why a number of the measures, which are now being taken, could not have been initiated earlier. If they had been taken earlier, they might have borne fruit by now."[69]

A few days later, Blix summarized much of this report to the Security Council. He noted that even more progress had been made during the last few days. More interviews with scientists were now being arranged. Some illegal missiles actually had been destroyed under UNMOVIC supervision. Iraq now was offering thoughtful suggestions on how to use advanced technology to calculate the amounts of anthrax and VX precursors that had been destroyed and dumped at various sites over the last decade. In brief, "there had been an acceleration of initiatives from the Iraqi side since the end of January." But these recent initiatives, Blix stressed, "cannot be said to constitute 'immediate' cooperation," as required under Resolution 1441. Nor do they "cover all the areas of relevance."[70]

Blix wanted more time. Bush, Powell, and Rice said the game was over. Although they observed that the inspectors were not finding significant evidence of prohibited weapons, they remained certain that the regime was cheating and deceiving. Their exasperation with the inspection process was partly the result of their entrenched beliefs and partly the consequence of the Iraqi regime's behavior. In a retrospective analysis of the agency's errors, the CIA noted that Iraqi leaders "did not understand that they would have to take specific steps . . . to overcome perceptions of dishonesty." They mistakenly believed that "just presenting the truth would be enough to rectify past problems." But they did not just present the truth. Some Iraqi officials continued to conceal and deceive, mostly on small matters. Their actions assumed disproportionate significance because they reinforced perceptions of past misbehavior. Their "extreme distrust of outsiders" and their "fanatical devotion to security" sabotaged their efforts to cooperate. It was hard to grasp "that the Iraqis had undergone a change in their behavior."[71]

As a result, the policy of coercive diplomacy, which Blix did not invent, but which he had endorsed, now was approaching a denouement of which he disapproved.[72] Although he still felt that Hussein had not demonstrated a "strategic" decision to comply, Blix angrily reproached the Bush administration. American officials appeared to be saying: "The witches exist; you are appointed to deal with these witches; testing whether there are witches is only a dilution of the witch hunt."[73]

From the Bush administration's perspective, however, neither the diplomacy nor the coercion could be sustained. On the Security Council, the French and Russians made clear that they would veto a second resolution. The diplomatic unity that was intended to intimidate Hussein collapsed. To sustain the pressure, the United States needed to keep talking in New York while maintaining its military presence in the Persian Gulf region. Few observers doubted that if the pressure were lifted, Hussein would resume his pursuit of the prohibited weapons. "A sustained inspection and monitoring system," Blix acknowledged, would be required over the long run "to strike an alarm if there were any sign of revival of forbidden weapons programs." ElBaradei agreed.[74] But such a force could not be maintained in the theater indefinitely. It would be too costly; the summer would be too hot.

Hussein was not chastened. Iraqi documents and postwar interviews with his former advisers indicate that he was playing for time, trying to divide his adversaries, and scheming to reveal as little as possible. He feared he would show his own weakness—not so much to the Americans as to the Iranians and his domestic foes. He also worried about exposing his past cheating. His advisers and subordinates, knowing that their leader often spoke in many voices, but never sure which one was intended for them, were never certain how far they should go to offer information to the inspectors—even after Hussein instructed them to do so. "The regime oscillated between initiatives to destroy or hide information that could provoke doubt about Iraqi compliance and 'crash efforts' to ensure greater cooperation with the UN inspectors," writes Målfrid Braut-Hegghammer, the foremost scholar of Iraqi behavior regarding weapons of mass destruction.[75]

Saddam Hussein still hoped to outmaneuver the inspectors, and outfox the Bush administration. The Iraqi dictator was more fearful of his domestic enemies—more worried about internal uprisings—than about his American adversaries. He deemed Americans cowardly. He thought they "would not fight a ground war because it would be too costly," Tariq Aziz told his inquisitors after the war. When diplomatic pressure began, Hussein calculated that Washington would "not strike, or maybe they will only strike military targets." As American forces deployed, his thinking evolved, but his confidence did not wane. Hostilities might become inevitable, but he thought the fighting would be limited. Iraqis would resist. Washington would try to avoid casualties. His friends at the United Nations—the French and Russians—would seek a compromise solution. He would survive. Americans, Hussein calculated, would accept an outcome short of regime change. They "would attack for three or four days," recalled one of his artillery officers, "and then it would be over." Hussein thought he would win the game of chicken with the Americans.[76]

He was wrong. Bush despised his defiance. The president knew he was being tested. By March, US troops were poised to take action. Summer was coming. Their readiness would decline. Arab partners in the region were growing impatient, communicating their uncertainty about US resolve. Cheney believed strongly that American credibility was at risk. Rumsfeld felt the same way: failure to confront Iraq would send "a message to other nations that neither America nor any other nation was willing to stand in the way of their support for terrorism and pursuit of WMD." Bush had to face reality: coercive diplomacy was failing: "If we were to tell Saddam he had another chance—after declaring this was his last chance—we would shatter our credibility and embolden him." The president had a fateful choice, Hadley explained: "use it, or lose it," and he commented, "Do you basically walk away and allow Saddam Hussein . . . [to make] us look like paper tigers," or do you enforce the resolutions that he had been violating for a dozen years?[77]

Bush resolved to go to war. On March 17, he told the American people that the day of decision had arrived. His aim now was clear: "Saddam

Hussein and his sons must leave Iraq within 48 hours. Their refusal to do so will result in military conflict, commenced at the time of our choosing." Exasperated by Hussein's charade, by his scheming to gain time, by his toying with American power, Bush would tolerate it no more. The regime, he said, "had a record of reckless aggression." It hated America and its friends. It trained and harbored terrorists, including operatives of al Qaeda. "The danger is clear: Using chemical, biological, or, one day, nuclear weapons obtained with the help of Iraq, the terrorists could fulfill their stated ambitions and kill thousands or hundreds of thousands of innocent people in our country or any other."[78] You have to grasp "the nature of the man," Bush told reporters ten days earlier. "The risk of doing nothing, the risk of hoping that Saddam Hussein changes his mind and becomes a gentle soul, the risk that somehow—that inaction will make the world safer, is a risk I'm not willing to take for the American people."[79] His motives clear—protecting the American people, safeguarding America's credibility—he expressed hope that his actions would "advance liberty and peace in the region."[80]

The threat was real, Bush insisted again and again. "If I thought we were safe from attack, I would be thinking differently. But I see a gathering threat." At the same time, he felt confident of the outcome—confident that American power would prevail. He also felt sure of American innocence: "We did nothing to provoke that terrorist attack on 9/11," he proclaimed. Americans were the victims of an attack by enemies who hated them—who hated freedom. "We love freedom, and we're not changing," he declared.[81] Recognizing the gravity of his decision to wage war, he visited Walter Reed Hospital. "You are asking your fellow citizens to be courageous. . . . You are committing them to harm's way," he explained to the journalist Bob Woodward a year later. A president, Bush said, had a duty to comfort wounded warriors and their families. Ruminating, he revealed much that stirred his soul. "I don't need to steel myself with grief. I mean I don't need to remind myself what grief is about. I've been through September the 11th to grieve with the nation. I am a president who has been through a lot of moments of grief."[82]

Sensing threat, sure of American power, convinced of American victimhood, and confident of American virtue and values, Bush pitted his resolve against Hussein's defiance. He assured reporters that he had calculated the costs of inaction against the risks of action.[83] In January and February 2003, at the request of the State Department's Policy Planning office, the National Intelligence Council (NIC) actually had produced two thoughtful assessments of the regional consequences and principal challenges of a post-Hussein Iraq. In these studies, intelligence analysts throughout the government identified prospective dangers as well as prospective benefits. While Iraq was not likely to break apart, they believed, there "was a significant chance that domestic groups would engage in violent conflict with each other unless an occupying force prevented them from doing so." A successor government would be unlikely to support terrorism, but "if Baghdad were unable to exert control over the Iraqi countryside, al Qaida and other terrorist groups could operate from remote areas." Although political Islam was likely to be bolstered, at least in the short run, the terrorist threat would probably decline in three to five years. According to the intelligence analysts, "The building of an Iraqi democracy would be a long, difficult and probably turbulent process." Even if successful, "the exemplar of a more politically liberal Iraq would not, by itself, be a catalyst for more wide-ranging political and economic change throughout the region." Policymakers must realize that an Iraqi defeat "would be a jarring event" in the Arab world, equivalent to the "psychological shocks" of 1948 (when Palestine was divided and Israel founded). War and occupation/liberation, concluded the NIC, might have "similarly wide-ranging and unpredictable consequences."[84]

The president and his principal advisers did not examine these studies carefully or calculate trade-offs systematically. But they were not unmindful of the weighty consequences of their intended use of military force. In fact, on February 28, as he was about to authorize military action, President Bush turned to his advisers and asked: had they thought enough about "what we want to see in Iraq"? Had they thought enough about how to "hold people accountable"? Had they thought enough about how to "keep things going within the country"? Had they thought enough about how to "provide services to the Iraqi people"?[85]

Had they thought enough?

9

Mission Awry

GENERAL TOMMY FRANKS, the head of CENTCOM, set the goals of his war plan in December 2001: change the regime and eliminate its weapons of mass destruction. Secretary of Defense Donald Rumsfeld put his imprimatur on those goals. If the president should decide to go to war, Saddam Hussein would no longer be the ruler of Iraq and his weapons of mass destruction would be seized and destroyed. "The aim," Rumsfeld said, "was not to bestow on it an American-style democracy, a capitalist economy, or a world-class military force." If Iraqis were inclined toward liberal democracy, that was well and good, but it was not Rumsfeld's central objective: "we could start them on their way and wish them well."[1]

Condoleezza Rice, George W. Bush's national security adviser, knew that the president for whom she worked had a different orientation. If he went to war, he wanted to help give birth to a free Iraq. Inspired by religious conviction, convinced that God wanted all humankind to be free, and recalling the joy expressed by East Germans, Poles, and Hungarians when the Berlin Wall came down, he thought in terms of a liberation strategy. In early August 2002, Rice injected Bush's thinking into a paper her team presented to the other principal makers of national strategy. It was not well received. Rumsfeld and his under secretary of defense, Douglas Feith, stressed that democracy was not their endgame. They would measure success by ending "the dangers posed by Iraq"—its possession of weapons of mass destruction (WMD), its support for terrorism, its threatening behavior, and its tyranny. If they accomplished those goals, "we would have achieved a highly valuable victory—even if the Iraqis were slow or unable to build a stable democracy."[2]

This paper, "Goals, Objectives, Strategy," was revised and approved by the president in late August 2002. Unfortunately, it did not clarify priorities. Feith acknowledged, "There was no actual meeting of the minds across the National Security Council on how to formulate our objectives for the post-Saddam Iraqi government."[3] The president himself did not communicate strong convictions, other than his contempt and hatred for Saddam Hussein, his wish to end oppression, and his zeal for freedom. His advisers knew he was motivated principally by his concerns about American security. They did not spend time discussing democracy-promotion, nation-building, or related matters. "I didn't hear rhetoric about democracy from Colin Powell or State Department officials," wrote Rumsfeld. "I know it did not come from those of us in the Department of Defense."[4]

There was discussion about a fundamental question—who would rule Iraq after Hussein was deposed—but no resolution. Officials in the Office of the Secretary of Defense and the Department of State clashed. Rumsfeld and his aides wanted to hand power to Iraqis as quickly as possible, meaning the leaders of the exile groups with whom they had long had contact. State Department officials in charge of Middle Eastern affairs, like Assistant Secretary of State William Burns, and his deputy, Ryan Crocker, believed that these Iraqi exiles were too divided among themselves. They hoped to identify leaders inside Iraq who could garner popular support, a process that would require time and patience. In the interval, they favored the establishment of a Transitional Civil Authority to govern Iraq. It would be led by the United States, in collaboration with other international authorities or institutions. These officials maintained that the United States and its coalition partners could not ignore the hard reality: they would constitute an occupation authority, even though they liked to talk about a liberation strategy.[5]

Feith and Peter Rodman, the assistant secretary of defense for international security affairs, disliked the State Department approach. Rodman warned Rumsfeld: "There are bad guys all over Iraq—radical Shia, Communists, Wahhabis, al-Qaeda—who will strive to fill the political vacuum. An occupation government will only delay the process of unifying the moderate forces. The best hope for filling the vacuum is to prepare Iraqis to do it." Rumsfeld needed little convincing. He did not plan to become enmeshed in postwar Iraqi politics and did not want the military to be tied down in protracted peacekeeping and stabilization missions, as had been the case in Bosnia and Kosovo. He said again and again that he wanted to relinquish governing responsibility to Iraqis as quickly as possible.[6]

But to which Iraqis? The debate within the administration got heated because State Department officials believed that their counterparts in OSD wanted to hand power to Ahmed Chalabi, the head of the Iraqi National Congress (INC). Chalabi was a controversial figure, with a distinguished ancestry inside Iraq, considerable wealth, impeccable English, and an unsavory reputation for financial chicanery and untrustworthiness. Educated in the United States and Great Britain, he grasped American idioms and instincts, talked about democracy, networked incessantly, and maintained ongoing contacts with Hussein's foes inside Iraq. Over the years, with the help of the CIA, his exile group—the INC—gained considerable visibility and influence. Nonetheless, George Tenet, the head of the CIA, and many of his subordinates inside the agency, as well as colleagues inside the State Department, deeply distrusted him. They also hated the influence that they thought Chalabi exerted inside the Pentagon.[7] The truth of the matter was that neither Rumsfeld nor Wolfowitz had a strong commitment to make Chalabi the new leader of a post-Saddam Iraq. But they did wish to transfer power rapidly to Iraqis they knew well, or believed they could trust. They constantly pushed the State Department to help arrange meetings with exile leaders.[8]

Marc Grossman, the under secretary of state; Ryan Crocker, the deputy assistant secretary of state for Near Eastern Affairs; and Zal Khalilzad, Rice's NSC expert, worked with Feith's subordinates to make these meetings a success—to try to establish a consensus among the Iraqi exile groups about the makeup and governing principles of a new Iraq. They helped orchestrate a successful meeting in London in December 2002. The State Department and NSC officials saw themselves as honest brokers among the disparate exile groups. They would not tip the scales in favor of Chalabi.[9]

President Bush knew his advisers were wrangling over the nature and composition of a post-Saddam government. He worried that too much publicity on this issue would undermine his efforts to conduct coercive diplomacy; too much talk about a postwar government would divert attention from inspections and disarmament. Bush, therefore, delayed the establishment of a formal planning group to resolve some of the issues bedeviling his advisers. Assuming he would be liberating Iraq, not occupying it, he instinctively shied away from determining who would run Iraq should an invasion take place and regime change occur. "I felt strongly," he later wrote, "that the Iraqis' first leader should be someone they selected." Notwithstanding all the talk about Chalabi, notwithstanding all the machinations that were orchestrated in his behalf, the US president did not intend to put him in charge of a provisional government. "No decisions have been reached on the post-Saddam governance of Iraq," OSD officials acknowledged in mid-January 2003.[10]

Bush and his principal advisers did meet frequently with General Tommy Franks to assess the evolution of the war plans. But they paid little attention to Phase IV, the stability operations that would be implemented after combat was over. Franks himself gave this matter little attention. At a meeting in December 2002, he astonished General Dick Myers, the chairman of the Joint Chiefs of Staff, when he declared that his job as CENTCOM commander was over once he took Baghdad. General John Abizaid, at the time the director of the Joint Staff, recognized that inadequate attention was being focused on the post-combat period. He, therefore, assigned General George Casey to take charge of planning for the period after hostilities would cease.[11]

Casey was a good choice because he had had extensive experience in the Balkans in the 1990s. He grasped the myriad problems that would need to be addressed, including food, electricity, oil production, water purification, and security. He was certain the postwar occupation would be prolonged, at least five years. Casey assumed the military would initially take control, a requirement that he believed could not be avoided under international law. Then, the military would hand off control to some civilian authority that, in turn, would relinquish power to Iraqis. Casey tried to coordinate inter-agency discussions between State and OSD officials, but lamented that they could not agree on which department would assume responsibility during the transition process. Nor (in his view) did they grasp the complex nature of many postwar issues.[12]

Although much remained unresolved, President Bush had reason to assume that serious planning was going on. Inside the Office of the Secretary of Defense, Feith established an Office of Special Plans to deal with the challenges the administration would face after a prospective invasion. Elsewhere in the military establishment, as noted above, there was Casey's team inside the Pentagon and Franks's planners at CENTCOM. In addition, Lieutenant General David D. McKiernan, in charge of the land forces assigned to the invasion of Iraq, dedicated part of his own staff to design post-combat operations. At the State Department, Secretary of State Powell authorized the Future of Iraq Project under the direction of Tom Warrick and his colleagues in the Office of Near Eastern Affairs. Warrick assembled seventeen working groups, composed of academicians, Iraqi émigrés, and State Department experts. In thirteen volumes and 2,000 pages they examined the most salient issues that Iraq would face after Hussein fell from power. The US Agency for International Development (AID) drew on its past experiences with humanitarian assistance and reconstruction efforts abroad and prepared its own studies on electricity, water, public health, education, and other critical matters. In the West Wing of the White House, Hadley assigned NSC staff members to study relief, refugees, oil, and security issues. He asked Elliott Abrams to head a group examining Iraq's humanitarian and reconstruction needs; and he tasked Franklin Miller, a longtime DoD civil servant and senior director for defense at the NSC, to work with General Casey to form an executive steering group to coordinate initiatives across the government.[13]

Yet neither Bush, nor Cheney, nor Rumsfeld, nor Powell, nor Rice, nor Tommy Franks paid a great deal of attention to all these efforts. They focused on the diplomacy at the United Nations, on the inspections in Iraq, and on the forces and tactics that would be required to vanquish Iraqi forces and topple Hussein. They did not concentrate on prospective developments inside Iraq after Hussein disappeared. "I did not think," wrote Rumsfeld, that "resolving other countries' internal political disputes, paving roads, erecting power lines, policing streets, building stock markets, and organizing democratic govern-mental bodies were missions for our men and women in uniform."[14]

Inside the State Department, even inside the Pentagon, and across the ocean inside British ministries, officials remonstrated about the inattention being paid to the post-hostilities period. Bill Burns, the assistant secretary of state for Near Eastern Affairs, informed Powell that key issues about postwar governance remained unresolved. In the Defense Department, Feith's subordinates alerted him to the treach-erous security situation US troops might face after combat ended. At CENTCOM, officers recognized that planning for civilian stabiliza-tion and reconstruction lacked clarity.[15] British prime minister Tony Blair was alerted to the differences among US departments and recog-nized that "aftermath planning was still quite immature." On January 24, 2003, he told President Bush that "the biggest risk" they faced in postwar Iraq would be "internecine fighting" and that they needed ad-ditional time to design more coherent plans.[16]

Nonetheless, the flawed process persisted through early 2003. The official US Army history of the war in Iraq says that the military planning for Phase IV was "insufficiently detailed and largely uncoordinated."[17] General Casey blamed Rumsfeld and Franks. Rumsfeld wanted to exit Iraq as soon as the wartime goals were achieved, and those aims were limited to finding Hussein's WMD arsenal and eliminating the evil dictator himself. His attitude, Casey stressed, "corroded postwar planning."[18] So did Feith's contempt for his counterparts at State and on Rice's NSC staff. Elliott Abrams remem-bered that when he and experts from the Office of Management and Budget assessed Iraq's food and health systems, DoD "just blew us off. We stopped, went away, and went home." The behavior of Rumsfeld and Feith infuriated many of their colleagues, but Bush and Rice and Hadley did little to heal the mounting tension.[19]

They did, however, seek to address the underlying, fundamental issue: coordinating the diffuse initiatives that were going on in many government agencies. In December 2002, Rice and Hadley decided to create a postwar planning office inside the Pentagon, reporting directly to Rumsfeld. Bush authorized this decision in a formal na-tional security policy directive. Secretary of State Powell agreed that this arrangement made sense. The new Office for Reconstruction and Humanitarian Assistance (ORHA) was charged with responsibility for "detailed planning across the spectrum of issues that the United States Government would face with respect to the post-war administration of Iraq." These tasks included the provision of humanitarian assistance; the dismantling of WMD; defeating terrorist networks; protecting natural resources and infrastructure; facilitating economic reconstruction; re-establishing civilian services like food supplies, water, and electricity; "reshaping" the Iraqi military and other security organizations; and "supporting the transition to Iraqi-led authority over time." The new "planning office" was to draw on previous interagency studies and receive "policy guidance" from the principal and deputy members of the national security council and their subordinates. According to the president's policy directive, the new office would deploy to Iraq and "form the nucleus of the administrative apparatus" that would help administer Iraq for a limited period of time. It would involve Iraqis themselves, initially in an advisory role, and would solicit advice from other governments as well as non-governmental and international organizations. The presidential directive requested other departments and agencies of the US government to assign "detailees" to the Department of Defense to staff the new office by January 24.[20]

Rumsfeld appointed Jay Garner to head the new office. He was a retired lieutenant general who had led a mission to northern Iraq in 1991 to help secure an autonomous region for the Kurds and to provide them with relief. Rumsfeld worked on a space commission with Garner in the 1990s and had been impressed. The secretary of defense asked Garner to serve for a short period, after which he would turn over his responsibilities to a more experienced diplomat or politician. "General Garner believed, as I did," wrote Rumsfeld, "in empowering local populations to do things for themselves. . . . I thought it was strategically important to put the United States in a supporting role to the Iraqis as soon as possible."[21]

Garner labored to put together a staff and assess the resources he would need. His mandate was short-term, but huge. He did not feel that Rumsfeld grasped the magnitude of the issues yet he praised the defense secretary for seeking to integrate the entire postwar civilian enterprise. Garner met several times with Rice to request resources, and found her polite yet unforthcoming. He spent most of his time during February struggling to recruit talent in particular agencies and departments. He was hampered by the "clash of titans," meaning the constant, never-ending bickering between Rumsfeld's subordinates and Powell's subordinates as well as between the secretaries themselves. Rumsfeld did not want various State Department people working for Garner; he wanted to pick and choose. Powell threatened to withhold all help. Garner navigated between them, trying hard to ignore their feuding.[22] He assembled as many experts as he could, almost 100, and convened them at Fort McNair, National Defense University, on February 21 and 22, 2003. They tried to review all the planning initiatives that had been going on. They knew they were "behind the curve in almost every aspect." They believed that postwar success was achievable, "*but* only if funds and full complement of staff are made available *now*."[23]

Although Garner thought it was a worthwhile meeting that underscored the many gaps and ambiguities that had to be resolved, many attendees judged it a disaster. Experts on Ryan Crocker's staff at the State Department's Bureau of Near Eastern Affairs told him the meeting "lacked organization, focus, direction, purpose." Seth Carus, one of Cheney's bioterrorist experts, said his friends who participated in the meeting were stunned: "Nobody in the room had a clue what we were going to be doing the day after we took Baghdad." Elliott Abrams, the NSC staffer who attended the meeting at Fort McNair, was appalled. He did not think that Garner knew what he was doing. He did not report that assessment to Hadley or Rice. But Eric Edelman, Cheney's assistant, told the vice president after the first day of the meeting that many issues remained unresolved, that supplemental funding was crucial, and that it was indispensable to determine who would be in charge after Hussein was removed.[24]

The two-day meeting "exposed problems created by the disjointed postwar preparations," the Inspector General's report on Iraqi reconstruction subsequently concluded. Most significantly, the attendees at Fort McNair highlighted the postwar security question. At one point during the discussions, Ambassador George Ward, ORHA's humanitarian overseer, asked, "How am I going to protect humanitarian convoys, humanitarian staging areas, humanitarian distribution points?" A CENTCOM officer replied flippantly, "Hire war lords." There are warlords in Afghanistan, thought Ward, not Iraq. "At that point," Ward ruminated, "I thought this was going to fail because no one is paying serious attention to civilian security." CENTCOM made it clear: they "would be strapped for forces." If the ground war went as fast as some expected, if the regime collapsed suddenly, if there was "catastrophic success" on the battlefield, coalition forces would not be in place for Phase IV stability operations, and overall US strategic objectives might be put at risk. Garner grasped the reality: "we wouldn't have enough security."[25]

Rumsfeld's subordinates also recognized the problem. Inside Feith's office, Chris Lamb, a deputy assistant secretary of defense for plans, informed his superiors that "Historically, the US has struggled with reestablishing and maintaining public order and safety during and after military operations. Civil disturbances, looting, and ethnic violence have marred operations in the past." He pointed out that, "currently, the fundamental planning assumption about maintaining order is that swift combat operations will limit large civil disturbances." The same fundamental assumption, he emphasized, had shaped "Operation Just Cause in Panama and proved wrong; massive civil disorder began almost immediately." Noting the shortage of forces that were being assigned to the entire Iraqi enterprise, Lamb thought "it is worth trying to use the Civil Police." Acknowledging that this effort might not work, he also recommended the preparation of a Quick Reaction Force and stressed that "US/Coalition forces must be effective at maintaining order and safety from the outset of the campaign." Feith told Lamb to rework the style of his memorandum yet paid little attention to its substance. He did not send the memo to Rumsfeld. Nor did he press the matter with General Franks. "I wished I had made more of our analysis on the importance of maintaining public order," Feith subsequently wrote in his memoir.[26]

Even if Lamb's ideas were prescient, he did not address critical details. Could coalition forces leverage the National Civil Police to maintain order? Could a Quick Reaction Force be mobilized in a timely way to "minimize the potential escalation of disorder"? Rice tried to get Bush to focus his own attention on such matters—on "rear area security," as she called the issue. When she arranged a meeting in early February with top generals, the president began the session in a totally dismissive way, "This is something that Condi has wanted to talk about," sending a signal that he himself was not much concerned. "If he wasn't interested in this issue," Rice realized, "why should they care?" She resolved to raise the matter anew. At subsequent meetings, the president did press Franks about whether he was on top of "the law and order issue." Franks told him not to worry. "It's covered," he insisted, "every village will have a mayor, a lieutenant, captains, a structure."[27]

Except that it wasn't covered. Decisions were not made about which headquarters would assume responsibility for stability operations once combat ended. The Third Infantry Division, for example, transitioned into Phase IV "in the absence of guidance," according to its "After-Action Report." "Higher headquarters did not provide [it] with a plan for Phase IV." On the eve of the invasion, as General David Petraeus was preparing to lead the 82nd Airborne Division into Iraq, he asked what he was supposed to do when he got to Baghdad. What then? He got no answer.[28]

Some Army officers were paying attention. At a committee hearing of the Armed Services Committee on February 25, Senator Carl Levin asked General Eric Shinseki, the Army's chief of staff, how large a force would be required to preserve stability after hostilities ended. Shinseki tried to evade the query. When pressed, he said, "Something on the order of several hundred thousand soldiers." Rumsfeld and Wolfowitz were outraged by the comment, which was widely reported in the press. A few days later, at another hearing, Wolfowitz raised the issue and said that number "was wildly off the mark."[29]

While President Bush did not pursue the matter, Jay Garner did not think that Shinseki was wildly off the mark. To preserve stability, Garner, too, thought the United States would require several hundred thousand troops. Garner was most worried about preventing oil fields from burning, feeding displaced refugees, and stopping the spread of cholera that might be catalyzed by damaged sewage systems, impure water supplies, and other sanitation problems. Beyond these issues, however, Garner knew that after combat ended the generals to whom he reported—Franks, Abizaid, and McKiernan—were counting on him to preserve civil order by bringing back the Iraqi army, some 250,000 soldiers.[30]

This matter—what to do with the Iraqi army—was among the most critical postwar issues that Bush and his top advisers addressed, however belatedly, during a series of meetings during the first two weeks of March. Feith's office had been studying the matter, along with the Joint Staff, since January. They recommended the elimination of Iraqi military organizations that were tainted by Ba'thite ideology and human rights abuses, like Hussein's bodyguards, the Special Security Organization, the Special Republican Guard, the Fedayeen, and the Qods force. While some individuals needed to be prosecuted, OSD officials recognized that most personnel of these organizations needed to be retrained and re-integrated: "employment is crucial to averting crime and terrorism." The Iraqi army, however, was not to be disbanded. In a March 7 paper, the Joint Staff noted that it was impossible "to immediately demobilize 250k–300k personnel and put [them] on the street." It made more sense to use the army "as a national reconstruction force" during the transitional phase of the postwar timetable. In a meeting on March 10, Garner presented these ideas to the president and his top advisers. He explained that Iraqi army personnel would be demobilized, reorganized, and put to work on the most important reconstruction projects. He envisioned something akin to the Civilian Conservation Corps during the Great Depression in the United States. Bush, Cheney, Powell, Tenet, and Rice embraced this vision, the core of which had emanated from the Pentagon.[31]

At the same time, the president decided to create an Iraq Interim Authority (IIA), an institutional apparatus to help govern Iraq in the immediate aftermath of war. The Department of State fought the proposal, believing that Rumsfeld and subordinates were conniving to anoint Chalabi as Hussein's successor. After overthrowing Hussein and defeating his forces, Powell, Armitage, and Burns wanted the US military to transfer control to some newly created international authority that would, in turn, eventually cede power to a more representative group of Iraqis. OSD officials bristled at these proposals. They favored a swift transition to Iraqis. They did not want international interference, and they hoped to give a "head start" to those Iraqis who shared American values. At an NSC meeting on March 10, President Bush said he supported "the formation of an Interim Iraq Authority as soon as possible after liberation." But it must not be handed over to the Iraqi exiles. The summary conclusion of the meeting stipulated that "The IIA should include internal Iraqis, Kurds, and external oppositionists. . . . We must ensure that internal Iraqis be fully represented." As for its responsibilities, the NSC conclusion was vague. The IIA could represent Iraq at the United Nations and claim Iraq's frozen assets. The ministries would migrate "to full Iraqi control as soon as possible." With the exception of the finance and "power" ministries, they would possess "limited but increasing authority." Rather than rejecting the entirety of the State Department's view, the NSC, with Bush's imprimatur, embraced the idea of a UN resolution that would, among other things, appoint a UN representative to "assist in political facilitation and national reconciliation."[32]

If the authority, responsibilities, and membership of the IIA remained vague, the administration's policy regarding de-Ba'thification was even more ambiguous. This topic was also addressed at the NSC meeting on March 10. Bush's advisers agreed that coalition forces would announce the termination of the Ba'th dictatorship and dissolve the Ba'th Party. Most "Iraqis despise the Ba'ath Party as a symbol of dictatorship," thought OSD officials. Although no one in administration circles disputed this notion, there was considerable uncertainty about how far the victorious forces should go in punishing its members. Those individuals responsible for crimes against humanity and for constituting pillars of the regime would need to be removed from office, but most members of the Ba'th Party were thought to be "opportunists." They had joined because it was expedient to do so and had no real ideological commitment to Hussein's brutal regime. Moreover, their competence was needed to administer and rebuild the country. De-Ba'thification, Feith's assistants said, should be a gradual process, left mostly to the Iraqis, and they might well be advised to establish a Truth and Reconciliation Committee to heal the wounds that permeated their society.[33]

At the NSC meeting on March 10, Frank Miller presented some guidelines that he and his NSC colleagues had designed to balance competing impulses: cleanse and penalize on the one hand; co-opt, reform, and employ on the other. The plan focused on the top 1 percent of a party that numbered approximately 1.5 to 2 million Iraqis. When President Bush questioned the wisdom of punishing as many as 25,000 Iraqis, Miller explained that most of these individuals would not be tried and imprisoned—they would simply be excluded from future government service. Nothing definite was resolved, but there was general accord that it would be prudent to take a lenient approach in order to preserve the future administrative capacity of the country.[34]

That was the state of postwar planning when President Bush informed his "fellow citizens" on March 19 that coalition forces had begun striking selected targets in Iraq to emasculate Hussein's ability to wage war.[35] That very night, Bush unexpectedly authorized a cruise missile attack on Dora Farms, the location where intelligence analysts thought they had spotted Hussein and his sons. The president hoped to take out the regime's leadership, spark a coup, and perhaps avoid a full-scale war.[36] Failing to do so, US military leaders realized the United States had alerted the regime to an impending invasion. Generals Franks and McKiernan determined to attack immediately. With the help of the British First Armored Division and Polish and Australian naval vessels, coalition forces moved swiftly from Kuwait, where they had been assembling, toward Basra, seized the port of Umm Qasr, and secured the southern oil fields. More than fifty detachments of Special Forces parachuted into northern and western Iraq. In the western desert, they captured airfields, searched for SCUD missile sites and weapons of mass destruction, and blocked escape routes. In the north, these Special Forces units linked up with troops from the Kurdish Democratic Party and the Patriotic Union of Kurdistan. They helped the Kurds fight Hussein's fleeing army, and then headed to Kirkuk to thwart any Kurdish attempt to take the city. They also destroyed the Ansar al-Islam terrorist enclaves near Halabjah and Sharqat.

The main thrust of the American attack, however, headed straight toward Baghdad, spearheaded by the US Army's Third Infantry Division, its 101st and 82nd Airborne Divisions, and the Marines First Expeditionary Force. They encountered scant resistance from the Iraqi army, but faced fierce assaults from Hussein's Fedayeen units that had been deployed secretly to southern cities. Initially, Generals McKiernan and William S. Wallace intended to bypass these cities, but realized they had to secure supply and communication lines. They did so during a terrible sandstorm that otherwise stymied the offensive from March 24 to 27. When conditions improved, the Third Infantry Division headed toward Najaf, seized bridges over the Euphrates, cleared the Karbala

Gap, and set its sights on Baghdad. On April 3 and 4, the division's First Brigade secured the airport. From April 5 to 10, US forces surrounded Baghdad. Daring raids—so-called thunder-runs—into the very heart of the city stunned Iraqi defenders, and emboldened US commanders to hold the center of the Iraqi capital. Iraqi resistance melted away and the regime collapsed. Hussein and his sons fled. On April 9, some US Marines symbolically helped Iraqis to pull down Hussein's statue in Firdos Square, while British forces consolidated their hold over Basra in the south. In less than three weeks, the war seemed won.[37]

Images of jubilant Iraqis celebrating in the streets of Baghdad thrilled US officials. Condi Rice hurried into the Oval Office while the president was meeting with Kanan Makiya, a prominent Iraqi exile, and Vice President Dick Cheney. It felt like 1991, Rice subsequently wrote, "when statues of Joseph Stalin were tumbling across Eastern Europe." Looking at the president, she exclaimed, "You did this." Bush seemed lost in his own thoughts, while Cheney and Makiya rejoiced and hugged one another.[38] Satisfaction, gratification, and vindication coursed through the halls of the Pentagon and the West Wing of the White House.

The very next day, April 10, the White House sent a videotaped message to the people of Iraq. "This is George W. Bush, the President of the United States. At this moment, the regime of Saddam Hussein is being removed from power, and a long era of fear and cruelty is ending. . . . Coalition forces will help maintain law and order so that Iraqis can live in security. We will respect your great religious traditions. . . . We will help you build a peaceful and representative government that protects the rights of all citizens. And then our military forces will leave."[39]

Rhetorical tropes of freedom and tantalizing visions of a transformed Iraq began punctuating President Bush's remarks. "If we must use force," President Bush declared in a speech at the American Enterprise Institute, he hoped a liberated Iraq "would show the power of freedom" to reshape the entire Middle East.[40] Visiting wounded warriors at Walter Reed Hospital and the National Naval Medical Center on April 11, he expressed appreciation for their sacrifices and exclaimed: "I don't think I'll ever forget . . . the statue of Saddam Hussein falling in Baghdad, and then seeing the jubilation on the faces of ordinary Iraqis as they realized . . . the first signs of freedom." He then underscored his original intent: "I committed our troops because I believe that Saddam Hussein and his regime posed a threat to the American people, posed a threat to anybody who loves freedom." With that danger removed, attention could shift to a brighter future. "We're working to make sure America is more secure, but we're also making sure that the Iraqi people can be free." Freedom was America's founding principle, its fundamental canon. "We believe in freedom," said Bush. "We believe that freedom is a gift from the Almighty God for every person." With freedom would come progress. "Day by day, hour by hour, life in Iraq is getting better for the citizens."[41]

On May 1, in an elaborately choreographed media event, the president donned a flight jacket, sat in the front seat of a fixed-wing jet aircraft, and chatted amiably as the plane's pilot landed the jet on an aircraft carrier near the coast of San Diego. Standing under a huge banner, "Mission Accomplished," President Bush announced the end of combat operations and thanked the crew that had recently returned from the Persian Gulf. "In the battle of Iraq, the United States and our allies have prevailed." Voicing pride in the accomplishment, he reminded everyone that "We have fought for the cause of liberty, and for the peace of the world." Yet no one should forget that "the liberation of Iraq is a crucial advance in the campaign against terror." Regimes that proffered aid to terrorists would remain at risk. But those who loved freedom could be sure that America would befriend them.[42]

Yet the mission was already going awry, and the president was mightily aware of it. At an NSC meeting in late April, behind closed doors with his top advisers, he exclaimed, "What the hell is happening? Why isn't anybody stopping the looters?"[43] Anarchy reigned in Baghdad. "We found the city in utter chaos," said one of the police advisers sent by the Justice Department to assist Garner's ORHA mission. "Corpses littered the streets, AK-47 fire was near constant, and looters operated with impunity." Rioters destroyed seventeen of the regime's twenty-three ministry buildings. "They stripped the electrical wires out of the wall," said one US adviser, and then "they stripped most of the plumbing out, and then they set the buildings on fire." Another ORHA adviser wryly noted, "We would say they took everything but the kitchen sink, [but] they took that too." The looting, moreover, morphed into organized theft by gangs. Millions of dollars in cash were stolen from the vaults of banks, as were the contents of safety deposit boxes. Munition depots around the country were raided; thousands of tons of munitions disappeared.[44]

US military commanders were completely unprepared for the situation they encountered. They had ruminated about the problems of "catastrophic success," but had not planned for them. Their quick victory avoided a humanitarian crisis and thwarted the burning of oil fields and the destruction of dams, yet left troops ill-positioned and short-handed to deal with the lawlessness and disorder. They were not prepared to declare martial law. They did not clarify the rules of engagement for dealing with private Iraqi citizens. They did not know how to deal with looters, dissidents, and violent demonstrators. They had tanks and artillery, but insufficient military police, engineers, and contractors. "The President announced that our national goal was 'regime change,'" commented the "After-Action" report of the Third Infantry Division, Mechanized. Yet there was no plan to deal with "the obvious consequences" of regime collapse. Although there was "virtual certainty" that the US forces would overthrow Hussein's government, "there was no plan for oversight and reconstruction, even after the division arrived in Baghdad." General Wallace, commander of US Army V Corps, agreed. "When we decapitated the regime, everything below it fell apart. The regime officials were gone; the folks that provided security of the ministry buildings had gone; the folks that operated the water treatment plants and the electricity grid were gone. There were no bus drivers, no taxi drivers, everybody just went home."[45]

The scenario was made worse by Rumsfeld's decisions.[46] The defense secretary kept a keen eye on the flow of forces, and remained committed to a light footprint. Sensing a quick victory, he "off-ramped" the First Cavalry Division and ordered the quick withdrawal of the Third Infantry Division, leaving General McKiernan with far fewer troops than he expected for Phase IV stability operations. According to the Army's official history, McKiernan was "dumbfounded" by this decision. When he discussed it with Tommy Franks, his commanding officer, he was given explicit guidance: "we're not staying and we're going to take as much risk leaving Iraq as we did attacking Iraq." As a result, far fewer forces were available to secure the country than had been anticipated. When Baghdad fell, commented General Petraeus, hundreds of thousands of people roamed the streets; mobs were in control; US troops could hardly move. There were insufficient forces to protect infrastructure and control ammunition dumps. "An orgy of looting" took place. "No one at CENTCOM," or in the military command inside Iraq, concluded a detailed postwar assessment by the Army's Combat Studies Institute, "had any concrete understanding" of what needed to be done and by whom.[47]

In Washington, Rice grasped the situation. She realized that "there was a serious manpower shortage in Baghdad." But when the president asked his secretary of defense if there were enough troops on the ground, Rumsfeld assured him there were. General Franks, the coalition's supreme commander, did not argue with his defense secretary. Franks was eager to celebrate his combat victory and retire. He did not deem civilian governance to be his responsibility. The newest version of the postwar plan, Eclipse II, assigned postwar governance and security to ORHA.[48]

Jay Garner, the head of ORHA, was experiencing great difficulty just getting into Iraq. He and his senior staff members left Washington on March 16. When they got to Kuwait, there was no room for them to encamp with the military planners working for Franks and McKiernan. "CENTCOM treated ORHA's requests as low priority," concluded the report of the Special Inspector General for Iraqi Reconstruction in 2009. Franks would not even allow Garner to go to Baghdad to begin his work, insisting that conditions in the capital were too dangerous. In an angry exchange, Garner told Franks that they both knew that "vacuums are being created" and were being filled with bad guys. "The only way to prevent" these threatening outcomes was "to get us in there."[49] Franks relented. On April 21, Garner and his team arrived in Baghdad. They were staggered by the chaos, looting, and disorder. They located in one of Hussein's palaces. Like so much else, it was in "shambles." There were no bathrooms; no running water; nothing![50]

Garner had three priorities: staffing the ministries, recruiting Iraqi army personnel and civilian police for reconstruction and security purposes, and facilitating the formation of the Iraqi Interim Authority. He had been sent detailed instructions for securing key Baghdad institutions including ministry buildings, the Central Bank, and the

Iraqi Museum, but by the time he arrived most ministry buildings had been destroyed. More than that, the files and records that he was told to secure already had vanished. Employees did not show up for work; indeed, there was nowhere for them to go. Worse yet, there was no way for ORHA officials to reach the Iraqi employees; communication systems did not exist, except among the US and coalition military entities. Robin Raphel, for example, the US designee to oversee the ministry of trade, walked the streets of Baghdad with an interpreter asking, "Do you know anybody who's in the ministry of trade?" Recruiting workers to staff the ministries, securing communications, acquiring paper, phones, and records were nightmares, especially when so few of the Americans knew any Arabic. "You [had] a case of the so-called Hobbesian world," said General Petraeus, "without the Leviathan to impose order."[51]

Garner wanted to grapple with the lawless environment, and start to restore infrastructure. He called Rumsfeld and said, "You've got to stop this. You can't pull troops out. In fact, we probably need more right now." Rumsfeld listened politely and did nothing. Coalition commanders grasped that they were facing an incipient insurrectionary environment. General John Abizaid, now the number two person at CENTCOM, exclaimed, "We've got a guerrilla war going on here, and we'd better get control of this thing."[52] Franks moved some additional troops to Baghdad to help restore order, but he and Rumsfeld nonetheless decided to replace McKiernan's headquarters and to further reduce combat forces. Garner's mission, they agreed, should take "precedence" over the military enterprise.[53]

Garner believed he had a mandate from the administration to mobilize Iraqi soldiers for the purposes of preserving order and expediting reconstruction. The Iraqi army, however, did not surrender; it disintegrated and evaporated. Organized units did not lay down their arms and return to their barracks, as Franks had ordered them to do. Instead, soldiers took off their uniforms and fled with their arms. Garner and local commanders, like General Petraeus, wanted to find these men and lure them back into service. Garner was trying to arrange salaries to pay them. He thought Franks was relying on him "to bring back the Iraqi army." His job, he thought, was not to disband the Iraqi army, but to reform and repurpose it.[54]

Garner also was trying to help configure the Iraqi Interim Authority. He was collaborating with Zal Khalilzad, the NSC staffer, whom the president had appointed as a special envoy for this purpose. Powell and Rice also had sent Ryan Crocker to assist Khalilzad. Although the special envoy was well aware that senior policymakers "were schizophrenic" about the degree of authority to be transferred to the Iraqis, Khalilzad believed his instructions were clear: "I was charged with organizing the process to enable Iraqis, both the external opposition and internal leaders, to form an interim government as soon as possible."[55] Garner thought that was precisely what he, too, aimed to accomplish. First, they met with over 100 Iraqi exiles and internal leaders at Nasiriyah on April 15. On April 22, Garner met with Kurdish leaders and appealed to them to heal their own feuding and join an interim authority that he was trying to assemble. On April 28, the Americans met with an even larger group of Iraqis in Baghdad. The Iraqis yearned to form a provisional government; Khalilzad and Garner seemed to be prodding them in that direction. Ali Allawi, one of the Iraqi exile leaders, felt that it was "Clear to the participants that the USA . . . was keen to accelerate the process that would lead to an Iraqi-led government."[56]

Yet Garner's intent might have been as schizophrenic, or conflicted, as that of his superiors in Washington. Although espousing the rhetoric of self-government, he told the Iraqis that the interim authority would be an "executive type organization." The coalition would use it "as an Iraqi face for the Iraqi people." The coalition, he stressed, "would still be in charge." If IIA functioned effectively, Garner said, it might evolve into a provisional government, pending elections. This seemed like hedging, causing dismay among his Iraqi interlocutors. They sensed that the Americans might be backtracking on their fervor for self-government, or disingenuous about its meaning.[57]

Change was underway. The administration in Washington had lost faith in Garner before he had arrived in Baghdad. Condi Rice was especially agitated by what she was hearing and seeing. "The nightmare that we had tried to get Defense to avoid through planning for rear-area security was unfolding. There was a serious manpower shortage in Baghdad," she recognized. She blamed Rumsfeld. After an NSC meeting in early April, she asked him if he realized that the Garner mission was failing. Rumsfeld said he grasped the problem, and, on April

11, he told her he would recommend a different model, one he had been contemplating since early March. He would appoint a new presidential envoy to head a Coalition Provisional Authority. The designee would report directly to him, not through the CENTCOM commander in Iraq, as Garner formally had been doing.[58] On April 16, in a special freedom message to the Iraqi people, General Franks announced the establishment of a Coalition Provisional Authority (CPA) that would assume governmental power temporarily. He assumed that General Garner, as the head of ORHA, would exercise that responsibility. But a few days later, on April 21, the very day Garner arrived in Baghdad, Rumsfeld called him, told him he was doing a great job, and then said he would be replaced in the next few weeks. Garner asked for more time, stressing that he was making progress toward the formation of the type of interim authority that Rumsfeld claimed to want. The secretary of defense ducked responsibility for Garner's removal, suggesting that it was not his call: "I don't think I can give you that [more time]."[59]

Unwilling to acknowledge how the inadequacy of his military planning for Phase IV and his cap on troop numbers were causing the turmoil the White House deplored, Rumsfeld removed Garner. Although the defense secretary never blamed him for the unfolding chaos, it was clear to Khalilzad and Crocker that Garner had lost the respect of the Pentagon and the trust of Wolfowitz and Feith. In a phone conversation with Wolfowitz over an innocuous request to the State Department for more communications equipment and more staff for ORHA, Wolfowitz reproached Khalilzad for seeking to undercut the Pentagon's authority in Baghdad. "In a long friendship," Khalilzad recalled, "I do not remember a conversation so tense."[60]

It reflected the deep suspicions and poisonous relations that had evolved between Rumsfeld and Powell, between Wolfowitz and Armitage, between Feith and Grossman. The administration was "hemorrhaging," Rumsfeld complained to the president's chief of staff, Andy Card. "It is clearly not disciplined."[61] OSD officials were convinced that the State Department was seeking to thwart the creation of the IIA; policymakers at Foggy Bottom were convinced that their counterparts inside the Pentagon were scheming to place Chalabi in power. Neither side correctly gauged the intentions of the other. The

State Department was not seeking to undercut the IIA. And Rumsfeld was not pressing for the anointment of Chalabi, even though the INC leader may have been Feith's favorite candidate.[62]

In mid-April 2003, the vitriol among Bush's advisers in Washington made it difficult to address the chaos in Iraq. In Kuwait and Baghdad, OSD and State Department representatives barely talked to one another.[63] In Washington, the vice president hosted a small private party to celebrate the victory in Iraq, to which neither Rice, the national security adviser, nor Powell, the secretary of state, was invited. When Rice pleaded for more inter-agency collaboration for the postwar period, Cheney snarkily replied: "The Pentagon just liberated Iraq. What has the State Department done?"[64]

Rice knew she had her work cut out. She hoped to shape a course correction by replacing Garner. When Rumsfeld recommended L. Paul Bremer—a former high-ranking State Department official, protégé of Henry Kissinger, and well-known counterterrorism expert—she and the president thought they saw a way forward. They thought they were handing responsibility and authority to a tough-minded manager with a commanding presence who could also bridge the divide between their warring Cabinet officials. In order to give Bremer maximum flexibility, Rice and Hadley shut down the NSC inter-agency process. "The coordination," Rice wrote, "would be done in Baghdad under the direction and guidance of the Pentagon in Washington."[65]

When Rumsfeld recommended Bremer to President Bush, the secretary of defense did not know Bremer. Wolfowitz and Cheney's two key assistants, Scooter Libby and Eric Edelman, urged his appointment. Rumsfeld met with Bremer on Thursday, April 24. The conversation was brief. Bremer hardly remembered it, except to say that Rumsfeld asked how he got along with other members of the national security team. Rumsfeld immediately wrote a short note to Andy Card, the president's chief of staff, "I like him. I think he is the man." Card set up a meeting for Bremer to meet Bush the very next day. They did not know one another. Again, the meeting was brief. Bush asked him why he wanted the job. Bremer replied, "Because I believe America has done something great in liberating the Iraqis, sir. And because I think I can help." The meeting was over, except on the way out, Bremer told the president that his wife wanted the president "to know that her favorite passage from your State of the Union message is 'Freedom is not America's gift to the world. It is God's gift to mankind.' "[66]

During the next two weeks, Bremer worked feverishly to prepare for his assignment as the head of the CPA. He was not a Middle East expert and did not know Arabic. He spent lots of time reading background papers and books and even more time assembling a senior staff and talking to key officials. He came to understand that his chief task was "helping Iraqis get control of the country again." He said there were three aspects to this: "Helping them on a path toward better government; helping them get the economy back on its feet; and . . . providing security." His initial focus was on the political process. Feith told him that the president's policy was to form the IIA quickly and to transfer ministries to full Iraqi control as soon as possible. "As far as we knew," Feith subsequently wrote, "he agreed with the policy and intended to put the IIA plan into practice." Bremer, however, most emphatically did not agree. He almost drove off the road when he heard a news report on the radio that Garner intended to appoint an Iraqi government by May 15. In his own mind, this was not possible.[67]

Bremer had a critical meeting with the president on May 6. Bush invited him for a private lunch. Two macho men, who prided themselves on their athletic ability and good physical conditioning, sat down for a lunch of pears and greens. After some small talk about overall policy, Bush crisply asked, "What can I do to help you?" Bremer was clear. He wanted uncontested authority in Iraq; there had to be unity of command. Khalilzad had to go, as well as Garner. "I must have full authority to bring all the resources of the American government to bear on Iraq's reconstruction." Bush said he understood, and agreed. Next, Bremer told the president that the transition to Iraqi self-government could not be quick; a ninety-day transition was out of the question. It was necessary to focus on the "shock-absorbers" of a free society—a free press, trade unions, political parties, professional organizations—as well as the formal institutions of democratic self-government. Bush emphatically agreed. Bremer then stated that, although he was no general, he felt more troops were needed for security—"to stabilize Iraq we'll probably need an awful lot more troops than we now have." The president said he would "mention it" to Powell, who was negotiating with other governments to lend help and troops. Bush then reassured Bremer that he knew it would take time to bring representative government to the Iraqi people. He stressed, "We're not going to abandon Iraq. We'll stay until the job is done."[68]

Lunch finished, the two men walked down to the Oval Office to meet with Rumsfeld, Cheney, Powell, Rice, and Card. Bush quipped, "I don't know whether we need this meeting after all. Jerry and I have just had it." Bremer was delighted. He got what he wanted: full authority over all personnel, activities, and funds in Iraq—over all executive, legislative, and judicial functions. Bremer would report to the president through the secretary of defense. But he knew, and so did everyone else, that "I was neither Rumsfeld's or Powell's man. I was the president's man." Rumsfeld was not happy.[69]

Bremer left Washington a few days later confident that he knew the president's wishes. He arrived in Iraq on May 12. Driving from the airport to the presidential palace, where the CPA was housed, he immediately witnessed the fragility of the security environment. There were tanks and armored vehicles and Humvees—and looters in pickup trucks, and civilians firing AK-47s. Conditions were beyond anything that had been reported to him, and anything that he had imagined. Even in Hussein's former presidential palace, there was now no electricity, no air conditioning, no running water. In the city, there was no trash disposal, no potable water; schools and universities were closed; hospitals were in shambles; malnutrition was widespread. Looters had machine guns, and even rocket-propelled grenades. The cops were home guarding their families. Violent crime had ramped up—burglaries, kidnapping, murders.[70]

Appalled, Bremer seized command. On the very first night he assembled the entire staff. He asserted that law and order must be restored. Looters should be shot. Ministries had to be guarded. Cops had to be put back on the streets. A vigorous private sector had to be nurtured. Elections could not be rushed. Civil society had to be reconstituted—an independent judiciary, a free press, political parties. These were society's shock absorbers, he emphasized. To underscore his attitude, he canceled the meeting with the seven Iraqi leaders, most of them former exiles, with whom Garner and Crocker had been working. "I wanted to signal to the Iraqi political leaders that I was not in a hurry to see them. . . . I wanted to show everybody that I, not Jay [Garner], was now in charge."[71]

On May 16, Bremer issued CPA Regulation Number 1. It defined the CPA's mission, responsibilities, and authority. It temporarily allocated to the CPA all governmental authority in order to provide "for the effective administration of Iraq." For an undefined transitional period, the CPA would strive to restore security, nurture self-governmental institutions, expedite reconstruction, and facilitate economic recovery. The edict vested the CPA administrator, Bremer, with all executive, legislative, and judicial authority to achieve the state's objectives. Iraqi law could continue "unless replaced or suspended by the CPA." Regulation Number 1 ended the illusion of liberation and accepted the reality of occupation.[72]

A week later, the UN Security Council passed Resolution 1483. It formally recognized the United States and the United Kingdom as occupation powers and assigned them the responsibilities that accompanied that status. Expressing hope for a quick return to self-government, the resolution authorized a mission to help occupation authorities create a transitional Iraqi governing council. At the same time, UNSCR 1483 terminated all the sanctions that had been applied to Hussein's regime and turned over the Oil-for-Food revenues to an Iraqi Developmental Fund, controlled by the CPA.[73]

On May 19, Bremer met with the seven Iraqi leaders, the so-called Iraqi Leadership Council, that Garner and Crocker had regarded as the nucleus of the IIA. Bremer knew that Khalilzad, who had now returned to Washington, had left them "with the impression that we would turn over governing power to them by mid-May." Bremer now told them that this was not going to happen: the process "would be incremental" and the goal was a truly representative group. This body, he told them, "is not representative." Composed of former exiles, mostly Shi'a, it had only one Sunni, no Turkmen, no Christians, and no women. It had to be reconstituted. It would take some time. "My request," Bremer later wrote, provoked "animated confusion." That was an understatement. The assembled Iraqi exile leaders expected to form a provisional government. They were "vehemently opposed" to the reversal of policy. One of them—Iyad Allawi, the head of the Iraqi National Accord—wrote that they "warned Bremer that the CPA would most certainly fail if there were no parallel Iraqi governmental authority with which it could liaise." Bremer was insistent. "I was exerting the authority President Bush had granted me, putting down the hammer. . . . I wasn't running in a popularity contest."[74]

The Iraqis "were stunned," wrote Khalilzad. "We had given our word that the United States would quickly restore their country's sovereignty. Breaking this promise would call into question our motives for intervening in Iraq."[75] Bremer's approach immediately reframed the war's aftermath not as a "liberation," but as an "occupation," in the Arabic language, an *ihtilal*. Iraqis bristled at the disrespect that inhered in the new American approach.[76] Bremer, however, felt confident that he was carrying out the president's intentions. Bush wrote him: "you have the backing of our Administration that knows our work will take time."[77]

Bremer moved forward. At the very same time that he assumed full authority over Iraq and postponed the creation of an Iraqi Interim Authority, Bremer issued his first official order calling for the de-Ba'thification of Iraqi society. Although General Franks already had dissolved the Ba'th Party, this new order banned the top four rungs of the party's leadership from government service and removed Ba'th members from the top three layers of management in government agencies, state enterprises, universities, and hospitals. This de-Ba'thification policy had been fully vetted through the NSC interagency process, and Bremer had discussed it with Feith before he left Washington. US officials were well aware that it would have a deleterious impact on the administrative capacity of the Iraqi state. But they wanted to underscore that they were eliminating the remnants of Saddam Hussein's regime.[78] When Bremer arrived in Baghdad, Garner warned him that it was too sweeping—that it would impede efforts to restore services and fix infrastructure. So did General Abizaid, the incoming CENTCOM commander. Bremer's proposals, Abizaid thought, "went far too deep into Iraqi society and were bound to cause problems." Bremer ignored this advice.[79]

Iraqi exile leaders, however, appreciated Bremer's de-Ba'thification order. They yearned to rid the country of Hussein's henchmen who had imprisoned, tortured, and exiled them. In fact, they feared their re-emergence. The deposed leader, they knew, was hiding somewhere and issuing calls "to rise against the occupier." "The Ba'th Party is regrouping," Dr. Ibrahim al-Jaafari told Bremer on the day they first met. Chalabi appealed for even more aggressive de-Ba'thification.[80]

The de-Ba'thification order was popular inside Iraq, well beyond the group of former exiles and their followers. Most Iraqi Shi'a—perhaps 70 percent of the population—wanted to rid themselves of their Ba'th overlords, composed mainly of Sunni. Winning Shi'a support was critical for the success of the occupation and the legitimation of any claims to nurturing representative government.[81] Yet de-Ba'thification undermined efforts to preserve order, restore services, and reconstruct the infrastructure because Ba'th members were critical to running the ministries and staffing state enterprises, agencies, and security services. De-Ba'thification also alienated some Sunnis who saw themselves disgraced and unemployed. US Army officers, like General Petraeus, strongly opposed the magnitude of de-Ba'thification, the implementation process, and the absence of a truth and reconciliation commission. Charles Duelfer, a former inspection monitor with close links to the CIA and the State Department, was in Baghdad in April and May. Resuming contacts with Iraqis and compiling lists of people to staff the various ministries, he was "dumbfounded" by the de-Ba'thification order. "Excising Bathists, particularly in a way that impugned their dignity," he wrote, "made enemies of the secular part of an Iraqi government, upon which the normal functioning of government depended."[82]

Although some de-Ba'thification was imperative, its negative repercussions were magnified by Bremer's next order disbanding the Iraqi army and security services. Unlike CPA Order #1 regarding de-Ba'thification, this edict had not been agreed upon in inter-agency discussions in Washington. As late as May 7, OSD policy was not to disband the Iraqi army. On May 9, Bremer and Walt Slocombe, the tax lawyer and experienced defense policymaker whom Rumsfeld had recruited to refashion and rebuild the Iraqi armed forces, convinced Feith to change course. Since the Iraqi army had disintegrated, it served no purpose to try to retain it. Slocombe wanted to start anew. Feith agreed, but did not bring the new policy to the attention of Hadley or to Feith's counterparts at Foggy Bottom.[83] On May 19, Bremer sent his plan from Baghdad directly to Rumsfeld. Believing there was no objection, he announced it in Baghdad on May 23. Rice and Powell were stunned when they read about it in the newspaper the next day; so was General Abizaid, the incoming CENTCOM commander. "The president," Rice subsequently wrote, "had made clear that he wanted Jerry to have flexibility in dealing with conditions on the ground. But something was wrong when a decision of that magnitude could be made without Washington's full and considered deliberation."[84] Something was wrong; the president knew it was wrong—but he did not intervene.

Bremer's CPA Order #2 regarding the Iraqi army was designed as part of his de-Ba'thification campaign. "It is a critical step," Bremer explained to Rumsfeld, "in our effort to destroy the underpinnings of the Saddam regime, to demonstrate to the Iraqi people that we have done so, and neither Saddam nor his gang is coming back." This order, he emphasized to the defense secretary, "will affect large numbers of people," including 400,000 employees of the MOD alone. He realized that he needed to design some means to provide them with compensation and pensions. Otherwise, he acknowledged, there was risk of serious discontent, increased terrorism, and much higher crime rates. He also knew there would "be some delay in making these payments, because . . . we do not have employee rosters, or contacts with administrative officials of the dissolved entities."[85] Bremer was willing to take that risk. It was a mistake.

Disbanding the Iraqi army complicated the security situation in two ways. It deprived the CPA of the services of trained personnel and it alienated many former officers whose salary and pension vanished. Although units had disintegrated and soldiers had fled, Garner, McKiernan, Petraeus, and other local commanders and ORHA officials were in the midst of contacting, recruiting, and reassembling army units for reconstruction and security. "They would have returned to their units," thought Duelfer, "if the word had been put out." Indeed, on the very day that Bremer issued his order, Brigadier General Mark Hertling met with 600 senior Iraqi officers in Baghdad to solicit their participation in a reconstituted Iraqi army.[86] Bremer, Slocombe, and Crocker nonetheless thought the decision made sense, given the realities on the ground and the popular clamor to demolish the formal institutions of Hussein's brutal regime. If it made sense, its good effects, acknowledged Crocker, were canceled by the CPA's failure to pay pensions quickly, rehire officers swiftly, and redesign the army to deal with internal security and reconstruction as well as border protection. "We created hundreds of thousands of enemies," said General Petraeus. They had "no incentive to support the new Iraq, they actually had every incentive to oppose it."[87]

To observers inside Iraq, like Duelfer, "Baghdad was at a tipping point," as early as May. Iraqi expectations were high; yet "there was no message about who was in charge. . . . There was no authority. There was complete freedom—to do absolutely anything, good or bad." Over the ensuing weeks, Duelfer believed, "The vacuum of power spawned wider chaos. There was no penalty for committing crimes and there was no reward for going to work." Bremer, he thought, with his commanding presence and overbearing demeanor "brought order to the Green Zone [the administrative compound of the CPA], but not beyond it." A British general surveying the situation reported back to London, "It is startlingly apparent that we are not delivering that which was deemed to be promised and is expected."[88] Iraqis watched, bewildered. They thought Americans were allowing the plunder. They wondered, wrote one well-informed journalist, "whether the condition of their country was the result of malicious inattention or inattentive malice."[89] In June, there were 250 attacks on coalition forces; in July the number doubled to roughly 500 (Figure 9.1).[90]

Bremer tried to put a positive spin on developments when he met with Bush in early June in Doha. But he was acutely aware of the incendiary, chaotic situation. On June 14, he informed the president that security had improved in most of the country, but noted that he still faced "virulent opposition in the triangle north and west of the capital."[91] In a video conference with the NSC, chaired by Bush, Bremer voiced his concern that "we may be drawing down our forces here too soon." He worried that "filling in with foreign troops [would] detract from our combat capability." The president tried to reassure Bremer, saying that the American troops would be replaced with other units from the US Army. Bremer did not contradict the president, but believed Bush did not accurately understand the situation. After the meeting, he called Rumsfeld's military aide to make sure the defense secretary grasped the urgency of his concerns. Bremer also called Rice, and stressed: "the

Figure 9.1 Secretary of Defense Rumsfeld (center) and Paul Bremer, the head of the Coalition Provisional Authority, walk in Baghdad as violence mounts and insurrection brews, February 23, 2004.

Getty Images, https://www.gettyimages.com/detail/news-photo/secretary-of-defense-donald-rumsfeld-and-coalition-news-photo/3031039

Coalition's got about half the number of soldiers we need here and we run a real risk of having this thing go south on us." On July 1, he reiterated to the president, "the security situation is not acceptable."[92]

The military situation on the ground in Iraq got worse, not better. The command headquarters led by General McKiernan was replaced and downsized. Major General Ricardo Sanchez, commander of the 1st Armored Division in Germany, replaced him. His staff was neither equipped nor trained to deal with the operational issues he had to confront in Iraq. Meanwhile, many of the units and officers that had gained some experience inside Iraq during these first tumultuous weeks were reassigned back to Kuwait, Qatar, or CENTCOM headquarters at MacDill Air Force Base in Florida. Sanchez remonstrated against the loss of experienced officers and intelligence analysts, but to no avail. His own superior officers—Franks, Abizaid, McKiernan, Wallace— were unwilling to fight with Rumsfeld. They knew he was determined to ratchet down the numbers. In May and June, Franks, McKiernan, and Wallace all departed; Abizaid became CENTCOM commander.

He did not press Rumsfeld or Bush for more troops. Officers did not buck their civilian boss. Sanchez remonstrated in private, but not publicly. The manpower shortage was perfectly clear to Bremer and Rice, but did not alter Rumsfeld's determination to lighten the American footprint.[93] Bush deferred to his defense secretary.

Rumsfeld, however, was not oblivious to the ominous developments. On June 9, he wrote Bremer urging him "to move quickly to create a leadership council for the Interim Administration." It was imperative, Rumsfeld wrote, to "put an Iraqi face on what is now a Coalition military presence." Ethnic groups inside Iraq were "restless. Standing still may lead to unraveling." He concluded: "Regime remnants are coalescing and stepping up sabotage. Their dream is a guerrilla insurgency. But guerrilla insurgencies depend on popular support. Progress toward an IIA will help neutralize if not dry up that popular support."[94] Bremer did not ignore Rumsfeld's wishes. He worked to create an Iraqi Governing Council. When formed in late July, it was a much more representative body than the original group of seven that Bremer had met with in May. Critical to its formation was the UN Special Representative for Iraq, Sérgio Vieira de Mello. He was a very able Brazilian who had served as UN High Commissioner for Refugees. After arriving in Baghdad on June 2, Vieira de Mello worked collaboratively with Bremer. Hoping to shift responsibility to Iraqis swiftly, Vieira de Mello urged Bremer to treat the Governing Council as more than an advisory body. Bremer was not so inclined. The Iraqis' work habits exasperated him; their inability to reach consensus infuriated him. The friction between him and the Governing Council was palpable. Several of its members felt "his distaste, bordering on contempt."[95]

Bremer, however, was not indifferent to Iraqis' desire to write a constitution, hold a referendum, conduct national elections, form a government, and regain their national sovereignty. But these goals, as important as they were, could not be achieved if chaos persisted and the economy stagnated. "We're in a race," he realized. "Economic recovery and reconstruction, as well as the creation of representative government, were intertwined with security." And security was not improving. Saboteurs were blowing up pipelines and halting fuel production; roadside bombings made it increasingly difficult to hire contractors. Bremer needed more resources, more skilled professionals, and more troops and police. The killing of Hussein's two sons at the end of July momentarily buoyed spirits, but did not alter the fundamental situation.[96]

Bremer's ability to get the assistance he desperately needed was hampered by the never-ending bureaucratic feuding in Washington and Baghdad. His relations with Rumsfeld soured. Sulking after being excluded from the private lunch between Bush and Bremer on May 6, the defense secretary now thought Bremer was maneuvering behind his back, refusing to report regularly, and defying his desire to transition responsibilities quickly to the Iraqis. Bremer, however, thought he was communicating regularly, sending timely memoranda, and carrying out the president's mandate.[97] Working prodigiously hard in oppressive living quarters and a fraught security environment, he complained that he was not getting enough resources from Washington. He remonstrated that the CIA and the military were not bold enough to arrest Shi'a leaders, like Muqtada al Sadr, who fomented opposition to the occupation.[98] Acting imperiously, he alienated the new Army commander, Ricardo Sanchez, and fought with him over such matters as who would control the training of the new Iraqi army.[99]

Bremer asked Andy Card, the president's chief of staff, to help him navigate through the bureaucratic morass in Washington. But that quagmire became more treacherous, not less. Rice's assistants complained that Bremer was not providing the information they needed.[100] Rumsfeld had the data, but sniped at Rice because her subordinates were going to the Joint Staff, rather than his office, for the information they required.[101] The defense secretary also raged at the State Department for not supporting his desire to recruit 7,000 policemen from Arab nations to help stifle the chaos and preserve order.[102] In turn, Powell remonstrated about OSD delays in processing qualified State Department personnel for service in Iraq.[103] Bremer knew that he had "to deal with the reality that you have Rumsfeld and Powell at each other's throats," but he may not have known that the boycott of some inter-agency meetings by OSD officials, and their behavior at others, interfered with the making of policy on some of the most salient issues he was tackling. According to participants in the process, OSD officials often skipped key meetings dealing with electricity supplies, security for humanitarian missions, and the recruitment of translators for US troops. Feith's assistants, they claimed, "never brought an issue to the table to be solved, nor sought to assist in resolving those that were on the table." The departmental animus extended to Baghdad, where OSD and State Department representatives often treated one another with abiding suspicion and hamstrung one another's efforts.[104]

"We're in a pretty deep hole in Iraq," Assistant Secretary of State Bill Burns wrote his boss, Secretary of State Powell, on July 11. American casualties were increasing because "of the disaffection of large numbers of former regular army officers." An ex–Iraqi army captain, Burns informed Powell, was arrested for leading an ambush on US troops. He said he had done so for a $50 payment. "They took away my job and my honor," he explained. "I can't feed my family. There are many more like me."[105]

Of course, Americans were not the only targets of disaffected Ba'thites and discharged Army officers. Iraqis keenly felt their insecurity. Shi'a protests mounted and revenge killings began. At one of Bremer's first meetings with Iraqi leaders, Iyad Allawi told the CPA administrator, "There is a security vacuum. . . . The people need more protection." When pollsters came to Baghdad during the summer, Iraqis told them that the streets were becoming more dangerous.[106] "There is no gas, no kerosene, no security," lamented an Iraqi friend of a *Washington Post* reporter.[107] Sunni started targeting Shi'a; Shi'a splintered among themselves; Kurds battled Arabs in the north; Iran conspired in the south; and, meanwhile, some of Hussein's Ba'thists hid, regrouped, and initiated acts of sabotage.[108]

Bremer grasped the reality: As the heavily armed coalition failed to preserve order, protect people, and ameliorate economic conditions, the confidence of Iraqis in America waned and the resolve of Iraqi insurgents and foreign terrorists increased. Trust and hope evaporated. "The awe of American power was being eroded," wrote Charles Duelfer, "by the growing realization that the United States had no idea what it was doing in Iraq."[109]

On August 16, insurgents blew up the Jordanian embassy. Three days later, they attacked the UN compound in Baghdad with a suicide truck bomb and destroyed much of the building (Figure 9.2). Bremer rushed to the scene. Many were dead, more were wounded. Vieira de Mello was trapped between slabs of concrete. He couldn't

Figure 9.2 Aftermath of the bombing of UN Headquarters in Baghdad, August 2003, signaling the onset of insurrectionary activity and highlighting the failure of US and coalition forces to preserve stability and order after overthrowing Saddam Hussein.
Getty Images, https://www.gettyimages.com/detail/news-photo/worker-stands-in-front-of-the-canal-hotel-blast-site-after-news-photo/939634820

move, but was conscious. Soldiers desperately tried to release him, but failed. He died. Soon thereafter, the UN pulled out most of its personnel; international agencies and non-governmental organizations followed.[110] Iraqis' confidence in the United States plummeted. Referencing the sputtering efforts to restore electricity—but applicable to much else—CENTCOM informed Rumsfeld in late August: "We are losing the consent of the Iraqi people by failing to meet their expectations. . . . [W]e risk losing the peace."[111]

The destruction of the UN headquarters highlighted America's faltering adventure in Iraq. Despite Bremer's prodigious efforts, its mission had gone awry. Having decided to invade Iraq to remove Saddam Hussein and promote US security, President Bush had promised Iraqis that regime change would bring freedom and prosperity. But the American military establishment not only had planned miserably for the postwar phase of operations, but also had exacerbated its poor planning with a series of disastrous staff changes, unit rotations, and troop cuts. Its civilian overseers bickered among themselves. Policymakers could not decide if they were liberators or occupiers, if they were staying briefly, or not. They argued over the Iraqis they could trust, and the institutions they could rely upon. They prepared for disasters that did not occur and failed to foresee the challenges that awaited them. They labored under assumptions that postulated an enthusiastic reception by Iraqis and the survival of the basic institutions of the state. But these assumptions were never carefully scrutinized or discussed. Had they planned enough, or wisely? No, they had not.

Secretary of Defense Donald Rumsfeld bears much of the responsibility. He oversaw the war planning. He scrutinized the combat phase of the mission again and again, asking for iteration after iteration of the attack plan, but showed scant interest in the stability operations following the end of hostilities. He insisted on ramping down troop numbers after combat. After seeking to control postwar operations, he eagerly shifted responsibility to Garner and then to Bremer. He talked incessantly about turning responsibilities quickly to the Iraqis, yet handed his CPA administrator a set of guidelines that gave him authority to dictate the future of Iraq. "There will be clarity that the coalition is in charge," read the instructions. "The Coalition will not 'let a thousand flowers bloom.' "[112] The contradictions between his rhetoric and his instructions were glaring, and Rumsfeld never resolved them. Subsequently, he railed against what Bremer was doing, but at the time he spoke with him frequently, responded to his queries, and praised his efforts: "You are doing a good job, my friend," he wrote Bremer on July 8.[113] Yet Rumsfeld hamstrung what Bremer cared most about—security—by accepting the disbandonment of the Iraqi army, scaling back American troops, and allowing a sequence of unit rotations and staff changes that undercut the capacity of occupation authorities to preserve order. He also disrupted inter-agency coordination by treating Rice with contempt, sending her snowflakes that criticized her procedures and processes, and encouraging his subordinates, perhaps inadvertently, to emulate his uncooperative behavior.[114] Rumsfeld was smart and demanding, incisive, curious, and hardworking, yet inconsistent, ambiguous, unforthcoming, and petulant. At times he infuriated, sometimes he intimidated, and frequently he exasperated many of his subordinates and interlocutors. He grabbed power, but did not exercise it effectively.

President Bush stood atop the morass of postwar planning, and did little to uplift it. He knew his top Cabinet officers were feuding, but for the most part did not interfere. He knew the challenges in Iraq were arduous, and his answer was to devolve responsibility to Bremer. Seeing the chaos in Iraq, he agreed that the Iraqis were not ready for self-government, and concurred that occupation authorities would need to create the "shock absorbers" of a civil society. Shifting his focus from security of the US homeland to democracy-promotion and nation-building in Iraq, President Bush failed to orchestrate the requisite planning. He did not resolve the divergent predilections of the two most consequential officials making Iraq policy—his newly appointed administrator of the Coalition Provisional Authority and his secretary of defense—or heal the animosity between his most important advisers: Cheney, Powell, and Rumsfeld.

Rice and Hadley, the president's top personal aides for national security, wanted to overcome the acrimony seething through the administration. Failing, they temporarily shut down the NSC inter-agency process on Iraq and left key decisions to Bremer.[115] They knew the president had confidence in his newly appointed CPA administrator. They knew Bush and Bremer were on the same page. They knew the president believed in delegating authority, trusting subordinates on the ground, and averting attempts to micromanage.[116] They hoped things would get better. They were wrong.

The president, however, remained undaunted. As Bremer hurried to the smoldering UN headquarters, President Bush called him. Tell the Iraqis, he instructed Bremer, "I admire their courage." Tell them, "The United States will not be deterred from carrying on in Iraq." A few hours later, they talked again. Reassure the Iraqis, Bush emphasized, "We would not be driven out of Iraq by terrorists."[117] A few days later, he reminded Americans, "Terrorists commit atrocities because they want the civilized world to flinch. . . . There will be no flinching."[118]

IO

Conclusion

Fear, Power, Hubris

CENTCOM TASKED THE 75th Field Artillery Brigade in January 2003 to find and secure Iraq's weapons of mass destruction (WMD). Soon to be known as the 75th Exploitation Task Force (XTF), its leaders had no training and no experience looking for WMD. Its commander, Colonel Richard McPhee, assembled experts and military personnel from a potpourri of agencies, including the Defense Intelligence Agency (DIA), the Federal Bureau of Investigation (FBI), and the Central Intelligence Agency (CIA). "We were comfortable shooting rockets," commented the leader of its command and control headquarters, Major Kevin Brown, "but dragging lab technicians and intel folks around the battlefield was kind of a unique prospect." Rather than follow a systematic plan, the task force responded to ongoing reports about suspect sites. With inadequate equipment and insufficient forces to protect the areas it investigated, many sites were poorly explored or quickly "compromised" by local looters. At other times, the task force digressed to explore the regime's humanitarian crimes. "We became the bastard stepchildren for all things strange within Iraq," recalled Major Brown.[1]

The failure of XTF to locate the stockpiles of weapons agitated policymakers in Washington. When President George W. Bush asked who was in charge of the hunt for Iraqi WMD, he did not receive a clear answer. Frustrated, he told George Tenet, the CIA director, to take charge. The CIA then worked closely with the DIA and the

Office of the Secretary of Defense (OSD). They assembled a large group of civilian experts and military personnel—the Iraq Survey Group (ISG)—under the leadership, first, of David Kay, and then Charles Duelfer.[2] Both men had extensive experience monitoring Iraqi weapons developments in the 1990s. After months of systematic exploration and long interviews with captured military officers and civilian advisers to Saddam Hussein, they came up empty-handed. They reported that they could find no stockpiles of chemical and biological weapons, no evidence of fissile material, and no signs of ongoing WMD programs.[3]

"Let me begin by saying that we were almost all wrong" about Iraqi WMD programs, David Kay told the Senate Armed Services Committee on January 28, 2004. Although chastened by the egregious misreading of Iraqi capabilities, Kay still did not think that intelligence analysts had misled policymakers about the fundamental threat. "I think the world is far safer with the disappearance and removal of Saddam Hussein. . . . I actually think this may be one of those cases where it was even more dangerous than we thought. . . . [I]n a world where we know others are seeking WMD, the likelihood at some point in the future of a seller and a buyer meeting up would have made that a far more dangerous country than even we anticipated."[4]

In September 2004, Duelfer delivered the final, comprehensive report of the Iraq Survey Group. The evidence appeared conclusive: Iraq did not have WMD stockpiles, nor any active programs. But in key respects, Duelfer sounded much like Kay. The absence of weapons had not changed his view of Saddam Hussein. His investigation and his interviews had confirmed his apprehensions and suspicions. "It was very clear," Duelfer wrote in his memoir, "that Saddam complied with UN disarmament restrictions only as a tactic."[5] The report stressed that Hussein's overriding objective was to terminate sanctions and move ahead with his WMD ambitions. "Virtually" no senior Iraqi leader "believed that Saddam had forsaken WMD forever."[6]

While Duelfer was preparing his comprehensive report, US forces captured Saddam Hussein on December 13, 2003. He was found hiding in a hole on a farm not far from Tikrit. He was imprisoned near Baghdad, and tried by an Iraqi court. Denied his desire to be executed by a firing squad, he was hanged in prison on December 30,

2006 (Figure 10.1). While detained, he was interviewed extensively by an FBI Special Agent named George Piro, a Lebanese-American fluent in Arabic.[7] Duelfer oversaw part of the process, and watched the former tyrant tangle with his captors. Shrewd and cagey, Duelfer observed, Hussein "had a controlling presence." When he "gazed upon you he conveyed the sense of decrypting you. . . . His stare was unnerving to his lieutenants. It was even unnerving to his captors." But Piro labored craftily over six months to get Hussein to talk about himself, his family, his rise to power, his leadership, and his goals. Duelfer studied the process and reflected on the dictator who had ruled Iraq, informally and formally, for almost thirty years. He "was not a cartoon. He was catastrophically brilliant and extremely talented in a black, insidious way," much like Joseph Stalin, the leader Hussein most wanted to emulate. He was obsessed with his legacy, eager to be seen in the tradition of Nebuchadnezzar and other great Iraqis. His aspirations were

Figure 10.1 Hanging of Saddam Hussein, December 30, 2006. Saddam Hussein was captured by US forces and tried by a Special Tribunal of five Iraqi judges. He was sentenced to death for his crimes against humanity and genocidal actions.
Getty Images, https://www.gettyimages.com/detail/news-photo/in-this-television-screen-grab-taken-from-iraqi-national-news-photo/72904085

clear: thwart Iran, defeat Israel, and dominate the region. To achieve his goals—to bequeath his imagined legacy—he still yearned to acquire weapons of mass destruction. His "ambitions remained."[8]

Ryan Crocker, the deputy assistant secretary of state in the office of Near Eastern Affairs, agreed with Duelfer. Few Americans knew the Middle East better than Crocker, an American foreign service officer who served as ambassador to Lebanon, Syria, Afghanistan, Pakistan, and Kuwait. He was in Iraq between 1978 and 1980, when Hussein seized total power. "I've lived in a lot of unsavory regimes," Crocker recalled, "but this was in a class by itself. It was a regime of terror, it ruled by terror." Over the years Hussein did not become more benign. "We Americans," Crocker stressed, too often "lose sight of just how awful that regime was and why we were up against such terrifically hard choices by 2002, 2003 as sanctions were crumbling, international consensus was dissipating, and Saddam was by no means getting any kinder or gentler." "What we really don't grasp," Crocker reiterated, "is just how evil that regime was. . . . It was a masterful system of total evil." Although he never supported an invasion, Crocker acknowledged, "it was a kind of Hobson's choice because leaving him in place meant he was only going to get stronger, and then what?"[9]

George W. Bush and his advisers had to wrestle with that choice. Until September 11, 2001, the administration could not decide how to handle the tyrant. The president reviled Hussein. He despised his character, his brutality, and his defiance. His advisers spent lots of time discussing what to do when Iraq shot at American planes enforcing the no-fly zones in northern and southern Iraq. They spent even more time pondering how to make sanctions more effective in punishing the Iraqi regime and more benign toward the Iraqi people, whose suffering inflamed anti-Americanism throughout the Arab world and beyond. Bush, however, did not dwell on these issues. His priorities were domestic. He was not planning a military invasion to bring down Saddam Hussein.[10]

9/11 shocked, saddened, and humiliated policymakers. The overwhelming emotion was fear, reinforced by a sense of guilt that 9/11 had occurred on their watch, and by a desire for revenge. US intelligence agencies were certain more attacks would follow. Officials in one department after another—Energy, Interior, Transportation,

Justice—highlighted the vulnerabilities of the nation's infrastructure, for example, its susceptibility to even more damaging attacks on nuclear plants or water systems. Military officers and intelligence chiefs warned the president that al Qaeda was a multifaceted organization with tentacles in dozens of countries, and innumerable affiliated groups. They told Bush that Osama bin Laden wanted to acquire nuclear, biological, and chemical weapons. They said he yearned to inflict more damage. Just a week after the 9/11 attack, letters with anthrax started circulating in Florida and then Washington. People died. Postal service was disrupted; government offices shut down. Alarm bells went off in the White House itself when signs of a biological attack were discovered. Policymakers and military officials began taking the antibiotic Cipro.

Fear wrapped itself around a sense of responsibility, a deep abiding conviction that the overwhelming duty of a government is to protect its citizens. Bush knew well that he had failed to do so. So did his advisers. Another attack, they recognized, would shatter the confidence of the American people, expose the vulnerability of American institutions, and catalyze calls for a garrison state—for vigilance bordering on repression. And lurking just beneath these fears was another certainty: should another attack occur, the administration's political viability would be crushed and the reputation of the Republican Party as the stalwart defender of American national security would be eviscerated. The American people might forgive one surprise attack, not a second.

Faced with these realities, during the days and weeks after the 9/11 attack, Bush took charge. His colleagues highlight his focus, determination, and self-confidence. At times, he conveyed his deeper emotions—outrage, sadness, grief. Those closest to him nonetheless comment on his almost preternatural calm, a quality that impressed British prime minister Tony Blair when they met on September 20.[11] None of his advisers doubted that George Bush was in command. Nobody in the administration thought Vice President Richard Cheney or Secretary of Defense Donald Rumsfeld or their assistants like Scooter Libby or Paul Wolfowitz were calling the shots. Upon joining Rice's staff in the summer of 2001, Elliott Abrams mused, "It took me just a few minutes . . . to see who was in charge. . . . [T]he caricature of

[Bush] as lacking in intelligence was itself a joke."[12] Like other advisers, Abrams appreciated the president's energy, discipline, intelligence, self-confidence, and good humor. Bush was straightforward, unpretentious, level-headed, honest, and easy to work with. He was a good listener, interactive in small groups, incisive, and probing. His spiritual sensibilities and locker-room candor, however incongruous, won praise. There was much that his advisers liked about George W. Bush, and they deferred to him.[13]

But his Iraq policy went awry and led to tragedy, and it demands more rigorous analysis than scholars, pundits, and journalists have given it. The interviews and memoirs provide some answers. President Bush had many positive qualities, but others that served him poorly. He delegated too much authority and did not monitor implementation of the policies he approved. He did not order people to do things or criticize them for their failures. He did not insist on rigorous process. He let issues linger in bureaucratic wonderlands, where their real-life outcomes had huge ramifications. He was indifferent to the nasty bickering among his subordinates, acrimony that went well beyond personality conflicts and adversely affected his policies. More important, Bush disliked heated arguments, and, therefore, did not invite systematic scrutiny of the policies he was inclined to pursue. He did not ask his advisers if invading Iraq was a good idea.[14] Many commentators think that was because his mind was made up from the outset. His closest associates, however, did not think so. They believe the outcome of his strategy of coercive diplomacy was more contingent than most observers have acknowledged.[15]

Saddam Hussein was critical to that outcome. He was a brutal tyrant who had acted monstrously and provocatively in the past. He murdered his foes at home and attacked his neighbors abroad (Iran and Kuwait). He developed chemical and biological weapons and used them to kill Iranian soldiers and murder Kurdish and Shi'a rebels. He repeatedly lied about his weapons, violated his pledges to the United Nations, cheated on the Oil-for-Food Program, challenged international sanctions, and shot at US and UK airplanes enforcing the no-fly zones that were designed to protect the Kurds in the north and the Shi'a in the south. He dealt with terrorist groups, celebrated the Palestinian intifada, and sponsored suicide attacks. His ambitions were to break free of the sanctions, build strength, restart his WMD programs, regain stature in his neighborhood, and challenge US hegemony in the region. He did little to reassure Bush that he wanted a new start, making grudging concessions under duress, and hoping to escape the forces circling around him.[16] Whether all this constituted reason to go to war was a confounding question. Few would dispute that getting rid of Hussein was desirable. But was it wise to try when there was opportunity to do so, as there was after 9/11?

Bush decided to confront Hussein—not invade Iraq. Fear, power, and hubris were determinative. The president feared another attack, perhaps one even more dramatic than the one that had occurred. If he had failed to connect the dots before 9/11, as his critics charged, were there now not even more dots suggesting the necessity of gaining control of Hussein's presumed WMD or changing the regime itself? Feeling guilt about the attack he failed to avert, he had a compelling motive to act, one he cited more than any other: his responsibility to protect the American people. 9/11 had exposed the nation's vulnerabilities. Oceans no longer protected the United States from attack as they had in the past. Rogue states like Iraq, Bush worried, might share the world's most deadly weapons with terrorists who desperately wanted to inflict more pain, puncture American power, erode American harmony, undermine American institutions, and make Americans themselves doubt the utility and efficacy of their freedoms.[17]

Fear alone did not shape the president's strategy of confrontation. Bush's sense of American power—its capacity to achieve what it needed to do—was equally important. From the onset of his administration, he embraced ideas of military transformation, wanted to hike the defense budget, and aimed to revamp American military capabilities, already far beyond the match of any combination of nations in the world. The use of air power, special forces, and new technologies to expel the Taliban from Kabul reinforced his sense of power. America's reach appeared to have no bounds.[18] If the United States could help reconfigure the government in Afghanistan, as it seemed to be doing, could it not enjoy equal success in Baghdad, and beyond? And if he failed to act, might he not allow rogue dictators, like Hussein, to use their (presumed) possession of the world's most destructive weapons to blackmail the United States and check its future exercise of power? Washington must not be dissuaded from helping its friends and protecting its interests, especially in regions harboring critical raw materials and energy reserves. It had the power to do so, and needed to demonstrate it.[19]

Fear and power were an intoxicating brew when reinforced by hubris, a sense of exceptional goodness and greatness. Bush believed that America's system of democratic capitalism had proved its superiority in the battles with Nazism and communism. People, he insisted, wanted to be free to say what they pleased and pray as they wished. If the United States had to act out of self-interest and use its awesome power to overthrow an evil dictator, American officials could take comfort in knowing that they would offer something superior to the benighted Iraqis whose lives Americans would be enriching. Bush read the UN Human Development Report on the Arab world that appeared in 2002 and thought that he would be redressing one of the three key deficits—the freedom deficit—that had contributed to the region's dysfunctionality, turbulence, and backwardness. More important, he read his Bible and believed that freedom was God's gift to humanity.[20]

Spurred by fear, buoyed by his growing confidence in American power, and inspired by a sense of victimhood and ideological purity, Bush embraced his strategy of coercive diplomacy. Exaggerating the likelihood of an attack on the United States—sponsored by Hussein—and inflating its consequences, he thought military intimidation might force Hussein to allow inspections, disclose his WMD, or flee, or alternatively, it might spur disaffected military officers to overthrow him. The strategy was appealing because almost everyone concurred that Hussein's defiance would not cease lest he be confronted with superior power. But the strategy was adopted without resolving its priority—regime change or WMD elimination, without a careful assessment of the diplomatic tactics and political inducements that might be necessary to make it a success, and without a thorough examination of its consequences should it not work. If Hussein did not disclose and relinquish Iraq's alleged WMD, or if he were not removed, the United States would have to invade because its credibility—the president's credibility—would now be at stake. But whether invasion and war were more desirable outcomes than the status quo, however frightening, had not been evaluated.

The president's advisers did not serve him well. Those who urged caution did so too hesitantly, and ineffectively. The "perfect storm" memo written in the State Department's bureau of Near Eastern Affairs was a laundry list of worries rather than a serious analysis of impending dangers. Secretary of State Powell used it to prepare for his meeting with the president on August 5, and then never asked for a redraft. Rice sat in on Powell's meeting, but the conversation spurred neither her nor the president to study the issues Powell raised. Caution was discounted because America's power appeared so awesome. CENTCOM assured Bush that the US military would prevail quickly; and the president's confidence in a swift victory discouraged careful analysis of the requisite diplomacy and of the war's aftermath, despite shrill warnings about its challenges. Certain that Iraqis would welcome their freedom, Bush could not imagine the distrust, ambivalence, and anger that an American invasion might arouse.

US and coalition forces toppled Hussein, but found no weapons of mass destruction, the catalyst for the invasion. American power overthrew the Taliban and disrupted al Qaeda training grounds in Afghanistan, but the numbers of terrorists grew.[21] The United States, Rumsfeld wrote Bush in June 2004, had misconstrued the conflict. The global war on terror, he now believed, placed too much emphasis on a tactic—terrorism—rather than on the source of the problem. The United States faced an ideological enemy, Rumsfeld stressed, spearheaded by a radical extremist minority within the Muslim world. These extremists wanted "to reshape the world—to cripple the US, drive us out of the Middle East, and overthrow all moderate and pro-Western governments in the Arab and Muslim world." To address the underlying challenge, Rumsfeld advised, the United States needed to go on the ideological offensive, support Islamic moderates, encourage institutional change, and promote reform, women's rights, and economic diversification.[22] Two years later, the secretary of defense—by then discredited by America's torturous behavior in Iraqi prisons, mounting insurrectionary strife in Iraq, and virulent anti-Americanism in the Muslim world—reminded Steve Hadley, now Bush's principal national security adviser, that they still had not given systematic thought to the fundamental challenge. "I continue to worry that we will never fully understand it ourselves, or organize to deal with it effectively, if we don't have NSC meetings on the Long War/Global War on Terror/the Struggle against Violent Extremists. . . . The difficulty of continuing on this path is that we fail to get clear what needs to be done, and who ought to be doing it. And as a result, we fail to organize, train, and equip to win the Long War."[23]

Rumsfeld's reflection, remorse, and critique were only partly right. From the outset of the global war on terror, Bush understood that he would need to wage an ideological war as well as a military one. As he practiced coercive diplomacy and ratcheted up the pressure on Hussein, he talked nobly about the need to tackle poverty, corruption, and disease, the wellsprings of alienation, radicalism, and terrorism. He boosted US aid, promoted women's rights, supported education, and launched a monumental war on disease, especially HIV/AIDS, that stretched well beyond the Middle East. These actions were almost always initiated at the same time he escalated pressure on Iraq and highlighted its possession of WMD, thereby obfuscating their significance.[24] When those weapons were not found, Bush shifted to a more ideological discourse, stressing that the United States had to make democracy work in Iraq. "The failure of Iraq democracy," he warned, "would embolden terrorists around the world. . . . [S]uccess will send forth the news, from Damascus to Teheran—that freedom can be the future of every nation."[25]

Bush's rhetoric grated and seemed insincere—an excuse for his failure to locate the WMD he had dwelled upon. When weapons were not found, when he got locked in an insurrectionary struggle, when Islamic fundamentalism surged and the terrorist threat mounted, rather than receded, neither his goals nor his strategy appeared to make sense. His critics flourished, often mocking his naïveté, stressing his dishonesty, minimizing his leadership skills, and ridiculing his new zealotry in behalf of a free Iraq and a democratic peace.

This portrait of the president obfuscates as much as it illuminates. It underestimates Bush's qualities, and misconstrues his calculations. Bush always was in charge of the administration's Iraq policy, and he did not rush to war. Haunted by the catastrophe on 9/11, he grappled with unprecedented threats, identified Iraq as a potential danger, developed a strategy of coercive diplomacy, and hoped Hussein would bow to American pressure. He went to war *not* out of a fanciful idea to make

Iraq democratic, but to rid it of its deadly weapons, its links to terrorists, and its ruthless, unpredictable tyrant.[26] Moreover, he did succeed at preventing another major attack on American soil and did remove a murderous dictator, a leader who had every intention of restarting his weapons programs, who was infatuated with suicide missions, and who cultivated links with terrorist groups, if not al Qaeda.[27]

Bush, however, did not achieve his goals at acceptable cost. He failed because his information was flawed, his assumptions inaccurate, his priorities imprecise, and his means incommensurate with his evolving ends. Inept planning, administrative dysfunction, and poor judgment plagued the early months of the occupation. To overcome these deficiencies, Bush required more accurate "intelligence," a more deliberate process, and a more intrusive managerial style. He needed advisers both more inclined to argue openly and honestly with one another and more disposed to work as a team. He did not get the help he needed. And, personally, he was unable to grasp the magnitude of the enterprise he was embracing, the risks that inhered in it, and the costs that would be incurred.[28] When one thinks too conventionally, when one knows too little about the country one is targeting, as was the case with Iraq, when one takes "a short cut on aligning ends, ways, and means," observed General Douglas Lute, a key adviser to the president at the end of his administration, "you end up with flawed strategy."[29]

Placing the story in proper perspective is necessary because the intervention in Iraq was so consequential. The occupation intensified sectarian strife and insurrectionary activity in Iraq. Although the Coalition Provisional Authority nurtured a political process, orchestrated the writing of a constitution, and held elections, fighting escalated and civil strife mounted. Over the years, around 235,000 Iraqis perished on account of the war and over nine million—more than a third of Iraq's prewar population—were internally displaced or fled abroad.[30] Bush decided to augment US troops in 2007 and supported a new array of counterinsurgency tactics. The "surge" worked to quell the killing and produced a modicum of political stability.[31] But when Bush's successor, Barack Obama, withdrew American troops in 2011, jihadists affiliated with the Islamic State (ISIS) regrouped, seized much of northern Iraq, and threatened the existence of the Iraqi government.

US troops returned to rescue the faltering regime, and a small number of American soldiers still remain to support a struggling democracy.

For the United States, the geopolitical, psychological, and domestic costs of the intervention persist and reverberate. The war enhanced Iranian power in the Persian Gulf, diverted attention and resources from the ongoing struggle inside Afghanistan, divided America's European allies, and provided additional opportunity for China's rise and Russia's revanchism. The conflict besmirched America's reputation and heightened anti-Americanism. It fueled the sense of grievance among Muslims, accentuated perceptions of American arrogance, complicated the struggle against terrorism, and dampened hopes for democracy and peace among Arabs and Jews in the Middle East.[32] Rather than enhancing the spread of liberty, the president and his advisers left office witnessing the worldwide recession of freedom.[33]

The war exacted a human, financial, economic, and psychological toll on the United States that hardly anyone had foreseen. Almost 9,000 American soldiers and contractors died in Iraq and over 32,000 Americans were wounded in action. Several hundred thousand veterans suffered brain injuries or experienced post-traumatic stress, and suicide rates among these GIs remain alarmingly high. Overall, the war will cost American taxpayers over $2 trillion.[34] It also distracted attention from mounting chicanery on Wall Street and a brewing financial crisis that precipitated the worst economic downturn since the Great Depression.[35] Sadly, then, the war divided rather than united Americans. It accentuated partisan rifts and sundered trust in government. Believing that Bush and his advisers had lied about their motives and then had acted incompetently, Americans grew more disillusioned with their leaders and their institutions.[36] Faith in the American way of life slipped.

Although it is appropriate to blame Bush and his advisers for this dismal trajectory, the failures in the aftermath of 9/11 should not be attributed to the president alone or exclusively to his administration. The failures were the nation's failures, the failures of the American people—not all, but many. When the president took the nation to war in mid-March 2003, 72 percent of the American people supported his decision. His own approval rating was at 71 percent; his disapproval rating, never more than 38 percent, dropped to 25 percent. Nor should anyone forget that in November 2001—long before there were any alleged "lies" or misinformation—74 percent of the American people favored the use of ground troops to remove Hussein from power. Support for war dropped from 61 percent in June 2002 to 54 percent in October and then hovered in the mid to high 50s until March 2003.[37] Twenty-nine Democrats in the Senate joined with 48 Republicans to authorize the president to use military force. In the House, 296 representatives, including 81 Democrats, voted to support the president. Although some of the nation's most eminent scholars of international relations argued that the war was not in America's interest, in March 2003 most Americans (64 percent) believed the war in Iraq would make the Middle East more stable and even more Americans (79 percent) thought it would improve the lives of Iraqis.[38]

Like most Americans, Bush and his advisers allowed their fears to overcome their prudence; their awe of American power to trump their judgment about the risks of employing it; their pride in American values—their hubris—to dwarf their understanding of the people they were allegedly seeking to help. Like most of their countrymen, Bush and his advisers never quite grasped that the anti-Americanism coursing through the Islamic world was not a result of Arabs hating American values but a consequence of their resentment of American deeds—Washington's support of repressive regimes, its embrace of Israel, its sanctions policy in Iraq, its military presence in Muslims' Holy Land (Saudi Arabia), its quest for oil, and its hegemonic role in their neighborhood.[39] Like most Americans, the president could not understand that his freedom agenda conjured up memories of American hypocrisy and Western imperialism and had little chance of transcending the divide between Islamists and secularists inside the Muslim world or allaying the distrust between ethnic, religious, and tribal groups inside Iraq.[40] Like most Americans, Bush and his advisers could not foresee how societal disorder, lawlessness, and personal vulnerability could trump the appeal of freedom for most Iraqis.[41] Like most Americans, administration policymakers could not imagine how secret prisons, black sites, waterboarding, and prisoner humiliation by white Christian women soldiers could undercut all the talk of freedom, human rights, and personal dignity. Like many Americans, the president and his advisers could not help but conflate the evil that Hussein personified with a magnitude of threat that he did not embody.

When critics blame Bush personally or his advisers more broadly, however, they tend to obfuscate the larger dilemmas of statecraft that inhered in the aftermath of 9/11. Bush failed not because he was a weak leader, a naïve ideologue, or a lying, manipulative politician. Critics forget how ominous the al Qaeda threat seemed and how evil and manipulative Hussein really was. They overlook how imprecise the intelligence was, and the difficulties of gathering it. They ignore Hussein's links to terrorists and the ongoing havoc caused by acts of suicidal terror. They trivialize how difficult it was to measure the threat Hussein constituted, how easy it was to magnify the danger he posed, how tempting it was to employ American power, and how consequential it would be if America was attacked again.

It is important to get the story right in order to grapple earnestly with the dilemmas of statecraft. By simplifying the story, we comfort ourselves to think that if we only had more honest officials, stronger leaders, wiser policymakers, all would be well. We did need such leaders then, and still do. Nonetheless, we must recognize that it is hard to collect actionable intelligence, measure threats, calculate the intentions of adversaries, set priorities, mobilize domestic support, and link means and ends. Tragedy occurs not because leaders are ill-intentioned, stupid, and corrupt; tragedy occurs when earnest people and responsible officials seek to do the right thing, and end up making things much worse. We need to think about that—to understand why. We need to ponder what happens when there is too much fear, too much power, too much hubris—and insufficient prudence.

NOTES

Chapter 1

1. These descriptive paragraphs regarding Saddam Hussein's childhood and upbringing are based on: Said K. Aburish, *Saddam Hussein: The Politics of Revenge* (London: Bloomsbury, 2000); Efraim Karsh and Inari Rautsi, *Saddam Hussein: A Political Biography* (New York: Grove Press, 1991); Con Coughlin, *Saddam: The Secret Life* (London: Macmillan, 2002).

2. For the role of the CIA, see Brandon Wolf-Hunnicutt, *The Paranoid Style in American Diplomacy: Oil and Arab Nationalism in Iraq* (Stanford, CA: Stanford University Press, 2021), 106–21.

3. Karsh and Rautsi, *Saddam Hussein*, 29–30.

4. Ibid., 33–34, quotation on 33.

5. Joseph Sassoon, *Saddam Hussein's Ba'th Party: Inside an Authoritarian Regime* (New York: Cambridge University Press, 2012), 169; also see Kanan Makiya, *Republic of Fear: The Politics of Modern Iraq* (Berkeley: University of California Press, 1998), 110–24, 225, 275; Aburish, *Saddam Hussein*, 126; Coughlin, *Saddam*, 73–98; Karsh and Rautsi, *Saddam Hussein*, 39–45.

6. Aburish, *Saddam Hussein*, 76, 93; Coughlin, *Saddam*, 59–63; Sassoon, *Ba'th Party*, 163–64, 278–79; Khidhir Hamza, "Saddam's Nuclear Program," in *The Saddam Hussein Reader*, ed. Turi Munthe (New York: Thunder's Mouth Press, 2002), 423.

7. For Hussein's strategic ambitions, see Kevin M. Woods, *The Mother of All Battles: Saddam Hussein's Strategic Plan for the Persian Gulf War* (Annapolis, MD: Naval Institute Press, 2008), 32–40; for his flexibility, see his interview in 1979 with Fuard Matar, in Munthe, *The Saddam Hussein Reader*, 18, 29–33; Sassoon, *Ba'th Party*, 277–79; Karsh and

Ratsui, *Saddam Hussein*, 144–45; illustratively, see "Saddam and Ba'ath Party Members Discussing the Status of the Party in the Arab World and Potential Cooperation with the Muslim Brotherhood," July 24, 1986, Conflict Records Research Center, SH-SHTP-A-001-167, https://conflict records.files.wordpress.com/2013/06/sh-shtp-a-001-167_english.pdf.

8. Aburish, *Saddam Hussein*, 99–102; Karsh and Rautsi, *Saddam Hussein*, 77–79; Wolfe-Hunnicutt, *Paranoid Style in American Diplomacy*, 204–14; Atif A. Kubursi, "Oil and the Iraqi Economy," *Arab Studies Quarterly* 10 (Summer 1988): 283–98.

9. For statistics, see Kubursi, "Oil and the Iraqi Economy," 293; also see Karsh and Rautsi, *Saddam Hussein*, 90–92; Aburish, *Saddam Hussein*, 105–18; Coughlin, *Saddam*, 111–16.

10. Aburish, *Saddam Hussein*, 135–37.

11. Ibid., 129–54, quotation on 147; also see Målfrid Braut-Hegghammer, *Unclear Physics: Why Iraq and Libya Failed to Build Nuclear Weapons* (Ithaca, NY: Cornell University Press, 2016), 46–64; Coughlin, *Saddam*, 127–37; Hamza, "Saddam's Nuclear Program," 417–27.

12. Karsh and Rautsi, *Saddam Hussein*, 84; also see Coughlin, *Saddam*, 118–22.

13. Karsh and Rautsi, *Saddam Hussein*, 97–98.

14. Ibid.; Aburish, *Saddam Hussein*, 122–23.

15. Coughlin, *Saddam*, 141–43.

16. Matar interview with Hussein, in Munthe, *Saddam Hussein Reader*, 23–24; Kevin M. Woods, David D. Palkki, and Mark E. Stout, eds., *The Saddam Tapes: The Inner Workings of a Tyrant's Regime, 1978–2001* (New York: Cambridge University Press, 2011), 118–21; Woods, *Mother of All Battles*, 33–37; Karsh and Rautsi, *Saddam Hussein*, 106–8; also see Saddam's interview with George L. Piro, February 10, 2004, "Saddam Hussein Talks to the FBI: Twenty Interviews and Five Conversations with High Value Detainee #1 in 2004," National Security Archive (NSA), EBB no. 279 (hereafter cited as Saddam's interviews with Piro).

17. Aburish, *Saddam Hussein*, 165–69; Karsh and Rautsi, *Saddam Hussein*, 106–9.

18. Coughlin, *Saddam*, 163–72; Karsh and Rautsi, *Saddam Hussein*, 113–18; Aburish, *Saddam Hussein*, 170–75; for Saddam's account, see his interview with Piro, February 20, 2004, NSA, EBB 279.

19. Hussein's interview with Piro, February 8, 2004, NSA, EBB 279.

20. Karsh and Rautsi, *Saddam Hussein*, 125–49; Pierre Razoux, *The Iran-Iraq War*, trans. Nicholas Elliott (Cambridge, MA: Harvard University Press, 2015), 1–87; Charles Tripp, *A History of Iraq*, 3rd ed. (New York: Cambridge University Press, 2007), 223–26; Phebe Marr, *The Modern History of Iraq* (Boulder, CO: Westview Press, 2012), 179–82.

21. Woods, *Saddam Tapes*, 31–33; Razoux, *Iran-Iraq War*, especially 381–87.

22. "Meeting between Saddam Hussein and His Senior Advisers Following the Israeli Attack on Osirak," circa 1981, CRRC Record Number: SH-SHTP-A-001-480.

23. For Hussein's feelings, see his conversation with Piro, February 8, 2004, NSA, EBB 279; Woods, *Saddam Tapes*, 220; also see Coughlin, *Saddam*, 210–11, 223–24; Razoux, *Iran-Iraq War*, 298–99, 437–42; Tripp, *History of Iraq*, 235–36.

24. Karsh and Rautsi, *Saddam Hussein*, 145–70; Coughlin, *Saddam*, 207–24; Razoux, *Iran-Iraq War*, 463–73.

25. Karsh and Rautsi, *Saddam Hussein*, 194–96.

26. Coughlin, *Saddam*, 236–37; Aburish, *Saddam Hussein*, 259–65; Marr, *Modern History of Iraq*, 200–9; Sassoon, *Ba'th Party*, 139–43.

27. For the quotation, see Aburish, *Saddam Hussein*, 254, also 259–62; Amatzia Baram, "The Effect of Iraqi Sanctions: Statistical Pitfalls and Responsibility," *Middle East Journal* 54 (Spring 2000): 221–22; Karsh and Ratsui, *Saddam Hussein*, 175–205.

28. Hussein's interview with Piro, February 10, 2004, NSA, EBB 279.

29. Ibid., February 10 and 24, 2004; Coughlin, *Saddam*, 243–50; Aburish, *Saddam Hussein*, 271–83; Karsh and Ratsui, *Saddam Hussein*, 201–15; Hal Brands and David Palkki, "'Conspiring Bastards': Saddam Hussein's Strategic View of the United States," *Diplomatic History* 36 (June 2012): 625–59.

30. Karsh and Ratsui, *Saddam Hussein*, 211–12; Amatzia Baram, "The Iraqi Invasion of Kuwait," in Munthe, *Saddam Reader*, 262–66; Lawrence Freedman and Efraim Karsh, *The Gulf Conflict, 1990–1991: Diplomacy and War in the New World Order* (Princeton, NJ: Princeton University Press, 1993), 42–50.

31. Robert K. Brigham, ed., *The United States and Iraq since 1990* (Malden, MA: Wiley-Blackwell, 2014), 10–15; George Bush and Brent Scowcroft, *A World Transformed* (New York: Vintage, 1998), 307–12; Jeffrey A. Engel, *When the World Seemed New: George H. W. Bush and the End of the Cold War* (Boston: Houghton, Mifflin, Harcourt, 2017), 376–83; for Tariq Aziz's comment, see Samuel Helfont, *Iraq against the World: How Saddam's Ba'thists Defied America and Shaped Post–Cold War Politics* (New York: Oxford University Press, forthcoming); for a strong critique of the equivocal policies pursued by the United States in the 1980s, see Bruce W. Jentleson, *With Friends Like These: Reagan, Bush, and Saddam, 1982–1990* (New York: W. W. Norton, 1994); for a more balanced assessment, see Zachary Karabell and Philip D. Zelikow, "Iraq 1988–1990: Unexpectedly Heading toward War," in *Dealing with Dictators: Dilemmas of U.S. Diplomacy and Intelligence Analysis, 1945–1990*, ed. Ernest R. May and Philip D. Zelikow (Cambridge, MA: MIT Press, 2006), 167–202; also Freedman and Karsh, *Gulf Conflict*, 50–55, 428–30.

32. Woods, *Saddam Tapes*, 114–15.

33. See the illuminating documents, "Gorbachev's 'Diplomatic Marathon' to Prevent the 1991 Persian Gulf War," National Security Archive, Briefing Book #745, February 26, 2021; Freedman and Karsh, *Gulf Conflict*, 110–27.

34. Woods, *Saddam Tapes*, 237, 240; Kevin M. Woods et al., *Iraqi Perspectives Project: A View of Operation Iraqi Freedom from Saddam's Senior Leadership* (Washington, DC: Institute for Defense Analysis, 2006), 5–7; Woods, *Mother of All Battles*, 52; Karsh and Ratsui, *Saddam Hussein*, 217–66; Peter Hahn, *Missions Impossible: The United States and Iraq since World War I* (New York: Oxford University Press, 2012), 94–102; Brigham, *United States and Iraq*, 15–22.

35. Bush and Scowcroft, *A World Transformed*, 302–492; Jon Meacham, *Destiny and Power: The American Odyssey of George Herbert Walker Bush* (New York: Random House, 2015), 462–69; Karsh and Freedman, *Gulf Conflict*, 201–442; Marr, *Modern History of Iraq*, 224–26; Brigham, *United States and Iraq*, 18–26.

36. Lawrence Freedman, *A Choice of Enemies: America Confronts the Middle East* (New York: Public Affairs, 2018), 251.

37. Saddam's interviews with Piro, March 13 and 16, 2004, NSA, EBB 279.

38. Marr, *Modern History of Iraq*, 228–34; Dina Rizk Khoury, *Iraq in Wartime: Soldiering, Martyrdom, and Remembrance* (New York: Cambridge University Press, 2013), 133–45.

39. Woods, *Mother of All Battles*, 299–305; Woods, *Iraqi Perspectives*, 14–16, 30.

40. Meacham, *Destiny and Power*, 541–42.

41. For Hussein's view, see his interview with Piro, May 13, 2004, NSA, EBB 279; Rolf Ekeus, "The United Nations Special Commission on Iraq," *SIPRI Yearbook 1992: World Armaments and Disarmament*, 509–24, https://www.sipri.org/sites/default/files/SIPRI%20Yearbook%201 992.pdf; for the work of UNSCOM, see SIPRI, "Iraq: The UNSCOM Experience: Fact Sheet, 1998," https://www.sipri.org/sites/default/files/ files/FS/SIPRIFS9810.pdf; for background on Hussein's atomic program, see Braut-Hegghammer, *Unclear Physics*, 103–23.

42. Iraq Survey Group, *Comprehensive Report of the Special Advisor to the DCI on Iraq's WMD*, September 30, 2004, 8–9, 26, 34, 43–46, http://www-perso nal.umich.edu/~graceyor/govdocs/duelfer.html (hereafter cited as Duelfer Report); also see Norman Cigar, "Saddam Hussein's Nuclear Vision: An Atomic Shield and Sword for Conquest," *Middle East Studies Occasional Papers* (Quantico, VA: Marine Corps University Press, 2011), 42, 52–53; "Meeting between Saddam Hussein and His Senior Advisers," circa 1981, CRRC, SH-SHTP-A-001-480; Hal Brands and David Palkki, "Saddam, Israel, and the Bomb," *International Security* 36(Summer 2011): 133–66; Coughlin, *Saddam*, 283–86, 294–95.

43. UN Security Council, "The Status of the Implementation of the Plan for the Ongoing Monitoring and Verification of Iraq's Compliance with . . .," Security Council Resolution 687 (1991), 19 October 1992, https://www.un.org/Depts/unscom/24661.pdf; UN Security Council, "Fourth Report of the Executive Chairman of the Special Commission . . .," December 17, 1992, https://www.un.org/Depts/unscom/24984.pdf; Arms Control Association, "A Chronology of UN Inspections," https://www.armscontrol.org/act/2002-10/features/iraq-chronology-un-inspections.

44. Marr, *Modern History of Iraq*, 238–41; Joy Gordon, *Invisible War: The United States and the Iraq Sanctions* (Cambridge, MA: Harvard University Press, 2010), 86–102; Sarah Graham-Brown, *Sanctioning Saddam: The Politics of Intervention in Iraq* (London: I. B. Tauris, 1999), 153–251; Baram, "Effect of Iraqi Sanctions," 194–223; Aburish, *Saddam Hussein*, 318–19.

45. Karsh and Ratsui, *Saddam Hussein*, 273–74; Gordon, *Invisible War*, 125–30.

46. Marr, *Modern History of Iraq*, 234–35; Offra Bengio, *Saddam's Word: Political Discourse in Iraq* (New York: Oxford University Press, 1998); Samuel Helfont, "Saddam and the Islamists: The Ba'athist Regime's Instrumentalization of Religion in Foreign Affairs," *Middle East Journal* 68 (Summer 2014): 352–66.

47. Woods, *Iraqi Perspectives*, 7–16; Duelfer Report, 11–23; Sassoon, *Ba'th Party*, 3–12.

48. Coughlin, *Saddam*, 293–98, 305, 317; Aburish, *Saddam Hussein*, 324–27.

49. Aburish, *Saddam Hussein*, 236, 326, 337–39; Duelfer Report, 17, 45–46.

50. Arms Control Association, "A Chronology of UN Inspections," 7; Braut-Hegghammer, *Unclear Physics*, 118–23.

51. Duelfer Report, 48–57; SIPRI, "Iraq: The UNSCOM Experience: Fact Sheet"; Arms Control Association, "A Chronology of UN Inspections," 7–23; for Saddam's view, see his interview with Piro, May 13, 2004, NSA, EBB 279; also see Steven Hurst, *The United States and Iraq since 1979: Hegemony, Oil and War* (Edinburgh: Edinburgh University Press, 2009), 126–41; Hahn, *Missions Accomplished*, 124–25.

52. Marr, *Modern History of Iraq*, 239–40; Duelfer Report, 55–60; for analysis of Hussein's strategy to divide his former enemies and undermine sanctions, see Helfont, *Iraq against the World,* chapter 8.

53. Jack Straw, "Statement on Sanctions," May 4, 2011, Iraq Inquiry, https://webarchive.nationalarchives.gov.uk/ukgwa/20171123123237/http://www.iraqinquiry.org.uk/; Duelfer Report, 48, also the section on "Regime Finance and Procurement."

54. World Bank data, https://data.worldbank.org/indicator/NY.GDP.PCAP.KD?locations=IQ; also see Marr, *Modern History of Iraq*, 239; Coughlin, *Saddam*, 314–16; Gordon, *Invisible War*, 131–32; Sassoon, *Ba'th Party*, 281.

55. Aburish, *Saddam Hussein*, 337–39.

56. Marr, *Modern History of Iraq*, 249–50.

57. *Human Rights Watch World Report 2000—Iraq*, https://www.refworld.org/docid/3ae6a8cdc.html.

58. Kevin M. Woods, Project Leader, with James Lacy, *Iraqi Perspectives Project: Saddam and Terrorism: Emerging Insights from Captured Iraqi Documents (Redacted)*, 5 vols. (Washington, DC: Institute for Defense Analysis, 2007), I:1–11, quote on I:10.

59. Duelfer Report, 57, 59.

60. Ibid., "Regime Finance and Procurement—Key Findings."

61. Tommy R. Franks, "Statement," March 28, 2001, U.S. House, Armed Services, http://www.reasons-for-war-with-iraq.info/tommy_franks_3-28-01.html.

62. Woods, *Iraqi Perspectives Project: Saddam and Terrorism*, 1: ES-2, 21; Helfont, "Saddam and the Islamists."

63. These quotations are from the Duelfer Report, 24. Most authors characterize Saddam's ambitions in precisely the same manner. See, for example, Woods, *Iraqi Perspectives Project*; Aburish, *Saddam Hussein*; Coughlin, *Saddam*; Karsh and Ratsui, *Saddam Hussein*; Sassoon, *Ba'th Party*.

64. Duelfer Report; also see Saddam's own comments in his conversations with Piro, May 10, 2004, May 13, 2004, June 11, 2004, NSA, EBB 279.

65. Arms Control Association, "Chronology of UN Inspections," especially 16, 18, 20.

66. Duelfer Report, 9, 51, 59; Woods, *Iraqi Perspective Project*, 91–95.

67. See especially three of his last four conversations with Piro, May 10, 2004, May 13, 2004, June 11, 2004, NSA, EBB 279.

68. Woods, *Iraqi Perspective Project*, 14.

69. *Ibid.*, 15–16; "Transcription of a Meeting between Saddam Hussein and U.S. Congressman Bill Richardson," July 16, 1995, CRRC Record Number: SH-SHTP-D-001-500; "Transmittal Message," 4, Duelfer Report; Saddam conversation with Piro, June 11, 2004, NSA, EBB 279.

70. Saddam's interviews with Piro, February 7, 2004, February 13, 2004, NSA, EBB 279.

71. Sassoon, *Ba'th Party*, 174; Duelfer Report, 22; Woods, *Iraqi Perspectives Project*, 6, 12–16.

72. Tripp, *History of Iraq*, 222.

Chapter 2

1. George W. Bush, *Decision Points* (New York: Crown Publishers, 2010); George W. Bush, *A Charge to Keep* (New York: William Morrow and Company, 1999); James Mann, *George W. Bush* (New York: Henry Holt and Company, 2015), 1–19; Jean Edward Smith, *Bush* (New York: Simon & Schuster, 2016).

2. Bush, *Decision Points*, 8.

3. Ibid., 7–8, 20–21; Jacob Weisberg, *The Bush Tragedy* (New York: Random House, 2008), 3–29; John Meacham, *Destiny and Power: The American Odyssey of George Herbert Walker Bush* (New York: Random House, 2015).

4. Bush, *Decision Points*, especially 22; Bush, *A Charge to Keep*, 46–66; Mann, *Bush*, 5–25.

5. Bush, *Decision Points*, 31; Bush, *A Charge to Keep*, 61–66, 132–35; Ann Gerhart, *The Perfect Wife: The Life and Choices of Laura Bush* (New York: Simon & Schuster, 2004), 45–87.

6. Bush, *Decision Points*, 30–34; Bush, *A Charge to Keep*, 1–13, 132–39; Gerhart, *Perfect Wife*, 71–79; David Aikman, *A Man of Faith: The Spiritual Journey of George W. Bush* (Nashville, TN: W. Publishing Group, 2004).

7. These generalizations are based on: Bush, *A Charge to Keep*; Mann, *Bush*; Weisberg, *Bush Tragedy*; Smith, *Bush*; Robert Draper, *Dead Certain: The Presidency of George W. Bush* (New York: Free Press, 2007).

8. Bush, *Decision Points*, 51.

9. Lauren F. Turek, "Religious Rhetoric and the Evolution of George W. Bush's Political Philosophy," *Journal of American Studies* 48 (May 2014): 975–98.

10. "Talking Points," Faith Based Bill Press Conference, March 11, 1997, 2002/151–67, Texas Governor George W. Bush Executive Office Speeches, Texas State Library and Archives Commission. I am indebted to Lauren Turek for sharing these documents with me; also see Gary Scott Smith, *Faith and the Presidency: From George Washington to George W. Bush* (New York: Oxford University Press, 2006), 365–72, 387–92.

11. "Talking Points," Faith Based Bills Signing, June 12, 1997, 2002/151–68, Texas Governor George W. Bush Executive Office Speeches, Texas State Library and Archives Commission.

12. "Bush Says G.O.P. Stresses Wealth at Expense of Tackling Social Ills," *New York Times*, October 6, 1999.

13. "Excerpts from Bush's Speech Outlining His Proposal to Revise Medicare," *New York Times*, September 6, 2000.

14. Bush, *A Charge to Keep*; Aikman, *Man of Faith*, 1–13; Smith, *Faith and the Presidency*, 365–92.

15. Bush, *Decision Points*, 82–83; Condoleezza Rice, *No Higher Honor: A Memoir of My Years in Washington* (New York: Crown Publishers, 2011), 1–2; Antonia Felix, *Condi: The Condoleezza Rice Story* (New York: Newmarket Press, 2005), 8–10; Marcus Mabry, *Twice as Good: Condoleezza Rice and Her Path to Power* (New York: Modern Times, 2007), 153–56.

16. Dov S. Zakheim, *A Vulcan's Tale: How the Bush Administration Mismanaged the Reconstruction of Afghanistan* (Washington, DC: Brookings Institution Press, 2011), 8, 14–15, 39; Stephen Hadley, interview, October 31–November 1, 2011, George W. Bush Oral History Project (hereafter GWB/OHP), Miller Center (MC), University of

Virginia, http://web1.millercenter.org/poh/transcripts/hadley_stephe
n_2011_1031.pdf; Rice, *No Higher Honor*, 1–8; James Mann, *Rise of the
Vulcans: The History of Bush's War Cabinet* (New York: Viking, 2004);
Condoleezza Rice, "Campaign 2000: Promoting the National Interest,"
Foreign Affairs, January/February 2000.

17. Hadley, Interview, October 31-November 1, 2011, GWB/OHP; Zakheim,
Vulcan's Tale, 15; Rice, *No Higher Honor*, 4.

18. Zakheim, *Vulcan's Tale*, 16, 19; Paul Wolfowitz, interview with author,
February 2, 2011, transcript of this interview—and most others cited
below—are in possession of author; Robert Zoellick, interview with
author, October 22, 2015; Hadley, interview, October 31-November 1,
2011, GWB/OHP; Eric Edelman, interview with author, March 10,
2011; Michael Gerson, *Heroic Conservatism: Why Republicans Need to
Embrace America's Ideals (and Why They Deserve to Fail If They Don't*
(New York: HarperCollins, 2007), 37–42; Michael Morell, *The Great War
of Our Time: The CIA's Fight against Terrorism from Al-Qa'ida to ISIS*
(New York: Twelve, 2015), 31–32; Donald Rumsfeld, Note, December
28, 2000, Rumsfeld Papers, https://www.rumsfeld.com/archives/;
Hugh Shelton, *Without Hesitation: The Odyssey of an American Warrior*
(New York: St. Martin's Press, 2010), 413–17; Michael Hayden, Interview,
November 20, 2012, GWB/OHP, MC, http://web1.millercenter.org/poh/
transcripts/hayden_michael_2012_1120.pdf.

19. Bush, "A Distinctly American Internationalism," November 19, 1999,
https://www.mtholyoke.edu/acad/intrel/bush/wspeech.htm; Bush, "A
Period of Consequences," September 23, 1999, http://www3.citadel.edu/
pao/addresses/pres_bush.html.

20. Michael Gerson, interview with author, March 9, 2016.

21. Bush, "A Distinctly American Internationalism"; Bush, "A Period of
Consequences."

22. Bush, "A Period of Consequences."

23. Gerson, interview with author, March 9, 2016; Zakheim, *A Vulcan's Tale*,
14–15; Zalmay Khalilzad, *The Envoy: From Kabul to the White House,
My Journey through a Turbulent World* (New York: St. Martin's Press,
2016), 110.

24. Samuel Helfont, *Iraq against the World: How Saddam's Ba'thists Defied
America and Shaped Post–Cold War Politics* (New York: Oxford University
Press, 2023).

25. Bush-Gore Second Presidential Debate, October 11, 2000, https://www.
debates.org/voter-education/debate-transcripts/october-11-2000-debate-tra
nscript/. Many of these points were reiterated in the third presidential
debate, October 17, 2000, https://www.debates.org/voter-education/deb
ate-transcripts/october-17-2000-debate-transcript/.

26. Michael Morell, interviews with author, December 18, 2013, and January
25, 2014; Gerson, interview with author, March 9, 2016.

27. Christopher Meyer, interview, November 26, 2019, 3–5, 19, Iraq Inquiry, https://webarchive.nationalarchives.gov.uk/20150122084505/http://www.iraqinquiry.org.uk/transcripts/oralevidence-bydate/091126.aspx.

28. Richard Cheney, interview with author, August 11, 2017; Scooter Libby, interview with author, December 9, 2010; Edelman, interview with author, March 10, 2011.

29. Bush, *Decision Points*, 49, 65–70; Dick Cheney, with Liz Cheney, *In My Time: A Personal and Political Memoir* (New York: Threshold Editions, 2011), 252–60; Peter Baker, *Days of Fire: Bush and Cheney in the White House* (New York: Doubleday, 2013), 52–64.

30. Libby, interviews with author, December 9, 2010, January 25, 2011; Richard Clarke, interview with author, December 31, 2010; Edelman, interview with author, March 10, 2011; Steve Biegun, lunchtime discussion with author, August 7, 2015; Franklin Miller, interview with author, July 15, 2011; Hadley, Interview, October 31-November 1, 2011, GWB/OHP, MC; Peter Wehner, comments at a colloquium sponsored by the Miller Center, October 21, 2015.

31. Bush, *Decision Points*, 81–94; Rice, *No Higher Honor*, 13–50; Hadley, Interview, October 31-November 1, 2011, GWB/OHP, MC. These generalizations are also based on the author's interviews with Libby, Edelman, Powell, Armitage, Clarke, and Miller, among others.

32. Bush, "Inaugural Address," January 20, 2001, https://www.presidency.ucsb.edu/documents/inaugural-address-52.

33. Ibid.

34. Rice to Bush, January 7, 2001, Philip D. Zelikow Papers, University of Virginia.

35. Clarke to Rice, January 25, 2001, Electronic Briefing Book [EBB] #147, National Security Archive [NSA]; Clarke, "Strategy for Eliminating the Threat from the Jihadist Networks of al Qida: Status and Prospects," December 2000, ibid.

36. Clarke, *Against All Enemies*, 227–38; Rice, *No Higher Honor*, 64–66; Hadley, Interview, October 31–November 1, 2011, GWB/OHP, MC; Clarke, interview with author. Among top officials in the office of the vice president, as well as on the NSC staff, there was widespread contempt for Clarke. See Edelman, interview with author, March 10, 2011; Biegun, lunchtime discussion with author, August 7, 2015.

37. Smith, *Bush*, 174; Rice, *No Higher Honor*, 17.

38. Smith, *Bush*, 174; Colin Powell, interview with author, January 24, 2011; Richard Armitage, interview with author, March 23, 2011. Powell and Armitage did not initially see Bush as favoring the advice of Cheney and Rumsfeld, although their perceptions started to change during the summer of 2001.

39. NSC Principals Meetings–Iraq, February 13, 16, 20 2001, Targeting Iraq, DNSA; Department of Defense Secret Cable to Sec of State, February 1,

2001, ibid.; Rice, *No Higher Honor*, 27–34; Bush, *Decision Points*, 225–26; Hugh Shelton, with Ronald Levinson and Malcolm McConnell, *Without Hesitation: The Odyssey of an American Warrior* (New York: St. Martin's Press, 2010), 421–23.

40. Memo of Conversation, Meeting with British Prime Minister Blair, February 23 2001, Targeting Iraq, DNSA; Christopher Meyer, interview, 3–5, 13, 18–19, 57–58, Iraq Inquiry, Nov 26, 2009.

41. Statement of Donald H. Rumsfeld, January 11, 2001, Senate, Armed Services, https://www.congress.gov/107/chrg/shrg75903/CHRG-107sh rg75903.htm; Statement, by Wolfowitz, February 27, 2001, Senate, Armed Services, https://www.globalsecurity.org/military/library/congress/2001 _hr/010227pw.pdf; also see "Executive Summary of the Report of the Commission to Assess the Ballistic Missile Threat to the United States," July 15, 1998, http://www.bits.de/NRANEU/BMD/documents/Rumsfel d150798.pdf.

42. Rumsfeld, Prepared Testimony, June 21, 2001, Senate, Armed Services, https://www.globalsecurity.org/military/library/congress/2001_hr/ 010621rumsfeld.pdf; Richard Myers, with Malcolm McConnell, *Eyes on the Horizon: Serving on the Front Lines of National Security* (New York: Threshold Editions, 2009), 140.

43. Memo, by Rumsfeld, May 31, 2001, Rumsfeld Papers; Rumsfeld, Draft-2, "The DOD Challenge," June 25, 2001, ibid.; Christopher Lamb, interview with author, September 2, 2011; Douglas Lute, Interview, August 3, 2015, GWB/OHP, MC; Shelton, *Without Hesitation*, 401–13; for a slightly more positive assessment, see Myers, *Eyes on the Horizon*, 134–36.

44. Department of Defense, *Quadrennial Defense Review Report*, September 30, 2001, iii, 13–14, https://archive.defense.gov/pubs/qdr2001.pdf; Rumsfeld, Draft-2, "The DOD Challenge"; Rumsfeld, Testimony, June 28, 2001, Senate, Armed Services Committee, https://www.globalsecurity. org/military/library/congress/2001_hr/010628rumsfeld.pdf.

45. Libby, interviews with author, December 9, 2010, January 25, 2011; Edelman, interviews with author, December 2, 2010, March 10, 2011; Seth Carus, interview with author, December 16, 2015; Cheney, *In My Times*, 318–21; "Dark Winter," June 22–23, 2001, Rumsfeld Papers.

46. Report of the National Energy Policy Development Group, *National Energy Policy*, May 2001, especially chapter 8, quotation on 8:1, http:// wtrg.com/EnergyReport/National-Energy-Policy.pdf; for Cheney's views on carbon commissions and the Kyoto Protocol on climate, see Cheney, *In Our Time*, 315–18; Rice, *No Higher Honor*, 41–43.

47. Edelman, interviews with author, December 2, 2010, March 10, 2011; Libby, interview with author, December 9, 2010; Rice, *No Higher Honor*, 64–66; Hadley, Interview, October 31-November 1, 2011, GWB/ OHP, MC.

48. Tenet, Statement, March 7, 2001, Senate, Armed Services Committee, https://fas.org/irp/congress/2001_hr/s010308t.html.

49. Morell, interview with author, December 18, 2013; Morell, *Great War*, 38–43; George Tenet, *At the Center of the Storm: My Years at the CIA* (New York: HarperCollins, 2007), 144–58; Clarke, *Against All Enemies*, 230–38.

50. Morell, interview with author, December 18, 2013; Armitage, interview with author, March 23, 2011; Tenet, *At the Center of the Storm*, 142–60.

51. Draft, "National Security Strategy," July 23, 2001, Zelikow Papers; Richard N. Haass, *War of Necessity, War of Choice: A Memoir of Two Iraq Wars* (New York: Simon & Schuster, 2009), 200–1.

52. Draft, "National Security Strategy," July 23, 2001.

53. Libby, interview with author, December 9, 2010; Cheney, interview with author, August 11, 2017; Edelman, interview with author, March 10, 2011; Biegun, lunchtime discussion with author, August 7, 2015; Gerson, interview with author, March 9, 2016.

54. Carl W. Ford to Powell, September 7, 2001, Targeting Iraq, DNSA; Bureau of Near Eastern Affairs and Policy Planning Staff, "Strategies for Preserving U.S. Political Capital in the Middle East," August 30, 2001, "The Archive" for *The Back Channel* by William J. Burns, https://carneg ieendowment.org/publications/interactive/back-channel/ (hereafter cited as Burns Papers); DIA report, "Possibility and Implications of Iraq Breaking Out of International Isolation," February 1, 2001, Reading Room, Office of the Secretary of Defense, www.esd.whs.mil (hereafter cited as OSD Reading Room). For evolving worries about Iraq's nuclear and biological programs, based on reports about aluminum tubes and biological warfare capabilities, see Report to the President of the United States, The Commission on the Intelligence Capabilities of the United States Regarding Weapons of Mass Destruction, March 31, 2005, 55, 83, 90, 93, https://govinfo.library.unt.edu/wmd/report/wmd_report. pdf. The problems and controversies regarding these findings were just beginning to percolate in spring 2001. Powell used the phrase "jail cell" in his conversation with the German foreign minister, February 20, 2001, Targeting Iraq, DNSA.

55. For Wolfowitz's views, see "Prepared Testimony," July 12, 2001, July 17, 2001, Senate, Armed Services Committee; Wolfowitz, interview with author, July 28, 2010; Khalilzad, *The Envoy*, 98–99.

56. Rumsfeld to Rice, July 27, 2001, Rumsfeld Papers.

57. Khalilzad, *The Envoy*, 99.

58. Edelman, interview with author, March 10, 2011; Hadley, interview with author, Feb. 22, 2011; Armitage, interview with author, March 23, 2011.

59. Khalilzad, *The Envoy*, 99.

60. Armitage, interview with author, March 23, 2011.

61. For an excellent assessment of the issues, see Anthony H. Cordesman, *Iraq's Military Capabilities in 2002: A Dynamic Net Assessment* (Washington, DC: Center for Strategic and International Studies, 2002).

62. Final Report of the National Commission on Terrorist Attacks upon the United States, *The 9/11 Commission Report* (New York: W. W. Norton, 2004), 211–14; Clarke, *Against All Enemies*, 237–38; J. Samuel Walker, *The Day That Shook America: A Concise History of 9/11* (Lawrence: University Press of Kansas, 2021), 75–77.

63. Bob Woodward, *Plan of Attack* (New York: Simon & Schuster, 2004), 24.

64. David L. Phillips, *Losing Iraq: Inside the Postwar Reconstruction Fiasco* (Boulder, CO: Westview Press, 2005), 17.

65. Clarke, *Against All Enemies*, 244; Morell, *Great War of Our Time*, 41; Walker, *Day That Shook America*, 66–77; *9/11 Commission Report*, 359–60.

66. Powell, written Remarks to the National Commission on Terrorist Attacks, March 23, 2004, https://govinfo.library.unt.edu/911/hearings/hearing8/powell_statement.pdf; Powell, interview with author, January 24, 2011; William Smullen, interview with author, February 23, 2011; Armitage, interview with author, March 23, 2011.

67. Rumsfeld to Wolfowitz, Cambone, and Feith, June 9, 2001, Targeting Iraq, DNSA; *9/11 Commission Report*, 208, 351; Tenet, *Center of the Storm*, 254; Morell, *Great War of Our Time*, 41.

68. Rice, *No Higher Honor*, 68–69; Hadley, Interview, October 31–November 1, 2011, GWB/OHP, MC; Biegun, lunchtime conversation with author, August 7, 2015.

69. Libby, interviews with author, December 9, 2010, January 25, 2011; Edelman, interview with author, March 10, 2011; Carus, interview with author, December 16, 2015; Cheney, *In My Time*, 318–19.

70. *9/11 Commission Report*, 254–77, 339–60, quotation on 265; Clarke, *Against All Enemies*, 254, 256.

71. Remarks Delivered by Rumsfeld, September 10, 2001, https://agovern mentofthepeople.com/2001/09/10/donald-rumsfeld-speech-about-burea ucratic-waste/.

Chapter 3

1. For a superb description of the events on 9/11, see J. Samuel Walker, *The Day That Shook America: A Concise History of 9/11* (Lawrence: University Press of Kansas, 2021).

2. Karl Rove, *Courage and Consequence: My Life as a Conservative in the Fight* (New York: Threshold Editions, 2010), 250–52.

3. Ibid., 250–57; George W. Bush, *Decision Points* (New York: Crown Publishers, 2010), 128–31.

4. Rove, *Courage and Consequence*, 259–63.

5. Michael Morell, interview with author, December 8, 2013.

6. Rove, *Courage and Consequence*, 261; Michael Morell, *The Great War of Our Time: The CIA's Fight against Terrorism from Al Qa'ida to ISIS* (New York: Twelve, 2015), 45–60; Morell, interview with author, December 8, 2013.

7. Morell, interview with author, December 8, 2013; Rove, *Courage and Consequence*, 256.

8. Bush, *Decision Points*, 128; Morell, *Great War of Our Time*, 63.

9. Karen Hughes, *Ten Minutes from Normal* (New York: Viking, 2004), 241; Rove, *Courage and Consequence*, 250–56; Morell, *Great War of Our Time*, 55.

10. Morell, interview with author, December 8, 2013; for allusions to Bush's spirituality, also see Michael Gerson, *Heroic Conservatism: Why Republicans Need to Embrace America's Ideals* (New York: HarperCollins, 2007), 1–10, 61; Colin Powell and Richard L. Armitage, Interview, March 28, 2017, George W. Bush, Oral History Project, Miller Center, University of Virginia (hereafter cited as GWB/OHP, MC).

11. Hughes, *Ten Minutes from Normal*, 239–40.

12. George W. Bush, "Address to the Nation on the Terrorist Attacks," September 11, 2001, https://www.presidency.ucsb.edu/documents/address-the-nation-the-terrorist-attacks (hereafter cited as APP).

13. Richard Clarke, *Against All Enemies: Inside America's War on Terror* (New York: Free Press, 2004), 24.

14. Bush, *Decision Points*, 138–39.

15. Gerson, *Heroic Conservatism*, 70.

16. Clarke, *Against All Enemies*, 28–30.

17. Hughes, *Ten Minutes from Normal*, 246.

18. Stephen J. Hadley, Interview, October 31–November 1, 2011, GWB/OHP, MC; Shelton, *Without Hesitation*, 439–42; Condoleezza Rice, *No Higher Honor: A Memoir of My Years in Washington* (New York: Crown Publishers, 2011), 80.

19. Hadley, Interview, October 31-November 1, 2011, GWB/OHP, MC; Rice, *No Higher Honor*, 85–86; Clarke, *Against All Enemies*, 29–32; Dick Cheney, with Liz Cheney, *In My Time: A Personal and Political Memoir* (New York: Threshold Editions, 2011), 329–34; Richard Myers, with Malcolm McConnell, *Eyes on the Horizon: Serving on the Front Lines of National Security* (New York: Threshold, 2009), 166; Shelton, *Without Hesitation*, 441–42; The 9/11 Commission Report, *Final Report of the National Commission on Terrorist Attacks upon the United States* (Washington, DC: New York: W. W. Norton, 2004), 330–36 (hereafter cited as *9/11 Commission Report*).

20. Alberto R. Gonzales, *True Faith and Allegiance: A Story of Service and Sacrifice in War and Peace* (Nashville, TN: Nelson Books, 206), 137–39; Rice, *No Higher Honor*, 86–87; Paul Wofowitz, "What Was and What Might Have Been: The Threats and Wars in Afghanistan and Iraq," 3,

February 22, 2022, Hoover Institution, https://www.aei.org/articles/what-was-and-what-might-have-been-the-threats-and-wars-in-afghanistan-and-iraq/.

21. John Negroponte, Interview, September 14, 2012, GWB/OHP, MC.

22. George W. Bush, "Address before a Joint Session of the Congress," September 20, 2001, APP.

23. George W. Bush, "The President's Press Conference," October 11, 2001, APP.

24. Donald Rumsfeld, *Known and Unknown: A Memoir* (New York: Sentinel, 2011), 361–62.

25. Rumsfeld, Memorandum, September 23, 2001, Rumsfeld Papers, http://library.rumsfeld.com/doclib/sp/2815/2001-09-23%20to%20(no%20recipient)%20re%20What%20is%20Victory.pdf (hereafter cited as Rumsfeld Papers); Wolfowitz, Interview with Fox News, September 13, 2001, http://www.defense.gov/transcripts/transcript.aspx?transcriptid=1909; Douglas J. Feith, *War and Decision: Inside the Pentagon at the Dawn of the War on Terrorism* (New York: Harper, 2008), 10, 12.

26. See, for example, Ron Suskind, *The Price of Loyalty: George W. Bush, the White House, and the Education of Paul O'Neill* (New York: Simon & Schuster, 2004); James Mann, *Rise of the Vulcans: The History of Bush's War Cabinet* (New York: Viking, 2004); Terry H. Anderson, *Bush's Wars* (New York: Oxford University Press, 2011); Michael J. Mazarr, *Leap of Faith: Hubris, Negligence, and America's Greatest Foreign Policy Tragedy* (New York: Public Affairs, 2019); Barton Gellman, *Angler: The Cheney Vice Presidency* (New York: Penguin, 2008); Jane Mayer, *The Inside Story of How the War on Terror Turned into a War on American Ideals* (New York: Doubleday, 2008).

27. George Tenet, *At the Center of the Storm: My Years at the CIA* (New York: HarperCollins, 2007), 171; Clarke, *Against All Enemies*, 23; Clarke, interview with author, December 31, 2010; Gonzales, *True Faith and Allegiance*, 139; Rumsfeld, *Known and Unknown*, 350–51: Rice, *No Higher Honor*, 83–84; also see Hughes, *Ten Minutes from Normal*, 252–53; Peter Pace, Interview, January 19, 2016, GWB/OHP, MC; Zalmay Khalilzad, *The Envoy: From Kabul to the White House, My Journey through a Turbulent World* (New York: St. Martin's Press, 2016), 108–13.

28. "Bush Job Approval Highest in Gallup History," September 24, 2001, https://news.gallup.com/poll/4924/bush-job-approval-highest-gallup-history.aspx.

29. The White House, "A National Security Strategy for a New Century," October 15–16, 1998, https://www.globalsecurity.org/military/library/policy/national/nss-9810.pdf.

30. Report of the National Commission on Terrorism, *Countering the Changing Threat of International Terrorism* (Washington,

DC: Government Printing Office, 2000), 6–8, https://fas.org/irp/threat/commission.html.

31. Tenet, Statement, March 8, 2001, U.S. Senate, Committee on Armed Services, https://fas.org/irp/congress/2001_hr/s010308t.html.

32. Thomas R. Wilson, Statement, March 8, 2001, U.S. Senate, Committee on Armed Services, https://fas.org/irp/congress/2001_hr/s010207w.html.

33. Shelton, *Without Hesitation*, 431.

34. Tommy R. Franks, Statement, March 22, 2001, Senate, Armed Services Committee, http://armed-services.senate.gov/hearings/2001/c010322.htm; Tommy Franks, with Malcolm McConnell, *American Soldier* (New York: Regan Books, 2004), 236; for terrorist networks and their linkages, also see "DCI's Worldwide Threat Briefing," enclosed in Rumsfeld to Andy Marshall, February 27, 2001, "Targeting Iraq," DNSA; "Strategy for Eliminating the Threat of Jihadist Networks of al Qida: Status and Prospects," December 2000, Electronic Briefing Book (EBB) #147, National Security Archive (NSA); Rice, *No Higher Honor*, 98; Kenneth Katman, Report for Congress, "Al Qaeda: Profile and Threat Assessment," Congressional Reference Service (CRS), Report for Congress, August 17, 2005, https://fas.org/sgp/crs/terror/RL33038.pdf.

35. Bush, *Decision Points*, 140; Cheney, *In My Time*, 33; Rumsfeld, *Known and Unknown*, 342.

36. Rumsfeld to Bush, September 19, 2001, Rumsfeld Papers; Wolfowitz, interview with Fox News, September 13, 2001; also see Feith, *War and Decision*, 50.

37. This notion was a staple of bipartisan national security reports in the late 1990s. See, for example, the one chaired by Rumsfeld, "Executive Summary of the Report of the Commission to Assess the Ballistic Missile Threat to the United States, July 15, 1998," https://missiledefenseadvocacy.org/wp-content/uploads/2016/07/Rumsfeld150798.pdf#:~:text=EXECUTIVE%20SUMMARY%20of%20the%20REPORT%20of%20the%20COMMISSION,the%20Speaker%20of%20the%20U.S.%20House%20of%20Representatives%2C; also see United States Commission on National Security/21st Century, "New World Coming: American Security in the 21st Century," September 15, 1999, https://govinfo.library.unt.edu/nssg/Reports/NWC.pdf.

38. Bush, *Decision Points*, 191; Rumsfeld, "Weakening of Deterrent," December 10, 2001, Rumsfeld Papers; Rumsfeld, *Known and Unknown*, 282, 297, 314, 342; Feith, *War and Decision*, 7, 18; Gerson, *Heroic Conservatism*, 81–83; Department of State, *Patterns of Global Terrorism, 2001*, May 2002, 171, 175, 176, https://www.globalsecurity.org/security/library/report/2002/patterns-of-global-terrorism2001.htm.

39. Tenet, *At the Center of the Storm*, 496, 187–88; John McLaughlin, interview with author, April 4, 2011; Morell, interview with author, December 8, 2013; Rice, *No Higher Honor*, 88; Rove, *Courage and*

Consequence, 259; Gerson, *Heroic Conservatism*, 74; Hughes, *Ten Minutes from Normal*, 246; for Laura Bush quote, see Bob Woodward, *Bush at War* (New York: Simon & Schuster, 2002), 171; John Ashcroft, *Never Again: Securing America and Restoring Justice* (New York: Center Street, 2006), 125; John B. Taylor, *Global Financial Warriors: The Untold Story of International Finance in the Post-9/11 World* (New York: W. W. Norton, 2007), 3–5; Pace, Interview, January 19, 2016, GWB/OHP, MC.

40.   Ashcroft, *Never Again*, 130; Jack Goldsmith, *The Terror Presidency: Law and Judgment inside the Bush Administration* (New York: W. W. Norton, 2007), 74–75; Rice, *No Higher Honor*, 79, 113.

41.   Rove, *Courage and Consequence*, 282; Hughes, *Ten Minutes from Normal*, 253–56.

42.   Rove, *Courage and Consequence*, 273.

43.   Woodward, *Bush at War*, 29.

44.   Dick Cheney, interview with author, August 11, 2017; Scooter Libby, interview with author, December 9, 2010; Seth Carus, interview with author, December 16, 2015; Eric Edelman, interview with author, March 10, 2011.

45.   Carl W. Ford Jr., review of Paul Pillar's book, June 4, 2012, https://issforum.org/ISSF/PDF/ISSF-Roundtable-3-15.pdf; Robert M. Gates, *Duty: Memoirs of a Secretary at War* (New York: Vintage Books, 2015), 93.

46.   Feith, *War and Decision*, 12.

47.   Morell, interview with author, January 25, 2014; also Gerson, interview with author, March 9, 2016.

48.   Cheney, *In My Time*, 318–19; Scooter Libby, interview with author, December 9, 2010.

49.   Goldsmith, *Terror Presidency*, 130–31.

50.   Rice, *No Higher Honor*, 121.

51.   Bush, *Decision Points*, 180.

52.   See, for example, Mike Hurley to Jaime Gorelick, April 5, 2004, box 7, team 3 files, Records of the National Commission on Terrorist Attacks upon the United States, Record Group 148 (Records of the Commissions of the Legislative Branch), National Archives (Washington, DC) (hereafter cited as 9/11 Commission Records); see the questions prepared for Bush, Cheney, Rice, and other top officials in box 7, team 2 files, also boxes 5 and 7, team 3 files; also see the chapter on failures in *9/11 Commission Report*, 339–60; Clarke, *Against All Enemies*, 26, 214–15; for warnings of attacks inside the United States, see Office of the Inspector General, "Report on Central Intelligence Accountability Regarding Findings and Conclusions of the Joint Inquiry into Intelligence Community Activities before and after the Terrorist Attacks of September 11, 2001," June 2005, 14, 21, 27, 29, https://www.cia.gov/library/readingroom/docs/DOC_0006184107.pdf; also see *9/11 Commission Report*, 118, 128, 141, 176, 179–80, 199, 212.

53. Clarke, *Against All Enemies*, 18.

54. For Rove, see Scott McClellan, *What Happened: Inside the Bush White House and Washington's Culture of Deception* (New York: Public Affairs, 2008), 112–14; Clarke, interview with the author, December 31, 2010; Feith, *War and Decision*, 514–15; Edelman, interview with author, March 10, 2011; Testimony of Armitage and Wolfowitz, Senate Select Committee on Intelligence and the House Permanent Select Committee on Intelligence, September 19, 2002, https://www.govinfo.gov/content/pkg/CHRG-107jhrg96166/html/CHRG-107jhrg96166.htm.

55. For Afghanistan as a training ground for a global network of terrorists, see Department of State, *Patterns of Global Terrorism, 2000*, https://2009-2017.state.gov/j/ct/rls/crt/2000/2419.htm.

56. Tommy Franks, Interview, October 22, 2014, GWB/OHP, MC; Myers, *Eyes on the Horizon*, 165–74; Feith, *War and Decision*, 106.

57. Wolfowitz to Rumsfeld, September 23, 2001, Rumsfeld Papers; Powell and Armitage, Interview, March 28, 2017, GWB/OHP, MC; Tenet, *Center of the Storm*, 207–10; Rumsfeld, *Known and Unknown*, 371–77; Myers, *Eyes on the Horizon*, 174–75; Franks, *American Soldier*, 276–77; Shelton, *Without Hesitation*, 446–47; Feith, *War and Decision*, 106–7; Carter Malkasian, *The American War in Afghanistan: A History* (New York: Oxford University Press, 2021), 54–65.

58. Tenet, *Center of the Storm*, 207–20; Feith, *War and Decision*, 80–115; Rumsfeld, *Known and Unknown*, 373–77.

59. Rumsfeld to Myers and Pace, October 10, 2001, Rumsfeld Papers.

60. Morell, interview with author, December 8, 2013; Steve Biegun, lunch discussion with author, August 7, 2015; Tenet, *At the Center of the Storm*, 229–40; Rice, *No Higher Honor*, 79; Bush, *Decision Points*, 153.

61. John McLaughlin, interview with author, April 4, 2011; Tenet, *Center of the Storm*, 230–31.

62. Bush, *Decision Points*, 157–59; "Timeline: How the Anthrax Terror Unfolded," National Public Radio, February 15, 2011, https://www.npr.org/2011/02/15/93170200/timeline-how-the-anthrax-terror-unfolded.

63. Bush, *Decision Points*, 152–53; Cheney, *In My Time*, 340–43; Powell and Armitage, Interview, March 28, 2017, GWB/OHP, MC; George Casey, Interview, September 25, 2014, GWB/OHP, MC; Jacob Weisberg, *The Bush Tragedy* (New York: Random House, 2008), 189–92.

64. Morell, interview with author, December 18, 2013; Gonzales, *True Faith and Allegiance*, 147–49; Seth Carus, interview with author, September 16, 2015; Cheney, *In My Time*, 319; Libby, interview with author, March 9, 2011; Casey, Interview, September 25, 2014, GWB/OHP, MC; McClellan, *What Happened*, 110–11; National Academy of Sciences, "Review of the Scientific Approaches Used during the FBI's Investigation of the 2001 Anthrax Letter," 2011, https://www.nap.edu/resource/13098/Anthrax-Report-Brief-Final.pdf.

65. Tenet, *Center of the Storm*, 259–60; Rolf Mowatt-Larssen, *A State of Mind: Faith and the CIA* (privately published, 2020), 216–20.

66. Biegun, lunchtime discussion with author, August 7, 2015.

67. Walker, *Day That Shook America*, 222–23; Tenet, *Center of the Storm*, 234; Gonzales, *True Faith and Allegiance*, 146; Gellman, *Angler*, 142–43; Mayer, *The Dark Side*, 66–67.

68. This paragraph is based on Bush, *Decision Points*, 157–60; Cheney, *In My Time*, 344–45; Tenet, *At the Center of the Storm*, 261–65; Myers, *Eyes on the Horizon*, 193; Rice, *No Higher Honor*, 102–3; Gellman, *Angler*, 157; David S. C. Chu to Rumsfeld and Wolfowitz, October 31, 2001, Rumsfeld Papers.

69. Rumsfeld, *Known and Unknown*, 398–400; Ahmed Rashid, *Descent into Chaos: The United States and the Failure of Nation Building in Pakistan, Afghanistan and Central Asia* (New York: Viking, 2008), 79–86; Malkasian, *American War in Afghanistan*, 56–72.

70. Bush, *Decision Points*, 200; Myers, *Eyes on the Horizon*, 180.

71. Rumsfeld to Myers and Pace, October 10, 2001, Rumsfeld Papers; Rumsfeld to Bush, September 30, 2001, Rumsfeld Papers; Malkasian, *American War in Afghanistan*, 74.

72. Feith, *War and Decision*, 220.

73. Ibid., 220–21; Rumsfeld to Bush, September 30, 2001, Rumsfeld Papers; Wolfowitz interview with Fox News, September 13, 2001; Wolfowitz, interviews with the author, July 28, 2010, February 2, 2011; Wolfowitz interview with National Public Radio, September 14, 2001, http://www.defense.gov/transcripts/transcript.aspx?transcriptid=1911; Wolfowitz, "What Was and What Might Have Been"; for a more thorough discussion of Iraq, see Chapter 4.

74. See, for example, "Remarks with Prime Minister Junichiro Koizumi," September 25, 2001, APP.

75. Armitage, interview with author, March 23, 2011; Woodward, *Bush at War*, 58–59; Rashid, *Descent into Chaos*, 27–28, 89–90; Nelly Lahoud, *The Bin Laden Papers* (New Haven, CT: Yale University Press, 2022), 43–44; Karen DeYoung, *Soldier: The Life of Colin Powell* (New York: Alfred A. Knopf, 2006), 349–50; Negroponte to author, October 7, 2021; "Transition Memorandum," January 16, 2009, re Pakistan, declassified memorandum in possession of Stephen Hadley.

76. See Bush, "Remarks with President Megawati Sukarnoputri of Indonesia," September 29, 2001, APP; Bush, "Remarks with Koizumi," September 25, 2001, APP; Rumsfeld to Bush, Cheney, Powell, and Rice, September 19, 2001, Rumsfeld Papers.

77. Khalilzad, *The Envoy*, 110–13.

78. "President's Press Conference," October 11, 2001, APP.

79. Terrorist organizations are described briefly in the annual reports of the Department of State, *Patterns of Global Terrorism*.

80. "Joint Statement between the United States and the Republic of Indonesia," September 19, 2001, APP; Bush, "Remarks prior to Discussions with Sukarnoputri," September 19, 2001, APP; Anthony L. Smith, "A Glass Half-Full: Indonesia-U.S. Relations in the Age of Terror," *Contemporary Southeast Asia: A Journal of International and Strategic Affairs* 25 (December 2003): 454.

81. Bush, *Decision Points*, 160–68; Cheney, *In Our Time*, 348–55; Mowatt-Larssen, *State of Mind*, 221–23; Tenet, *Center of the Storm*, 264, 268–69; Hadley, Interview, October 31-November 1, 2011, GWB/OHP, MC; for devastating critiques of Cheney and his associates, see Gellman, *Angler*, 160–62, 171; Mayer, *Dark Side*, 72–125. These critiques often minimize the threat perception of officials.

82. Mowatt-Larssen, *State of Mind*, 236.

83. Bush, "Remarks with Prime Minister Juichiro Koizumi," September 25, 2021, APP; Bush, "Address before a Joint Session of Congress," September 20, 2001, APP.

84. For motives of the jihadists, see Glenn E. Robinson, *Global Jihad: A Brief History* (Stanford, CA: Stanford University Press, 2021); Louise Richardson, *What Terrorists Want: Understanding the Enemy, Containing the Threat* (New York: Random House, 2006); Abdel Bari Atwan, *The Secret History of al Qaeda* (Berkeley: University of California Press, 2008); Richard Crockatt, *America Embattled: September 11 and Anti-Americanism and World Order* (London: Routledge, 2003).

85. Bin Laden stated his motives clearly. See World Islamic Front Statement, February 23, 1998, "Jihad against Jews and Crusaders," https://fas.org/irp/world/para/docs/980223-fatwa.htm; Osama bin Laden, "Declaration of War against the Americans Occupying the Land of the Two Holy Places," 1996, https://ctc.usma.edu/wp-content/uploads/2013/10/Declaration-of-Jihad-against-the-Americans-Occupying-the-Land-of-the-Two-Holiest-Sites-Translation.pdf; for Arab public opinion, see Shibley Telhami, "Arab Public Opinion on the United States and Iraq: Postwar Prospects for Changing Prewar Views," June 1, 2003, https://www.brookings.edu/articles/arab-public-opinion-on-the-united-states-and-iraq-postwar-prospects-for-changing-prewar-views/; also see Anonymous [Michael Scheuer], *Imperial Hubris: Why the West is Losing the War on Terror* (Washington, DC: Brassyey's, 2004). Ussama Makdisi, *Faith Misplaced: The Broken Promise of U.S.-Arab Relations, 1820–2001* (New York: Public Affairs, 2010), 353–60.

86. World Islamic Front Statement, February 23, 1998, "Jihad against Jews and Crusaders"; Peter Bergen, *The Rise and Fall of Osama Bin Laden* (New York: Simon & Schuster, 2021), 74–99; Lahoud, *Bin Laden Papers*, 283.

87. Lawrence Wright, *The Looming Tower: Al-Qaeda and the Road to 9/11* (New York: Alfred A. Knopf, 2006), 187; Lahoud, *Bin Laden Papers*, 283.

88. For approval ratings from 2001 to 2003, see CNN/USA/Gallup poll numbers, "Seventy-Two Percent of Americans Support War against Iraq," March 24, 2003, https://news.gallup.com/poll/8038/seventytwo-percent-americans-support-war-against-iraq.aspx; David W. Moore, "Eight of Ten Americans Support the Ground War in Afghanistan," November 1, 2001, https://news.gallup.com/poll/5029/eight-americans-support-ground-war-afghanistan.aspx.

89. Mowatt-Larssen, *Leap of Faith*, 236.

Chapter 4

1. Steve Cambone, handwritten notes, September 11, 2001, "Targeting Iraq, Part I: Planning, Invasion and Occupation, 1997–2004," Digital National Security Archive (DNSA).

2. Condoleezza Rice, *No Higher Honor: A Memoir of My Years in Washington* (New York: Crown Publishers, 2001), 85–88; Hugh Shelton, with Ronald Levinson and Malcolm McConnell, *Without Hesitation: Odyssey of an American Warrior* (New York: St. Martin's Press, 2010), 438–42; Richard B. Myers, with Malcolm McConnell, *Eyes on the Horizon: Serving on the Front Lines of National Security* (New York: Threshold Editions, 2009), 166.

3. Richard A. Clarke, *Against All Enemies: Inside America's War on Terror* (New York: Free Press, 2004), 32.

4. For Bush's conversation with Blair, September 14, 2001, see comments by Bruce Riedel, a member of Rice's NSC staff, September 10, 2021, https://www.rawstory.com/george-w-bush-iraq-war/; Paul Wolfowitz, "What Was and Might Have Been," Hoover Institution, February 2022, 3, https://www.aei.org/articles/what-was-and-what-might-have-been-the-threats-and-wars-in-afghanistan-and-iraq/.

5. Michael Morell, interview with author, December 8, 2013; Stephen J. Hadley, Interview, October 31, 2011- November 1, 2011, George W. Bush, Oral History Project, Miller Center, University of Virginia, https://millercenter.org/the-presidency/presidential-oral-histories/george-w-bush (hereafter cited as GWB/OHP, MC).

6. Richard D. Cheney, interview with author, August 11, 2017; Scooter Libby, interview with author, December 9, 2010.

7. See, for example, his speeches on September 11, 2011, September 15, 2011, and September 20, 2001, American Presidency Project, https://www.presidency.ucsb.edu (hereafter cited as APP).

8. Michael Gerson, interview with author, March 9, 2016.

9. George W. Bush, "Remarks with President Megawati Sukarnoputri," September 19, 2001, APP.

10. Final Report of the National Commission on Terrorist Attacks upon the United States, *The 9/11 Commission Report* (New York: W. W. Norton, 2004), 236.

11. Donald Rumsfeld, *Known and Unknown: A Memoir* (New York: Sentinel, 2011), 425–26.

12. Rumsfeld to Bush, September 30, 2001, Rumsfeld Papers, https://www.rumsfeld.com/archives/.

13. Peter Rodman to Rumsfeld, September 20, 2001, 06-F-2658, OSD Reading Room, https://www.esd.whs.mil/FOID/Reading-Room/.

14. Carl Ford to Powell, September 7, 2011, "Targeting Iraq," DNSA.

15. Feith to Rumsfeld, September 18, 2001, "Targeting Iraq," DNSA; Paul Wolfowitz, interviews with author, July 28, 2010 and February 2, 2011.

16. Paul Wolfowitz, "Think Again: Realism," *Foreign Policy*, August 24, 2009; Wolfowitz, Testimony, October 4, 2001, U.S. Senate, Committee on Armed Services, https://www.globalsecurity.org/military/library/congress/2001_hr/011004wolf.pdf; Wolfowitz, interview with author, July 28, 2010; Wolfowitz, "What Was and Might Have Been."

17. Wolfowitz, interview with author, February 2, 2011; Rumsfeld, *Known and Unknown*, 347.

18. "Saddam Hussein in His Own Words: Quotes from Saddam and Iraq's Regime-Controlled Media," October 22, 2002, Rumsfeld Papers; Rodman to Wolfowitz, November 7, 2001, "Targeting Iraq," DNSA; U.S. Department of State, *Patterns of Global Terrorism, 2001*, 65, https://2009-2017.state.gov/j/ct/rls/crt/2001/pdf/index.htm.

19. Morell, interview with author, December 8, 2013; Gerson, interview with author, March 9, 2016.

20. Bush, "The President's News Conference," October 11, 2001, APP.

21. Gerson, interview with author, March 9, 2016.

22. Memorandum of Conversation, February 23, 2001, "Targeting Iraq," DNSA.

23. "President's News Conference with Tony Blair," February 23, 2001, APP.

24. Tony Blair, *A Journey: My Political Life* (New York: Alfred A. Knopf, 2011), 345–55 (quotations on 349, 348, 354); George W. Bush, *Decision Points* (New York: Crown Publishers, 2010), 230–31; Alastair Campbell, *The Blair Years: Extracts from the Alastair Campbell Diaries* (New York: Alfred A. Knopf, 2007), 505–7, 571–75.

25. "President's News Conference," October 11, 2001, APP.

26. The Commission on the Intelligence Capabilities of the United States Regarding Weapons of Mass Destruction, *Report to the President of the United States*, March 31, 2005, 55–56, https://fas.org/irp/offdocs/wmd_report.pdf (hereafter cited as the Robb-Silberman Report).

27. Ibid., 83–84.

28. Rolf Mowatt-Larssen, *A State of Mind: Faith and the CIA* (self-published, 2020), 242–45.

29. Seth Carus, interview with author, December 16, 2015.

30. Morell, interviews with author, December 8, 2013 and January 25, 2014.

31. Ibid.; also see Michael Hayden, Interview, November 20, 2012, GWB/
    OHP, MC; for an extremely good contemporary assessment, see Anthony
    H. Cordesman, *Iraq's Military Capabilities in 2002: A Dynamic Net
    Assessment* (Washington, DC: Center for Strategic and International
    Studies, 2002), 30–39.

32. Colin Powell, interview with author, January 24, 2011; Richard Armitage,
    interview with author, March 23, 2011.

33. Rice, *No Higher Honor*, 150, 171; Stephen, J. Hadley, interviews with
    author, February 22, 2011 and December 4, 2019.

34. Carl W. Ford review of Paul Pillar's book, H-Diplo, Vol. III, No. 15,
    https://issforum.org/ISSF/PDF/ISSF-Roundtable-3-15.pdf; Hayden,
    Interview, November 20, 2012, GWB/OHP, MC; Michael Morell, *The
    Great War of Our Time* (New York: Twelve, 2015), 99–107.

35. Morell, interview with author, December 8, 2013 and January 25, 2014;
    Franklin Miller, interview with author, July 15, 2011; Ford to Powell, July
    31, 2001, December 20, 2001, and May 8, 2002, "Targeting Iraq," DNSA;
    Robb-Silberman Report, 3.

36. See, for example, Paul Pillar, *Intelligence and U.S. Foreign Policy: Iraq, 9/
    11 and Misguided Reform* (New York: Columbia University Press, 2011),
    13–68; Robert Draper, *To Start a War: How the Bush Administration Took
    America into Iraq* (New York: Random House, 2020), 276–80.

37. Morell, interviews with author, December 8, 2013 and January 25, 2014;
    Cheney, interview with author, August 11, 2017; Hadley, interview with
    author, February 22, 2011; Wolfowitz, interview with author, July 28,
    2010; Gerson, interview with author, March 9, 2016; Robb-Silberman
    Report, 53–56, 58, 82, 86, 92.

38. Department of State, *Patterns of Global Terrorism*, 2001, 64–65;
    Cordesman, *Iraq's Military Capabilities*, 48.

39. Defense Intelligence Agency, September 29, 2001, "Targeting Iraq,"
    DNSA; Defense Intelligence Agency, October 23, 2001, "Targeting
    Iraq," DNSA.

40. Morell, *Great War of Our Time*, 80–81; Dick Cheney, with Liz Cheney, *In
    My Time* (New York: Threshold Editions, 2011), 415.

41. Morell, interviews with author, December 8, 2013 and January 25, 2014;
    Morell, *Great War of Our Time*, 81.

42. Edelman, interview with author, March 10, 2011; Gerson, interview with
    author, March 9, 2016.

43. Tommy Franks, with Malcolm McConnell, *American Soldier*
    (New York: Regan Books, 2004), 332–33. General Shelton, for
    example, thought Saddam was contained—in his box. See Shelton,
    Without Hesitation, 479; so did General Douglas Lute, Shelton's
    military assistant. See Lute, Interview, August 3, 2015, GWB/
    OHP, MC.

44. Peter Pace, Interview, January 19, 2016, GWB/OHP, MC; Myers, *Eyes on the Horizon*, 219; also see George Casey, Interview, September 25, 2014, GWB/OHP, MC; Cordesman, *Iraq's Military Capabilities*, 48–50.

45. Wolfowitz, interview with author, July 28, 2010.

46. Douglas J. Feith, *War and Decision: Inside the Pentagon at the Dawn of the War on Terrorism* (New York: Harper, 2008), 179–229, 274–99.

47. Carus, interview with author, December 16, 2015; Libby, interviews with author, January 25, 2011 and March 9, 2011.

48. Feith, *War and Decision*, 308; Wolfowitz, Testimony, October 4, 2001, U.S. Senate, Committee on Armed Services, 5, https://www.globalsecur ity.org/military/library/congress/2001_hr/011004wolf.pdf.

49. Rumsfeld, *Known and Unknown*, 343; Rumsfeld, "Weakening of Deterrent," December 10, 2001, Rumsfeld Papers; Libby, interview with author, January 25, 2011; Wolfowitz, interview with author, July 28, 2010.

50. Powell, Interview, March 28, 2017, GWB/OHP, MC; William J. Burns, *The Back Channel: A Memoir of American Diplomacy and the Case for Its Renewal* (New York: Random House, 2019), 158–60; Richard Haass, *War of Necessity, War of Choice: A Memoir of Two Iraq Wars* (New York: Simon & Schuster, 2009), 181.

51. Myers, *Eyes on the Horizon*, 217; Shelton, *Without Hesitation*, 479; Lute, Interview, August 3, 2015, GWB/OHP, MC.

52. Ford to Powell, July 31, 2001 and September 7, 2001, "Targeting Iraq," DNSA; Libby, interviews with author, December 9, 2010 and January 25, 2011; Cheney, interview with author, August 11, 2017; Edelman, interview with author, March 10, 2011.

53. Kofi Annan, with Nader Mousavizadeh, *Interventions: A Life in War and Peace* (New York: Penguin Press, 2012), 345; for the British perspective on sanctions, see JIC Assessment, "Iraq: Economic Sanctions Eroding," February 14, 2001, The Iraq Inquiry: The Official Records of the Public Inquiry, 2009–2016, https://webarchive.nationalarchives.gov.uk/ukgwa/20170831105118/http://www.iraqinquiry.org.uk/media/203152/2001-02-14-jic-assessment-iraq-economic-sanctions-eroding.pdf.

54. For an excellent assessment of the uncertainties, see Cordesman, *Iraq's Military Capabilities*, 14–19.

55. Tommy Franks, Statement, March 28, 2001, Senate, Armed Services Committee, http://www.reasons-for-war-with-iraq.info/tommy_franks_3-28-01.html.

56. Thomas R. Wilson, Statement, "Global Threats and Challenges through 2015," March 8, 2001, Senate, Armed Services Committee, https://fas.org/irp/congress/2001_hr/s010308w.html; George J. Tenet, Statement, "The Worldwide Threat in 2001: National Security in a Changing World," March 7, 2001, Senate, Armed Services Committee, https://fas.org/irp/congress/2001_hr/s010308t.html.

57. Clarke, *Against All Enemies*, 267–68; Burns to Armitage, November 19, 2001, *The Back Channel*, https://carnegieendowment.org/publications/inte ractive/back-channel/?lang=en&qry=November+19%2C+2001 (hereafter cited as Burns Papers); Haass, *War of Necessity*, 192, 210–14; Burns, *Back Channel*, 162–67.

58. Armitage, interview with author, March 23, 2011; Shelton, *Without Hesitation*, 419, 479; Franks, *American Soldier*, 332; Myers, *Eyes on the Horizon*, 215.

59. Wolfowitz, interview with author, July 28, 2010; Morell, interview with author, December 8, 2013; Hadley, interview with author, December 4, 2019; Rice, *No Higher Honor*, 170.

60. JIC Assessment, "Iraq after September 11—The Terrorist Threat," November 28, 2001, Iraq Inquiry, https://webarchive.nationalarchives.gov. uk/20170919105634/http://www.iraqinquiry.org.uk/media/236911/2001-11- 28-jic-assessment-iraq-after-september-11-the-terrorist-threat.pdf.

61. Blair to Bush, October 11, 2001.

62. Rice, "Press Briefing," November 8, 2001, APP.

63. This paragraph summarizes the conflicting information that Bush was hearing from his advisers. It is based upon the evidence already cited above, and especially the author's interviews with Morell, Libby, Wolfowitz, Edelman, Carus, and McLaughlin.

64. Statistical data from the fall of 2001 to the spring of 2003 can be found in Frank Newport, "Seventy-Two Percent of Americans Support War against Iraq," March 24, 2003, https://news.gallup.com/poll/8038/seventytwo- percent-americans-support-war-against-iraq.aspx.

65. See, for example, Blair's comments about Bush's tranquility in Blair, *A Journey*, 354; Franks, *American Soldier*, 280; Rove, *Courage and Consequence*, 258, 265; Myers, *Eyes on the Horizon*, 163.

66. Bush, *Decision Points*, 200.

67. Ibid.

68. Several officials commented on the sense of power, even "hubris," that the quick collapse of the Taliban infused. McLaughlin, interview with author, April 4, 2011; Edelman, interview with author, March 10, 2011; Armitage, interview with author, April 7, 2011.

69. Myers, *Eyes on the Horizon*, 196; Rumsfeld, *Known and Unknown*, 408–9; Shelton, *Without Hesitation*, 482.

70. David Manning, Private Hearing, June 24, 2010, Iraq Inquiry, https://web archive.nationalarchives.gov.uk/20171123123616/http://www.iraqinquiry. org.uk/the-evidence/witnesses/m/sir-david-manning/.

71. Bush, *Decision Points*, 201.

72. Rumsfeld, *Known and Unknown*, 427.

73. Ibid., 427–28; Cheney, *In My Time*, 369; Myers, *Eyes on the Horizon*, 217. Wolfowitz stressed that after the meeting at Camp David on September

16, his focus was on Afghanistan and the GWOT, not Iraq. Wolfowitz, interview with author, July 28, 2010.

74. Bush explained this to the journalist Bob Woodward. See Bob Woodward, *Plan of Attack* (New York: Simon & Schuster, 2004), 30; Rice, *No Higher Honor*, 171–72.

75. Rumsfeld, *Known and Unknown*, 457; Rice, *No Higher Honor*, 186; Hadley, interview with author, February 22, 2011; Myers, *Eyes on the Horizon*, 229.

76. "President's News Conference with Blair," February 23, 2001.

77. For differences over sanctions, see Armitage, interview with author, March 23, 2011; Wolfowitz, interview with author, July 28, 2010; Haass, *War of Necessity*, 174–75, 180, 274.

78. Rumsfeld to Rice, October 3, 2001 and December 13, 2001, Rumsfeld Papers; Biegun, lunchtime discussion with author, August 7, 2015; Rice, *No Higher Honor*, 19–21.

79. Shelton, *Without Hesitation*, 401–13.

80. Armitage, interview with author, March 23, 2011; Wolfowitz interview with author, July 28, 2010.

81. Powell, Interview, March 28, 2017, GWB/OHP, MC.

82. Cheney, the subject of bitter criticism in much of the literature, impressed many of his colleagues. See Hayden, Interview, November 20, 2012, GWB/OHP, MC; Edelman, interview with author, March 10, 2011; Carus, interview with author, December 16, 2015; Mowatt-Larssen, *State of Mind*, 244–45; Tenet, *Center of the Storm*, 301–2, 264–65.

83. Haass, *War of Necessity*, 184–86, 218–22; Rice, *No Higher Honor*, 17–18.

84. Powell, Interview, March 28, 2017, GWB/OHP, MC; for the rifts within the administration, also see James Mann, *The Great Rift: Dick Cheney, Colin Powell, and the Broken Friendship That Defined an Era* (New York: Henry Holt, 2020).

85. Bush, "Remarks with Reporters," November 26, 2001, APP.

86. Draper, *To Start a War*, 46.

87. Human Rights Watch, *World Report*, 2002, "Iraq and Iraqi Kurdistan," https://www.hrw.org/legacy/wr2k2/mena4.html; United Nations, Security Council, Seventh Quarterly Report of the Executive Chairman of the United Nations Monitoring, Verification and Inspection Commission, November 29, 2001, https://www.un.org/depts/unmovic/documents/1126eng.pdf; Special Advisor to the DCI on Iraq's WMD, *Comprehensive Report*, September 30, 2004, 57, https://www.globalsecurity.org/wmd/library/report/2004/isg-final-report/ (hereafter cited as Duelfer Report).

88. Duelfer Report, 11, 56–57; Ford to Powell, September 7, 2001, "Targeting Iraq," DNSA.

89. Kevin Woods, with James Lacy, *Iraqi Perspectives Project: Saddam and Terrorism: Emerging Insights from Captured Iraqi Documents*, November 2007, 20, 24–25, 32–34, 40, https://fas.org/irp/eprint/iraqi/vi.pdf.

90. Human Rights Watch, *World Report*, 2002, "Iraq and Iraqi Kurdistan"; *Amnesty International Report 2002*, May 28, 2002, 131–33, https://www.amnesty.org/download/Documents/POL10000012002ENGLISH.PDF; US Department of State, *Country Report on Human Rights Practices, 2001*, March 4, 2002, https://www.refworld.org/cgi-bin/texis/vtx/rwmain?page=search&docid=3c84d99d4.

91. Rumsfeld, *Known and Unknown*, 499–500; Casey, Interview, September 25, 2014, GWB/OHP, MC.

92. Bush, "Remarks with President Pervez Musharraf," November 10, 2001, APP; Bush, "Remarks with Prime Minister Atal Bihari Vajpayee," November 9, 2001, APP.

93. Cheney, interview with author, August 11, 2017.

94. Feith to Rumsfeld, September 18, 2001, "Targeting Iraq," DNSA; also Rumsfeld to Bush, September 30, 2001, Rumsfeld Papers; Rumsfeld to Feith, October 30, 2001, Rumsfeld Papers; Wolfowitz, Testimony, October 4, 2001; Wolfowitz, Interview with Fox News, September 13, 2001, http://www.defense.gov/transcripts/transcript.aspx?transcriptid=1909; Wolfowitz, interview with National Public Radio, September 14, 2001, http://www.defense.gov/transcripts/transcript.aspx?transcriptid=1911; Feith, *War and Decision*, 234; for a typical account stressing missionary impulses, see Mazaar, *Leap of Faith*.

Chapter 5

1. Donald Rumsfeld, *Known and Unknown: A Memoir* (New York: Sentinel, 2011), 438.

2. Ibid., 426–27; Richard B. Myers, with Malcolm McConnell, *Eyes on the Horizon: Serving on the Front Lines of National Security* (New York: Threshold Editions, 2009), 216–18.

3. Talking Points for Rumsfeld-Franks Meeting, November 27, 2001, "The Iraq War—Part I: The US Prepares for Conflict," Electronic Briefing Book [EBB] 326, National Security Archive [NSA], https://nsarchive2.gwu.edu/NSAEBB/NSAEBB326/index.htm; Michael Gordon and Bernard E. Trainor, *Cobra II: The Inside Story of the Invasion and Occupation of Iraq* (New York: Pantheon Books, 2006), 21–22.

4. Myers, *Eyes on the Horizon*, 217; Tommy Franks, with Malcolm McConnell, *American Soldier* (New York: Regan Books, 2004), 315.

5. Franks, *American Soldier*, 277, 410; Myers, *Eyes on the Horizon*, 168; Bob Woodward, *Plan of Attack* (New York: Simon & Schuster, 2004), 117–19.

6. Woodward, *Plan of Attack*, 38.

7. Myers, *Eyes on the Horizon*, 218, 222.

8. Gordon and Trainor, *Cobra II*, 27–31; Woodward, *Plan of Attack*, 41–44.

9. Woodward, *Plan of Attack*, 52–66.

10. Ibid., 63–64.

11. Franks, *American Soldier*, 354; George W. Bush, *Decision Points* (New York: Crown Publishers, 2010), 234–35.

12. Tommy Franks, Interview, October 22, 2014, George W. Bush, Oral History Project, Miller Center, University of Virginia [hereafter cited as GWB/OHP, MC]; Franks, *American Soldier*, 359; Woodward, *Plan of Attack*, 66.

13. Simon MacDonald to David Manning, December 3, 2001, Foreign and Commonwealth Office, Iraq Inquiry, https://webarchive.nationalarchives. gov.uk/20130206044351/http://www.iraqinquiry.org.uk/transcripts/decla ssified-documents.aspx.

14. "The War against Terrorism: The Second Phase," December 4, 2001, Iraq Inquiry.

15. Report of a Committee of Privy Counsellors, *Report of the Iraq Inquiry*, 12 vols., Volume 1, Section 3.1, "Development of UK Strategy and Options, 9/11 to Early January 2002," Numbered Paragraphs 324– 402 [hereafter cited as Chilcot Report, volume, section: numbered paragraphs], https://www.thegroovygroup.org/chilcot-report.php.

16. Rumsfeld, *Known and Unknown*, 443; Hadley, interview with author, December 4, 2019.

17. Bush, "Remarks Welcoming General Franks," December 28, 2001, American Presidency Project [hereafter cited as APP], https://www.preside ncy.ucsb.edu/people/president/george-w-bush.

18. Rolf Mowatt-Larssen, *A State of Mind: Faith and the CIA* (privately published, 2020), 242; for a summary of these events, see Condoleezza Rice, *No Higher Honor: A Memoir of My Years in Washington* (New York: Crown Publishers, 2011), 98–198; George Tenet, with Bill Harlow, *At the Center of the Storm: My Years at the CIA* (New York: HarperCollins, 2007), 229–333.

19. Mowatt-Larssen, *State of Mind*, 250–52; Tenet, *Center of the Storm*, 270–71.

20. US Senate, Select Committee on Intelligence [SSCI], *Report on the US Intelligence Community's Pre-War Intelligence Assessments on Iraq*, 334– 37, https://fas.org/irp/congress/2004_rpt/ssci_iraq.pdf; Ford to Powell, January 22, 2002, "Targeting Iraq," Digital National Security Archive [DNSA]; DIA, "Special Analysis: Iraqi Chemical/Biological Support to al-Qaida Unlikely," February 28, 2002, "Targeting Iraq," DNSA. For the ambiguity of the relationship between al Qaeda movements into Iraq and Hussein's attitude, also see Abdel Bari Atwan, *The Secret History of al Qaeda* (Berkeley: University of California Press, 2008), 190–91.

21. SSCI, *Pre-War Intelligence Assessments on Iraq*, 339; DIA, "Special Analysis," February 28, 2002.

22. US Department of State, *Patterns of Global Terrorism, 2002*, 79, https://2009-2017.state.gov/documents/organization/20117.pdf.

23. "Briefer's Tasking for Richard Cheney," February 13, 2002, "Targeting Iraq," DNSA; Ford to Armitage, March 1, 2002, "Targeting Iraq," DNSA.

24. Ford to Powell, December 20, 2001, "Targeting Iraq," DNSA.

25. Ibid.; Department of State, Bureau of Intelligence and Research, "Europe: Key Views on Iraqi Threat and Next Steps," December 18, 2001, EBB 326, NSA; Ford to Powell, January 22, 2002, "Targeting Iraq," DNSA; Ford to Armitage, March 22, 2002, "Targeting Iraq," DNSA; DIA, "Special Analysis," February 28, 2002.

26. MacDonald to Manning, December 11, 2001, including Annex A, FCO, Iraq Inquiry.

27. JIC Assessment, "Iraq: Saddam under the Spotlight," February 27, 2002, Iraq Inquiry.

28. Woodward, *Plan of Attack*, 67–73.

29. Edelman to author, May 21, 2021.

30. Rice, *No Higher Honor*, 171.

31. Bush, "Remarks prior to Discussions with Ecevit," January 16, 2002, APP.

32. Bush, "Address before a Joint Session of the Congress on the State of the Union," January 29, 2002, APP.

33. In interviews with the author, both Libby and Wolfowitz expressed surprise and disapproval about the phrase "axis of evil."

34. Gerson, interview with author, March 9, 2016; Peter Baker, *Days of Fire: Bush and Cheney in the White House* (New York: Doubleday, 2013), 186; David Frum, *The Right Man: An Inside Account of the Bush White House* (New York: Random House, 2003), 230–45.

35. Rice, *No Higher Honor*, 172; Bush, *Decision Points*, 229–30.

36. JIC Assessment, "Iraq: Saddam under the Spotlight," February 27, 2002, Iraq Inquiry; DIS, Political-Military Memorandum, "Removing Saddam," March 5, 2002, Iraq Inquiry.

37. Cheney, *In My Time*, 371.

38. Senate, Committee on Foreign Relations, *Foreign Policy Overview and the President's Fiscal Year 2003 Foreign Affairs Budget Request*, February 5, 2002, 107th Cong., 2nd Sess. (Washington, DC: Government Printing Office, 2002), 37.

39. Senate, Committee on Foreign Relations, *What's Next in the War on Terrorism?*, February 7, 2002, 107th Cong., 2nd Sess. (Washington, DC: Government Printing Office, 2002), 9, 29–30; Madeleine Albright, *Madame Secretary: A Memoir* (New York: Miramax Books, 2003), 287.

40. Bush, "News Conference with Musharraf," January 13, 2002, APP.

41. Woodward, *Plan of Attack*, 108–9, 116; Tenet, *Center of the Storm*, 386.

42. Woodward, *Plan of Attack*, 159–63; Gordon and Trainor, *Cobra II*, 36–37.

43. Franks, *American Soldier*, 369.

44. Joel D. Rayburn and Frank K. Sobchak, eds., *The US Army in the Iraq War*, 2 vols. (Carlisle, PA: US Army War College Press, 2019), 1:37–38; George Casey, Interview, September 25, 2014, GWB/OHP, MC; Christopher Lamb, interview with author, September 2, 2011.

45. Trainor and Gordon, *Cobra II*, 45–46; Gregory Hooker, *Shaping the Plan for Operation Iraqi Freedom: The Role of Military Intelligence Assessments* (Washington, DC: Washington Institute for Near East Policy, 2005), 10–11; Rayburn and Sobchak, *Official History*, 36–38; for the quotation, see Woodward, *Plan of Attack*, 281.

46. Myers, *Eyes on the Horizon*, 219; Casey, Interview, September 25, 2014, GWB/OHP, MC.

47. Rumsfeld to Rice, December 27 and December 31, 2001, Rumsfeld Papers, https://www.rumsfeld.com/archives/library_catalog.asp?name=complete-document-collection&page=3.

48. Cheney, interview with author, August 11, 2017.

49. Frederick C. Smith and Franklin C. Miller, "The Office of the Secretary of Defense: Civilian Matters?" in *The National Security Enterprise: Navigating the Labyrinth*, ed. Roger Z. George and Harvey Rishikof (Washington, DC: Georgetown University Press, 2011), 111–12.

50. Abrams, interview with author, August 28, 2015; Edelman, interview with author, March 10, 2011; John McLaughlin, interview with author, April 4, 2011; Libby, interview with author, January 25, 2011; Stephen Biegun, lunch with author, August 7, 2015; Franklin Miller, interview with author, July 15, 2011.

51. Rumsfeld to Feith, February 8, 2002, 06-F-1731, ESD.WHS.Mil/FOID/Reading Room; "Vice President's Trip to the Middle East: Recommended Tasks," February 25, 2002, ESD.WHS.Mil/FOID/Reading Room; Rumsfeld, "Talking Paper," February 13, 2002, "Targeting Iraq," DNSA; "Jordan: Talking Points," February 23, 2002, EBB 328, NSA; Burns to Powell, February 26, 2002, Burns Papers; Woodward, *Plan of Attack*, 111.

52. Burns to Powell, February 14, 2002, Burns Papers; Ford to Powell, February 15 and March 8, 2002, "Targeting Iraq," DNSA.

53. Elliott A. Abrams, *Tested by Zion: The Bush Administration and the Israeli-Palestinian Conflict* (New York: Cambridge University Press, 2013), 13.

54. Ibid., 1–33; William J. Burns: *The Back Channel: A Memoir of American Diplomacy and the Case for Its Renewal* (New York: Random House, 219), 166–67, 179–80; Daniel C. Kurtzer, Scott B. Lasensky, William B. Quandt, Steven L. Spiegel, and Shibley Z. Telhami, *The Peace Puzzle: America's Quest for Arab-Israeli Peace, 1989–2011* (Ithaca, NY: Cornell University Press, 2013), 166–67; Woodward, *Plan of Attack*, 111–12; Edelman to author, September 9, 2021.

55. For Burns's report, see his cable, March 29, 2002, "Targeting Iraq," DNSA.

56. "Remarks with Reporters," March 21, 2002, APP.

57. Bush, "News Conference with Vicente Fox," March 22, 2002, APP.
58. Bush, "Remarks on the Situation in the Middle East," April 4, 2002, APP; Kurtzer, *Peace Puzzle*, 164–71; Abrams, *Tested by Zion*, 32–37.
59. Bush, "Interview," April 4, 2002, APP.
60. Scott McClelland, *What Happened: Inside the Bush White House and Washington's Culture of Deception* (New York: Public Affairs, 2008), 128; Gerson, interview with author, March 9, 2016; Edelman, interview with author, March 10, 2011.
61. The quotations are from his two speeches. See Bush, "Remarks at the Inter-American Development Bank," March 14, 2002, APP; "Remarks to the UN Conference in Monterrey," March 22, 2002, APP.
62. "Iraq Report," April 26, 2002, Radio Free Europe, Radio Liberty, https://www.rferl.org/a/1343162.html; for Bush's reference to Hussein's support of the suicide bombers, see his "Remarks on the Situation in the Middle East," April 4, 2002.
63. UNMOVIC, *Quarterly Report*, May 31, 2002, https://www.un.org/depts/unmovic/new/documents/quarterly_reports/s-2002-606.pdf; Iraq Survey Group, *Comprehensive Report of the Special Advisor to the DCI on Iraq's WMD* [hereafter cited as Duelfer Report], September 30, 2004, 61–63, https://www.globalsecurity.org/wmd/library/report/2004/isg-final-rep ort/; Arms Control Association, "A Chronology of UN Inspections," no date, 13, https://www.armscontrol.org/act/2002-10/features/iraq-chronol ogy-un-inspections; Ford to Armitage, February 7, 2002, "Targeting Iraq," DNSA.
64. Independent Inquiry Committee into the United Nations Oil-for-Food Programme, October 27, 2005, http://www.humanrightsvoices.org/assets/attachments/documents/volcker_report_10-27-05.pdf; Duelfer Report, 59.
65. Duelfer Report, 60.
66. Jim Jeffrey cable, April 9, 2002, "Targeting Iraq," DNSA; DIA, "Special Analysis," February 28, 2002.
67. Human Rights Watch, *World Report, 2003*, https://www.hrw.org/legacy/wr2k3/; "Iraq Report," April 26, 2002, Radio Free Europe, Radio Liberty.
68. In interviews and discussions with the author, many key advisers stressed their uncertainty about what Bush would do, including Hadley, Edelman, Libby, and Feith. Illustratively, Rumsfeld wrote in his memoir: "Up until the very minute the president authorized the first strike, there was no moment when I felt with razor-sharp certainty that Bush had fully decided." Rumsfeld, *Known and Unknown*, 457.

Chapter 6

1. Tony Blair, *A Journey: My Political Life* (New York: Alfred A. Knopf, 2010), 354–55, 392–94, 399–401; Alastair Campbell, *The Blair Years: The Alastair Campbell Diaries* (New York: Alfred A. Knopf, 2007), 505–7.

2. Meyer to Manning, February 13, 2002, Report of a Committee of Privy Counsellors, *Report of the Iraq Inquiry*, 12 vols., Volume 1, Section 3.2, "Development of UK Strategy and Options, January to April 2002," Numbered Paragraphs 39–41 [hereafter cited as Chilcot Report, volume, section: numbered paragraphs], https://www.thegroovygroup.org/chilcot-report.php.

3. DIS, "Politico-Military Memorandum, Removing Saddam," March 5, 2002, Iraq Inquiry, https://webarchive.nationalarchives.gov.uk/ukgwa/20130206044351/http:/www.iraqinquiry.org.uk/transcripts/declassified-documents.aspx; also JIC Assessment, "Iraq: Saddam Under the Spotlight," February 27, 2002, ibid.; "Iraq Briefing for the Parliamentary Labour Party," March 5, 2002, ibid.

4. "Conclusions of a Meeting of the Cabinet," March 7, 2002, ibid.; also see Chilcot Report, 1, 3.2: 183–256.

5. "Conclusions of a Meeting of the Cabinet," March 7, 2002, Iraq Inquiry; also see Chilcot Report, 1, 3.2: 183–256.

6. "Conclusions of a Meeting of the Cabinet," March 7, 2002, Iraq Inquiry; also see Chilcot Report, 1, 3.2: 183–256.

7. "Iraq: Options Paper," March 8, 2002, "Iraq War—Part II: Was There Even a Decision?" Electronic Briefing Book [EBB] #328, National Security Archive [NSA], https://nsarchive2.gwu.edu/NSAEBB/NSAEBB328/index.htm.; also see Simon Webb, "Axis of Evil," February 27, 2002, Iraq Inquiry; Gordon Hoon to Blair, March 22, 2002, ibid.; Straw to Blair, March 25, 2002, ibid.; Chilcot Report, 1, 3.2: 257–350.

8. Manning to Blair, March 14, 2002, EBB #328, NSA.

9. David Manning, Testimony, June 24, 2010, Iraq Inquiry.

10. Ibid.; Manning to Blair, March 14, 2002, EBB #328, NSA.

11. Blair to Jonathan Powell, March 17, 2002, Iraq Inquiry.

12. Hoon to Blair, March 22, 2002, ibid.

13. Straw to Blair, March 25, 2002, ibid.; also see Straw's interview, January 21, 2010, ibid.; and his "Statement," January 19, 2011, ibid.

14. Blair, Interview, January 29, 2010, 24, ibid.

15. Blair, Interview, January 29, 2010, 47, 66–70, ibid.; Blair, Interview, January 21, 2011, 85–91, ibid.; Blair to Jonathan Powell, March 17, 2002, ibid.; Blair, *Journey*, 398–99.

16. Blair, Interview, January 29, 2010, 42–49, Iraq Inquiry; Manning, Interview, June 24, 2010, 30–33, ibid.

17. "President's News Conference with Blair," April 6, 2002, American Presidency Project [hereafter cited as APP], https://www.presidency.ucsb.edu/documents/the-presidents-news-conference-with-prime-minister-tony-blair-the-united-kingdom-crawford.

18. Blair, Interview, January 29, 2010, 50–51, Iraq Inquiry; Jonathan Powell, Interview, January 18, 2010, 40–41, ibid.; Manning, Interview, June 24, 2010, 27, ibid.; Manning to Simon MacDonald, April 8, 2002, *Middle*

East Eye, January 13, 2022, https://www.middleeasteye.net/news/iraq-war-full-secret-memo-how-bush-blair-plotted.

19. Manning, Interview, June 24, 2010, 27, 37–38, Iraq Inquiry; Powell, Interview, January 18, 2010, 22–24, ibid.; Extracts from FCO Diptel 73, April 10, 2002, ibid.

20. William J. Burns, *The Back Channel: A Memoir of American Diplomacy and the Case for Its Renewal* (New York: Random House, 2019), 180–82; Elliott Abrams, *Tested by Zion: The Bush Administration and the Israeli-Palestinian Conflict* (New York: Cambridge University Press, 2013), 32–33.

21. Abrams, *Tested by Zion*, 32–40; Dick Cheney, with Liz Cheney, *In My Time: A Personal and Political Memoir* (New York: Threshold Editions, 2011), 380–82; Scooter Libby, interview with author, January 25, 2011.

22. Peter Rodman, "Read Ahead for Secretary Rumsfeld PC Meeting, April 16, 2002," April 12, 2002, EBB #328, NSA; Rodman to Rumsfeld, May 9, 2002, Donald Rumsfeld Papers, https://www.rumsfeld.com/archives/page/about-the-rumsfeld-archive-2; Rumsfeld to Feith, May 17, 2002, ibid.; Rumsfeld to Cheney, Powell, Tenet, and Rice, July 1, 2002, ibid.; Rumsfeld to Rice, August 12, 2002, ibid.; Rodman to Wolfowitz, July 3, 2002, "Targeting Iraq, Part I: Planning, Invasion, and Occupation, 1997–2004," Digital National Security Archive [DNSA]; Burns to Richard Armitage, July 19, 2002, William J. Burns Papers, https://carnegieendowment.org/publications/interactive/back-channel/.

23. Joel D. Rayburn and Frank K. Sobchak, eds., *The U.S. Army in the Iraq War: Invasion, Insurgency, Civil War*, 2 vols. (Carlisle, PA: Strategic Studies Institute and US Army War College Press, 2019), 1:36–41; Gregory Hooker, *Shaping the Plan for Operation Iraqi Freedom* (Washington, DC: Washington Institute for Near Eastern Policy, 2005).

24. Simon Webb, "Iraqi Objectives," May 16, 2002, Iraq Inquiry.

25. John Holmes to FCO, May 28, 2002, ibid.

26. Tommy Franks, with Malcolm McConnell, *American Soldier* (New York: Regan Books, 2004), 425; Cheney, *In My Time*, 383; Michael R. Gordon and Bernard E. Trainor, *Cobra II: The Inside Story of the Invasion and Occupation of Iraq* (New York: Pantheon, 2006), 50–51.

27. For Cheney, see Alberto R. Gonzales, *True Faith and Allegiance: A Story of Service and Sacrifice in War and Peace* (Nashville, TN: Nelson Books, 2016), 231–32; Libby, interview with author, December 9, 2010; Cheney, "Interview with Tim Russert," March 24, 2002, APP; quotation from his graduation speech at the Naval Academy, May 24, 2002, APP; Cheney, *In My Time*, 383.

28. Douglas J. Feith, *War and Decision: Inside the Pentagon at the Dawn of the War on Terrorism* (New York: Harper, 2008), 300–1.

29. Rumsfeld to Cheney, Powell, and Rice, ND [mid-May 2002?], EBB #328, NSA; OSD, "Dealing with Iraqi WMD: the Inspection Option,"

[ND], EBB #328, NSA; Rumsfeld, "V.P. and Rice Lunch," May 8, 2002, "Targeting Iraq," DNSA.

30. Bush, "Press Conference," April 26, 2002, July 8, 2002, APP.
31. Radio Free Europe, Radio Liberty, *Iraq Report*, 5(April 19, 2002), 4–5.
32. Hans Blix, *Disarming Iraq* (New York: Pantheon Books, 2004), 62–63.
33. Bush, "Interview with European Journalists," May 21, 2002, APP.
34. Ford to Powell, May 24, 2002, "Targeting Iraq," DNSA.
35. US Senate, Select Committee on Intelligence, *Report on the Intelligence Community's Prewar Intelligence Assessments on Iraq*, July 7, 2004, 326–45 (quotation on 329), https://nsarchive2.gwu.edu//NSAEBB/ NSAEBB234/SSCI_phaseI_excerpt.pdf; Tenet, *Center of the Storm*, 344–45; for Zarqawi, Joby Warrick, *Black Flags: The Rise of ISIS* (New York: Doubleday, 2015), 15–71; also see Mary Anne Weaver, "The Short, Violent Life of Abu Musab al Zarqawi," *The Atlantic*, July/August 2006, https://www.theatlantic.com/magazine/archive/2006/07/the-short-violent-life-of-abu-musab-al-zarqawi/304983/.
36. Robert Draper, *To Start a War: How the Bush Administration Took America into Iraq* (New York: Penguin Press, 2020), 258–59; Woodward, *Plan of Attack*, 246.
37. Scott McClellan, *What Happened: Inside the Bush White House and Washington's Culture of Deception* (New York: Public Affairs, 2008), 114.
38. Cheney, *In My Time*, 385.
39. Ford to Powell, May 8, 2002, "Targeting Iraq," DNSA.
40. Illustratively, see Bush, "News Conference with Gerhard Schroeder," May 23, 2002, APP.
41. Bush, "Commencement Address," June 1, 2002, APP.
42. Bush, "Remarks Announcing HIV Prevent Initiative," June 19, 2002, APP; Gary Edson, "Press Briefing," June 25, 2002, APP; Bush, *Decision Points*, 336–40; Rice, *No Greater Honor*, 225–29; John Donnelly, "The President's Emergency Plan for Health Relief," *Health Affairs* 31 (July 2012): 1389–96.
43. Bush, "Remarks on the Middle East," June 24, 2002, APP; Abrams, *Tested by Zion*, 39–45.
44. Burns, "President's Speech: Short-Term Follow-Up," June 25, 2002, Burns Papers.
45. Abrams, *Tested by Zion*, 42–45; Bush, *Decision Points*, 404–5.
46. Manning to Blair, July 3, 2002, Iraq Inquiry; P. D. Watkins to Manning, July 2, 2002, ibid.; "CDS Discussion with CJCS, General Myers, 3 July," ibid.; Straw to Blair, July 8, 2002, ibid.
47. Mike Tucker and Chares S. Faddis, *Operation Hotel California: The Clandestine War inside Iraq* (Guilford, CT: Lyons Press, 2009), 1–10, 26; Warrick, *Black Flags*, 70-71, 86–91; Micah Zenko, "Foregoing Limited Force: The George W. Bush Administration's Decision Not to Attack Ansar Al-Islam," *Journal of Strategic Studies* 32 (August 2009): 615–49;

Tenet, *At the Center of the Storm*, 350–54; Woodward, *Plan of Attack*, 139–44; SSCI, *Prewar Intelligence*, 334–39.

48. Zenko, "Foregoing Limited Force," 629; Edelman, interview with author, March 10, 2011; Wolfowitz, interview with author, July 28, 2010; for Zarqawi's presence in Baghdad, also see Ford to Powell, May 24, 2002, "Targeting Iraq," DNSA.

49. For Bush's quote, see Woodward, *Plan of Attack*, 137; also see Gonzales, *True Faith and Allegiance*, 232–41; Zenko, "Foregoing Limited Force," 631–34; Rumsfeld, *Known and Unknown*, 447; Haass, *War of Necessity*, 213–14; Burns to Powell, July 29, 2002, Burns Papers; Manning, Interview, 42, Iraq Inquiry; Chilcot Report, 2, 3.3: 403–13.

50. Chilcot Report, 2, 3.3: 301–315; Matthew Rycroft to Manning, July 23, 2002, Iraq Inquiry.

51. Watkins to Hoon, July 22, 2002, Iraq Inquiry; Simon MacDonald to Peter Ricketts, "Iraq," July 26, 2002, ibid.; Rycroft to Manning, July 23, 2002, ibid.; Chilcot Report, 2, 3.3: 342, 346.

52. Rycroft to Manning, July 23, 2002, Iraq Inquiry; Chilcot Report, 2, 3.3: 342–47.

53. Blair, Interview, January 29, 2010, 6–7, 98–99, 112, 199, 245–47, Iraq Inquiry.

54. Blair to Bush, July 28, 2002, ibid.

55. Chilcot Report, 2, 3.3: 462–82; 5, 6.1: 446–51.

56. Ibid., 2, 3.3: 439–85, 506, 534; Blair, *Journey*, 404; Manning, Interview, 56, Iraq Inquiry; Blair to Bush, "Note on Iraq," July 28, 2002, ibid.

57. Blair, Interview, January 29, 2010, 29, 24, ibid.

58. Blair, *Journey*, 384.

59. See, e.g., Manning to Blair, "Iraq: Conditions for Military Action," July 19, 2002, Iraq Inquiry; DIS, "Politico-Military Memorandum, Removing Saddam," March 5, 2002, ibid.

60. Blair, Statement, January 14, 2011, 6, Iraq Inquiry.

61. Blair, Interview, January 21, 2011, 51, ibid.

62. Bush, "Remarks Prior to Discussions with Blair," June 26, 2002, APP.

63. Blair, *Journey*, 404; Chilcot Report, 2, 3.3: 415–85, 503–35.

Chapter 7

1. Alberto R. Gonzales, *True Faith and Allegiance: A Story of Service and Sacrifice in War and Peace* (Nashville, TN: Nelson Books, 2016), 236–39.

2. George W. Bush, *Decision Points* (New York: Crown Publishers, 2010), 235–37; Gonzales, *True Faith and Allegiance*, 235–41.

3. Joel D. Rayburn and Frank K. Sobchak, eds., *The US Army in the Iraq War: Invasion, Insurgency, Civil War, 2003–2006*, 2 vols. (Carlisle, PA: Strategic Studies Institute and US Army War College Press, 2019), 1:41–43; Michael R. Gordon and Bernard E. Trainor, *Cobra II: The Inside Story of the Invasion and Occupation of Iraq* (New York: Pantheon

Books, 2006), 66–77; Bush, *Decision Points*, 235–36; Tommy Franks, with Malcolm McConnell, *American Soldier* (New York: Regan Books, 2004), 388–91; Bob Woodward, *Plan of Attack* (New York: Simon & Schuster, 2004), 145–48.

4. Franks, *American Soldier*, 388–91; Rayburn and Sobchak, *US Army in the Iraq War*, 42–43; Bush, *Decision Points*, 235–36; Gordon and Trainor, *Cobra II*, 66–77.

5. Woodward, *Plan of Attack*, 148–53; Karen DeYoung, *Soldier: The Life of Colin Powell* (New York: Alfred A. Knopf, 2006), 401–3.

6. William Burns to Powell, July 29, 2002, *The Back Channel*: The Archive, https://carnegieendowment.org/publications/interactive/back-channel [hereafter cited as Burns Papers].

7. Powell, interview with author, January 24, 2011; DeYoung, *Soldier*, 401–3; Bush, *Decision Points*, 238; Woodward, *Plan of Attack*, 150–51.

8. Bush, *Decision Points*, 238.

9. Douglas J. Feith, *War and Decision: Inside the Pentagon at the Dawn of the War on Terrorism* (New York: Harper, 2008), 284–304.

10. Memo for Myers, by Rumsfeld, Aug 12, 2002, Rumsfeld Papers, https://www.rumsfeld.com/archives/; Feith, *War and Decision*, 284–86; Scooter Libby, interview with author, December 9, 2010.

11. Thomas Fingar to Richard Armitage, July 14, 2002, "Targeting Iraq," Digital National Security Archive [DNSA]; CIA, Directorate of Intelligence, "The Postwar Occupations of Germany and Japan: Implications for Iraq," Iraq War, Part II, Electronic Briefing Book [EBB] #328, National Security Archive [NSA]; Burns to Armitage, September 30, 2002, Burns Papers; Richard N. Haass, *War of Necessity, War of Choice: A Memoir of Two Iraqi Wars* (New York: Simon & Schuster, 2009), 224–27, 279–93.

12. The unwillingness or inability of Rice and Hadley to resolve issues was a persistent theme of the interviews the author conducted with Eric Edelman, Scooter Libby, Richard Armitage, Elliott Abrams, and Franklin Miller.

13. George Casey, Interview, September 25, 2014, George W. Bush, Oral History Project, Miller Center, University of Virginia [hereafter cited as GWB/OHP, MC]; Feith, *War and Decision*, 290–93.

14. Brent Scowcroft, "Don't Attack Saddam," August 15, 2002, https://www.wsj.com/articles/SB1029371773228069195; Bush, *Decision Points*, 238.

15. Bush, *Decision Points*, 238; Condoleezza Rice, *No Higher Honor: A Memoir of My Years in Washington* (New York: Crown Publishers, 2011), 179–80.

16. Eric Edelman, interview with author, March 10, 2011; Dick Cheney, with Liz Cheney, *In My Time: A Personal and Political Memoir* (New York: Threshold Editions, 2011), 390; Donald Rumsfeld, *Known and Unknown: A Memoir* (New York: Sentinel, 2011), 437–43; Richard B. Myers, with Malcolm McConnell, *Eyes on the Horizon: Serving on*

the Front Lines of National Security (New York: Threshold Editions, 2009), 229.

17.   Cheney, "Remarks to the Veterans of Foreign Wars," August 26, 2002, https://www.americanrhetoric.com/speeches/dickcheney103rdvfw.htm; Cheney, *In My Time*, 388–90.

18.   Feith, *War and Decision*, 259–73; Joby Warrick, *Black Flags: The Rise of ISIS* (New York: Doubleday, 2015), 76–80; for a thorough analysis, see Senate Select Committee on Intelligence [SSCI], Report of the US Intelligence Community's Prewar Intelligence Assessments on Iraq, July 7, 2004, 304–49, https://fas.org/irp/congress/2004_rpt/ssci_concl. pdf; Defense Intelligence Agency, Joint Intelligence Task Force, "Special Analysis," July 31, 2002, September 18, 2002, "Targeting Iraq," DNSA; for Feith's briefing that stirred so much controversy, see "Assessing the Relationship between Iraq and al Qaida," September 16, 2002, https:// fas.org/irp/news/2007/04/feithslides.pdf; DoD Background Paper, "Framework for Thinking about Iraq's Relationship with Al Qaida," July 2003, "Targeting Iraq," DNSA; also Edelman, interview with author, March 10, 2011; Paul Wolfowitz, interview with author, July 28, 2010.

19.   For assessments that analysts were not cowed or intimidated, see SSCI, *Prewar Intelligence*, 34, 284, 363; also see The Commission on the Intelligence Capabilities of the United States Regarding Weapons of Mass Destruction, *Report to the President of the United States*, March 31, 2005, 188–90, https://irp.fas.org/offdocs/wmd_report.pdf [hereafter cited as Robb-Silberman Report]; Michael V. Hayden, Interview, November 20, 2012, GWB/OHP, MC; Carl Ford's review of Paul Pillar's book, H-Diplo, June 4, 2012, https://issforum.org/ISSF/PDF/ISSF-Roundtable-3-15.pdf.

20.   Rice, *No Higher Honor*, 170–71.

21.   DIA, Joint Intelligence Task Force [JITF], Special Analysis: "Iraq's Inconclusive Ties to Al-Qaida," "Targeting Iraq," DNSA; "JITF-CT Response to DUSD (PS) Assessment on Iraq/Al-Qaida Ties," August 14, 2002, ibid.; "IC Meeting on Iraq," August 21, 2002, ibid.

22.   SSCI, *Prewar Intelligence*, 307–30 (quotation on 330); George Tenet, with Bill Harlow, *At the Center of the Storm: My Years at the CIA* (New York: HarperCollins, 2007), 341–56; Michael Morell, with Bill Harlow, *The Great War of Our Time: The CIA's Fight against Terrorism from Al Qa'ida to ISIS* (New York: Twelve, 2015), 86–88; Michael V. Hayden, Interview, November 20, 2012, GWB/OHP, MC; Feith, *War and Decision*, 260–73; Cheney, *In My Time*, 384–86, 388; John McLaughlin, interview with author, April 4, 2011.

23.   Rice, *No Higher Honor*, 171; Morell, interview with author, December 18, 2013. The State Department's Intelligence and Research Division offered its own muddied reading of the intelligence and noted that it did not assign the same credibility to some of Tenet's sources. See Ford to Powell, September 26, 2002, "Targeting Iraq," DNSA.

24. Feith, *War and Decision*, 308; the Cheney quotation is from his speech to the Veterans of Foreign Wars, August 26, 2002.

25. Feith, "Sovereignty and Anticipatory Self-Defense," August 24, 2002, "Targeting Iraq," DNSA; "The Case against Iraq," August 23, 2002, ibid.

26. Department of State, "A Decade of Deception and Defiance," September 12, 2002, EBB, #80, NSA.

27. Bush, September 17, 2002, letter accompanying "The National Security Strategy of the United States of America," https://nssarchive.us/national-security-strategy-2002/.

28. "Rumsfeld Says Link between Iraq, al Qaeda 'Not Debatable,'" September 27, 2002, http://www.defense.gov/news/newsarticle.aspx?id= 43413.

29. Rumsfeld, "Parade of Horribles," October 15, 2002, https://nsarchive2.gwu.edu/NSAEBB/NSAEBB418/docs/7%20-%20Iraq%20-%20An%20illustrative%20list%20of%20potential%20problems%20-%2010-15-2002.pdf; Rumsfeld, *Known and Unknown*, 479–81.

30. Rumsfeld, *Known and Unknown*, 525; Cheney, *In My Time*, 448–49; Feith, *War and Decision*, 143–44; Tenet, *At the Center of the Storm*, 305; Steve Biegun, lunch with author, August 7, 2015; Franklin Miller, interview with author, July 15, 2011; Elliott Abrams, interview with author, August 28, 2015; also John McLaughlin, interview with author, April 4, 2011; Edelman, interview with author, March 10, 2011.

31. Rice, *No Higher Honor*, 180; Biegun, lunchtime discussion with author, August 7, 2015.

32. Edelman to the author, October 5, 2021.

33. Tony Blair, *A Journey: My Political Life* (New York: Alfred A. Knopf, 2010), 403–4; Report of a Committee of Privy Counsellors, *Report of the Iraq Inquiry*, 12 vols., Volume 2, Section 3.4, "Development of UK Strategy and Options, Late July to 14 September 2002," Numbered Paragraphs 570, 179, 186, https://www.thegroovygroup.org/chilcot-report.php [hereafter cited as Chilcot Report, volume, section: numbered paragraphs].

34. Chilcot Report, 2, 3.5, "Development of UK Strategy and Options, September to November 2002—the Negotiation of Resolution 1441," 95, 107–22; DeYoung, *Soldier*, 406.

35. David Manning to Blair, August 28, 2002, Iraq Inquiry, https:// web arch ive.natio nala rchi ves.gov.uk/ ukgwa/ 201 3020 6044 351/ http:/ www.iraq inqu iry.org.uk/ tran scri pts/ decla ssif ied- docume nts.aspx.

36. Manning to Blair, September 6, 2002, Iraq Inquiry; Chilcot Report, 2, 3.4: 322–28.

37. Rice, *No Higher Honor*, 180–81; Gonzales, *True Faith and Allegiance*, 243–45.

38. Tenet, *At the Center of the Storm*, 319.

39. Chilcot Report, 2, 3.4: 571–78, 480.

40. Manning, Interview, 73, Iraq Inquiry; Meyer, Interview, 49–51, ibid.
41. Gonzales, *True Faith and Allegiance*, 245–47; Rumsfeld to Rice, September 13, 2002, "Targeting Iraq," DNSA; Bush, "Remarks prior to Discussions with Blair," September 7, 2002, The American Presidency Project, https://www.presidency.ucsb.edu/documents [hereafter cited as APP].
42. Blair to Iraq Inquiry, January 14, 2011, Iraq Inquiry; Chilcot Report, 2, 3.4: 452.
43. For the Powell-Straw conversation, see Meyer to FCO, September 16, 2002, Iraq Inquiry; also see Straw's speech to House of Commons, September 24, 2002, quoted in Chilcot Report, 2, 3.5: 206.
44. Chilcot Report, 2, 3.5: 153; also see UK, SPG Paper, "Force or Mind," ibid., 5, 6.1, "Development of the Military Options for an Invasion of Iraq": 727–30, 1017.
45. Hans Blix, *Disarming Iraq* (New York: Pantheon Books, 2004), 81–82, also 116, 125, 130; Chilcot Report, 2, 3.4: 345, 348, 559; for Jacques Chirac's views, see Matthew Rycroft to Mark Sedwill, September 6, 2002, Iraq Inquiry; for Blair's conversation with Vladimir Putin, Chilcot Report, 2, 3.5: 100.
46. Rice, *No Higher Honor*, 180–81; Hadley, interview with author, December 4, 2019.
47. Radio Free Europe, Radio Liberty, *Iraq Report*, October 12, 2002, https://www.rferl.org/a/1343186.html.
48. For Rice, see Chilcot Report, 2, 3.5: 751; for Rumsfeld, see his snowflake, September 30, 2002, Rumsfeld Papers; for Edelman's speculative comment, see his interview with author, March 10, 2011.
49. Bush, "Address to the UN General Assembly," September 12, 2002, APP.
50. The negotiations over the UN resolution can be followed most closely in Chilcot Report, 3, 3.5; for Rumsfeld's unhappiness with the delays and with Bush's concessions, see Rumsfeld to Bush, October 14, 2002 and November 2, 2002, "Targeting Iraq," DNSA; Gonzales, *True Faith and Allegiance*, 248–53.
51. Blix, *Disarming Iraq*, 86–87. Mohamed ElBaradei, the director of the International Atomic Energy Agency, was not so pleased with the meeting. See ElBaradei, *The Age of Deception: Nuclear Diplomacy in Treacherous Times* (New York: Metropolitan Books, 2011), 50–54.
52. Chilcot Report, 3.5: 893–895, 901, 751, 752, 753.
53. Rice, *No Higher Honor*, 184–86. Rumsfeld's carping about the NSC process grew significantly during this period. See, e.g., Rumsfeld to Rice, October 16, 2002, January 6, 2003, Rumsfeld Papers; John Negroponte, interview with author, June 18, 2021.
54. For an excellent brief discussion of coercive diplomacy, see Jack S. Levy, "Deterrence and Coercive Diplomacy," *Political Psychology* 29

(2008): 537–52. Note, though, that Bush and Rice were seeking to use "coercive diplomacy" for compellence, not deterrence.

55. Rice, *No Higher Honor*, 184.

56. See, e.g., Bush, "Remarks in South Bend," September 5, 2002; Bush, "Remarks at a Dinner for Chris Chocola," September 5, 2002; Bush, "Radio Address," September 28, 2002; Bush, "Radio Address," October 5, 2002; also Bush, "Remarks with Congressional Leaders," September 4, 2002, APP.

57. "The National Security Strategy," September 17, 2002; for my previous analysis of this national security strategy statement, see Melvyn P. Leffler, "9/11 and American Foreign Policy," *Diplomatic History* 19 (June 2005): 395–413.

58. National Intelligence Estimate, "Iraq's Continuing Programs of Mass Destruction," October 2002, https://www.jewishvirtuallibrary.org/jsou rce/images/Iraq/IraqWMDs.pdf.

59. See Carl Ford's review of Paul Pillar's book, H-Diplo, June 4, 2012, https://issforum.org/ISSF/PDF/ISSF-Roundtable-3-15.pdf; regarding the irrelevance of the NIE to policymakers, Pillar agrees. See Paul R. Pillar, *Intelligence and US Foreign Policy: Iraq, 9/11, and Misguided Reform* (New York: Columbia University Press, 2011), 252; also see Tenet, *At the Center of the Storm*, 336, 370; Cheney, *In My Time*, 368; Robb-Silberman Report, 49–51, 181.

60. These generalizations are based on the Robb-Silberman Report; SSCI, *Prewar Intelligence*; Hayden, Interview, November 20, 2012, GWB/OHP, MC; Morell, *Great War of Our Time*, 89–90; Tenet, *At the Center of the Storm*, 322–30; and author's interviews with Morell, McLaughlin, Hadley, Edelman, Libby, and Wolfowitz. Much of the controversy regarding the intelligence collection and analysis can be seen in the review of Pillar's book, H-Diplo, 4 June 2012, cited above; also see, e.g., James P. Pfiffner and Mark Pythian, eds., *Intelligence and National Security Policymaking on Iraq: British and American Perspectives* (College Station: Texas A&M University Press, 2008); Robert Jervis, *Why Intelligence Fails: Lessons from the Iranian Revolution and the Iraq War* (Ithaca, NY: Cornell University Press, 2010); Frank P. Harvey, *Explaining the Iraq War: Counter-Factual Theory, Logic and Evidence* (New York: Cambridge University Press, 2012); Joshua Rovner, *Fixing the Facts: National Security and the Politics of Intelligence* (Ithaca, NY: Cornell University Press, 2015).

61. Ford to Powell, August 29, 2002, September 11, 2002, "Targeting Iraq," DNSA; Ford's review of Pillar, June 4, 2012, H-Diplo.

62. DIA, Joint Intelligence Task Force for Combating Terrorism, "Iraq/ Worldwide: Iraqi Terrorist Threat in Anticipation/Response to Hostilities with US," September 18, 2002, "Targeting Iraq," DNSA; DIA, "Iraq's Reemerging Nuclear Weapons Program," September 2002, "Targeting Iraq," DNSA. For a strong critique of the intelligence analysts and

their superiors, see Robert Draper, *To Start a War: How the Bush Administration Took America into Iraq* (New York: Penguin Press, 2020), especially 200–20, 257–83; for thorough and illuminating critiques that do not highlight political motives, see the Robb-Silberman Report and SSCI, *Prewar Intelligence*. This author participated in one review of the agency's conclusions.

63. Rumsfeld, *Known and Unknown*, 288; Cheney, *In My Time*, 402–17; Cheney, interview with author, August 11, 2017; Libby, interview with author, December 9, 2010; Edelman, interview with author, March 10, 2011; Feith, phone interview with author, September 9, 2020.

64. Glen D. Shafer to CJCS, VCJCS, ACJS, DJS, September 9, 2002, Rumsfeld Papers.

65. Rumsfeld to Myers, September 9, 2002, ibid.

66. The criticisms are systematically explored in SSCI, *Prewar Intelligence*; also Robb-Silberman report. For the analysts' acknowledgment of their errors, see Morrell, *Great War of Our Time*, 95–97; Tenet, *At the Center of the Storm*, 330–36; Hayden, interview, November 20, 2012, GWB/OHP, MC.

67. This was the view of Robert Jervis, one of the smartest and best informed students of the CIA. See Jervis, *Why Intelligence Fails*, 146.

68. Haass, *War of Necessity, War of Choice*, 230; Miller, interview with author, July 15, 2011; Franks, interview, October 22, 2014, GWB/OHP, MC.

69. For Hussein's speech, see Radio Free Europe, Radio Liberty, *Iraq Report*, August 16, 2002, 2; also see *Iraq Report*, September 6, 2002, 1–2; for views of Hussein and Iraqi defense officials, see Samuel Helfont, *Iraq against the World: How Saddam's Ba'thists Defied America and Shaped Post–Cold War Politics* (New York: Oxford University Press, 2023), chapter 9.

70. Resolution 1441, November 8, 2002, https://www.un.org/Depts/unmovic/documents/1441.pdf.

71. Chilcot Report, 2, 3.5: 313.

72. "Coalition Forces Strike Military Mobile Radar," October 3, 2002, Global Security Archives, https://www.globalsecurity.org/wmd/library/news/iraq/2002/iraq-021001-centcom01.htm; "Coalition Forces Strike Air Defense Radar and Surface-to-Air Missile Sites," October 10, 2002, ibid.

73. OSD, "Post-UNSCR Strategy for Iraq," [ND], OSD Reading Room, https://www.esd.whs.mil/Portals/54/Documents/FOID/Reading%20Room/Homeland_Defense/07-F-1332_first_interim_release.pdf.

74. Morell, interview with author, December 8, 2013; Department of State, *Patterns of Global Terrorism, 2002*, iv, viii, ix, 76, 79; for an illustrative list of terrorist incidents in 2002, see https://en.wikipedia.org/wiki/List_of_terrorist_incidents_in_2002.

75. Bush, "Address to the Nation on Iraq," October 7, 2002, https://www.presidency.ucsb.edu/documents/address-the-nation-iraq-from-cincinnati-ohio

[hereafter cited as APP]; for Bush's feelings, I have relied especially on my interviews with Gerson, Morell, and Hadley.

76. Gerson, interview with author, March 9, 2016; Rice, *No Higher Honor*, 183–86; Ari Fleischer, *Taking Heat: The President, the Press and My Years in the White House* (New York: Harper LargePrint, 2005), 507; the quotation is in the Cincinnati speech.

77. Lydia Saad, "Top Ten Findings about Public Opinion and Iraq," October 8, 2002, https://news.gallup.com/poll/6964/top-ten-findings-about-pub lic-opinion-iraq.aspx.

78. See, e.g., Dan Balz, "Democrats Speak Up on Foreign Policy: Reluctance to Criticize Bush Fades," *Washington Post*, July 15, 2002; James Dao, "Call in Congress for Full Airing of Iraq Policy," *New York Times*, July 18, 2002; Carla Anne Robbins, Leila Abboud, and Greg Jaffe, "Democrats to Pose Careful Questions on Iraq: Public Support for Bush Approach Means Political Risks in Senate Hearings," *Wall Street Journal*, July 31, 2002. In mid-October about 65 percent of people polled approved Bush's job performance and about 55 percent favored invading Iraq with US ground troops. See the numbers in Frank Newport, "Seventy-Two Percent of Americans Support War against Iraq," March 24, 2003, https://news.gal lup.com/poll/8038/seventytwo-percent-americans-support-war-against-iraq.aspx. Also see Harvey, *Explaining the Iraq War*.

79. Testimony by Wolfowitz and Armitage, "Joint Inquiry Hearing on Counterterrorist Center Customer Perspective," September 19, 2002, 37, 42.

80. Gonzales, *True Faith and Allegiance*, 247.

81. For his scorn of political motives, see Fleischer, *Taking Heat*, 482; Gonzales, *True Faith and Allegiance*, 250.

82. Bush, "News Conference," November 7, 2002, APP.

83. Bush, "Radio Address," September 28, 2002, APP; Bush, "Press Conference," November 7, 2002, APP.

84. Bush, "Remarks to Community in South Bend," September 5, 2002, APP.

85. Ibid.

86. Bush, "Remarks at the Embassy of Afghanistan," September 10, 2002, APP; Bush, "Remarks at a Dinner," September 5, 2002, APP.

87. UN Security Council Resolution 1441, November 8, 2002. Rumsfeld outlined all the concessions the administration had made. See Rumsfeld to Bush, November 2, 2002, "Targeting Iraq," DNSA.

88. Rumsfeld to Bush, November 2, 2002, "Targeting Iraq," DNSA.

89. Rayburn and Sobchak, *US Army in the Iraq War*, 1:55–57; Gordon and Trainor, *Cobra II*, 75–91.

90. Gordon and Trainor, *Cobra II*, 77; Woodward, *Plan of Attack*, 173–74; Franks, *American Soldier*, 394–96; Colin Powell and Richard Armitage, interview, March 28, 2017, GWB/OHP, MC.

91. Gordon and Trainor, *Cobra II*, 74.

Chapter 8

1. George W. Bush, "Radio Address," November 9, 2002, The American Presidency Project [hereafter cited as APP], https://www.presidency.ucsb.edu; Bush, "Radio Address," November 16, 2002, APP.

2. Radio Free Europe, Radio Liberty, *Iraq Report*, 5 (November 15, 2002), 1–5, https://www.rferl.org/a/1343191.html (hereafter cited as *Iraq Report*); Naji Sabri to Kofi Annan, November 13, 2002, "Targeting Iraq," Digital National Security Archive [DNSA].

3. Kevin M. Woods, with Michael R. Pease, Mark E. Stout, Williamson Murray, and James G. Lacey, *Iraqi Perspectives Project: A View of Operation Iraqi Freedom from Saddam's Senior Leadership* (Washington, DC: Joint Center for Operational Analysis, 2006); 25–32; Iraq Survey Group, *Comprehensive Report of the Special Advisor to the DCI on Iraq's WMD*, September 30, 2004, 62–67, http://www-personal.umich.edu/~graceyor/govdocs/pdf/duelfer1.pdf [hereafter cited as Duelfer Report]; CIA, "Misreading Intentions: Iraq's Reaction to Inspections Created Picture of Deception," January 5, 2006, ii, 13, https://nsarchive2.gwu.edu/news/20120905/CIA-Iraq.pdf; Michael R. Gordon and Bernard E. Trainor, *Cobra II: The Inside Story of the Invasion and Occupation of Iraq* (New York: Pantheon Books, 2006), 64–66.

4. Woods, *Iraqi Perspectives*, 28–29.

5. Ibid., 16, 25–31; DIS, "Iraq: Psychological Portrait of Saddam," November 14, 2002, Iraq Inquiry, https://webarchive.nationalarchives.gov.uk/ukgwa/20130206044351/http:/www.iraqinquiry.org.uk/transcripts/declassified-documents.aspx [hereafter cited as Iraq Inquiry]; JIC, "Iraq: Regime Cohesion under Pressure," November 14, 2002, ibid.; Gordon and Trainor, *Cobra II*, 62–66, 118–23, 135; Målfrid Braut-Hegghammer, "Cheater's Dilemma: Iraq, Weapons of Mass Destruction, and the Path to War," *International Security* 45 (Summer 2020): 51–89.

6. Hans Blix, *Disarming Iraq* (New York: Pantheon Books, 2004), 94–95; United Nations Security Council [UNSC] Resolution 1441, https://2001-2009.state.gov/p/nea/rls/15016.htm.

7. Report of a Committee of Privy Counsellors, *Report of the Iraq Inquiry*, 12 vols., Volume 3, Section 3.6, "Development of UK Strategy and Options, November 2002 to January 2003," Numbered Paragraphs 142–44 [hereafter cited as Chilcot Report, volume, section: numbered paragraphs], https://www.thegroovygroup.org/chilcot-report.php; Jonathan Powell, Interview, January 18, 2010, 52, Iraq Inquiry.

8. Senate Select Committee on Intelligence (SSCI), *Report on the US Intelligence Community's Prewar Intelligence Assessments on Iraq*, July 7, 2004, 316–17, https://fas.org/irp/congress/2004_rpt/ssci_intro.pdf.

9. The Commission on the Intelligence Capabilities of the United States Regarding Weapons of Mass Destruction, *Report to the President of the United States*, March 31, 2005, 81–89, 108–9, 115–27, https://fas.org/irp/offd

ocs/wmd_report.pdf [hereafter cited as Robb-Silberman Report]; George
Tenet, "DCI's World Threat Briefing," February 11, 2003, "Targeting Iraq,"
DNSA; JIC, Current Intelligence Group Assessment, "Global Chemical
and Biological Weapons Survey," October 28, 2002, Chilcot Report, 4, 4.3,
"Iraq's WMD Assessments, October 2002 to March 2003": 45–53.

10. Robb-Silberman Report, 105, 127–31; SSCI, *Prewar Intelligence*, 14–
35; Michael V. Hayden, Interview, November 20, 2012, GWB/OHP,
MC; Raphael Perl, "Terrorism, the Future and US Foreign Policy,"
Congressional Reference Service [CRS], April 11, 2003, https://digital.
library.unt.edu/ark:/67531/metacrs4127/; for the debate over Curveball,
see George Tenet, with Bill Harlow, *At the Center of the Storm: My Years
at the CIA* (New York: HarperCollins, 2007), 375–83; Robert Draper,
To Start a War: How the Bush Administration Took America into Iraq
(New York: Penguin Press, 2020), 276–80.

11. Carl Ford to Colin Powell, December 12, 2002, "Targeting Iraq," DNSA;
DIA/JITF/CT Analytical Product, "Iraq: Terrorism/C.I. Update for 5
March 2002," "Targeting Iraq," DNSA; JIC Assessment, "International
Terrorism: The Threat from Iraq," October 10, 2002, Iraq Inquiry.

12. Bob Woodward, *Plan of Attack* (New York: Simon & Schuster,
2004), 237–39; Dick Cheney, with Liz Cheney, *In My Time*
(New York: Threshold Editions, 2011), 384–85; George W. Bush, *Decision
Points* (New York: Crown Publishers, 2010), 252–53; for funding of the
Biosphere initiative, see Bush, "State of the Union," January 28, 2003,
APP. As will become evident, in speech after speech, press conference
after press conference, Bush cited this concern. Interviews confirmed
this as an overriding preoccupation. Steve Hadley, interview with author,
December 4, 2019; Michael Morell, interview with author, December
8, 2013, and January 25, 2014; Michael Gerson, interview with author,
March 9, 2016; Scooter Libby, interview with author, January 25, 2011.

13. Rumsfeld to Bush, ND [November 13, 2002?], "Targeting Iraq," DNSA.

14. Ibid.; Donald Rumsfeld, *Known and Unknown: A Memoir*
(New York: Sentinel, 2011), 440; Woodward, *Plan of Attack*, 228–35;
Gordon and Trainor, *Cobra II*, 95–100; Condoleezza Rice, interview with
author, July 19, 2021.

15. Gordon and Trainor, *Cobra II*, 75–94; Joel D. Rayburn and Frank K.
Sobchak, eds., *The US Army in the Iraq War: Invasion, Insurgency, Civil
War* (Carlisle, PA: US Army War College, 2019), 62–63.

16. W. Robert Pearson to Department of State, December 3, 2002, "Targeting
Iraq," DNSA.

17. Chilcot Report, 5, 6.1, "Development of the Military Options for an
Invasion of Iraq": 1052–170, esp. 1138–39.

18. Alberto R. Gonzales, *True Faith and Allegiance: A Story of Service and
Sacrifice in War and Peace* (Nashville, TN: Nelson Books, 2016), 259;
Bush, "Radio Address," December 7, 2002, APP; Bush, *Decision Points*,

242; for "granular detail," Morell, interview with author, January 25, 2014; Tenet, "Worldwide Threat," February 11, 2003, "Targeting Iraq," DNSA.

19. Blix, *Disarming Iraq*, 106–9.
20. Ford to Powell, December 18, 2002, "Targeting Iraq," DNSA; JIC, "An Initial Assessment of Iraq's WMD Declaration," December 18, 2002, Iraq Inquiry.
21. Gonzales, *True Faith and Allegiance*, 259–61; Condoleezza Rice, *No Higher Honor: A Memoir of My Years in Washington* (New York: Crown Publishers, 2011), 184–85.
22. Woodward, *Plan of Attack*, 242–43.
23. For Blair's thinking, see Blair, Interview, January 29, 2010, 98–99, Iraq Inquiry; Blair, Interview, January 21, 2011, 70–85, ibid.; for British thinking, Ministry of Defense, "UK Military Strategic Thinking on Iraq," December 13, 2002, especially "Box 2: Change in Regime Posture of Behaviour," ibid.
24. Blix, *Disarming Iraq*, 116, 130.
25. Woodward, *Plan of Attack*, 247–50; Tenet, *At the Center of the Storm*, 360–62; Draper, *To Start a War*, 264–66.
26. Tenet, *Center of the Storm*, 369–71; Draper, *To Start a War*, 268; Rice, *No Higher Honor*, 199–200.
27. Bush, *Decision Points*, 242. Libby also stressed how daily briefings were much more alarming than the NIE. Libby, interview with author, December 9, 2010. Rice emphasized that the president's doubts were not about whether Iraq had WMD, but about the persuasiveness of the public presentation. Rice, interview with author, July 19, 2021.
28. Woodward, *Plan of Attack*, 251.
29. Bush, *Decision Points*, 243.
30. Woodward, *Plan of Attack*, 253–54; Rice, *No Higher Honor*, 186. Rice, Hadley, Morell, Libby, Edelman, and Gerson indicated in interviews with the author that the president was not rushing to war.
31. Woodward, *Plan of Attack*, 258–60.
32. *Iraq Report*, 6 (January 13, 2003), 3–7; ibid., 6 (January 20, 2003), 15–16; for Hussein's rhetoric, see Ofra Bengio, *Saddam's Word: Political Discourse in Iraq* (New York: Oxford University Press, 1998).
33. *Iraq Report*, 6 (January 13, 2003), 12; ibid., 6 (January 20, 2003), 10–14.
34. Woodward, *Plan of Attack*, 263–66; Cheney, *In My Time*, 396–97.
35. Rumsfeld, *Known and Unknown*, 439–40, 443, 450, 457.
36. For slightly different versions of this conversation, see Karen DeYoung, *Soldier: The Life of Colin Powell* (New York: Knopf, 2006), 429; Bush, *Decision Points*, 251; Woodward, *Plan of Attack*, 269–73. In his Miller Center interview, Powell misstated the date, but provides his own account, from which I quote. Colin L. Powell and Richard L. Armitage, Interview, March 28, 2017, George W. Bush, Oral History Project, Miller Center, University of Virginia [hereafter cited as GWB/OHP, MC].

37. Powell, Interview, March 28, 2017, GWB/OHP, MC.

38. Blix, *Disarming Iraq*, 115–16.

39. Ibid., 129–42; Duelfer Report, 62–63; Mohamed ElBaradei, *The Age of Deception: Nuclear Diplomacy in Treacherous Times* (New York: Metropolitan Books, 2011), 59–72.

40. Rice, interview with author, July 19, 2021; Hadley, interview with author, December 4, 2019; Morell, interview with author, December 8, 2013; McLaughlin, interview with author, April 4, 2011; Gonzales, *True Faith and Allegiance*, 252–72.

41. Gonzales, *True Faith and Allegiance*, 262; Rumsfeld, *Known and Unknown*, 443–44; DeYoung, *Soldier*, 433–34.

42. Christopher Meyer to FCO, January 23, 2003, Iraq Inquiry; Peter Ricketts, Memorandum, "Iraq: Planned Presentation for President Bush," January 23, 2003, ibid.

43. Meyer to FCO, January 23, 2003, ibid.

44. "Deputy Secretary Wolfowitz Speech on Iraq Disarmament," January 23, 2003, https://www.nytimes.com/2003/01/23/international/full-text-in-wol fowitzs-words.html.

45. Rice, "Why We Know Iraq Is Lying," January 23, 2003, "Targeting Iraq," DNSA; The White House, "What Disarmament Looks Like," January 23, 2003, Electronic Briefing Book [EBB] #80, National Security Archive [NSA].

46. Hans Blix, "Update on Inspection," January 27, 2003, https://www.un.org/depts/unmovic/Bx27.htm; *Iraq Report*, 6 (February 2, 2003), 13–14; Blix, *Disarming Iraq*, 137–42.

47. JIC, "Iraq: The Emerging View from Baghdad," January 29, 2003, Iraq Inquiry; John Scarlett to David Manning, January 30, 2003, ibid.

48. Gonzales, *True Faith and Allegiance*, 263–64.

49. Bush, "Address on the State of the Union," January 28, 2003, APP.

50. Gonzales, *True Faith and Allegiance*, 263–64; Rumsfeld, *Known and Unknown*, 453.

51. Bush, *Decision Points*, 244; Woodward, *Plan of Attack*, 296–97; a poll conducted by the Chicago Council on Foreign Relations and the German Marshall Fund of the United States suggested Americans' strong preference for multilateral action through the United Nations. See "A World Transformed: Foreign Policy Attitudes of the US Public after September 11," September 4, 2002, www.icpsr.umich.edu/web/ICPSR/studies/3821.

52. Bush, "News Conference," January 31, 2003, APP.

53. Gonzales, *True Faith and Allegiance*, 264, 268; Rumsfeld, *Known and Unknown*, 457; Gerson, interview with author, March 9, 2016; Hadley, interview with author, December 4, 2019; Rice, interview with author, July 19, 2021; Bush, *Decision Points*, 244–45; Chilcot Report, 3, 3.6: 862–977.

54. Tenet, *At the Center of the Storm*, 371–75; Edelman, interview with author, March 10, 2011; Libby, interview with author, January 25, 2011; Powell, Interview, March 28, 2017, GWB/OHP, MC.

55. For Powell's speech, February 5, 2003, https://www.washingtonpost.com/wp-srv/nation/transcripts/powelltext_020503.html.

56. Pew Research Center, "What the World Thinks in 2002," December 4, 2002, https://www.pewresearch.org/global/2002/12/04/what-the-world-thinks-in-2002/; also see "Not Even the Reputable Powell Could Alter Opinion in Europe," *Los Angeles Times*, February 10, 2003, https://www.latimes.com/archives/la-xpm-2003-feb-10-fg-eurpowell10-story.html; Richard Sobel, Peter Furia, and Bethany Barratt, eds., *Public Opinion and International Intervention: Lessons from the Iraq War* (Washington, DC: Potomac Books, 2012).

57. Blix, *Disarming Iraq*, 163–66; Chilcot Report, 3, 3.7, "Development of UK Strategy and Options, 1 February to 7 March 2003": 172.

58. Blix, *Disarming Iraq*, 160–78; Chilcot, 3, 3.7: 316, 361–83, 435–40. For the issue of US cooperation with the inspectors, see SSCI, *Prewar Intelligence*, 404–22.

59. Blix, *Disarming Iraq*, 167.

60. Rice, interview with author, July 19, 2021; Hadley, interview with author, December 4, 2019; Gerson, interview with author, March 9, 2016.

61. Myers, Memorandum for the Record, February 6, 2003, "Targeting Iraq," DNSA.

62. Chilcot Report, 3, 3.7: 555.

63. Rice, phone interview with author, August 2, 2021; Hadley, interview with author, December 4, 2019; Chilcot Report, 3, 3.7: 1076, 1079.

64. Bush, "Radio Address," February 8, 2003, APP; Bush, "News Conference," February 22, 2003, APP; Bush, "News Conference," March 6, 2003, APP.

65. Blix, *Disarming Iraq*, 207.

66. Ibid., 185.

67. *Iraq Report*, 6 (February 20, 2003), 1; ibid., 6 (February 27, 2003), 1; Blix, *Disarming Iraq*, 187–90.

68. Chilcot Report, 3, 3.7: 649, 839–41; Blix, *Disarming Iraq*, 187–205.

69. UNMOVIC, *Twelfth Quarterly Report*, February 28, 2003, https://www.globalsecurity.org/wmd/library/news/iraq/un/iraq-unmovic_report12_2003.htm.

70. Blix, "Oral Introduction of the 12th Quarterly Report," March 7, 2003, https://www.un.org/Depts/unmovic/SC7asdelivered.htm; Blix, *Disarming Iraq*, 205–13.

71. CIA, "Misreading Intentions," especially 11–14; Braut-Hegghammer, "Cheater's Dilemma," 84–89; also illuminating is SSCI, *Prewar Intelligence*, 14–28.

72. Blix, *Disarming Iraq*, 192–221; Chilcot Report, 3, 3.7: 436–39, 843, 1086–88, 1091.

73. Blix, *Disarming Iraq*, 202, 242–43.

74. Ibid., 210–11; for the best insight into Hussein's "strategic intent," see Duelfer Report, 1–66.

75. Braut-Hegghammer, "Cheater's Dilemma," 84–89 (quotation on 86); CIA, "Misreading Intentions," 14.

76. Braut-Hegghammer, "Cheater's Dilemma," 84; Duelfer Report, 62–68; Woods, *Iraqi Perspectives*, 25–35 (quotation on 31); CIA, "Misreading Intentions," ii, 10–14; the quote is from Mark Kukis, *Voices from Iraq: A People's History, 2003–2009* (New York: Columbia University Press, 2011), 3.

77. Gonzales, *True Faith and Allegiance*, 267–68; for Cheney's views, see Meyer to FCO, January 23 and 29, 2003, Iraq Inquiry; Bush, *Decision Points*, 252; Rumsfeld, *Known and Unknown*, 717; Hadley, interviews with author, December 4, 2019 and February 22, 2011; Gerson, *Heroic Conservatism*, 142–43; for the importance of credibility, see , e.g., Hal Brands, Eric Edelman, and Thomas Mahnken, "Credibility Matters: Strengthening American Deterrence in an Age of Geopolitical Turmoil" (Washington, DC: Center for Strategic and Budgetary Assessment, 2018), 1-10, https://csbaonline.org/uploads/documents/Credibility_Paper_FINAL_format.pdf.

78. Bush, "Address to the Nation," March 17, 2003, APP.

79. Bush, "News Conference," March 6, 2003, APP.

80. Bush, "Address to the Nation," March 17, 2003, APP; also see Bush, "Address at the American Enterprise Institute," February 26, 2003, APP.

81. Bush, "News Conference," March 6, 2003, APP.

82. Woodward, *Plan of Attack*, 280.

83. Bush, "News Conference," March 6, 2003, APP.

84. These quotes are strung together from the two most important intelligence studies of post-Hussein Iraq: National Intelligence Council, "Regional Consequences of Regime Change in Iraq," January 2003, https://www.cia.gov/readingroom/docs/DOC_0005299385.pdf; "Principal Challenges in Post-Saddam Iraq," January 2003, https://www.cia.gov/readingroom/docs/DOC_0005674817.pdf; also see SSCI, *Prewar Intelligence*, 371–93.

85. Gonzales, *True Faith and Allegiance*, 271.

Chapter 9

1. Donald Rumsfeld, *Known and Unknown: A Memoir* (New York: Sentinel, 2011), 482, 428–30; Tommy Franks, with Malcolm McConnell, *American Soldier* (New York: Regan Books, 2004), 350; Joel D. Rayburn and Frank K. Sobchak, eds., *The US Army in the Iraq War: Invasion, Insurgency, Civil*

War, 2 vols. (Carlisle Barracks, PA: Strategic Studies Institute and US Army War College Press, 2003–2006), 1:31–36.

2. Douglas J. Feith, *War and Decision: Inside the Pentagon at the Dawn of the War on Terrorism* (New York: Harper, 2008), 283–85.

3. Ibid., 288–89.

4. Ibid., 304; Rumsfeld, *Known and Unknown*, 499; George W. Casey, Interview, September 25, 2014, George W. Bush, Oral History Project, Miller Center, University of Virginia, https://millercenter.org/the-preside ncy/presidential-oral-histories/george-casey-oral-history (hereafter cited as GWB/OHP, MC).

5. William Burns to Colin Powell, January 16, 2003 and February 12, 2003, *The Back Channel*: The Archive, https://carnegieendowment.org/publicati ons/interactive/back-channel/ (hereafter cited as Burns Papers).

6. Peter Rodman to Rumsfeld, August 15, 2002, The Rumsfeld Archive, https://www.rumsfeld.com/archives/catalog/complete-document-collect ion (hereafter cited as Rumsfeld Papers); Feith, *War and Decision*, 401–2; Rumsfeld, *Known and Unknown*, 481–85.

7. George Tenet, *At the Center of the Storm: My Years at the CIA* (New York: HarperCollins, 2007), 397–98; Feith, *War and Decision*, 189–92; Ryan Crocker, Interview, September 9–10, 2010, GWB/OHP, MC; William Burns, *The Back Channel: A Memoir of American Diplomacy and the Case for Its Renewal* (New York: Random House, 2019), 164.

8. Feith, *War and Decision*, 379–86, 396–401; Rumsfeld, *Known and Unknown*, 489; Paul Wolfowitz, interview with author, July 28, 2010; Jay Garner, Interview, July 17, 2003, *Frontline*, https://www.pbs.org/wgbh/ pages/frontline/shows/truth/interviews/garner.html; Crocker, Interview, September 9-10, 2010, GWB/OHP, MC; Zalmay Khalilzad, *The Envoy: From Kabul to the White House, My Journey through a Turbulent World* (New York: St. Martin's Press, 2016), 165–67.

9. Condoleezza Rice, *Democracy: Stories from the Long Road to Freedom* (New York: Hachette, 2017), 281–87; Crocker, Interview, September 9-10, 2010, GWB/OHP, MC; Khalilzad, *Envoy*, 160–67; Feith, *War and Decision*, 280–82.

10. George W. Bush, *Decision Points* (New York: Crown Publishers, 2010), 249; Special Inspector General for Iraq Reconstruction, *Hard Lessons: The Iraq Reconstruction Experience* (Washington, DC: Government Printing Office, 2009), 12–13; Robert Draper, *To Start a War: How the Bush Administration Took America into Iraq* (New York: Penguin, 2020), 383; Douglas J. Feith, Interview, March 22–23, 2012, GWB/OHP, MC; "Considerations for Post-Liberation Iraq," January 17, 2003, OSD Reading Room, 07-F-1332, https://www.esd.whs.mil/FOID/Reading-Room/.

11. Rayburn and Sobchak, *US Army in the Iraq War*, 66–67.

12. Casey, Interview, September 25, 2014, GWB/OHP, MC; Feith, Interview, March 22-23, 2012, GWB/OHP, MC.

13. Nora Bensahel et al., *After Saddam: Prewar Planning and the Occupation of Iraq* (Santa Monica, CA: Rand, 2008), xvii–xxi, 21–27; Condoleezza Rice, *No Higher Honor: A Memoir of My Years in Washington* (New York: Crown, 2011), 190–91; Feith, Interview, March 22–23, 2012, GWB/OHP, MC.

14. Rumsfeld, *Known and Unknown*, 482.

15. Lorne Cramer, Arthur Dewey, and Paul Simons to Paula Dobriansky, February 7, 2003, Electronic Briefing Book (EBB) 163, National Security Archive (NSA), https://nsarchive2.gwu.edu/NSAEBB/NSAEBB163/iraq-state-03.pdf; Burns to Powell, January 16, 2003 and February 12, 2003, Burns Papers; Chris Lamb to Feith, February 9, 2003, cited in Feith, *War and Decision*, 362–63; Gregory Hooker, *Shaping the Plan for Operation Iraqi Freedom: The Role of Military Intelligence Assessments* (Washington, DC: Washington Institute for Near East Policy, 2005), 37.

16. "Record of a Meeting on January 15, 2003," dated January 22, 2003, Ministry of Defense Papers, Iraq Inquiry, https://webarchive.nationalarchives.gov.uk/ukgwa/20130206044351/http:/www.iraqinquiry.org.uk/transcripts/declassified-documents.aspx [hereafter cited as Iraq Inquiry]; Dominic Chilcot to Edward Chaplin, January 17, 2003, Foreign and Commonwealth Office, ibid.; Report of a Committee of Privy Counsellors, *The Report of the Iraq Inquiry* (hereafter cited as Chilcot Report), Executive Summary, Paragraph 629, https://www.thegroovygroup.org/chilcot-report.php.

17. Rayburn and Sobchak, *US Army in the Iraq War*, 68.

18. Casey, Interview, September 25, 2014, GWB/OHP, MC.

19. Elliott Abrams, interview with author, August 18, 2015; Franklin Miller, interview with author, July 15, 2011; Rice, *No Higher Honor*, 192; Inspector General, *Hard Lessons*, 16.

20. National Security Presidential Directive/NSPD-24, January 20, 2003, https://irp.fas.org/offdocs/nspd/nspd-24.pdf; Feith to Rumsfeld, January 8, 2003, "Targeting Iraq, 1997–2004," Digital National Security Archive (DNSA); Colin L. Powell and Richard L. Armitage, Interview, March 28, 2017, GWB/OHP, MC; Powell, interview with author, January 24, 2011.

21. Rumsfeld, *Known and Unknown*, 488; Feith, *War and Decision*, 348–49.

22. Garner, Interview, July 17, 2003, *Frontline*; Garner, Interview, August 11, 2006, *Frontline*, https://www.pbs.org/wgbh/pages/frontline/yeariniraq/interviews/garner.html; Powell and Armitage, Interview, March 28, 2017, GWB/OHP, MC; Inspector General, *Hard Lessons*, 41–42.

23. Office of Reconstruction and Humanitarian Assistance (ORHA), "Inter-Agency Rehearsal and Planning Conference," February 21–22, 2003, https://web.archive.org/web/20131103044321/http://www.waranddecision.com/docLib/20080404_ORHAConferencebriefing.pdf; Inspector General, *Hard Lessons*, 38–43.

24. Garner, Interviews, July 17, 2003 and August 11, 2006, *Frontline*; Crocker, Interview, September 9–10, 2010, GWB/OHP, MC; Seth Carus, interview with author, December 16, 2015; Abrams, interview with author, August 18, 2015; Edelman to Leffler, October 27, 2021; Bensahel, *After Saddam*, 53–64; James Dobbins et al., *Occupying Iraq: A History of the Coalition Provisional Authority* (Santa Monica, CA: Rand, 2009), 34–36.

25. Inspector General, *Hard Lessons*, 43; Bensahel, *After Saddam*, 64, 35, 13–14; Garner, Interview, August 11, 2006, *Frontline*.

26. Lamb to Feith, February 9, 2003, in possession of author; Feith, *War and Decision*, 362–66; Christopher J. Lamb, interview with author, September 2, 2011.

27. Steve Busby, "Summary of Public Order Plan: Phase One," [ND], Rumsfeld Papers; Rice, *No Higher Honor*, 189–90; Rice, *Democracy*, 290; Inspector General, *Hard Lessons*, 35.

28. Bensahel, *After Saddam*, 14; Third Infantry Division, Mechanized, *After Action Report*, 2003, 292, https://www.globalsecurity.org/military/libr ary/report/2003/3id-aar-jul03.pdf; David Petraeus, "Reflections," *Prism* 7(2017): 151–52; Rayburn and Sobchak, *US Army in the Iraq War*, 111–25.

29. Peter Baker, *Days of Fire: Bush and Cheney in the White House* (New York: Doubleday, 2013), 248; Bradley Graham, *By His Own Rules: The Ambitions, Successes, and Ultimate Failures of Donald Rumsfeld* (New York: Public Affairs, 2009), 384–86; Rumsfeld, *Known and Unknown*, 452–56.

30. Garner, Interview, August 11, 2006, *Frontline*.

31. SP/NESA, "Rebuilding the Iraqi Military," January 21, 2003, Rumsfeld Papers; Joint Staff, "Reshaping the Iraqi Military," March 7, 2003, ibid.; Rodman to Rumsfeld, May 24, 2006, ibid.; Inspector General, *Hard Lessons*, 44.

32. Burns to Powell, February 12, 2003, Burns Papers; "Summary of Conclusion for NSC Meeting" (on March 10, 2003), March 11, 2003, in author's possession; Rumsfeld to Bush, March 26, 2003, "Targeting Iraq," DNSA; Feith, *War and Decision*, 403–9; Hadley, interview with author, February 22, 2011.

33. OSD, "Key Principles for Post-Conflict Governance," March 11, 2003, OSD Reading Room.

34. Ibid.; Inspector General, *Hard Lessons*, 44; Feith, *War and Decision*, 418–28; Dobbins, *Occupying Iraq*, 112–14.

35. Bush, "Address to the Nation," March 19, 2003, American Presidency Project (hereafter cited as APP), https://www.presidency.ucsb.edu/people/ president/george-w-bush.

36. Rice, interviews with author, July 19, 2021 and August 2, 2021.

37. Rayburn and Sobchak, *US Army in the Iraq War*, 81–105; Michael R. Gordon and Bernard E. Trainor, *Cobra II: The Inside Story of the Invasion and Occupation of Iraq* (New York: Pantheon Books, 2006), 164–456.

38. Rice, *Democracy*, 274; Rice, *No Higher Honor*, 208.

39. Bush, "Videotaped Remarks to the Iraqi People," April 10, 2003, APP.

40. Bush, "President Discusses the Future öf Iraq," February 26, 2003, https://geor gewbush-whitehouse.archives.gov/news/releases/2003/02/20030226-11.html.

41. Bush, "Remarks in Bethesda, Maryland," April 11, 2003; Bush, "Remarks in Canton, Ohio," April 24, 2003; Bush, "Remarks in Dearborn, Michigan," April 28, 2003, APP.

42. Bush, "Remarks on the Deck of USS Abraham Lincoln," May 1, 2003, https://www.cbsnews.com/news/text-of-bush-speech-01-05-2003/.

43. Bush, *Decision Points*, 258.

44. Inspector General, *Hard Lessons*, 59–60; Rayburn and Sobchak, *US Army in the Iraq War*, 111–15.

45. William Scott Wallace, Interview, February 26, 2004, *Frontline*, https://www.pbs.org/wgbh/pages/frontline/shows/invasion/interviews/wallace.html; Third Infantry Division, *After-Action Report*, 289–90; Rayburn and Sobchak, *US Army in the Iraq War*, 111–27.

46. For lessons learned, see Defense Science Board, 2004 Summer Study, "Transition to and from Hostilities," December 2004, https://dsb.cto.mil/reports/2000s/ADA430116.pdf.

47. For McKiernan and Franks, see Rayburn and Sobchak, *US Army in Iraq War*, 121; Petraeus, "Reflections," 152; Donald P. Wright and Timothy R. Reese, *On Point II: Transition to the New Campaign: The United States Army in Operation Iraqi Freedom, May 2003–January 2005* (Ft. Leavenworth, KS: Combat Studies Institute Press, 2008), 76; Ricks, *Fiasco*, 144–46; Crocker, Interview, September 9-10, 2010, GWB/OHP, MC.

48. Rice, *No Higher Honor*, 210; Rayburn and Sobchak, *US Army in Iraq War*, 117–22; Inspector General, *Hard Lessons*, 57–58, 61; Gordon and Trainor, *Cobra II*, 457–60.

49. Inspector General, *Hard Lessons*, 58.

50. Ibid., 46–64; Garner, Interviews, July 17, 2003 and August 11, 2006, *Frontline*.

51. Petraeus, "Reflections," 173; Inspector General, *Hard Lessons*, 61–62; Garner, Interviews, *Frontline*, July 17, 2003 and August 11, 2006; for Garner's instructions, Mike Mobbs to Garner, March 25, 2003, OSD Reading Room.

52. Inspector General, *Hard Lessons*, 61; Garner, Interview, *Frontline*, August 11, 2006.

53. Franks to Rumsfeld, April 16, 2003, Rumsfeld Papers; Benashel, *After Saddam*, 90; Gordon and Trainor, *Cobra II*, 459–62.

54. Garner, Interview, *Frontline*, August 11, 2006; Khalilzad, *Envoy*, 168–69; for Franks's appeal to Iraqi soldiers, see "Instructions to Iraqi Armed Forces," draft, March 18, 2003, OSD Reading Room.

55. Khalilzad, *Envoy*, 168.

56. Ibid., 160–73; Inspector General, *Hard Lessons*, 61–62; Ali A. Allawi, *The Occupation of Iraq: Winning the War, Losing the Peace* (New Haven, CT: Yale University Press, 2007), 104.

57. Garner, Interview, *Frontline*, July 17, 2003; Dobbins, *Occupying Iraq*, 35–39; Khalilzad, *Envoy*, 166–67, 172; Allawi, *Occupation of Iraq*, 103–4.

58. Rice, *No Higher Honor*, 208–12; Rice, *Democracy*, 279–80; Rumsfeld, *Known and Unknown*, 502–5; Feith, *War and Decision*, 420–23; Edelman to Leffler, October 27, 2021.

59. Garner, Interview, *Frontline*, August 11, 2006; Office of General Counsel to L. Paul Bremer, May 22, 2003, OSD Reading Room.

60. Khalilzad, *Envoy*, 172–73.

61. Rumsfeld to Andrew Card, April 7, 2003, "Targeting Iraq," DNSA.

62. Khalilzad, *Envoy*, 172–73; Garner, Interview, *Frontline*, August 11, 2006; Crocker, Interview, September 9–10, 2010, GWB/OHP, MC; Feith, *War and Decision*, 397–411.

63. Charles Duelfer, *Hide and Seek: The Search for Truth in Iraq* (New York: Public Affairs, 2004), 267–68.

64. Rice, *No Higher Honor*, 208.

65. Ibid., 211; for Bremer's thinking and background, see L. Paul Bremer III, Interview, August 28–29, 2012, GWB/OHP, MC.

66. L. Paul Bremer III, with Malcolm McConnell, *My Year in Iraq: The Struggle to Build a Future of Hope* (New York: Simon & Schuster, 2006), 7–8; Rumsfeld, *Known and Unknown*, 502–7; Bremer, Interview, August 28-29, 2012, GWB/OHP, MC; Eric Edelman, interview with author, March 10, 2011.

67. Bremer, Interview, August 28-29, 2012, GWB/OHP, MC; Feith, *War and Decision*, 424; Bremer, *My Year in Iraq*, 12. OSD policy is most clearly laid out in Rumsfeld to Cheney, Powell, Tenet, and Rice, March 29, 2003, "Targeting Iraq," DNSA.

68. Bremer, *My Year in Iraq*, 12.

69. Ibid., 11–12; Bush, *Decision Points*, 258–59; Bremer, Interview, August 28–29, 2012, GWB/OHP MC; Rumsfeld, *Known and Unknown*, 506.

70. Bremer, *My Year in Iraq*, 10–20, 32–35; Duelfer, *Hide and Seek*, 274–84; for a vivid description of conditions as experienced by Iraqis, see Anthony Shadid, *Night Draws Near* (New York: Henry Holt & Company, 2005).

71. Bremer, *My Year in Iraq*, 43; for conditions when Bremer arrived, see Radio Free Europe/Radio Liberty, *Iraq Report*, 6 (May 16, 2003): 1–10.

72. Inspector General, *Hard Lessons*, 70–71.

73. For UNSCR 1483, May 22, 2003, see https://digitallibrary.un.org/record/495555?ln=en.

74. Bremer, *My Year in Iraq*, 48–49; Illawi, *Occupation of Iraq*, 110.

75. Khalilzad, *Envoy*, 174–75; Dobbins, *Occupying Iraq*, 39–49.

76. Shadid, *Night Draws Near*, 235–37.

77. Inspector General, *Hard Lessons*, 72; Bremer, Interview, August 28–29, 2012, GWB/OHP, MC.

78. Feith, *War and Decision*, 427–31; "Principles for Iraq—Policy Guidelines," May 13, 2003, Rumsfeld Papers.

79. Inspector General, *Hard Lessons*, 73–74; Rayburn and Sobchak, *US Army in Iraq War*, 141.

80. Bremer, *My Year in Iraq*, 48; for Hussein, see Radio Free Europe/Radio Liberty, *Iraq Report* 6 (May 2, 2003): 1.

81. Dobbins, *Occupying Iraq*, 114–16; Inspector General, *Hard Lessons*, 73–74.

82. Petraeus, "Reflections," 154; Duelfer, *Hide and Seek*, 309–10; Rajiv Chandrasekaran, *Imperial Life in the Emerald City: Inside Iraq's Green Zone* (New York: Alfred A. Knopf, 2006), 70–73.

83. Feith, *War and Decision*, 431–35; Rodman to Rumsfeld, May 24, 2006, Rumsfeld Papers.

84. Rice, *No Higher Honor*, 237–38; Rice, *Democracy*, 291–92; Rayburn and Sobchak, *US Army in Iraq War*, 141–44.

85. Bremer to Rumsfeld, May 19, 2003, Rumsfeld Papers.

86. Duelfer, *Hide and Seek*, 311; Rayburn and Sobchak, *US Army in Iraq War*, 142–44.

87. Petraeus, "Reflections," 154; Crocker, Interview, September 9–10, 2010, GWB/OHP.

88. Duelfer, *Hide and Seek*, 279–81; Mike Jackson, "Declassified Extracts from a Report of a Visit to Iraq," May 13, 2003, Iraq Inquiry.

89. Shadid, *Night Draws Near*, 236.

90. Wright and Reese, *On Point II*, 322; Rayburn and Sobchak, *US Army in Iraq War*, 154–55.

91. Bremer to Bush, June 14, 2003, "Targeting Iraq," DNSA.

92. Bremer, *My Year in Iraq*, 105–7; Dobbins, *Occupying Iraq*, 95–96.

93. Rayburn and Sobchak, *US Army in Iraq War*, 137–38, 146–47, 160–62; Wright and Reese, *On Point II*, 29–30, 156–59; Gordon and Trainor, *Cobra II*, 457–62; Ricardo Sanchez, with Donald T. Phillips, *Wiser in Battle: A Soldier's Story* (New York: Harper, 2008), 194, 197–98, 209; Bremer, Interview, August 28-29, 2012, GWB/OHP, MC; Graham, *By His Own Rules*, 385–86.

94. Rumsfeld to Bremer, June 9, 2003 and June 19, 2003, Rumsfeld Papers.

95. Bremer, *My Year in Iraq*, 122–23; Allawi, *Occupation of Iraq*, 166.

96. Bremer, *My Year in Iraq*, 115–18; Rayburn and Sobchak, *US Army in Iraq War*, 140–57.

97. Rumsfeld, *Known and Unknown*, 511–19; Feith, *War and Decision*, 440–47; Bremer, Interview, August 28-29, 2012, GWB/OHP, MC.

98. Bremer, *My Year in Iraq*, 113–36.

99. Rayburn and Sobchak, *US Army in Iraq War*, 144; Sanchez, *Wiser in Battle*, 177–220.

100. Dobbins, *Occupying Iraq*, 103.
101. Rumsfeld to Rice, July 22, 2003, "Targeting Iraq," DNSA.
102. Rumsfeld to Feith, July 25, 2003, OSD Reading Room, https://www.esd. whs.mil/Portals/54/Documents/FOID/Special_Collection/Rumsfeld/ DocumentsReleased_to_Rumsfeld_Under_FOIA.pdf?ver=2017-05-05- 104646-373.
103. Powell and Armitage, Interview, March 28, 2017, GWB/OHP, MC; Rumsfeld to Feith, July 31, 2003, "Targeting Iraq," DNSA.
104. Bremer, Interview, GWB/OHP, MC; Fredric C. Smith and Franklin C. Miller, "The Office of the Secretary of Defense: Civilian Masters?" in *The National Security Enterprise*, ed. Roger Z. George and Harvey Rishikof (Washington, DC: Georgetown University Press, 2011), 111–13; also see Marc Grossman, "The State Department: Culture as Interagency Destiny," in ibid., 86, 89; Duelfer, *Hide and Seek*, 268–69.
105. Burns to Powell, July 11, 2003, Burns Papers.
106. Bremer, *My Year in Iraq*, 48; Dobbins, *Occupying Iraq*, 96.
107. Shadid, *Night Draws Near*, 168, 180.
108. Rayburn and Sobchak, *US Army in Iraq War*, 169–88.
109. Bremer, *My Year in Iraq*, 112; Duelfer, *Hide and Seek*, 286.
110. Bremer, *My Year in Iraq*, 140–41; Ricks, *Fiasco*, 215–16.
111. Dobbins, *Occupying Iraq*, 101.
112. "Principles for Iraq—Policy Guidelines," May 13, 2003, Rumsfeld Papers.
113. See, e.g., Rumsfeld to Bremer, July 8, 2003, Rumsfeld Papers; Bremer, Interview, August 28-29, 2012, GWB/OHP, MC.
114. Rumsfeld's contempt for Rice was widely recognized and apparent in many of the snowflakes he wrote to her. See, e.g., Rumsfeld to Rice, July 8, 2003, "Targeting Iraq," DNSA; Powell and Armitage, Interview, March 28, 2017, GWB/OHP, MC.
115. Dobbins, *Occupying Iraq*, 103.
116. Rayburn and Sobchak, *US Army in Iraq War*, 143–44; Bush, *Decision Points*, 22, 66.
117. Bremer, *My Year in Iraq*, 139–41.
118. Bush, "Radio Address," August 23, 2003, APP.

Chapter 10

1. Kevin Brown, Interview, October 17, 2005, Combat Studies Institute (Fort Leavenworth, KS), https://www.armyupress.army.mil/Portals/7/ online-publications/documents/interview-with-maj-kevin-brown-75th- exploitation-task-force-operation-iraqi-freedom.pdf; Joel D. Rayburn and Frank K. Sobchak, eds., *The US Army in the Iraq War: Invasion, Insurgency, Civil War* (Carlisle, PA: US Army War College, 2019), 139.
2. George Tenet, with Bill Harlow, *At the Center of the Storm: My Years at the CIA* (New York: HarperCollins, 2007), 401–15.
3. David Kay, Testimony, January 28, 2004, US Senate, Armed Services Committee, "Iraqi Weapons of Mass Destruction Programs," https://

nsarchive2.gwu.edu/NSAEBB/NSAEBB80/kaytestimony.pdf; David Kay, "Iraq's Weapons of Mass Destruction," *Miller Center Report*, Spring/Summer 2004, 7–12; Iraq Survey Group, *Comprehensive Report of the Special Advisor to the DCI on Iraq's WMD*, September 30, 2004, http://www-personal.umich.edu/~graceyor/govdocs/pdf/duelfer1_a.pdf [hereafter cited as Duelfer Report].

4. Kay, Testimony, January 28, 2004; David Kay, Statement, October 2, 2003, US House of Representatives, House Permanent Select Committee on Intelligence, Subcommittee on Defense, and Senate Select Committee on Intelligence, https://www.cnn.com/2003/ALLPOLITICS/10/02/kay.report/.

5. Charles Duelfer, *Hide and Seek: The Search for Truth in Iraq* (New York: Public Affairs, 2004), 381.

6. Duelfer Report, 8–9; Kay, "Iraq's Weapons of Mass Destruction."

7. "Saddam Hussein Talks to the FBI: Twenty Interviews and Five Conversations with 'High Value Detainee #1' in 2004," Electronic Briefing Book No. 279, National Security Archive, https://nsarchive2.gwu.edu/NSAEBB/NSAEBB279/.

8. Duelfer, *Hide and Seek*, 380–412; for a very different view, see John Nixon, *Debriefing the President: The Interrogation of Saddam Hussein* (New York: Blue Ridge Press, 2016); for rebuttal of Nixon, see Charles Duelfer and Judith Miller, *City Journal*, March 5, 2017, https://www.city-journal.org/html/self-serving-history-15043.html.

9. Ryan Crocker, Interview, September 9-10, 2010, George W. Bush, Oral History Project, Miller Center, University of Virginia, 130–35, https://millercenter.org/the-presidency/presidential-oral-histories/ryan-crocker-oral-history (hereafter cited as GWB/OHP, MC).

10. These points are developed in Chapter 2.

11. Tony Blair, *A Journey: My Political Life* (New York: Knopf, 2010), 354.

12. Elliott Abrams, *Tested by Zion: The Bush Administration and the Israeli-Palestinian Conflict* (New York: Cambridge University Press, 2013), 64.

13. For appreciation of Bush, see, for example, interviews with Hadley, Wolfowitz, Franks, Hayden, Pace, Paul Bremer, George Casey, GWB/OHP, MC; Wolfowitz, interview with author, February 2, 2011; Gerson, interview with author, March 9, 2016; for favorable assessments in memoirs, see Hugh Shelton, with Ronald Levinson and Malcolm McConnell, *Without Hesitation: The Odyssey of an American Warrior* (New York: St. Martin's Press, 2010), 414–19; Donald Rumsfeld, *Known and Unknown: A Memoir* (New York: Sentinel, 2011), 317–19; Richard B. Myers, with Malcolm McConnell, *Eyes on the Horizon: Serving on the Front Lines of National Security* (New York: Threshold Editions, 2009), 145; Tenet, *At the Center of the Storm*, 171; David Frum, *The Right Man: An Inside Account of the Bush White House* (New York: Random House, 2003).

14. Powell, interview with author, January 24, 2011; Armitage, interview with author, March 23, 2011; Abrams, interview with author, August 28, 2015; Edelman, interview with author, March 10, 2011; Miller, interview

with author, July 15, 2011; Clarke, interview with author, December 31, 2010; Burns, interview with author, June 23, 2020; Pace, interview, January 19, 2016, GWB/OHP, MC.

15. Rice, interview with author, August 2, 2021; Hadley, interview with author, December 4, 2019; Gerson, interview with author, March 9, 2016.

16. For Hussein, see Chapters 1 and 8.

17. For Bush's motivations, see especially Chapters 2, 3, 7, and 8.

18. For Bush's views on military power and defense transformation, see Chapters 2, 3, 4, and 5.

19. This argument is made by Ahsan I. Butt, "Why Did the United States Invade Iraq in 2003?" *Security Studies* 28 (2019): 250–85.

20. For Bush's faith and his beliefs about the superiority of democratic capitalism and American institutions, see Chapters 2, 8, and 9. These beliefs are beautifully captured in his introduction to the National Security Strategy Statement of 2002, "National Security Strategy of the United States of America," September 17, 2002, https://georgewbush-whitehouse.archives.gov/nsc/nss/2002/; also see his "remarks" on the twentieth anniversary of the National Endowment for Democracy, November 6, 2003, APP; for the UN Arab Human Development Report, 2002, see https://www.arabstates.undp.org/content/rbas/en/home/library/huma_development/arab-human-development-report-2003-building-a-knowledge-society.html; for Bush's interest in it, Edelman, interview with author, March 10, 2011.

21. Nelly Lahoud, *The Bin Laden Papers* (New Haven, CT: Yale University Press, 2022); National Intelligence Estimate, "The Terrorist Threat to the US Homeland," July 2007, https://www.dni.gov/files/documents/NIE_terrorist%20threat%202007.pdf; also see the British JIC Assessment, "International Terrorism: Impact of Iraq," April 13, 2005, Iraq Inquiry, https://webarchive.nationalarchives.gov.uk/ukgwa/20130206044351/http:/www.iraqinquiry.org.uk/transcripts/declassified-documents.aspx; Aaron O'Connell, "The Global Wars on Terror," in *The Cambridge History of America and the World*, vol. 4, eds. David C. Engerman, Max Paul Friedman, and Melani McAlister (Cambridge: Cambridge, 2021), 707–30.

22. Rumsfeld to Bush, June 18, 2004, Rumsfeld Archive.

23. Rumsfeld to Hadley, August 4, 2006, ibid.

24. An excellent example was the president's State of the Union message, January 28, 2003, in which his initiative to battle HIV/AIDS was dwarfed by his focus on Iraq. See Bush, "State of the Union," January 28, 2003, APP.

25. "Remarks" on the twentieth anniversary of the National Endowment for Democracy, November 6, 2003, APP.

26. In addition to the evidence presented in the previous chapters, see the transition memos on counterproliferation policy, on WMD terrorism, and on Iraq in Stephen Hadley, *Hand-Off: The Foreign Policy George W. Bush Passed to Barack Obama* (Washington, DC: Brookings Institution Press, 2023).

27. For Hussein's links to terror, see Kevin M. Woods, Project Leader, with James Lacy, *Iraqi Perspectives Project: Saddam and Terrorism: Emerging Insights from Captured Iraqi Documents*, Vol. 1 (Redacted), https://irp.fas. org/eprint/iraqi/v1.pdf.

28. In addition to the arguments made in this book, see the comments by Megan O'Sullivan in her discussion of Iraq in Hadley, *Hand-Off.*

29. Douglas Lute, Interview, August 3, 2015, GWB/OHP, MC; for an incisive critique of Bush's strategy, see Hal Brands, *What Good Is Grand Strategy: Power and Purpose in American Statecraft from Harry S. Truman to George W. Bush* (Ithaca, NY: Cornell University Press, 2014), 144–89.

30. See data on the "Costs of War" website, https://watson.brown.edu/cos tsofwar/costs/human/military/wounded; for the evolution of the war, see especially Michael R. Gordon and Bernard E. Trainor, *The Endgame: The Inside Story of the Struggle for Iraq, from George W. Bush to Barack Obama* (New York: Pantheon Books, 2012).

31. For the "surge," see Timothy Andrews Sayle, Jeffrey A. Engel, Hal Brands, and William Inboden, eds., *The Last Card: Inside George W. Bush's Decision to Surge in Iraq* (Ithaca, NY: Cornell University Press, 2019); for a critique, see, e.g., Robert Brigham, "The Lessons and Legacies of the War in Iraq," in *Understanding the US Wars in Iraq and Afghanistan*, ed. Beth Bailey and Richard H. Immerman (New York: New York University Press, 2015), 286–307.

32. For perceptions and reactions, see, e.g., Shibley Telhami, "Arab Public Opinion on the United States and Iraq: Postwar Prospects for Changing Prewar Views," June 1, 2003, https://www.brookings.edu/articles/ arab-public-opinion-on-the-united-states-and-iraq-postwar-prospects-for-changing-prewar-views/; Pew Research Center, "America's Image in the World: Findings from the Pew Global Attitudes Project, 2007," March 14, 2007, https://www.pewresearch.org/global/2007/03/14/ameri cas-image-in-the-world-findings-from-the-pew-global-attitudes-proj ect/; American Political Science Association, Task Force Report, Jeffrey W. Legro and Peter J. Katzenstein, *US Standing in the World: Causes, Consequences, and the Future* (Washington, DC: American Political Science Association, 2009).

33. Freedom House, *Freedom in the World, 2008* (New York: Rowman and Littlefield, 2008), 3–11; Freedom House, *Freedom in the World, 2009* (New York: Rowman and Littlefield, 2009), 3–12.

34. For data and articles on the dead and wounded and on the financial costs, see the "Costs of War" website, https://watson.brown.edu/costsofwar/ costs/human/military/wounded; also Dan Froomkin, "How Many US Soldiers Were Wounded in Iraq? Guess Again," *Huffington Post*, February 29, 2012, https://www.huffpost.com/entry/iraq-soldiers-wounded_b_1176 276; for suicide numbers, see US Department of Veterans Affairs, "Suicide Risk and Risk of Death Among Recent Veterans," https://www.publichea lth.va.gov/epidemiology/studies/suicide-risk-death-risk-recent-veterans.asp; US Department of Veteran Affairs, *National Veteran Suicide Prevention,*

Annual Report, September 2021, https://www.mentalhealth.va.gov/docs/data-sheets/2021/2021-National-Veteran-Suicide-Prevention-Annual-Report-FINAL-9-8-21.pdf.

35. See, e.g., Henry M. Paulson Jr., *On the Brink: Inside the Race to Stop the Collapse of the Global Financial System* (New York: Business Plus, 2010); Adam Tooze, *Crashed: How a Decade of Financial Crises Changed the World* (New York: Viking, 2018).

36. In February 2008, 53 percent of Americans polled said the administration had "deliberately misled the American public" about Iraqi weapons of mass destruction. See Ole R. Holsti, "The United States," in *Public Opinion and International Intervention: Lessons from the Iraq War*, ed. Richard Sobel, Peter Furia, and Bethany Barratt (Washington, DC: Potomac Books, 2012), 30; for declining faith in government, see Pew Research Center, "Public Trust in Government: 1958–2021," May 17, 2021, https://www.pewresearch.org/politics/2021/05/17/public-trust-in-government-1958-2021/.

37. Frank Newport, "Seventy-Two Percent of Americans Support War against Iraq," March 24, 2003, https://news.gallup.com/poll/8038/seventytwo-percent-americans-support-war-against-iraq.aspx; for other polls, see "Media Polls on the Iraq War between 2003 and 2007," https://www.politicalfact.com/Iraq-war-polls; AEI Public Opinion Studies, "Public Opinion on the War in Iraq," January 11, 2007, https://www.aei.org/wp-content/uploads/2012/01/-aeipublicopinioniraq2009_133351682593.pdf.

38. "America's Image Further Erodes, Europeans Want Weaker Ties: But Post-War Iraq Will Be Better Off, Most Say," March 18, 2003, https://www.pewresearch.org/politics/2003/03/18/additional-findings-and-analyses-10/; for opposition to the war, see "War with Iraq Is Not in America's National Interest," *New York Times*, September 26, 2002, https://sadat.umd.edu/sites/sadat.umd.edu/files/iraq_war_ad_2002_2.pdf; John J. Mearsheimer and Stephen M. Walt, "An Unnecessary War," *Foreign Policy* (January/February 2003): 51–59.

39. Telhami, "Arab Public Opinion," June 1, 2003; Anonymous [Michael Scheuer], *Through Our Enemies' Eyes: Osama Bin Laden, Radicl Islam, and the Future of America* (Washington, DC: Potomac Books, 2002); Anonymous [James Scheuer], *Imperial Hubris: why the West is Losing the War on Terror* (Washington, DC: Brassey's, 2004).

40. John M. Own IV, *The Clash of Ideas in World Politics: Transnational Networks, States, and Regime Change, 1510–2010* (Princeton, NJ: Princeton University Press, 2010), 6–7, 202–39, 263; Ussama Makdisi, *Age of Coexistence: The Ecumenical Frame and the Making of the Modern Arab World* (Oakland: University of California Press, 2019); Gareth Stansfield, *Iraq: People, History, Politics* (Cambridge: Polity Press, 2007), 159–91.

41. This is beautifully portrayed in Anthony Shadid, *Night Draws Near: Iraq's People in the Shadow of America's War* (New York: Henry Holt, 2005).

BIBLIOGRAPHY

Interviews

Combat Studies Institute
Brown, Kevin. October 17, 2005.

Interviews with Author
Abrams, Elliott. August 18, 2015.
Armitage, Richard. March 23, 2011 and April 7, 2011.
Beigun, Steve. August 7, 2015.
Burns, William J. June 23, 2020.
Carus, Seth. December 16, 2015.
Cheney, Richard. August 11, 2017.
Clarke, Richard. December 31, 2010.
Edelman, Eric. December 2, 2010 and March 10, 2011.
Feith, Douglas J. September 9, 2020.
Gerson, Michael. March 9, 2016.
Hadley, Stephen. February 22, 2011 and December 4, 2019.
Lamb, Christopher. September 2, 2011.
Libby, I. Lewis (Scooter). December 9, 2010, January 25, 2011, and March 9, 2011.
McLaughlin, John. April 4, 2011.
Miller, Franklin. July 15, 2011.
Morrell, Michael. December 8, 2013 and January 25, 2014.
Negroponte, John. June 18, 2021.
Powell, Colin. January 24, 2011.

Rice, Condoleezza. July 19, 2021 and August 2, 2021
Smullen, William. February 23, 2011.
Wolfowitz, Paul. July 28, 2010 and February 2, 2011.
Zoellick, Robert. October 22, 2015.

Frontline (PBS) Interviews
Garner, Jay. July 17, 2003 and August 11, 2006.
Wallace, William Scott. February 26, 2004.

Miller Center Interviews, George W. Bush Oral History Project
Bremer, Paul L., III. August 28–29, 2012.
Casey, George W. September 25, 2014.
Crocker, Ryan. September 9–10, 2010.
Feith, Douglas J. March 22–23, 2012.
Franks, Tommy. October 22, 2014.
Hadley, Stephen. October 31–November 1, 2011.
Hayden, Michael. November 20, 2012.
Lute, Douglas. August 3, 2015.
Pace, Peter. January 19, 2016.
Powell, Colin, and Richard L. Armitage. March 28, 2017.

UN Documents

Blix, Hans. "An Update on Inspection." Speech, New York. January 27, 2003.
    UN Security Council. https://www.un.org/Depts/unmovic/Bx27.htm.
"Independent Inquiry Committee into the United Nations Oil-for-Food
    Programme: Manipulation of the Oil-for-Food Programme by the Iraqi
    Regime" [Volcker Report]. October 27, 2005. http://www.humanrightsvoices.
    org/assets/attachments/documents/volcker_report_10-27-05.pdf.
Monitoring, Verification and Inspection Commission (UNMOVIC). "Twelfth
    Quarterly Report of the Executive Chairman of the United Nations
    Monitoring, Verification and Inspection Commission in Accordance with
    Paragraph 12 of Security Council Resolution 1284 (1999)." Annex. Draft.
    February 28, 2003. https://www.globalsecurity.org/wmd/library/news/iraq/
    un/iraq-unmovic_report12_2003.htm.
Security Council. "Fourth Report of the Executive Chairman of the Special
    Commission Established by the Secretary-General Pursuant to Paragraph
    9 (b) (i) of Security Council Resolution 687 (1991), on the Activities of the
    Special Commission." December 17, 1992. https://www.un.org/Depts/uns
    com/24984.pdf.
Security Council. "Ninth Quarterly Report of the Executive Chairman of the
    United Nations Monitoring, Verification and Inspection Commission under
    Paragraph 12 of Security Council Resolution 1284 (1999)." May 31, 2002.

https://www.un.org/depts/unmovic/new/documents/quarterly_reports/s-2002-606.pdf.

Security Council. "Resolution 1441 (2002)." November 8, 2002. https://www.un.org/Depts/unmovic/documents/1441.pdf.

Security Council. "Resolution 1483 (2003)." May 22, 2003. https://digitallibrary.un.org/record/495555?ln=en.

Security Council. "Seventh Quarterly Report of the Executive Chairman of the United Nations Monitoring, Verification and Inspection Commission under Paragraph 12 of Security Council Resolution 1284 (1999)." November 29, 2001. https://www.un.org/depts/unmovic/documents/1126eng.pdf.

Security Council. "The Status of the Implementation of the Plan for the Ongoing Monitoring and Verification of Iraq's Compliance with Relevant Parts of Section C of Security Council Resolution 687 (1991)." October 19, 1992. https://www.un.org/Depts/unscom/24661.pdf.

US Government Documents

The American Presidency Project [APP]. University of California at Santa Barbara. https://www.presidency.ucsb.edu/documents.

Burns, William J. Papers. https://carnegieendowment.org/publications/interactive/back-channel.

Central Intelligence Agency. Electronic Reading Room. https://www.cia.gov/readingroom/search/site.

Commission on National Security/21st Century. "New World Coming: American Security in the 21st Century." September 15, 1999. https://govinfo.library.unt.edu/nssg/Reports/NWC.pdf.

Commission on the Intelligence Capabilities of the United States regarding Weapons of Mass Destruction [Robb-Silberman Report]. *Report to the President of the United States.* March 31, 2005. https://irp.fas.org/offdocs/wmd_report.pdf.

Commission to Assess the Ballistic Missile Threat to the United States. "Executive Summary of the Report of the Commission to Assess the Ballistic Missile Threat to the United States." July 15, 1998. http://www.bits.de/NRANEU/BMD/documents/Rumsfeld150798.pdf.

Department of Defense. Washington Headquarters Services. Freedom of Information Act. OSD Reading Room. https://www.esd.whs.mil/FOID/Reading-Room/.

Department of State. *Patterns of Global Terrorism 2000.* May 2001. https://2009-2017.state.gov/j/ct/rls/crt/2000/2419.htm.

Department of State. *Patterns of Global Terrorism 2001.* May 2002. https://2009-2017.state.gov/documents/organization/10319.pdf.

Department of State. *Patterns of Global Terrorism 2002.* April 2003. https://2009-2017.state.gov/documents/organization/20177.pdf.

Department of State. US *Department of State Country Report on Human Rights Practices 2001—Iraq*. March 4, 2002. https://www.refworld.org/cgi-bin/texis/vtx/rwmain?page=search&docid=3c84d99d4&skip=0&query=Human%252 0Rights, %25202001&coi=IRQ.

Digital National Security Archive. "Targeting Iraq, Part 1: Planning, Invaion, and Occupation,1997–2004." https://proquest.libguides.com/dnsa/iraq97.

Feith, Douglas J. *War and Decision*. Related Documents and Articles. https://web.archive.org/web/20090107022111/http://www.waranddecision.com/documents_and_articles/.

Hadley, Stephen, ed. *Hand-Off: The Foreign Policy George W. Bush Passed to Barack Obama*. Washington, DC: Brookings Institution Press, 2023.

Iraq Survey Group. *Comprehensive Report of the Special Advisor to the DCI on Iraq's WMD* [Duelfer Report]. 3 vols. September 30, 2004. http://www-perso nal.umich.edu/~graceyor/govdocs/duelfer.html.

Joint Inquiry into Intelligence Community Activities before and after the Terrorist Attacks of September 11, 2001: Hearings before the Select Committee on Intelligence US Senate and the Permanent Select Committee on Intelligence House of Representatives. Vol. 1. Washington, DC: US Government Printing Office, 2004.

National Archives. Washington, DC, Record Group 148, Records of the Commission of the Legislative Branch.

National Commission on Terrorism. *Countering the Changing Threat of International Terrorism*. Washington, DC: US Government Printing Office, 2000.

National Energy Policy Development Group. *National Energy Policy: Report of the National Energy Policy Development Group*. Washington, DC: US Government Printing Office, 2001. http://wtrg.com/EnergyReport/Natio nal-Energy-Policy.pdf.

National Security Archive. Electronic Briefing Books. Numbers 80, 147, 163, 279, 326, 328, 745.

Office of the Inspector General. *Report on the Central Intelligence Accountability regarding Findings and Conclusions of the Joint Inquiry into Intelligence Community Activities before and after the Terrorist Attacks of September 11, 2001*. Washington, DC: Office of the Inspector General, Central Intelligence Agency, 2005.

Rumsfeld, Donald. The Rumsfeld Archive. https://www.rumsfeld.com/archi ves/page/about-the-rumsfeld-archive-2.

US Office of the Inspector General. *Hard Lessons: The Iraq Reconstruction Experience*. Washington, DC: US Government Printing Office, 2009.

US Senate. Committee on Foreign Relations. *Foreign Policy Overview and the President's Fiscal Year 2003 Foreign Affairs Budget Request: Hearing before the Committee on Foreign Relations, United States Senate*, 107th Congress, 2nd Session, February 5, 2002. Washington, DC: Government Printing Office, 2002.

US Senate. Committee on Foreign Relations. *What's Next in the War on Terrorism? Hearing before the Committee on Foreign Relations, United States Senate*, 107th Congress, 2nd Session, February 7, 2002. Washington, DC: Government Printing Office, 2002.

US Senate. Select Committee on Intelligence. *Report on the US Intelligence Community's Prewar Intelligence Assessments on Iraq.* 108th Congress, July 7, 2004.

White House. *A National Security Strategy for a New Century.* October 1998. https://www.globalsecurity.org/military/library/policy/national/nss-9810.pdf.

White House. *The National Security Strategy of the United States of America.* September 2002. https://nssarchive.us/wp-content/uploads/2020/04/2002.pdf.

Zelikow, Philip D. Papers. University of Virginia.

Other Primary Sources

Bin Laden, Usamah bin Muhammad. "Declaration of Jihad against the Americans Occupying the Land of the Two Holiest Sites." 1996. https://www.911memorial.org/sites/default/files/inline-files/1996%20Osama%20bin%20Laden%27s%201996%20Fatwa%20against%20United%20States_0.pdf.

Conflict Records Research Center. https://conflictrecords.wordpress.com/collections/sh/.

Federation of American Scientists. Intelligence Resource Program. https://irp.fas.org.

Global Security.org. https://www.globalsecurity.org/org/index.html.

Human Rights Watch. *Human Rights Watch World Report 2000—Iraq.* December 1, 1999. https://www.refworld.org/docid/3ae6a8cdc.html.

Human Rights Watch. *Human Rights Watch World Report 2003.* 2003. https://www.hrw.org/legacy/wr2k3/.

Human Rights Watch. "Iraq and Iraqi Kurdistan." In *Human Rights Watch World Report 2002.* https://www.hrw.org/legacy/wr2k2/mena4.html.

The National Archives of the United Kingdom. The Iraq Inquiry. Evidence and Documents. https://webarchive.nationalarchives.gov.uk/ukgwa/20130206044351/http:/www.iraqinquiry.org.uk/transcripts/declassified-documents.aspx.

Radio Free Europe, Radio Liberty, *Iraq Reports*, vols. 5–6. https://www.rferl.org.

Report of a Committee of Privy Counsellors. *The Report of the Iraq Inquiry* [Chilcot Report]. 12 vols. 2016. https://www.thegroovygroup.org/chilcot-report.php.

"The Second Gore-Bush Presidential Debate: October 11, 2000 Debate Transcript." Winston Salem. NC, October 11, 2000. https://www.debates.org/voter-education/debate-transcripts/october-11-2000-debate-transcript/.

Texas State Library and Archives Commission. George W. Bush Executive
    Office Speeches. *Austin, TX.*
"The Third Gore-Bush Presidential Debate: October 17, 2000 Debate
    Transcript." Saint Louis, MO. October 17, 2000. https://www.debates.org/
    voter-education/debate-transcripts/october-17-2000-debate-transcript/.
Woods, Kevin M., with James Lacy. *Iraqi Perspectives Project: Saddam and
    Terrorism: Emerging Insights from Captured Iraqi Documents (Redacted).* 5
    vols. Washington, DC: Institute for Defense Analysis, 2007.

Periodicals

Foreign Affairs
Foreign Policy
Los Angeles Times
New York Times
Wall Street Journal
Washington Post

Websites

"Costs of War." Watson Institute of Public and International Affairs. Brown
    University. https://watson.brown.edu/costsofwar/costs/human/military/
    wounded.
Freedom House. "Freedom in the World." https://freedomhouse.org/report/free
    dom-world.
Pew Research Center. https://www.pewresearch.org.

Memoirs, Diaries, and Personal Accounts

Abrams, Elliott A. *Tested by Zion: The Bush Administration and the Israeli-
    Palestinian Conflict.* New York: Cambridge University Press, 2013.
Albright, Madeleine, with Bill Woodward. *Madame Secretary: A Memoir.*
    New York: Miramax Books, 2003.
Allawi, Ali A. *The Occupation of Iraq: Winning the War, Losing the Peace.* New
    Haven, CT: Yale University Press, 2007.
Annan, Kofi, with Nader Mousavizadeh. *Interventions: A Life in War and Peace.*
    New York: Penguin Press, 2012.
Anonymous [Michael Scheuer], *Imperial Hubris, Why the West is Losing the War
    on Terror.* Washington, DC: Brassey's, 2004.
Anonymous [Michael Scheuer], *Through Our Enemies' Eyes: Osama bin Laden,
    Radical Islam, and the Future of Amerca.* Washington, DC: Potomac
    Books, 2002.

Ashcroft, John. *Never Again: Securing America and Restoring Justice.* New York: Center Street, 2006.

Blair, Tony. *A Journey: My Political Life.* New York: Alfred A. Knopf, 2011.

Blix, Hans. *Disarming Iraq.* New York: Pantheon Books, 2004.

Bremer, Paul L., III, with Malcolm McConnell. *My Year in Iraq: The Struggle to Build a Future of Hope.* New York: Simon & Schuster, 2006.

Burns, William J. *The Back Channel: A Memoir of American Diplomacy and the Case for Its Renewal.* New York: Random House, 2019.

Bush, George W. *A Charge to Keep.* New York: William Morrow, 1999.

Bush, George W. *Decision Points.* New York: Crown, 2010.

Campbell, Alastair. *The Blair Years: Extracts from the Alastair Campbell Diaries.* New York: Alfred A. Knopf, 2007.

Cheney, Dick, with Liz Cheney. *In My Time: A Personal and Political Memoir.* New York: Threshold Editions, 2011.

Clarke, Richard A. *Against All Enemies: Inside America's War on Terror.* New York: Free Press, 2004.

Duelfer, Charles. *Hide and Seek: The Search for Truth in Iraq.* New York: Public Affairs, 2004.

ElBaradei, Mohammed. *The Age of Deception: Nuclear Diplomacy in Treacherous Times.* New York: Metropolitan Books, 2011.

Feith, Douglas J. *War and Decision: Inside the Pentagon at the Dawn of the War on Terrorism.* New York: Harper, 2008.

Fleischer, Ari. *Taking Heat: The President, the Press and My Years in the White House.* New York: Harper LargePrint, 2005.

Ford, Carl W., Jr. Review of *Intelligence and US Foreign Policy: Iraq, 9/11, and Misguided Reform*, by Paul R. Pillar. *H-Diplo* with *ISSF* 3, no. 15 (2002): 13–21. https://issforum.org/ISSF/PDF/ISSF-Roundtable-3-15.pdf.

Franks, Tommy, with Malcolm McConnell. *American Soldier.* New York: Regan Books, 2004.

Frum, David. *The Right Man: An Inside Account of the Bush White House.* New York: Random House, 2003.

Gates, Robert M. *Duty: Memoirs of a Secretary at War.* New York: Vintage Books, 2015.

Gerson, Michael. *Heroic Conservatism: Why Republicans Need to Embrace America's Ideals (And Why They Deserve to Fail If They Don't).* New York: HarperCollins, 2007.

Goldsmith, Jack. *The Terror Presidency: Law and Judgment inside the Bush Administration.* New York: W. W. Norton, 2007.

Gonzales, Alberto R. *True Faith and Allegiance: A Story of Service and Sacrifice in War and Peace.* Nashville, TN: Nelson Books, 2016.

Grossman, Marc. "The State Department: Culture as Interagency Destiny?" In *The National Security Enterprise: Navigating the Labyrinth*, edited by Roger Z. George and Harvey Rishikof, 81–96. Washington, DC: Georgetown University Press, 2017.

Haass, Richard. *War of Necessity, War of Choice: A Memoir of Two Iraq Wars.* New York: Simon & Schuster, 2009.

Hughes, Karen. *Ten Minutes from Normal.* New York: Viking, 2004.

Khalilzad, Zalmay. *The Envoy: From Kabul to the White House, My Journey through a Turbulent World.* New York: St. Martin's Press, 2016.

McClellan, Scott. *What Happened: Inside the Bush White House and Washington's Culture of Deception.* New York: Public Affairs, 2008.

Morell, Michael. *The Great War of Our Time: The CIA's Fight against Terrorism from Al Qa'ida to ISIS.* New York: Twelve, 2015.

Mowatt-Larssen, Rolf. *A State of Mind: Faith and the CIA.* Self-published, 2010.

Myers, Richard, with Malcolm McConnell. *Eyes on the Horizon: Serving on the Front Lines of National Security.* New York: Threshold Editions, 2009.

Nixon, John. *Debriefing the President: The Interrogation of Saddam Hussein.* New York: Blue Ridge Press, 2016.

Paulson, Henry M., Jr. *On the Brink: Inside the Race to Stop the Collapse of the Global Financial System.* New York: Business Plus, 2010.

Petraeus, David, Joseph Collins, and Nathan White. "Reflections by General David Petraeus, USA (ret.) on the Wars in Afghanistan and Iraq." *Prism* 7, no. 1 (2017): 150–67.

Pillar, Paul. *Intelligence and US Foreign Policy: Iraq, 9/11 and Misguided Reform.* New York: Columbia University Press, 2011.

Rice, Condoleezza. *Democracy: Stories from the Long Road to Freedom.* New York: Hachette, 2017.

Rice, Condoleezza. *No Higher Honor: A Memoir of My Years in Washington.* New York: Crown Publishers, 2011.

Riedel, Bruce. "9/11 and Iraq: The Making of a Tragedy." Brookings, September 17, 2012. https://www.brookings.edu/blog/order-from-chaos/2021/09/17/9-11-and-iraq-the-making-of-a-tragedy/.

Rove, Karl. *Courage and Consequence: My Life as a Conservative in the Fight.* New York: Threshold Editions, 2010.

Rumsfeld, Donald. *Known and Unknown: A Memoir.* New York: Sentinel, 2011.

Sanchez, Ricardo, with Donald T. Phillips. *Wiser in Battle: A Soldier's Story.* New York: Harper, 2008.

Shelton, Hugh, with Ronald Levinson and Malcolm McConnell. *Without Hesitation: The Odyssey of an American Warrior.* New York: St. Martin's Press, 2010.

Smith, Frederick C., and Franklin C. Miller. "The Office of the Secretary of Defense: Civilian Matters?" In *The National Security Enterprise: Navigating the Labyrinth*, edited by Roger Z. George and Harvey Rishikof, 120–41. Washington, DC: Georgetown University Press, 2017.

Taylor, John B. *Global Financial Warriors: The Untold Story of International Finance in the Post-9/11 World.* New York: W. W. Norton, 2007.

Tenet, George, with Bill Harlow. *At the Center of the Storm: My Years at the CIA.* New York: HarperCollins, 2007.

Tucker, Mike, and Charles S. Faddis. *Operation Hotel California: The Clandestine War inside Iraq.* Guilford, CT: Lyons Press, 2009.

Wolfowitz, Paul. "What Was and What Might Have Been: The Threats and Wars in Afghanistan and Iraq." Stanford: Hoover Institution Essay, 2022.

Woods, Kevin M., David Palkki, and Mark E. Stout, eds. *The Saddam Tapes: The Inner Workings of a Tyrant's Regime, 1978–2001.* New York: Cambridge University Press, 2011.

Woods, Kevin M., with Michael R. Pease, Mark E. Stout, Williamson Murray, and James G. Lacey. *Iraqi Perspectives Project: A View of Operation Iraqi Freedom from Saddam's Senior Leadership.* Washington, DC: Joint Center for Operational Analysis, 2006.

Zakheim, Dov S. *A Vulcan's Tale: How the Bush Administration Mismanaged the Reconstruction of Afghanistan.* Washington, DC: Brookings Institution Press, 2011.

Books and Articles

9/11 Commission Report. *Final Report of the National Commission on Terrorist Attacks upon the United States.* New York: W. W. Norton, 2004.

Aburish, Said K. *Saddam Hussein: The Politics of Revenge.* London: Bloomsbury, 2000.

Aikman, David. *A Man of Faith: The Spiritual Journey of George W. Bush.* Nashville, TN: W Publishing Group, 2004.

Anderson, Terry H. *Bush's Wars.* New York: Oxford University Press, 2011.

Atwan, Abdel Bari. *The Secret History of Al Qaeda.* Berkeley: University of California Press, 2008.

Bailey, Beth, and Richard H. Immerman, eds. *Understanding US Wars in Iraq and Afghanistan.* New York: New York University Press, 2015.

Baker, Peter. *Days of Fire: Bush and Cheney in the White House.* New York: Doubleday, 2013.

Bamford, James. *A Pretext for War: 9/11, Iraq, and the Abuse of America's Intelligence Agencies.* New York: Doubleday, 2004.

Baram, Amatzia. "The Effect of Iraqi Sanctions: Statistical Pitfalls and Responsibility." *Middle East Journal* 54, no. 2 (Spring 2000): 194–223.

Baram, Amatzia. "The Iraqi Invasion of Kuwait." In *The Saddam Reader,* edited by Turi Munthe, 251–87. New York: Thunder's Mouth Press, 2002.

Bensahel, Nora, et al. *After Saddam: Prewar Planning and the Occupation of Iraq.* Santa Monica, CA: Rand, 2008.

Bergen, Peter. *The Longest War: The Enduring Conflict between America and Al-Qaeda.* New York: Free Press, 2011.

Bergen, Peter. *The Rise and Fall of Osama Bin Laden.* New York: Simon & Schuster, 2021.

Blaydes, Lisa. *State of Repression: Iraq under Saddam Hussein.* Princeton, NJ: Princeton University Press, 2018.

Bozo, Frederic, translated by Susan Emanuel. *A History of the Iraq Crisis: France, the United States and Iraq, 1991–2003*. Washington, DC: Woodrow Wilson Center Press, 2016.

Brands, Hal. *What Good Is Grand Strategy: Power and Purpose in American Statecraft from Harry S. Truman to George W. Bush*. Ithaca, NY: Cornell University Press, 2014.

Brands, Hal, and Peter Feaver. "The Case for Reassessing America's 43rd President," *Orbis* 62, no. 1 (2018): 76–90.

Brands, Hal, and David Palkki. "'Conspiring Bastards': Saddam Hussein's Strategic View of the United States." *Diplomatic History* 36, no. 3 (June 2012): 625–59.

Brands, Hal, and Eric Edelman and Thomas G. Mahnken. "Credibility Matters: Strengthening American Deterrence in an Age of Geopolitical Turmoil." Washington, DC: Center for Strategic and Budgetary Assessments, May 2018. https://csbaonline.org/research/publications/credibility-matters-strengthening-american-deterrence-in-an-age-of-geopolit.

Brands, Hal, and David Palkki. "Saddam, Israel and the Bomb: Nuclear Alarmism Justified?" *International Security* 36, no. 1 (Summer 2011): 133–66.

Braut-Hegghammer, Målfrid. "Cheater's Dilemma: Iraq, Weapons of Mass Destruction, and the Path to War." *International Security* 45, no. 1 (2020): 51–89.

Braut-Hegghammer, Målfrid. *Unclear Physics: Why Iraq and Libya Failed to Build Nuclear Weapons*. Ithaca, NY: Cornell University Press, 2016.

Brigham, Robert K., ed. *The United States and Iraq since 1990*. Malden, MA: Wiley-Blackwell, 2014.

Butt, Ahsan I. "Why Did the United States Invade Iraq in 2003?" *Security Studies* 28, no. 2 (April/May 2019): 250–85.

Chandrasekaran, Rajiv. *Imperial Life in the Emerald City: Inside Iraq's Green Zone*. New York: Alfred A. Knopf, 2006.

Cigar, Norman. "Saddam Hussein's Nuclear Vision: An Atomic Shield and Sword for Conquest." *Middle East Studies Occasional Papers*. Quantico, VA: Marine Corps University Press, 2011.

Coll, Steve. *Ghost Wars: The Secret History of the CIA, Afghanistan, and Bin Laden, from the Soviet Invasion to September 10, 2001*. New York: Penguin Press, 2004.

Cook, Michael. "Is Political Freedom an Islamic Value?" In *Freedom and the Construction of Europe*, edited by Quentin Skinner and Martin van Gelderen, 2 vols., 2:283–310. New York: Cambridge University Press, 2013.

Cordesman, Anthony H. *Iraq's Military Capabilities in 2002: A Dynamic Net Assessment*. Washington, DC: Center for Strategic and International Studies, 2002.

Coughlin, Con. *Saddam: The Secret Life*. London: Macmillan, 2002.

Crockatt, Richard. *America Embattled: September 11, Anti-Americans, and the Global Order*. London: Routledge, 2003.

Croft, Stuart. *Culture, Crisis, and America's War on Terror.*
    Cambridge: Cambridge University Press, 2006.

Crosston, Matthew. *Fostering Fundamentalism: Terrorism, Democracy and
    American Engagement in Central Asia.* Burlington, VT: Ashgate Publishing
    Company, 2006.

DeYoung, Karen. *Soldier: The Life of Colin Powell.* New York: Alfred
    A. Knopf, 2006.

Dietrich, Christopher R. W. *Oil Revolution: Anticolonial Elites, Sovereign
    Rights, and the Economic Culture of Decolonization.* Cambridge: Cambridge
    University Press, 2017.

Dobbins, James, et al. *Occupying Iraq: A History of the Coalition Provisional
    Authority.* Santa Monica, CA: Rand, 2009.

Donnelly, John. "The President's Emergency Plan for AIDS Relief: How
    George W. Bush and Aides Came to 'Think Big' on Battling HIV." *Health
    Affairs* 31, no. 7 (July 2012): 1389–96.

Downes, Alexander B., and Lindsey A. O'Rourke. "You Can't Always Get
    What You Want: Why Foreign-Imposed Regime Change Seldom Improves
    Interstate Relations." *International Security* 41, no. 2 (Fall 2016): 43–89.

Draper, Robert. *Dead Certain: The Presidency of George W. Bush.*
    New York: Free Press, 2007.

Draper, Robert. *To Start a War: How the Bush Administration Took America into
    Iraq.* New York: Random House, 2020.

Dyson, Stephen. *Leaders in Conflict: Bush and Rumsfeld in Iraq.*
    Manchester: Manchester University Press, 2014.

Engel, Jeffrey A. *When the World Seemed New: George H. W. Bush and the End
    of the Cold War.* Boston: Houghton, Mifflin, Harcourt, 2017.

Fallows, James. "Blind into Baghdad." *The Atlantic.* January/February, 2004.

Felix, Antonia. *Condi: The Condoleezza Rice Story.* New York: Newmarket
    Press, 2005.

Freedman, Lawrence. *A Choice of Enemies: America Confronts the Middle East.*
    New York: Public Affairs, 2018.

Freedman, Lawrence, and Efraim Karsh. *The Gulf Conflict, 1990–
    1991: Diplomacy and War in the New World Order.* Princeton, NJ: Princeton
    University Press, 1993.

Gardner, Lloyd C., and Marilyn B. Young, eds. *The New American Empire: A
    21st Century Teach-In on US Foreign Policy.* New York: New Press, 2005.

Gellman, Barton. *Angler: The Cheney Vice Presidency.* New York: Penguin
    Press, 2008.

Gerges, Fawaz A. *The Rise and Fall of Al-Qaeda.* New York: Oxford University
    Press, 2011.

Gerhart, Ann. *The Perfect Wife: The Life and Choices of Laura Bush.*
    New York: Simon & Schuster, 2004.

Gordon, Joy. *Invisible War: The United States and the Iraq Sanctions.*
    Cambridge, MA: Harvard University Press, 2010.

Gordon, Michael, and Bernard E. Trainor. *Cobra II: The Inside Story of the Invasion and Occupation of Iraq*. New York: Pantheon, 2006.

Gordon, Michael, and Bernard E. Trainor. *The Endgame: The Inside Story of the Struggle for Iraq, from George W. Bush to Barack Obama*. New York: Pantheon Books, 2012.

Graham, Bradley. *By His Own Rules: The Ambitions, Successes, and Ultimate Failures of Donald Rumsfeld*. New York: Public Affairs, 2009.

Graham-Brown, Sarah. *Sanctioning Saddam: The Politics of Intervention in Iraq*. London: I. B. Tauris, 1999.

Greenstein, Fred. "The 'Strong Leadership' of George W. Bush." *International Journal of Applied Psychoanalytic Studies* 5, no. 3 (September 2008): 171–90.

Hahn, Peter. *Missions Impossible: The United States and Iraq since World War I*. New York: Oxford University Press, 2012.

Hamid, Shadi. *The Problem of Democracy: America, the Middle East and the Rise and Fall of an Idea*. New York: Oxford University Press, 2021.

Hamza, Khidhir. "Saddam's Nuclear Program." In *The Saddam* Hussein Reader, edited by Turi Munthe, 417–30. New York: Thunder's Mouth Press, 2002.

Harvey, Frank P. *Explaining the Iraq War: Counter-Factual Theory, Logic and Evidence*. New York: Cambridge University Press, 2012.

Helfont, Samuel. *Iraq against the World: How Saddam's Ba'thists Defied America and Shaped Post-Cold War Politics*. Forthcoming.

Helfont, Samuel. "Saddam and the Islamists: The Ba'thist Regime's Instrumentalization of Religion in Foreign Affairs." *Middle East Journal* 68, no. 3 (Summer 2014): 352–66.

Hooker, Gregory. *Shaping the Plan for Operation Iraqi Freedom: The Role of Military Intelligence Assessments*. Washington, DC: Washington Institute for Near East Policy, 2005.

Hooker, Richard D., Jr., and Joseph J. Collins, eds. *Lessons Encountered: Learning from the Long War*. Washington, DC: National Defense University Press, 2015.

Hurst, Steven. *The United States and Iraq since 1979: Hegemony, Oil and War*. Edinburgh: Edinburgh University Press, 2009.

Isikoff, Michael, and David Corn. *Hubris: The Inside Story of Spin, Scandal, and the Selling of the Iraq War*. New York: Three Rivers Press, 2006.

Jentleson, Bruce W. *With Friends Like These: Reagan, Bush, and Saddam, 1982–1990*. New York: W. W. Norton, 1994.

Jervis, Robert. *Why Intelligence Fails: Lessons from the Iranian Revolution and the Iraq War*. Ithaca, NY: Cornell University Press, 2010.

Jones, Toby Craig. "America, Oil, and War in the Middle East." *Journal of American History* 99, no. 1 (June 2012): 208–18.

Karabell, Zachary and Philip D. Zelikow, "Iraq, 1988-1990: Unexpectedly Heading toward War," In *Dealing with Dictators: Dilemmas of U.S.*

Diplomacy and Intelligence Analysis, 1945-1990, edited by Ernest R. May and Philip D. Zelikow, 167-202. Cambridge, MA: MIT Press, 2006.

Karsh, Efraim, and Inari Rautsi. *Saddam Hussein: A Political Biography*. New York: Grove Press, 1991.

Khoury, Dina Rizk. *Iraq in Wartime: Soldiering, Martyrdom, and Remembrance*. New York: Cambridge University Press, 2013.

Kubursi, Atif A. "Oil and the Iraqi Economy." *Arab Studies Quarterly* 10 (Summer 1988): 283–98.

Kukis, Mark. *Voices from Iraq: A People's History, 2003–2009*. New York: Columbia University Press, 2011.

Kurtzer, Daniel C., Scott B. Lasensky, William B. Quandt, Steven Spiegel, and Shibley Z. Telhami. *The Peace Puzzle: America's Quest for Arab-Israeli Peace, 1988–2011*. Ithaca, NY: Cornell University Press, 2013.

Lahoud, Nelly. *The Bin Laden Papers*. New Haven, CT: Yale University Press, 2022.

Leffler, Melvyn P. "9/11 and American Foreign Policy." *Diplomatic History* 19, no. 3 (June 2005): 395–413.

Legro, Jeffrey W., and Peter J. Katzenstein. US *Standing in the World: Causes, Consequences, and the Future*. Washington, DC: American Political Science Association, 2009.

Levy, Jack S. "Deterrence and Coercive Diplomacy: The Contributions of Alexander George." *Political Psychology* 29, no. 4 (2008): 537–52.

Lusane, Clarence. *Colin Powell and Condoleezza Rice: Foreign Policy, Race, and the New American Century*. Westport, CT: Praeger, 2006.

Mabry, Marcus. *Twice as Good: Condoleezza Rice and Her Path to Power*. New York: Modern Times, 2007.

Makdisi, Ussama. *Age of Coexistence: The Ecumenical Frame and the Making of the Modern Arab World*. Oakland: University of California Press, 2019.

Makdisi, Ussama. *Faith Misplaced: The Broken Promise of US–Arab Relations, 1820–2001*. New York: Public Affairs, 2010.

Makiya, Kanan. *Republic of Fear: The Politics of Modern Iraq*. Berkeley: University of California Press, 1998.

Malkasian, Carter. *The American War in Afghanistan: A History*. New York: Oxford University Press, 2021.

Malone, David M. *The International Struggle over Iraq: Politics in the UN Security Council, 1980–2005*. New York: Oxford University Press, 2005.

Mann, James. *George W. Bush*. New York: Times Books, 2013.

Mann, James. *The Great Rift: Dick Cheney, Colin Powell, and the Broken Friendship That Defined an Era*. New York: Henry Holt, 2020.

Mann, James. *Rise of the Vulcans: The History of Bush's War Cabinet*. New York: Viking, 2004.

Marr, Phebe. *The Modern History of Iraq*. Boulder, CO: Westview Press, 2012.

Mayer, Jane. *The Dark Side: The Inside Story of How the War on Terror Turned into a War on American Ideals*. New York: Doubleday, 2008.

Mazarr, Michael J. *Leap of Faith: Hubris, Negligence, and America's Greatest Foreign Policy Tragedy.* New York: Public Affairs, 2019.

Meacham, Jon. *Destiny and Power: The American Odyssey of George Herbert Walker Bush.* New York: Random House, 2015.

Mearsheimer, John J., and Stephen M. Walt. "An Unnecessary War." *Foreign Policy* (January/February 2003): 51–59.

"Media Polls on the Iraq War between 2003 and 2007." Politifact. The Poynter Institute. https://www.politifact.com/iraq-war-polls/.

Moore, David W. "Eight of Ten Americans Support the Ground War in Afghanistan." Gallup, November 1, 2001. https://news.gallup.com/poll/5029/eight-americans-support-ground-war-afghanistan.aspx.

Newport, Frank. "Seventy-Two Percent of Americans Support War against Iraq." Gallup, March 24, 2003. https://news.gallup.com/poll/8038/seventy two-percent-americans-support-war-against-iraq.aspx.

O'Connell, Aaron B. *Our Latest Longest War: Losing Hearts and Minds in Afghanistan.* Chicago: University of Chicago Press, 2017.

O'Connell, Aaron B. "The Global Wars on Terror." In *The Cambridge History of America and the World, Vol IV, 1945 to the Present,* edited by David C. Engerman, Max Paul Friedman, and Melani McAlister, 707-30. Cambridge: Cambridge University Press, 2021.

Otterman, Sharon. "Iraq: Debaathification." Council on Foreign Relations, February 22, 2005. https://www.cfr.org/backgrounder/iraq-debaathification.

Owen, John M., IV. *The Clash of Ideas in World Politics: Transnational Networks, States, and Regime Change, 1510–2010.* Princeton, NJ: Princeton University Press, 2010.

Packer, George. *The Assassins' Gate: America in Iraq.* New York: Farrar, Straus and Giroux, 2005.

Perl, Raphael. "Terrorism, the Future and US Foreign Policy." Washington, DC: Congressional Research Service, March 6, 2003.

Pfiffner, James P., and Mark Pythian, eds. *Intelligence and National Security Policymaking on Iraq: British and American Perspectives.* College Station: Texas A&M University Press, 2008.

Phillips, David L. *Losing Iraq: Inside the Postwar Reconstruction Fiasco.* Boulder, CO: Westview Press, 2005.

Pollack, Kenneth. *The Threatening Storm: The Case for Invading Iraq.* New York: Random House, 2002.

Randall, Stephen J. *United States Foreign Oil Policy since World War I: For Profits and Security.* Montreal: McGill-Queen's University Press, 2005.

Rashid, Ahmed. *Descent into Chaos: The United States and the Failure of Nation Building in Pakistan, Afghanistan and Central Asia.* New York: Viking, 2008.

Rayburn, Joel D., and Frank K. Sobchak, eds. *The US Army in the Iraq War.* 2 vols. Carlisle, PA: US Army War College Press, 2019.

Razoux, Pierre, translated by Nicholas Elliott. *The Iran-Iraq War.* Cambridge, MA: Harvard University Press, 2015.

Richardson, Louise. *What Terrorists Want: Understanding the Enemy, Containing the Threat*. New York: Random House, 2006.

Ricks, Thomas E. *Fiasco: The American Military Adventure in Iraq*. New York: Penguin Press, 2006.

Risen, James. *State of War: The Secret History of the CIA and the Bush Administration*. New York: Free Press, 2006.

Robinson, Glenn E. *Global Jihad: A Brief History*. Stanford, CA: Stanford University Press, 2021.

Rovner, Joshua. *Fixing the Facts: National Security and the Politics of Intelligence*. Ithaca, NY: Cornell University Press, 2015.

Saad, Lydia. "Top Ten Findings about Public Opinion and Iraq." Gallup, October 8, 2002.https://news.gallup.com/poll/6964/top-ten-findings-about-public-opinion-iraq.aspx.

Sassoon, Joseph. *Saddam Hussein's Ba'th Party: Inside an Authoritarian Regime*. New York: Cambridge University, 2012.

Sayle, Timothy Andrews, Jeffrey A. Engel, Hal Brands, and William Inboden. *The Last Card: Inside George W. Bush's Decision to Surge in Iraq*. Ithaca, NY: Cornell University Press, 2019.

Shadid, Anthony. *Night Draws Near*. New York: Henry Holt, 2005.

SIPRI. "Iraq: The UNSCOM Experience." Fact Sheet, October 1998. https://www.sipri.org/sites/default/files/files/FS/SIPRIFS9810.pdf.

Smith, Anthony L. "A Glass Half-Full: Indonesia-US Relations in the Age of Terror." *Contemporary Southeast Asia: A Journal of International and Strategic Affairs* 25, no. 3 (December 2003): 449–72.

Smith, Gary Scott. *Faith and the Presidency: From George Washington to George W. Bush*. New York: Oxford University Press, 2006.

Smith, Jean Edward. *Bush*. New York: Simon & Schuster, 2016.

Sobel, Richard, Peter Furia, and Bethany Barratt, eds. *Public Opinion & International Intervention: Lessons from the Iraq War*. Washington, DC: Potomac Books, 2012.

Stansfield, Gareth. *Iraq: People, History, Politics*. Cambridge: Polity Press, 2007.

Stokes, Doug, and Sam Raphael. *Global Energy and American Hegemony*. Baltimore: Johns Hopkins University Press, 2010.

Suskind, Ron. *The One Percent Doctrine: Deep inside America's Pursuit of Its Enemies since 9/11*. New York: Simon & Schuster, 2006.

Suskind, Ron. *The Price of Loyalty: George W. Bush, the White House, and the Education of Paul O'Neil*. New York: Simon & Schuster, 2004.

"Timeline: How the Anthrax Terror Unfolded." NPR, February 15, 2011. https://www.npr.org/2011/02/15/93170200/timeline-how-the-anthrax-terror-unfolded.

Tooze, Adam. *Crashed: How a Decade of Financial Crises Changed the World*. New York: Viking, 2018.

Tripp, Charles. *A History of Iraq*. 3rd ed. New York: Cambridge University Press, 2007.

Turek, Lauren F. "Religious Rhetoric and the Evolution of George W. Bush's Political Philosophy." *Journal of American Studies* 48, no. 4 (2014): 975–98.

Volger, Gary. *Iraq and the Politics of Oil*. Lawrence: University Press of Kansas, 2017.

Walker, J. Samuel. *The Day That Shook America: A Concise History of 9/11*. Lawrence: University Press of Kansas, 2021.

Warrick, Joby. *Black Flags: The Rise of ISIS*. New York: Doubleday, 2015.

Warshaw, Shirley Anne. *The Co-Presidency of Bush and Cheney*. Stanford, CA: Stanford University Press, 2009.

Weaver, Mary Anne. "The Short, Violent Life of Abu Musab al-Zarqawi," *The Atlantic*, July/August 2006. https://www.theatlantic.com/magazine/archive/2006/07/the-short-violent-life-of-abu-musab-al-zarqawi/304983/

Weisberg, Jacob. *The Bush Tragedy*. New York: Random House, 2008.

"What the World Thinks in 2002." Pew Research Center, December 4, 2002. https://www.pewresearch.org/global/2002/12/04/what-the-world-thinks-in-2002/.

Wolfe-Hunnicutt, Brandon. *The Paranoid Style in American Diplomacy: Oil and Arab Nationalism in Iraq*. Stanford, CA: Stanford University Press, 2021.

Woods, Kevin M. *The Mother of All Battles: Saddam Hussein's Strategic Plan for the Persian Gulf War*. Annapolis, MD: Naval Institute Press, 2008.

Woodward, Bob. *Bush at War*. New York: Simon & Schuster, 2002.

Woodward, Bob. *Plan of Attack*. New York: Simon & Schuster, 2004.

Wright, Donald P., and Timothy R. Reese. *On Point II: Transition to the New Campaign: The United States Army in Operation in Iraqi Freedom, May 2003–January 2005*. Fort Leavenworth, KS: Combat Studies Institute Press, 2008.

Wright, Lawrence. *The Looming Tower: Al-Qaeda and the Road to 9/11*. New York: Alfred A. Knopf, 2006.

Wright, Steven. *The United States and Persian Gulf Security: The Foundation of the War on Terror*. Reading, UK: Ithaca Press, 2007.

Yetiv, Steve A. *The Absence of Grand Strategy: The United States in the Persian Gulf, 1972–2005*. Baltimore: Johns Hopkins University Press, 2008.

Zelikow, Philip D. "U.S. Strategic Planning in 2001-02." In *In Uncertain Times: American Foreign Policy after the Berlin Wall and 9/11*, edited by Melvyn P. Leffler and Jeffrey W. Legro, 96–116. Ithaca, NY: Cornell University Press, 2011.

Zenko, Micah. "Foregoing Limited Force: The George W. Bush Administration's Decision Not to Attack Ansar Al-Islam." *Journal of Strategic Studies* 32, no. 4 (August 2009): 615–49.

INDEX

For the benefit of digital users, indexed terms that span two pages (e.g., 52–53) may, on occasion, appear on only one of those pages.

Page numbers followed by *f* indicate figures and photographs.